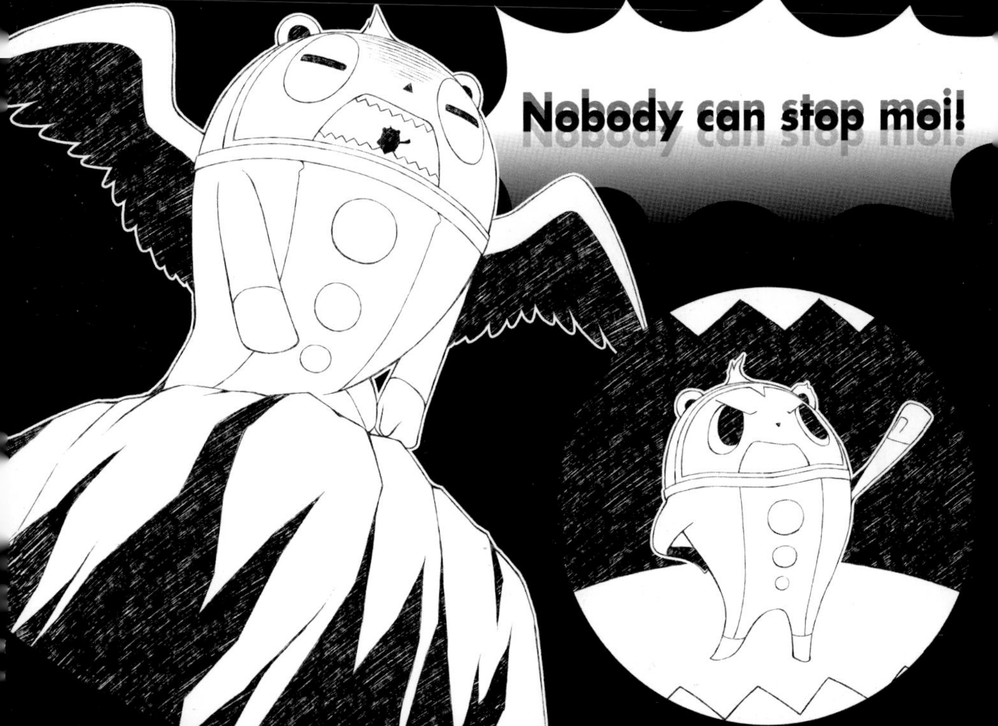
Nobody can stop moi!

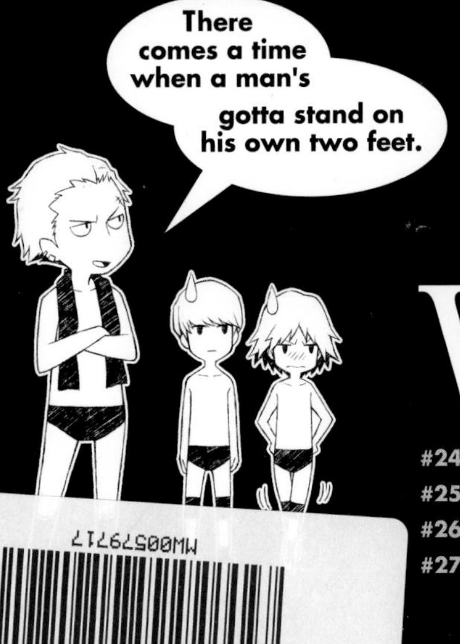
There comes a time when a man's gotta stand on his own two feet.

V Persona 4

Persona4

*Vol.5: Shuji SOGABE / ATLUS

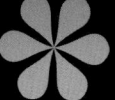

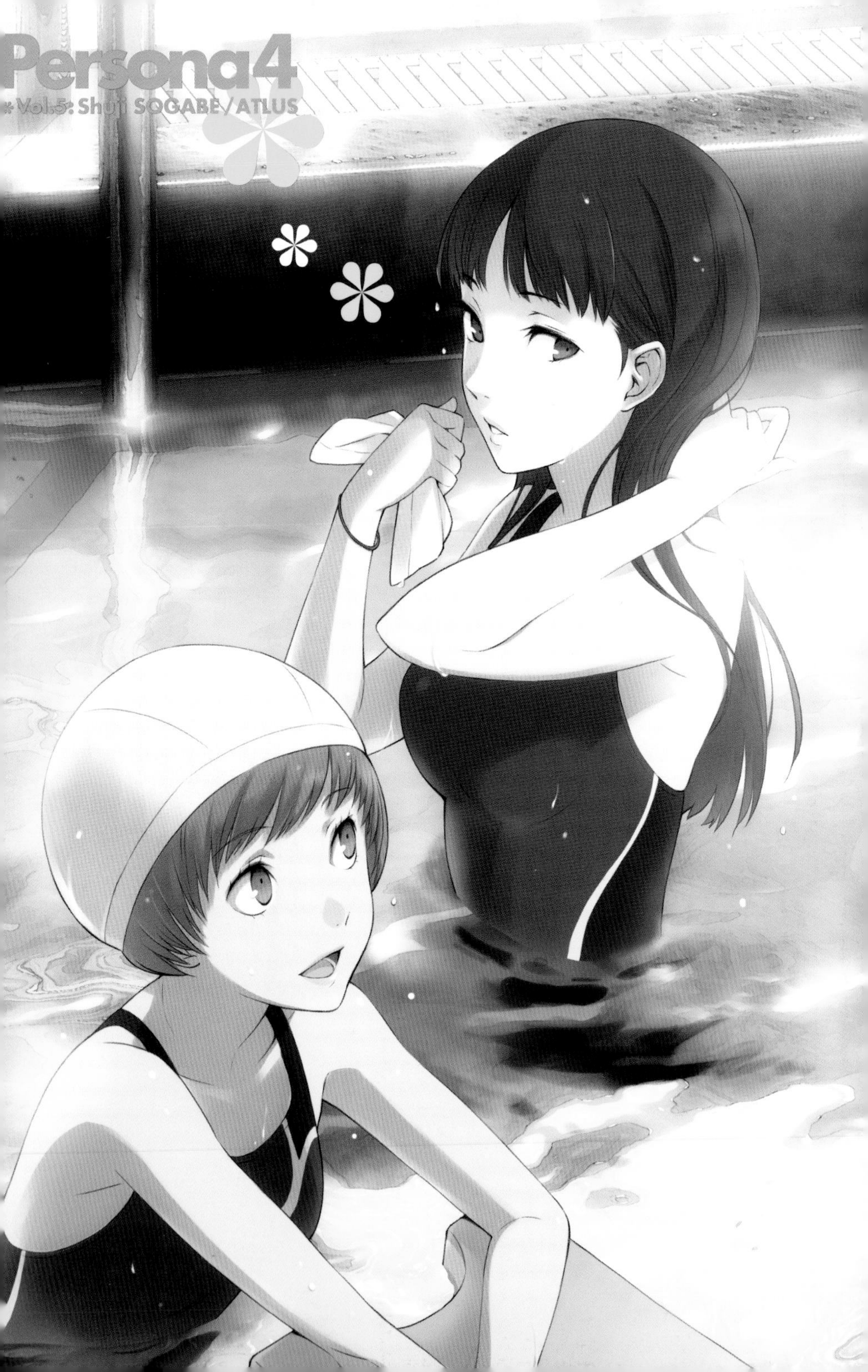
Persona4
Vol.5: Shuji SOGABE/ATLUS

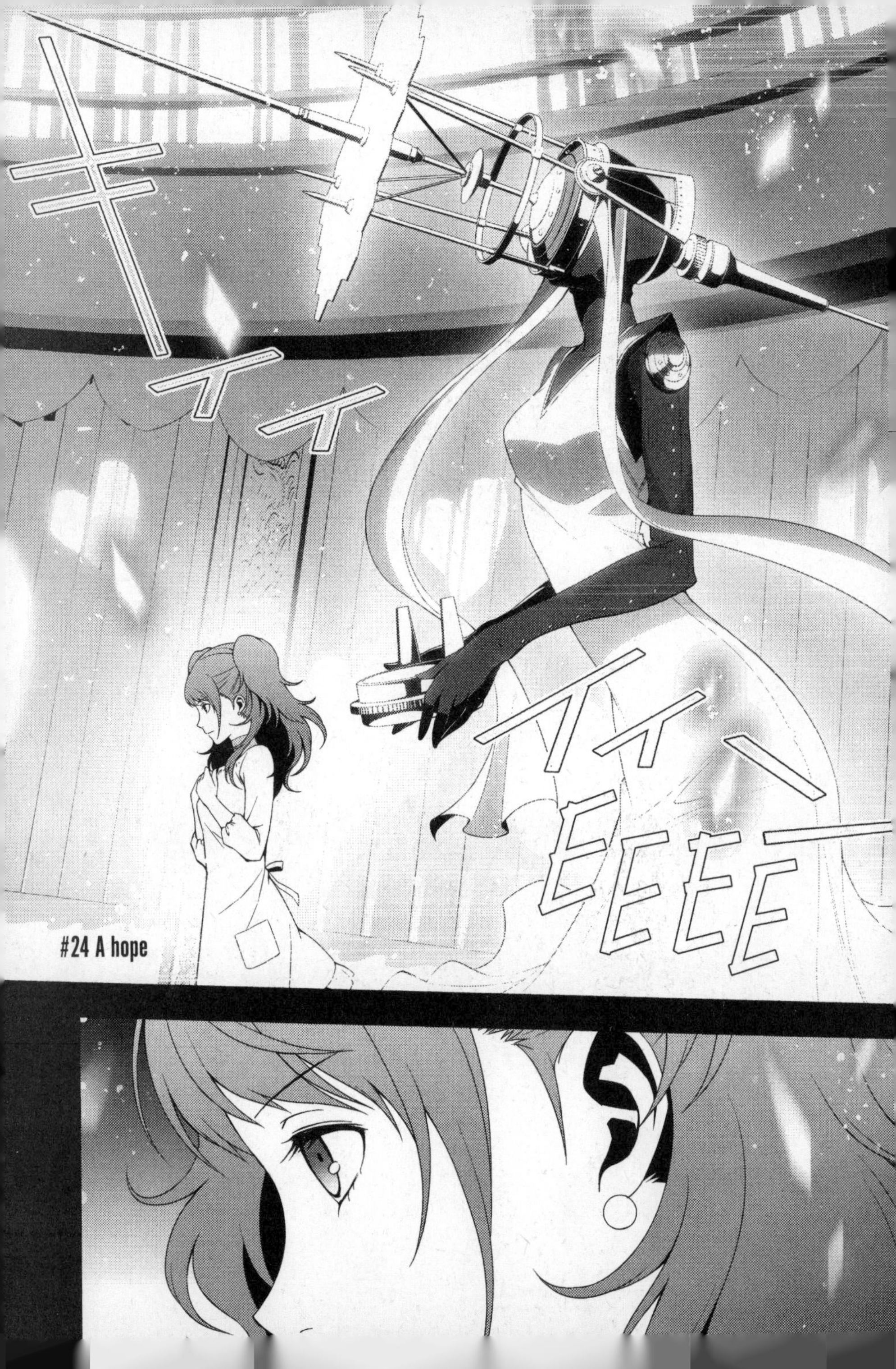
キィィィィーEEEE
#24 A hope

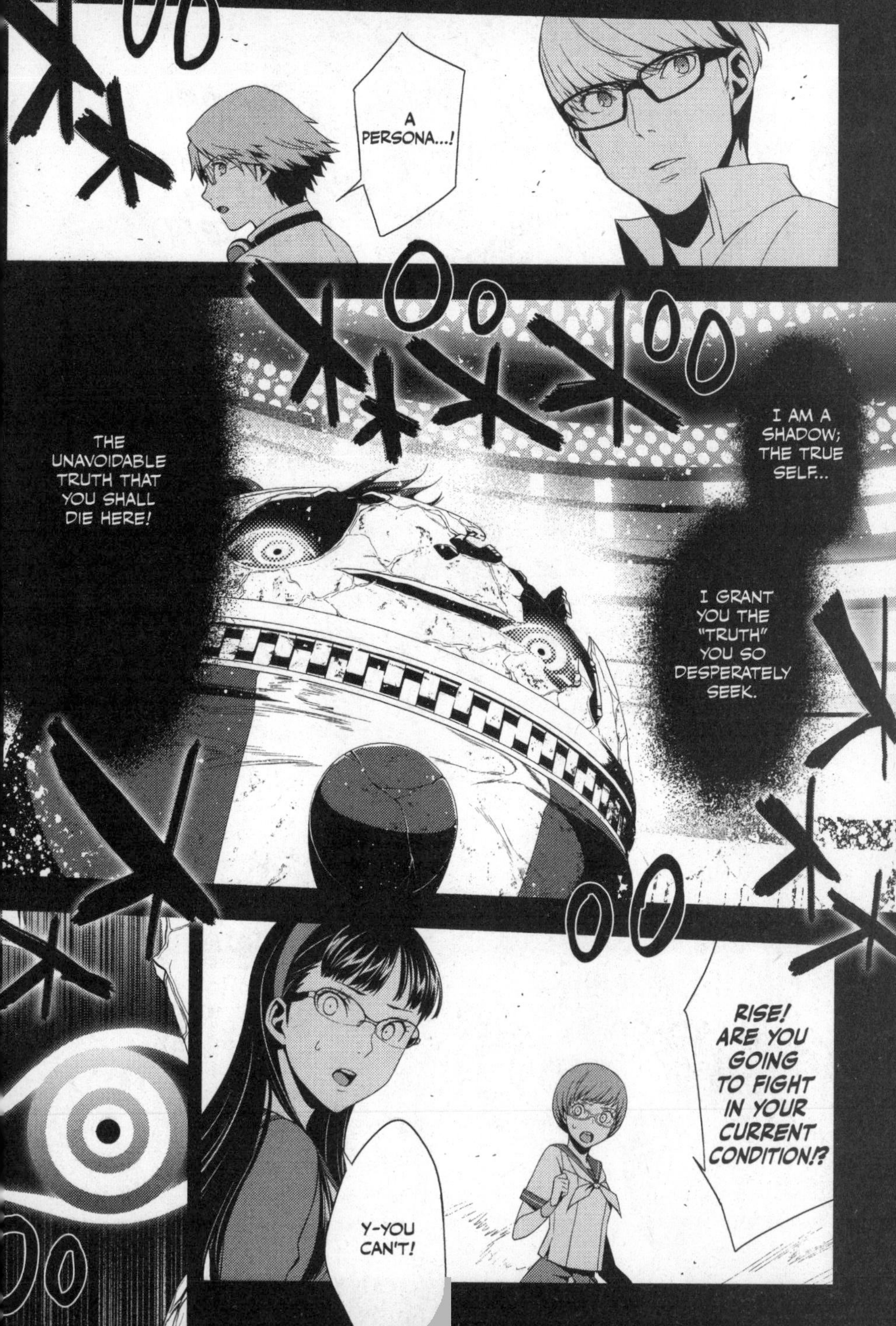
A PERSONA...!
I AM A SHADOW; THE TRUE SELF...
I GRANT YOU THE "TRUTH" YOU SO DESPERATELY SEEK.
THE UNAVOIDABLE TRUTH THAT YOU SHALL DIE HERE!
RISE! ARE YOU GOING TO FIGHT IN YOUR CURRENT CONDITION!?
Y-YOU CAN'T!

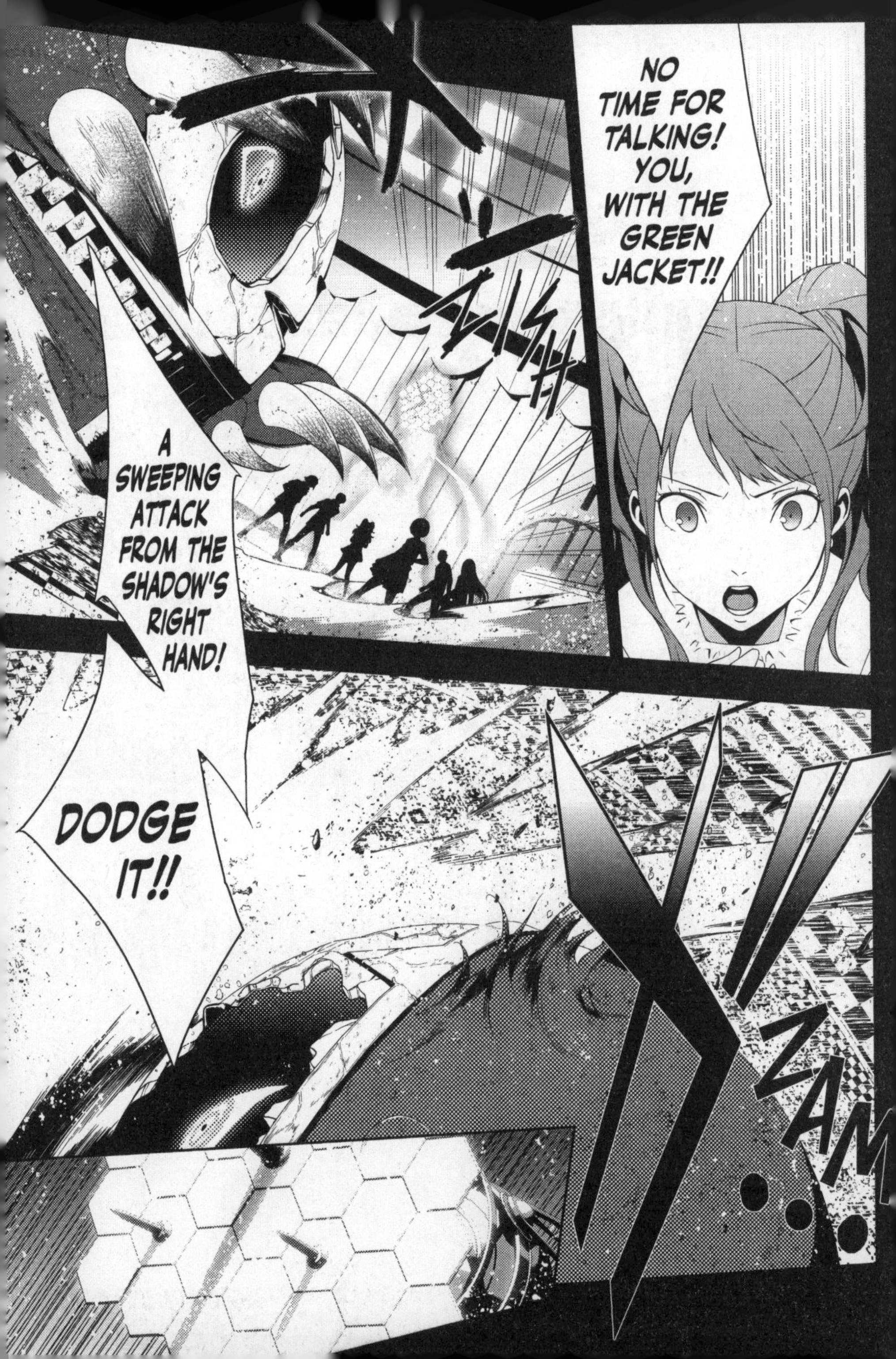
NO TIME FOR TALKING! YOU, WITH THE GREEN JACKET!!
ZISHH
A SWEEPING ATTACK FROM THE SHADOW'S RIGHT HAND!
DODGE IT!!
ZWAM
...

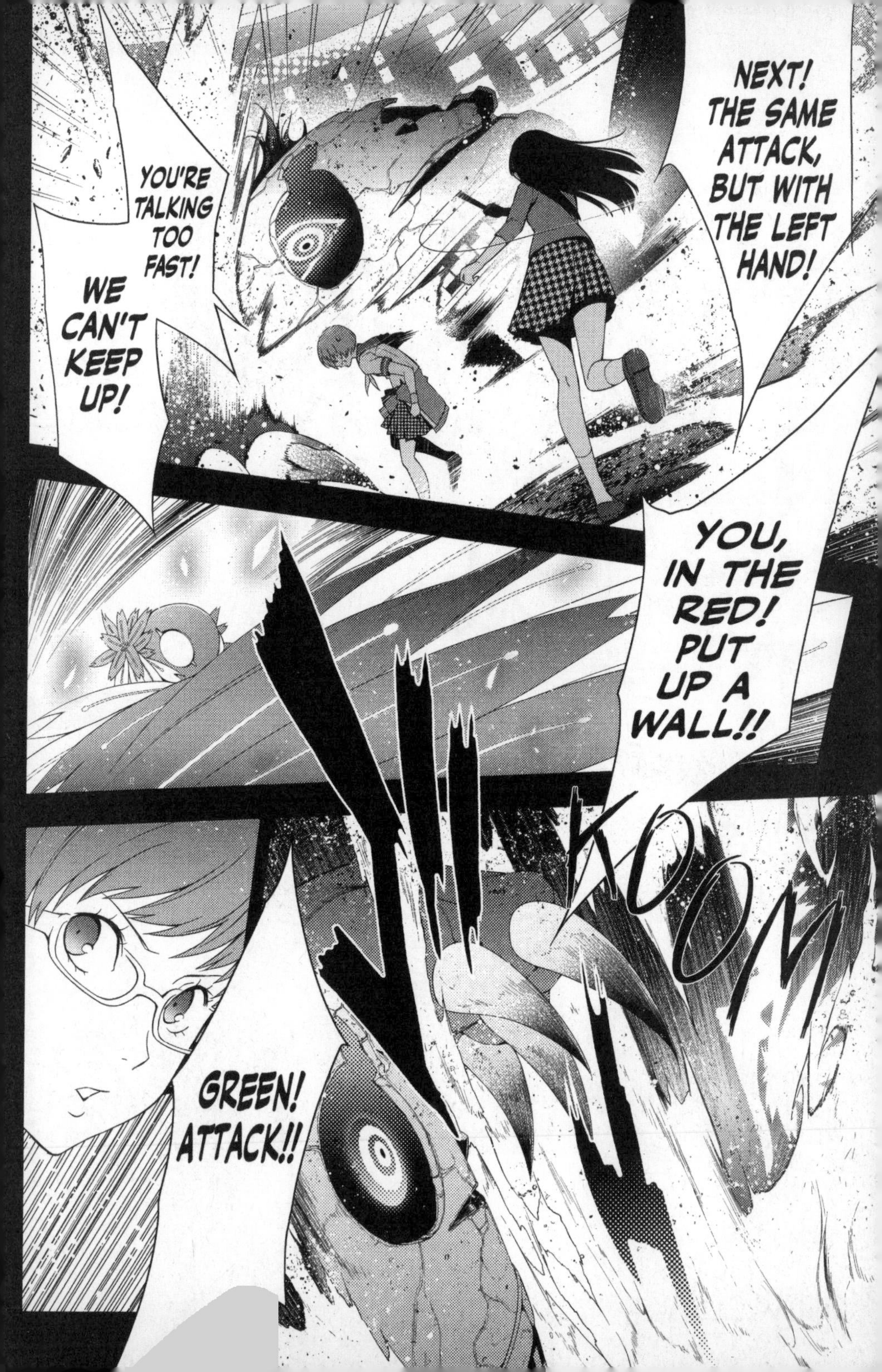
NEXT! THE SAME ATTACK, BUT WITH THE LEFT HAND!
YOU'RE TALKING TOO FAST!
WE CAN'T KEEP UP!
YOU, IN THE RED! PUT UP A WALL!!
KOOOM
GREEN! ATTACK!!

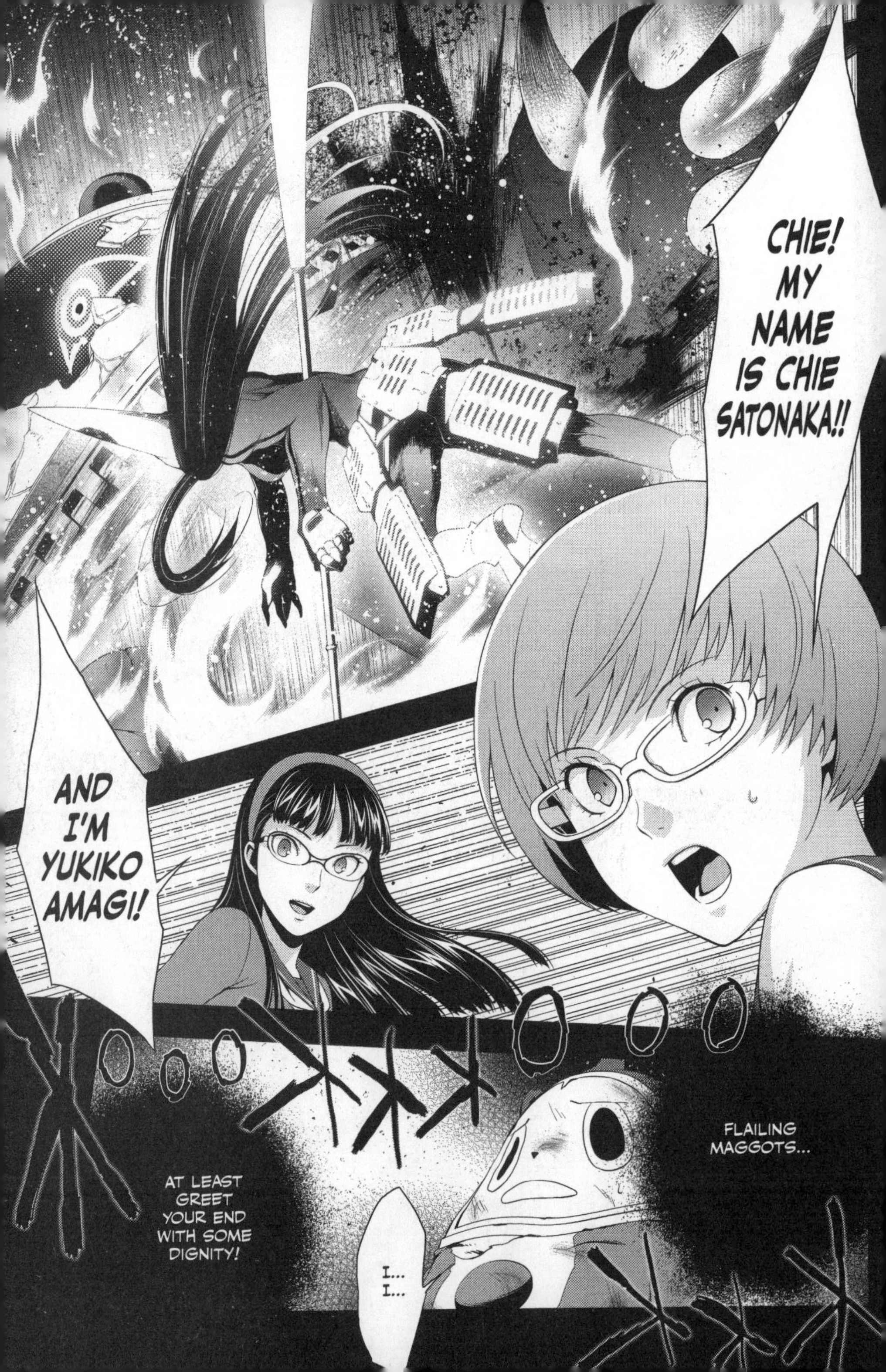
CHIE! MY NAME IS CHIE SATONAKA!!
AND I'M YUKIKO AMAGI!
FLAILING MAGGOTS...
AT LEAST GREET YOUR END WITH SOME DIGNITY!
I... I...

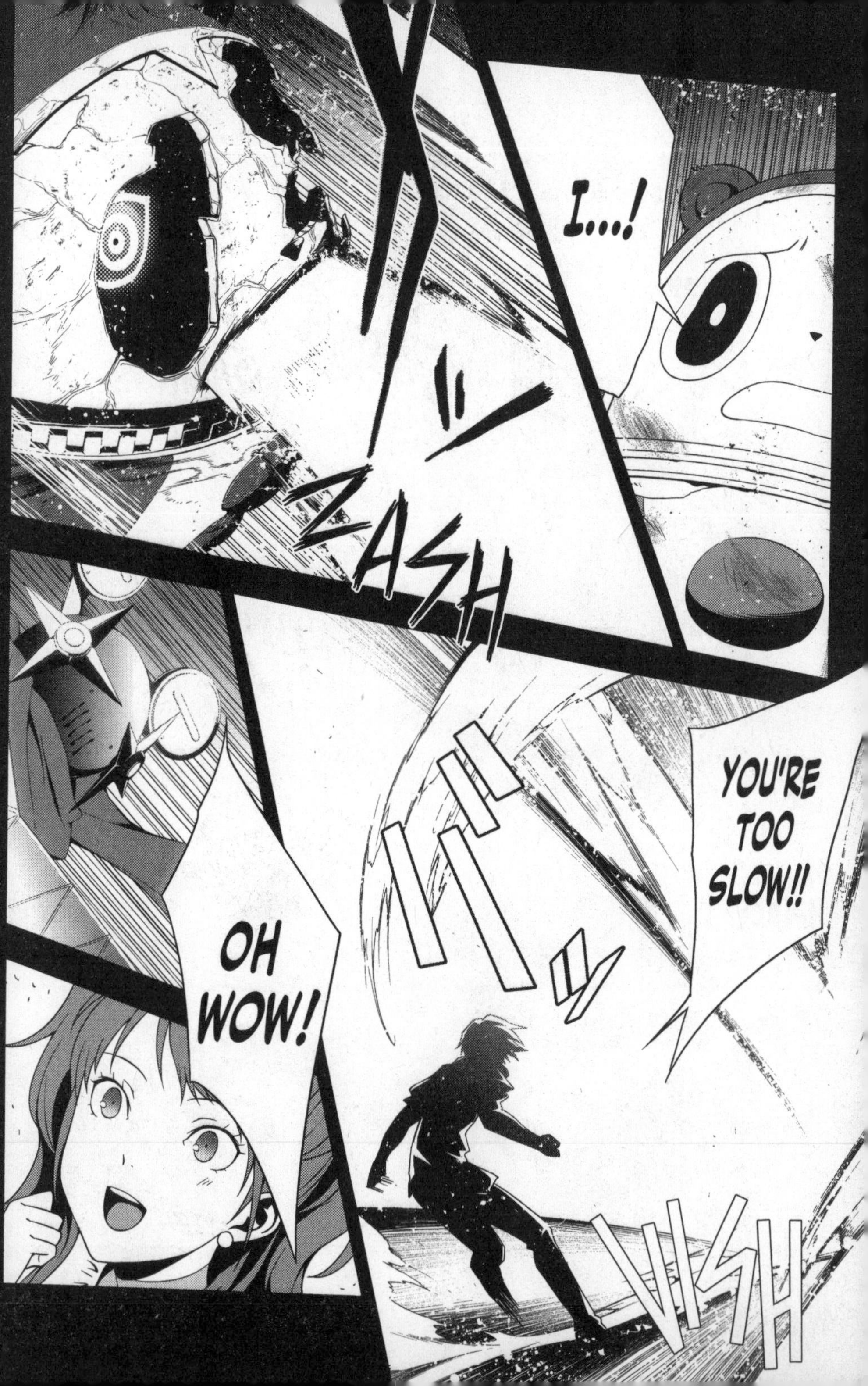
I...!
ZASH
YOU'RE TOO SLOW!!
VISH
OH WOW!

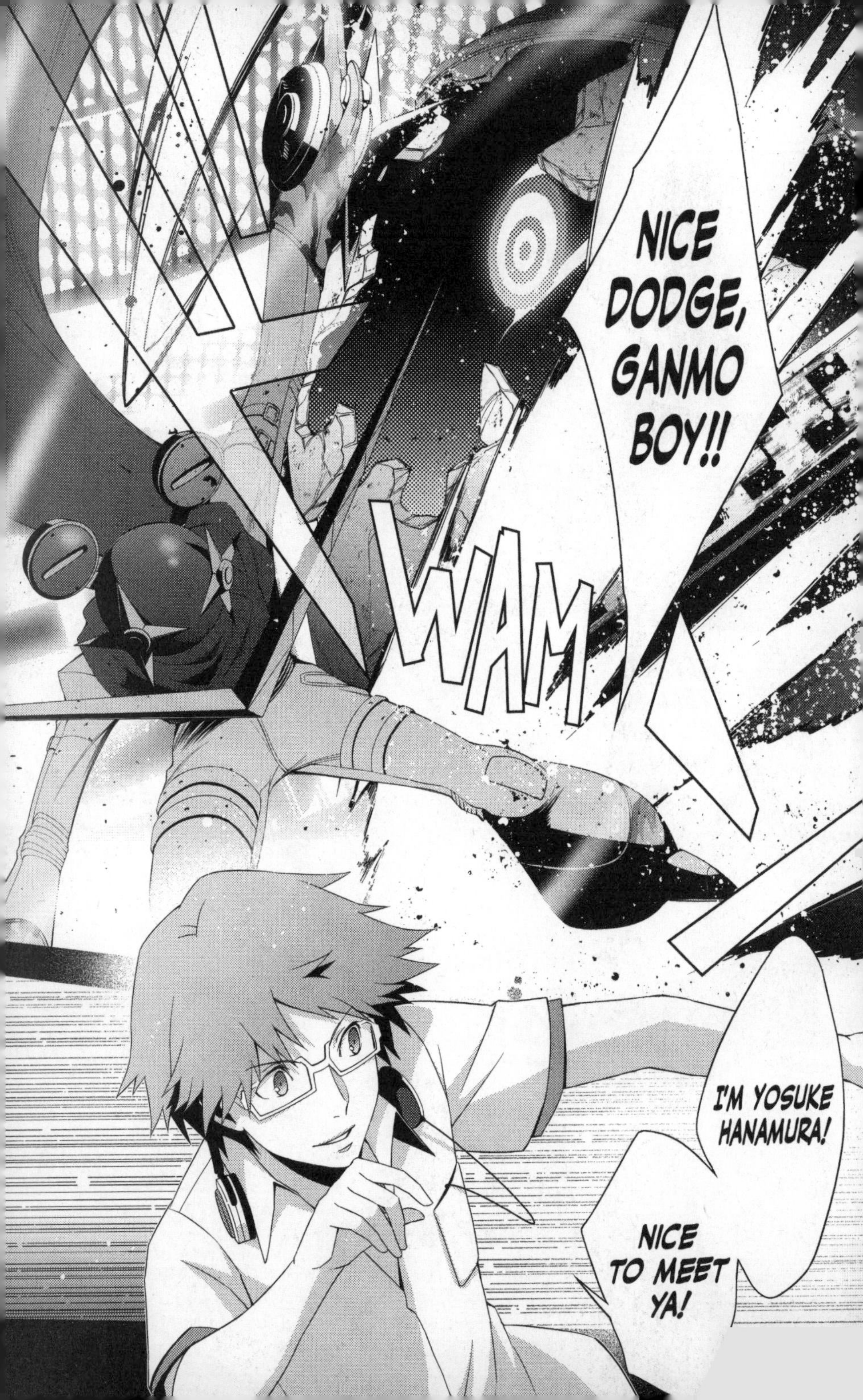
NICE DODGE, GANMO BOY!!
WAM
I'M YOSUKE HANAMURA!
NICE TO MEET YA!

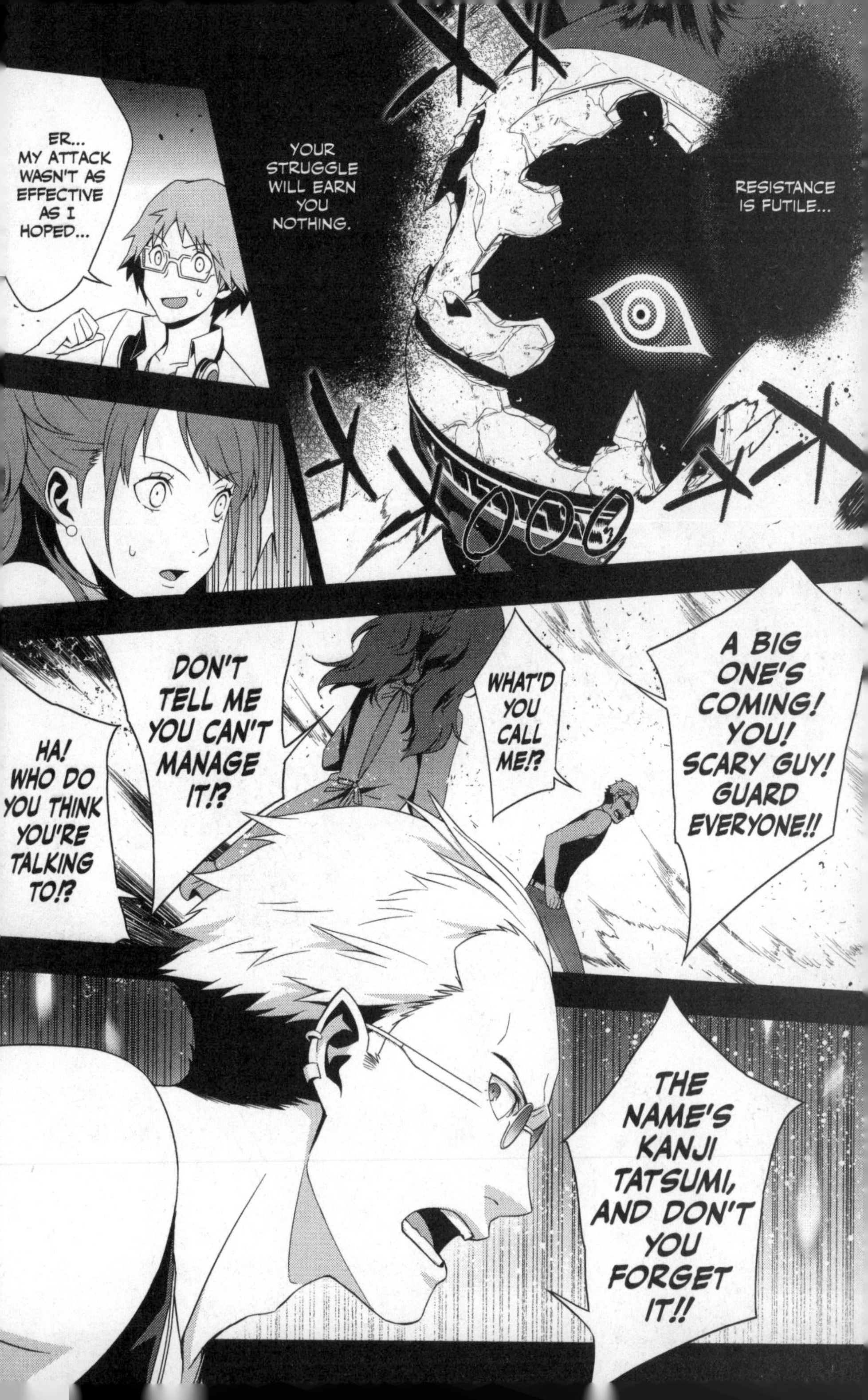
RESISTANCE IS FUTILE...
YOUR STRUGGLE WILL EARN YOU NOTHING.
ER... MY ATTACK WASN'T AS EFFECTIVE AS I HOPED...
A BIG ONE'S COMING! YOU! SCARY GUY! GUARD EVERYONE!!
WHAT'D YOU CALL ME!?
DON'T TELL ME YOU CAN'T MANAGE IT!?
HA! WHO DO YOU THINK YOU'RE TALKING TO!?
THE NAME'S KANJI TATSUMI, AND DON'T YOU FORGET IT!!

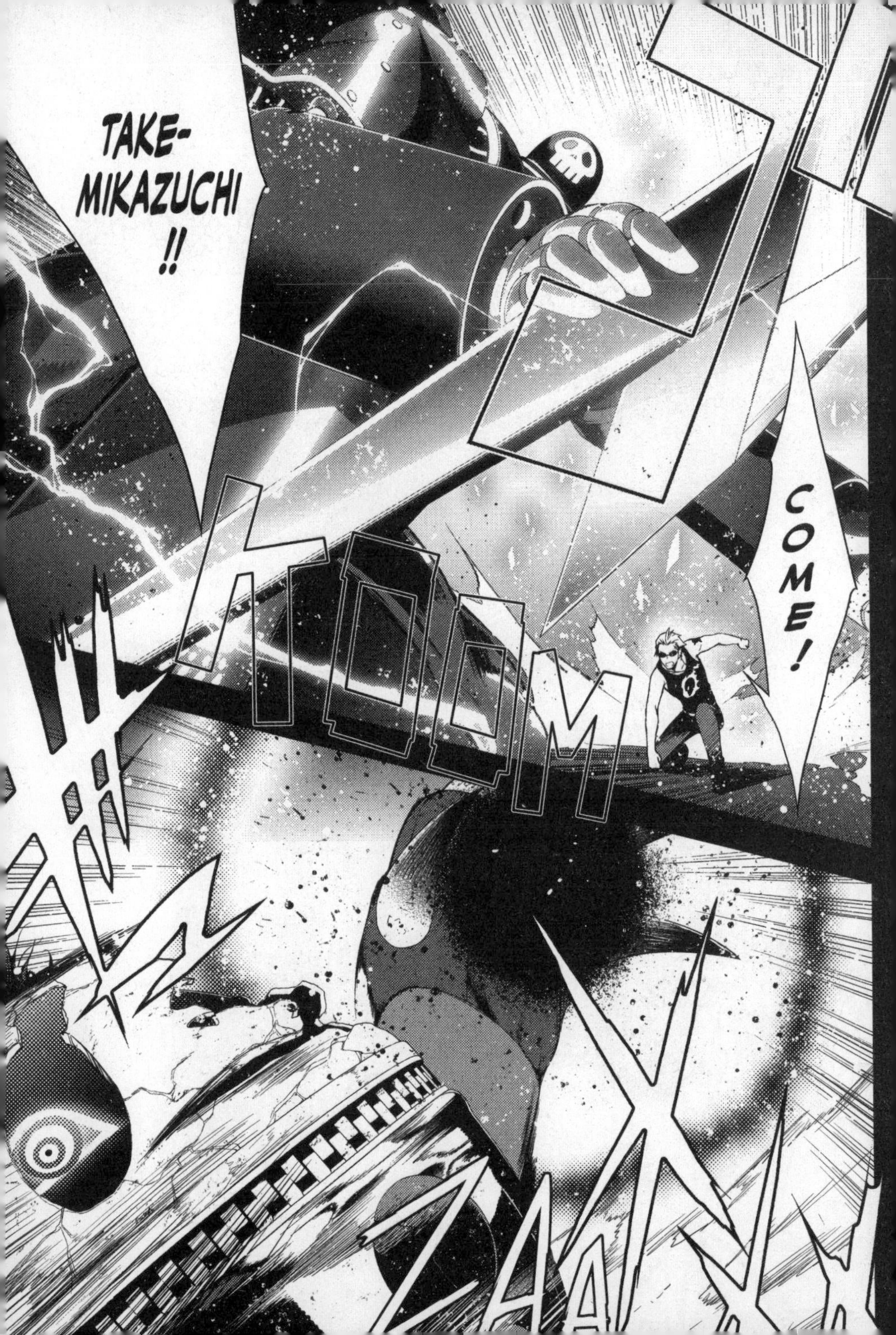
COME!
TAKE-
MIKAZUCHI
!!

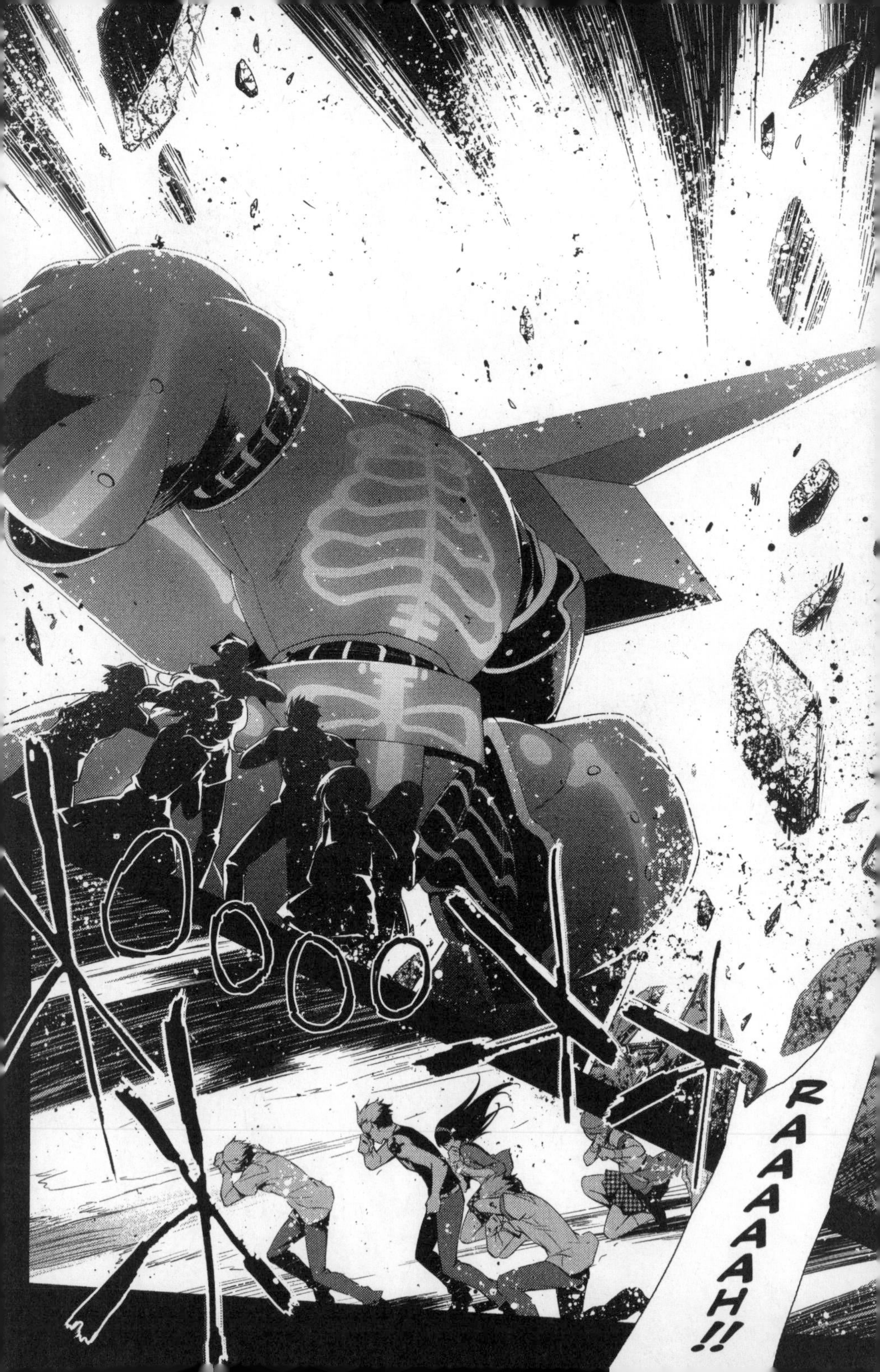
RAAAAAH!!

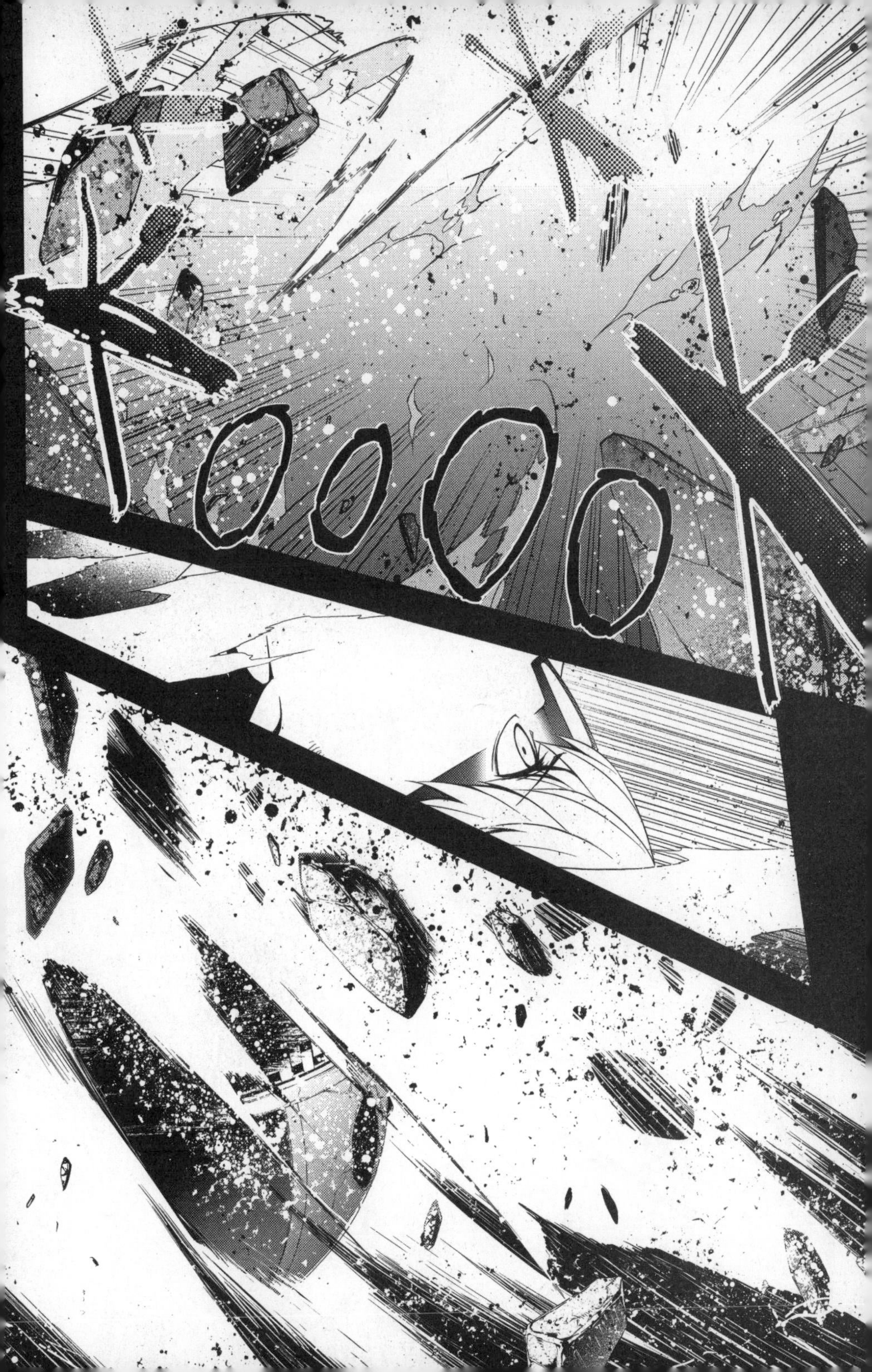

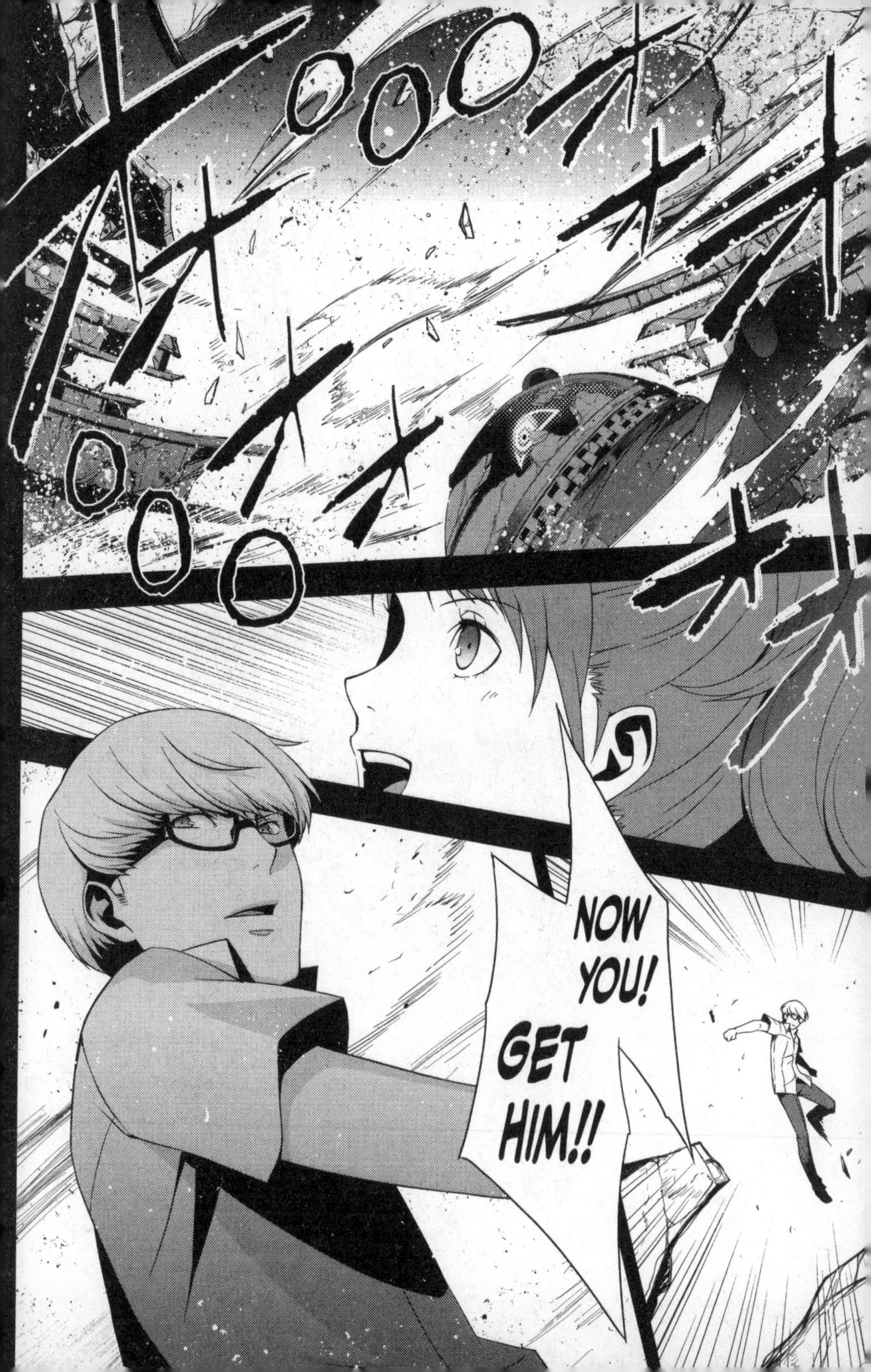
NOW YOU! GET HIM!!

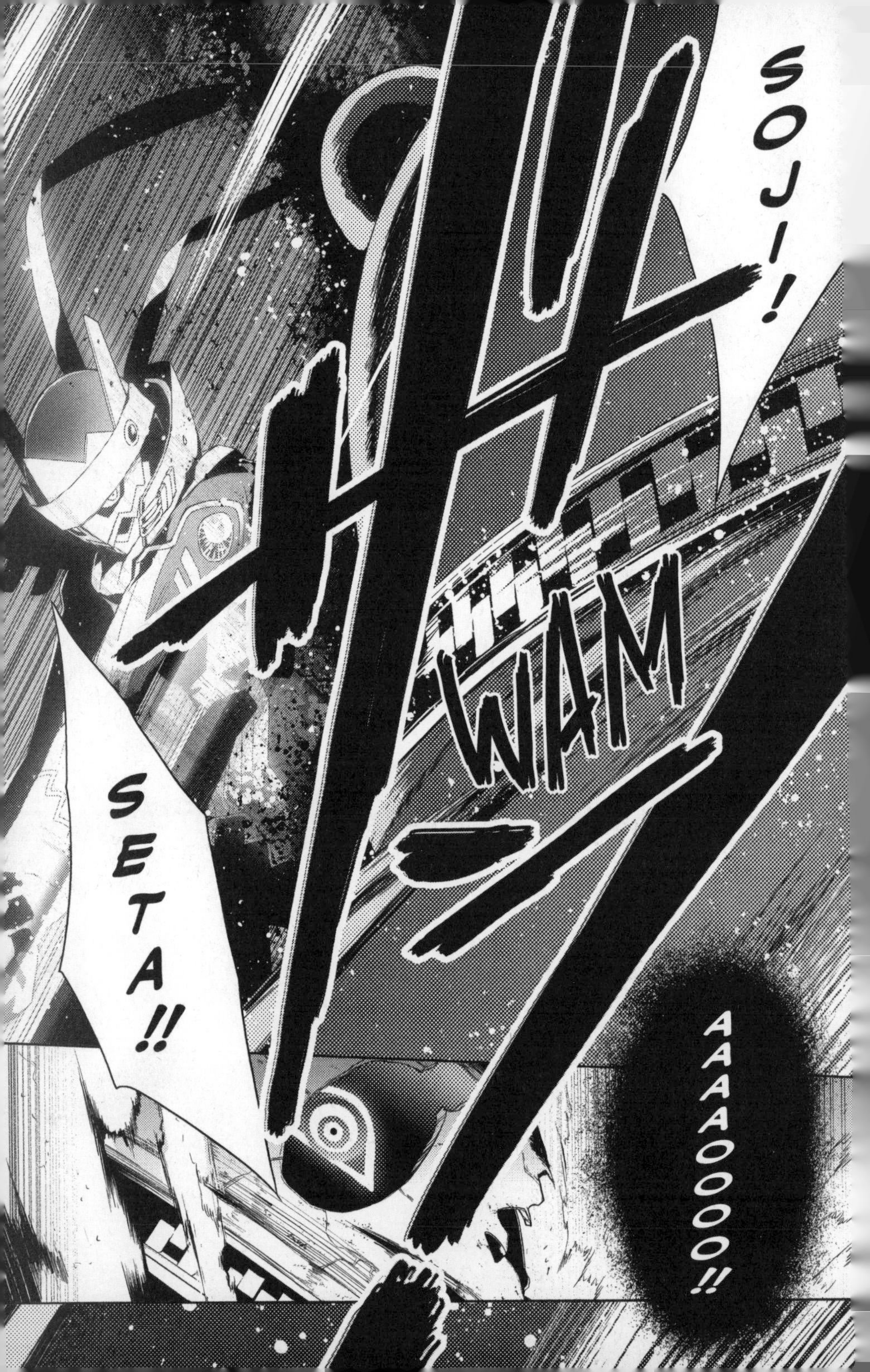
SOJI!!
WAM
SETA!!
AAAAAOOOOO!!

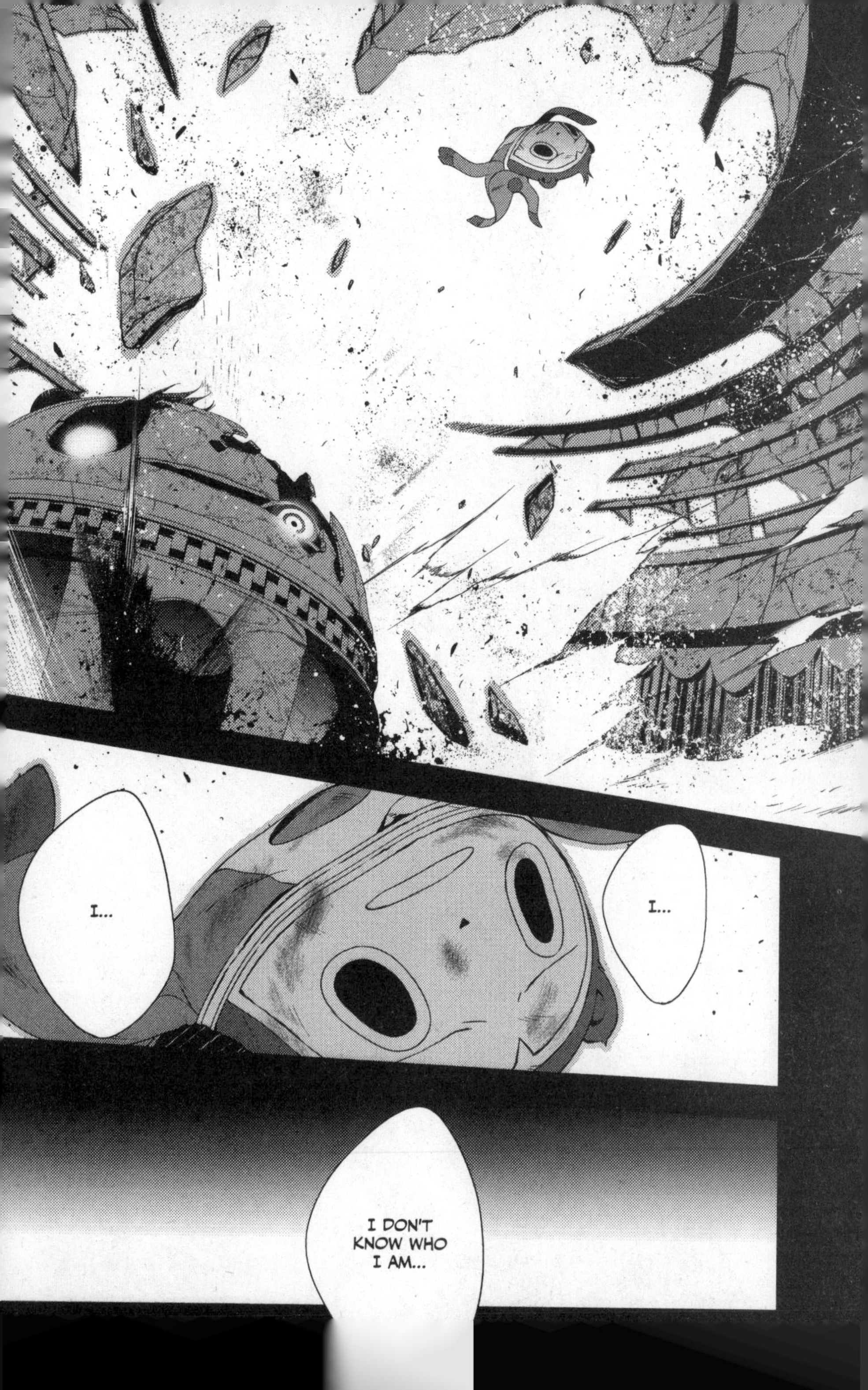
I...
I...
I DON'T KNOW WHO I AM...

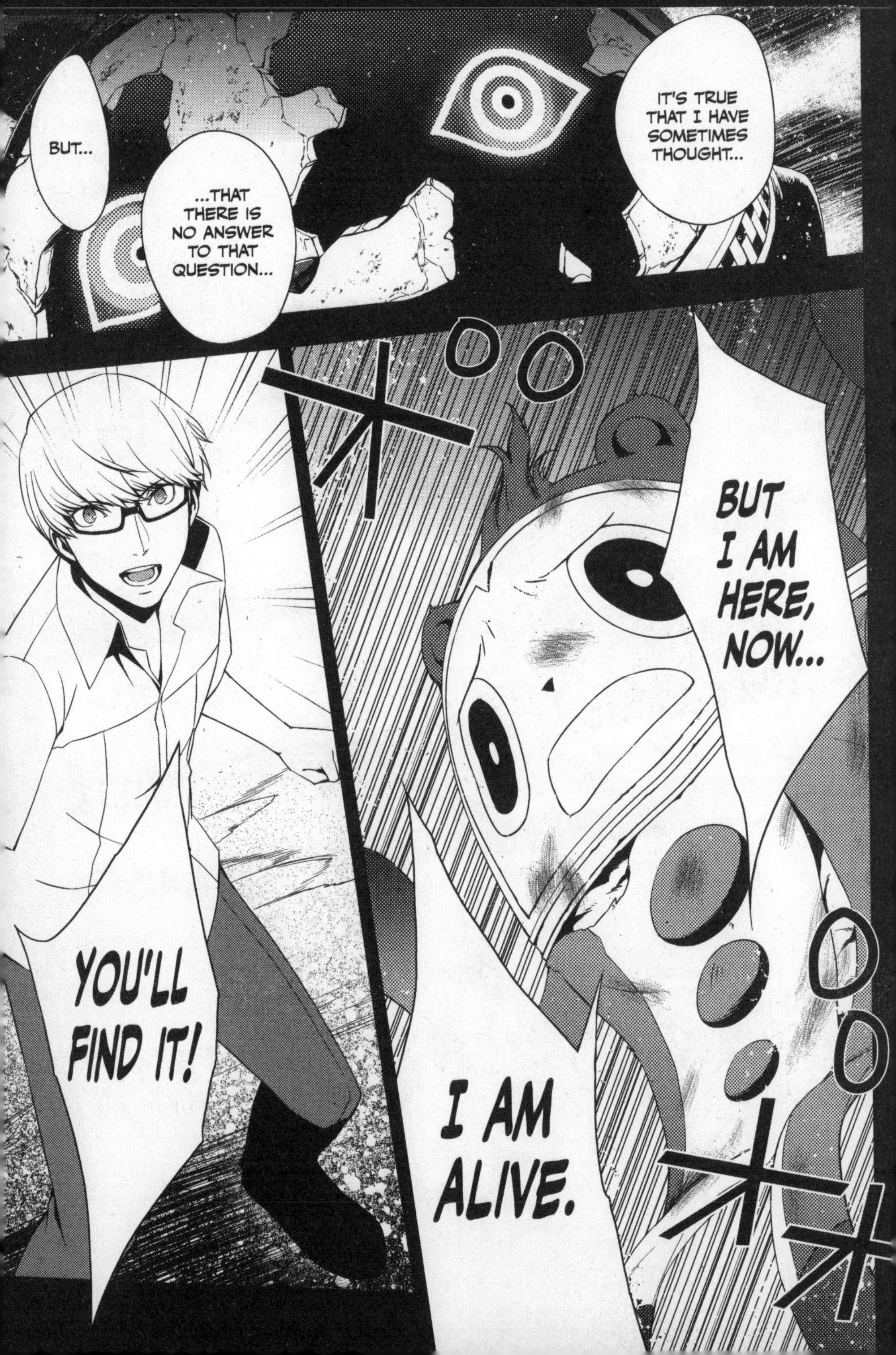
IT'S TRUE THAT I HAVE SOMETIMES THOUGHT...
...THAT THERE IS NO ANSWER TO THAT QUESTION...
BUT...
BUT I AM HERE, NOW...
I AM ALIVE.
YOU'LL FIND IT!

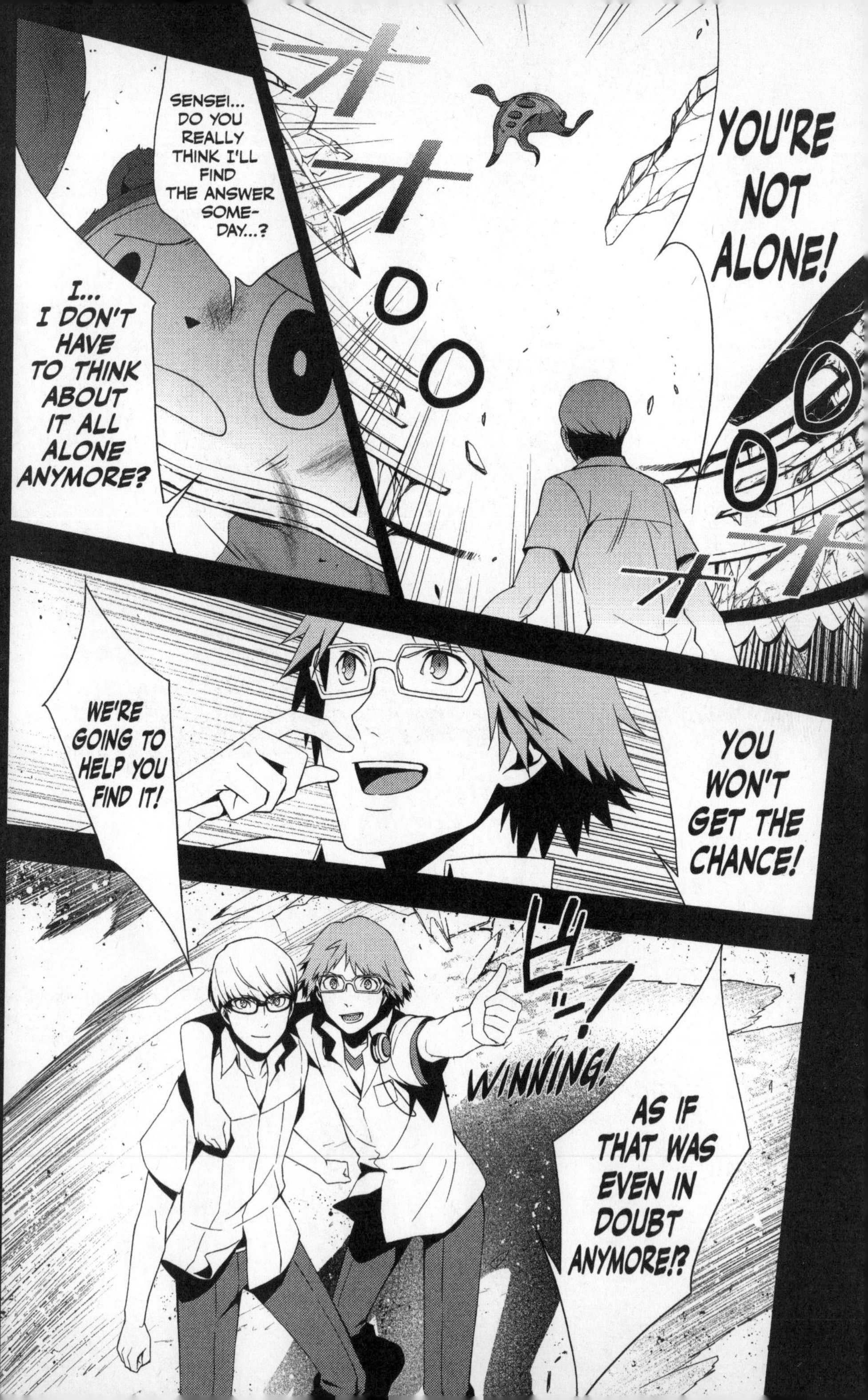
YOU'RE NOT ALONE!
SENSEI... DO YOU REALLY THINK I'LL FIND THE ANSWER SOME-DAY...?
I... I DON'T HAVE TO THINK ABOUT IT ALL ALONE ANYMORE?
YOU WON'T GET THE CHANCE!
WE'RE GOING TO HELP YOU FIND IT!
WINNING!
AS IF THAT WAS EVEN IN DOUBT ANYMORE!?

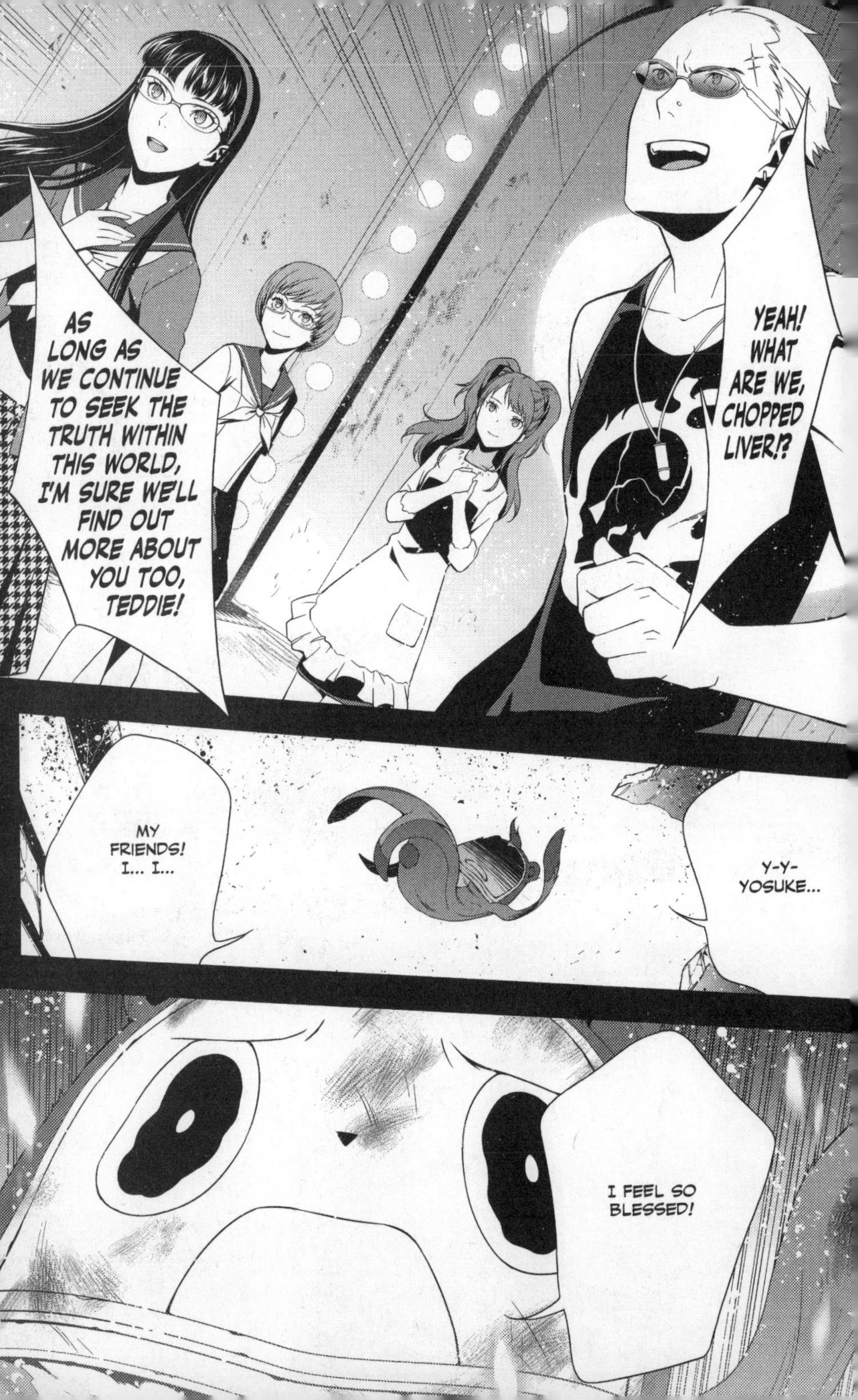
YEAH! WHAT ARE WE, CHOPPED LIVER!?
AS LONG AS WE CONTINUE TO SEEK THE TRUTH WITHIN THIS WORLD, I'M SURE WE'LL FIND OUT MORE ABOUT YOU TOO, TEDDIE!
Y-Y-YOSUKE...
MY FRIENDS! I... I...
I FEEL SO BLESSED!

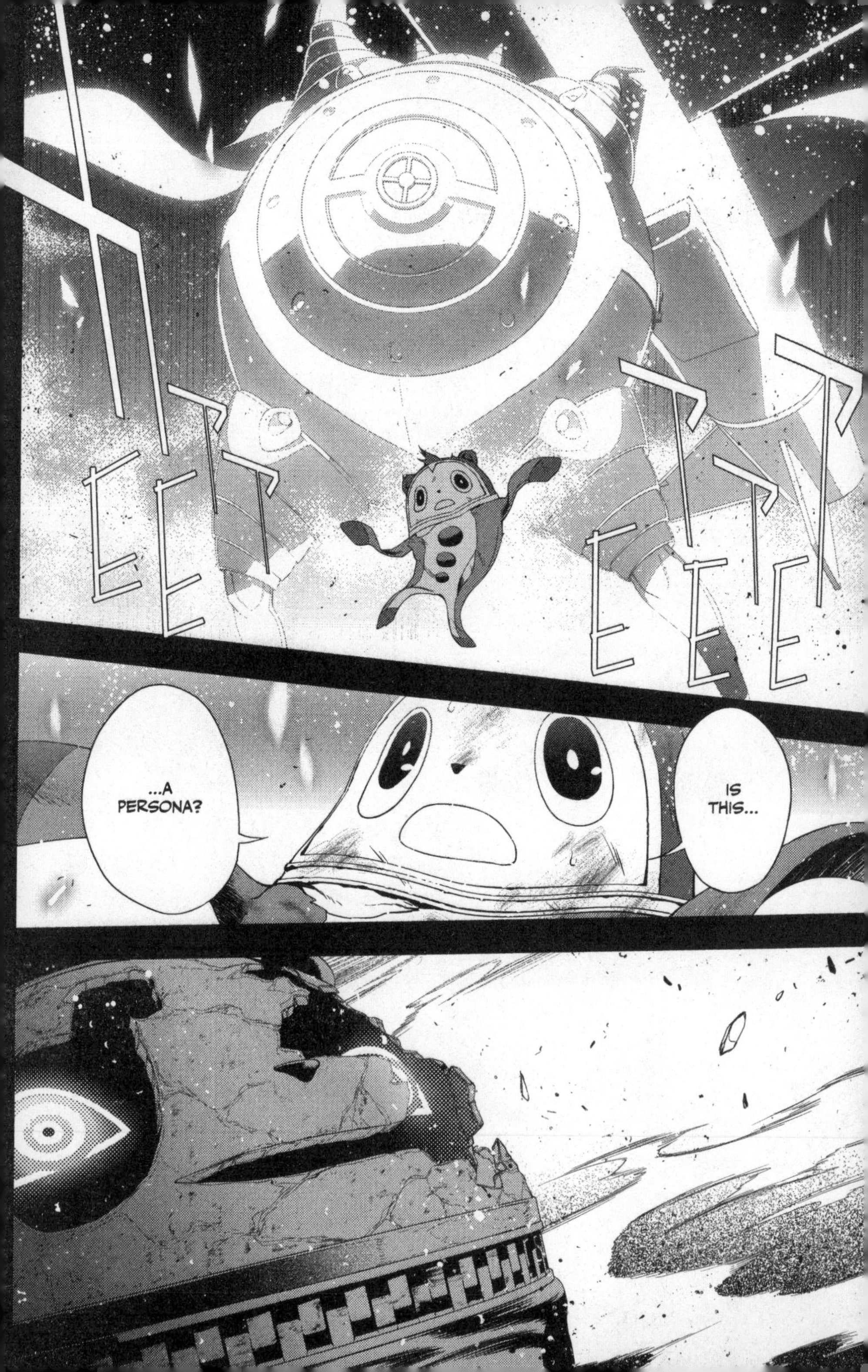
IS THIS...
...A PERSONA?

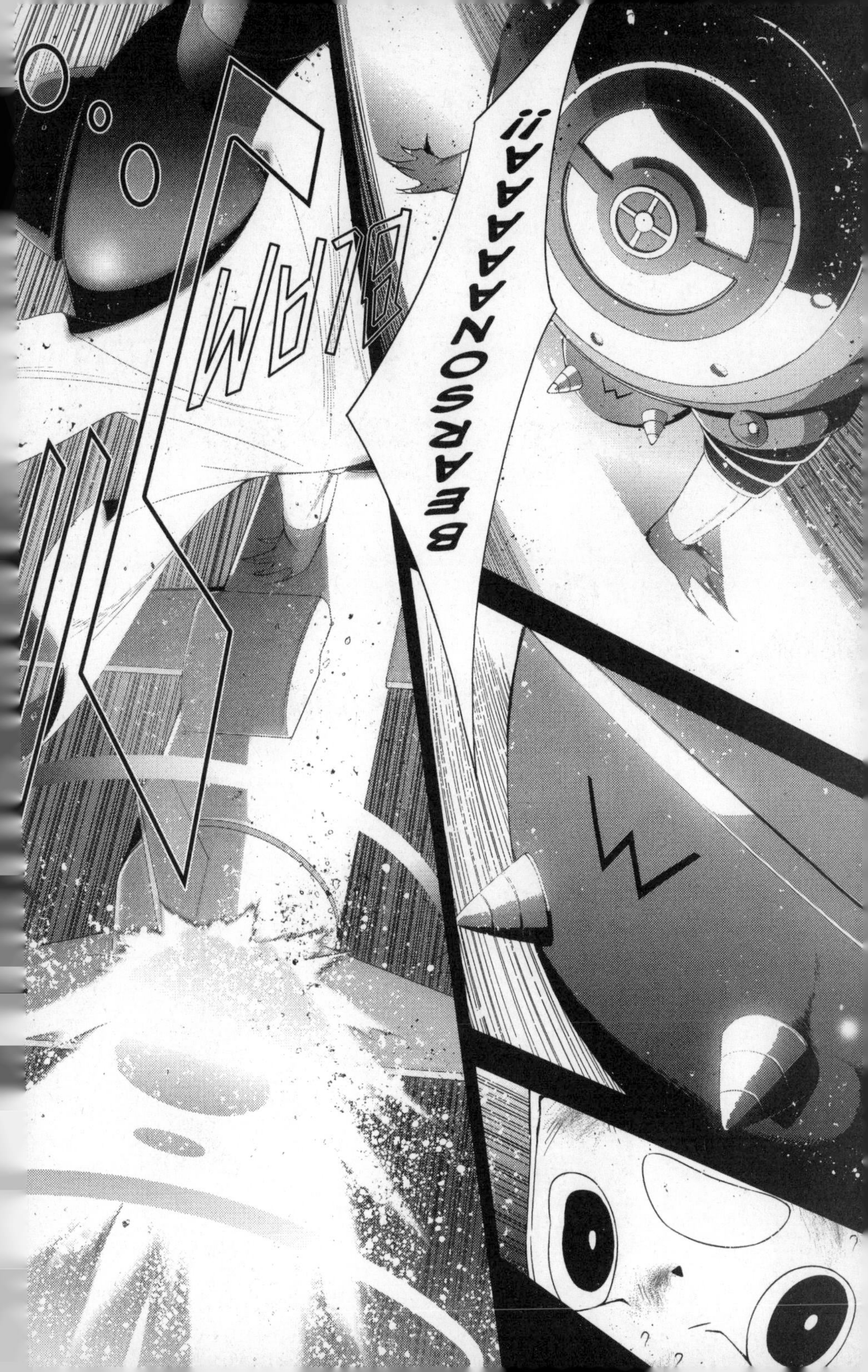
BEARSONAAAAA!!
BLAM

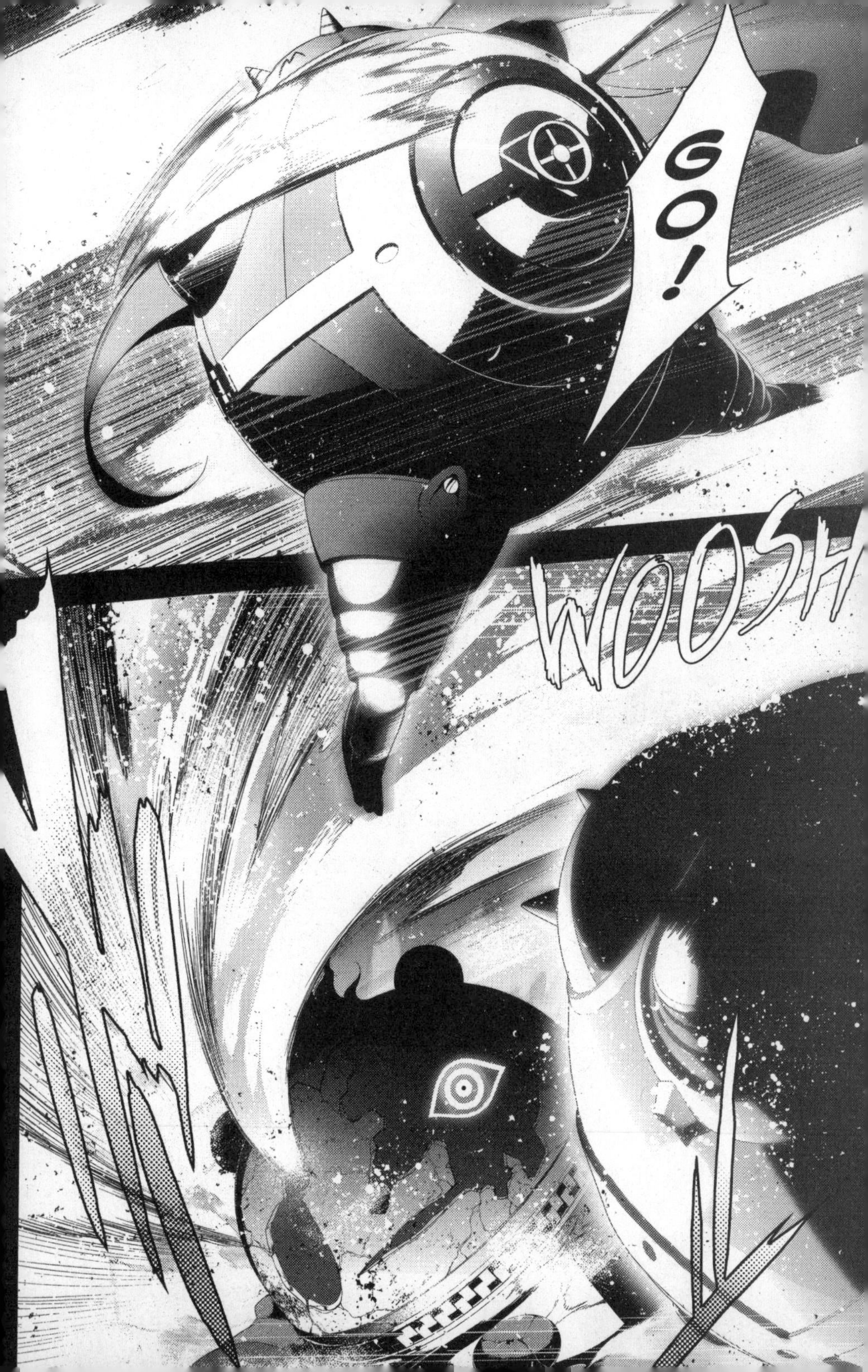
GO!
WOOSH

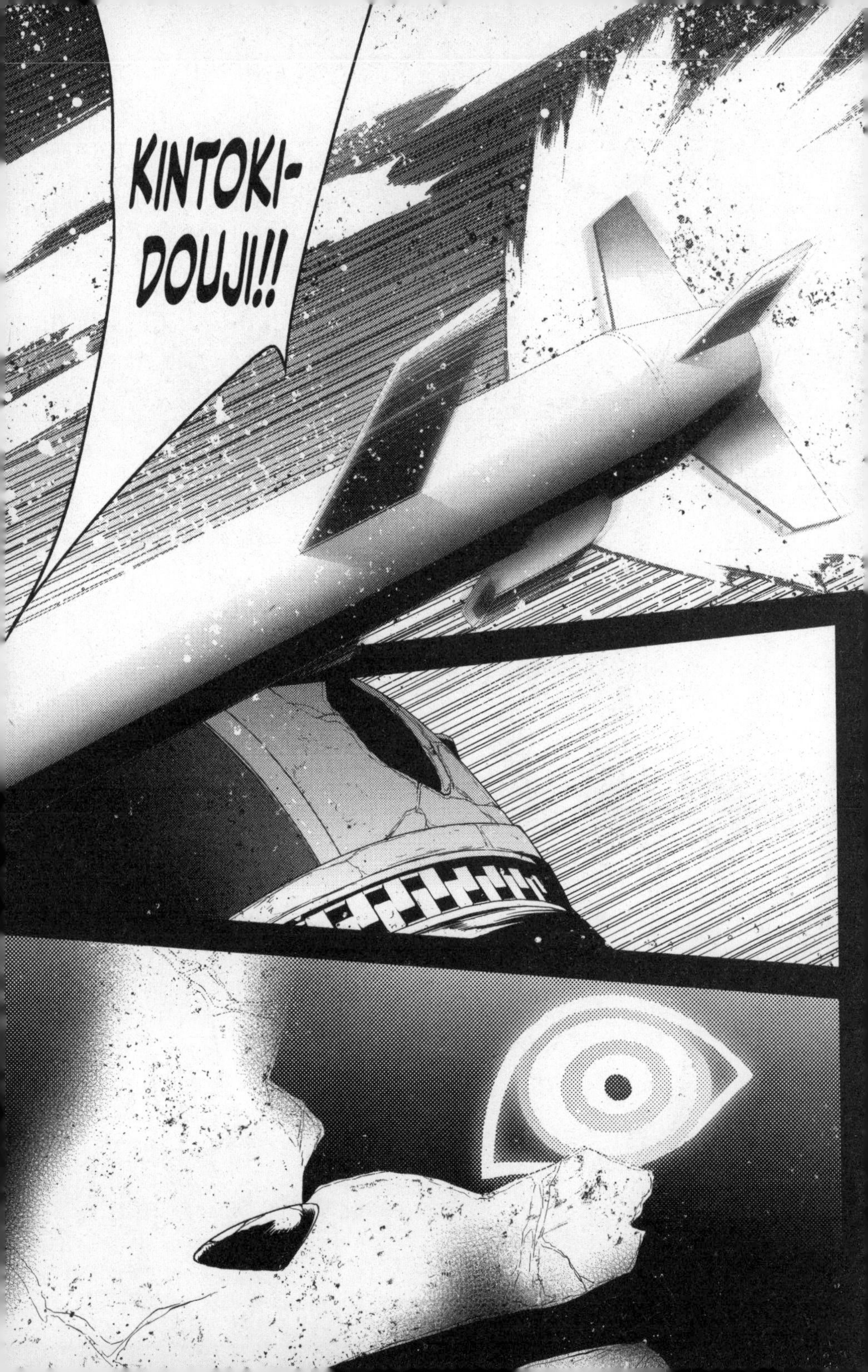
KINTOKI-DOUJI!!

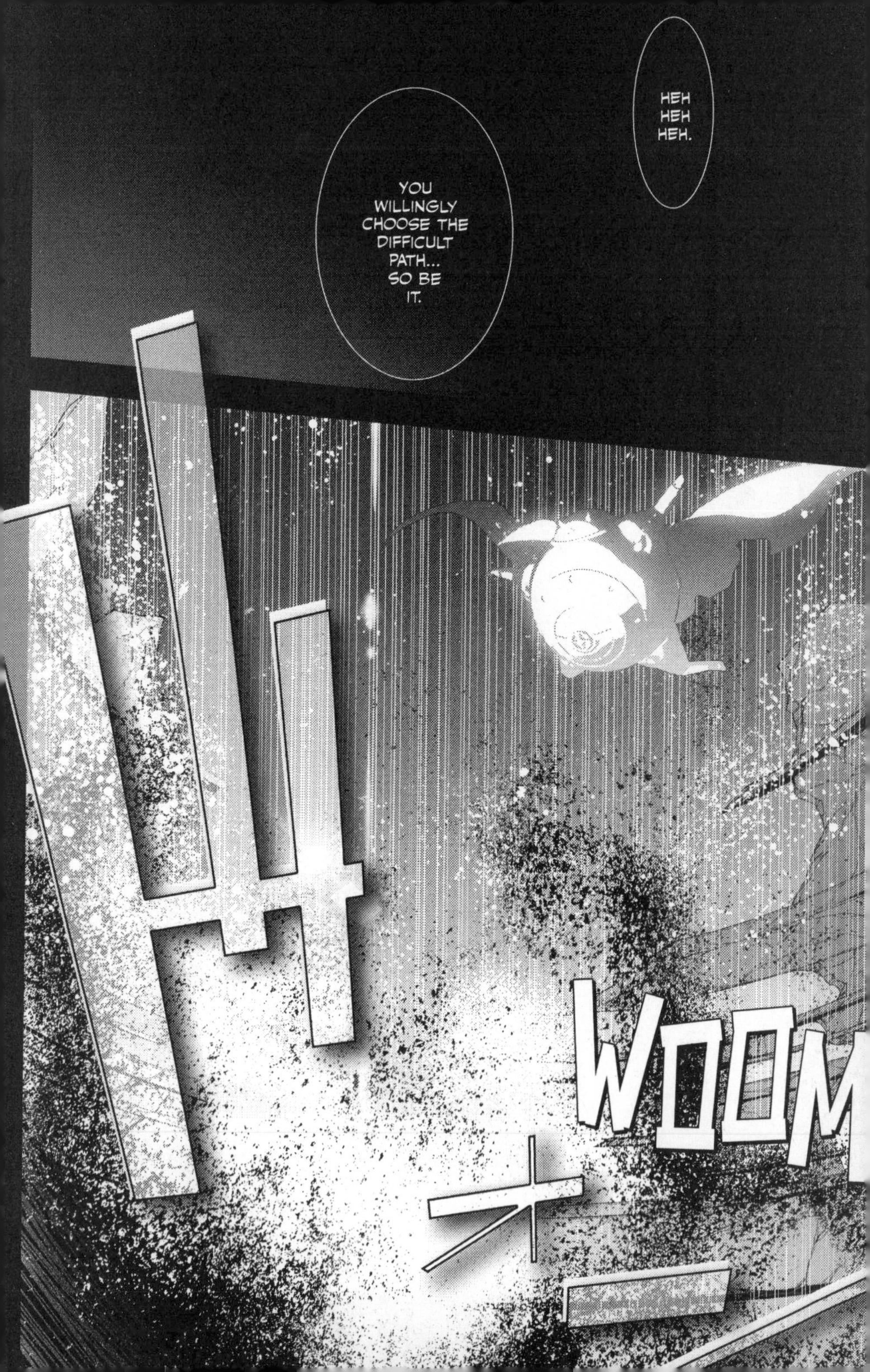
HEH HEH HEH.
YOU WILLINGLY CHOOSE THE DIFFICULT PATH... SO BE IT.
WOOM

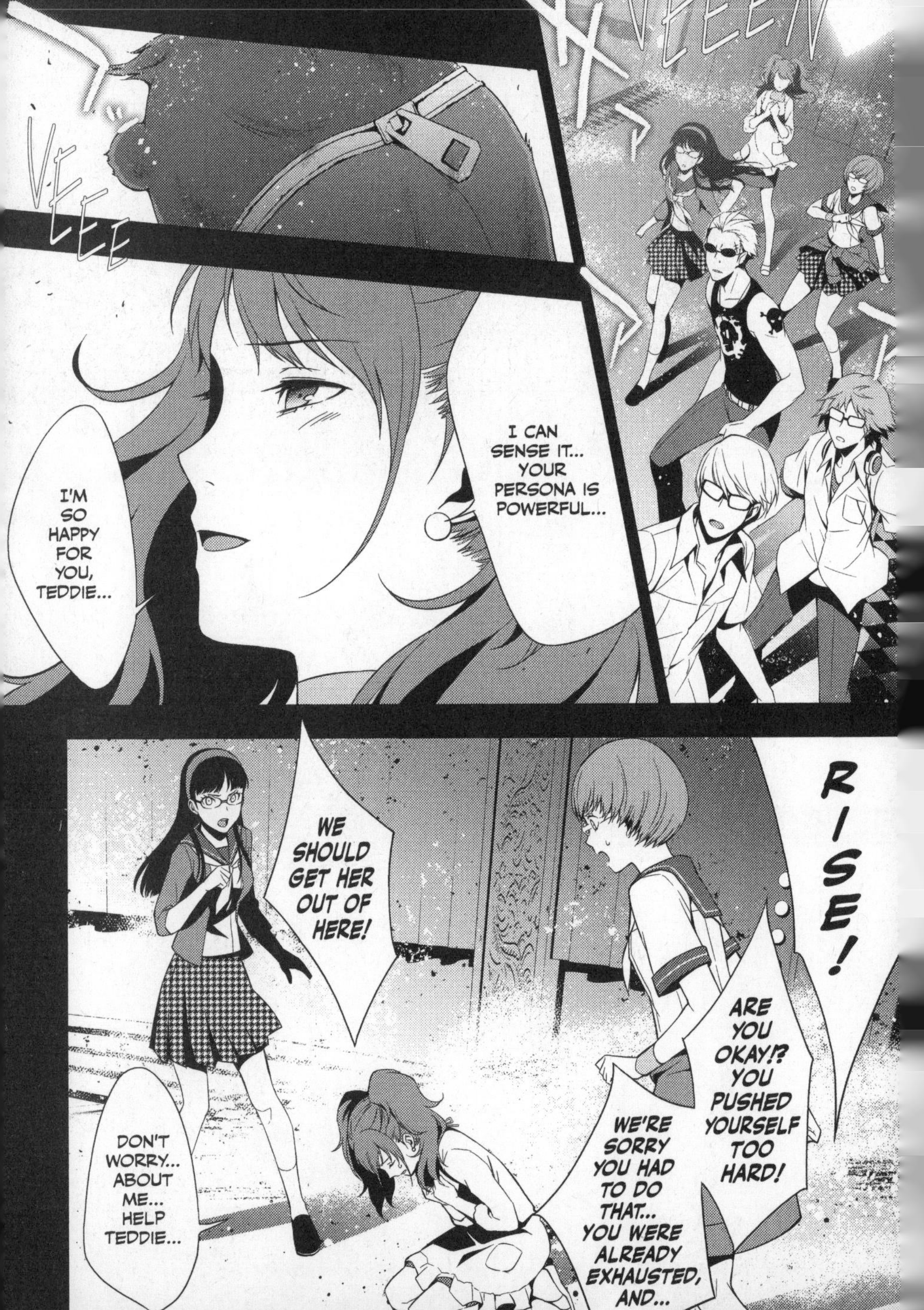
VEEEN
VEEE
I CAN SENSE IT... YOUR PERSONA IS POWERFUL...
I'M SO HAPPY FOR YOU, TEDDIE...
RISE!
ARE YOU OKAY!? YOU PUSHED YOURSELF TOO HARD!
WE'RE SORRY YOU HAD TO DO THAT... YOU WERE ALREADY EXHAUSTED, AND...
WE SHOULD GET HER OUT OF HERE!
DON'T WORRY... ABOUT ME... HELP TEDDIE...

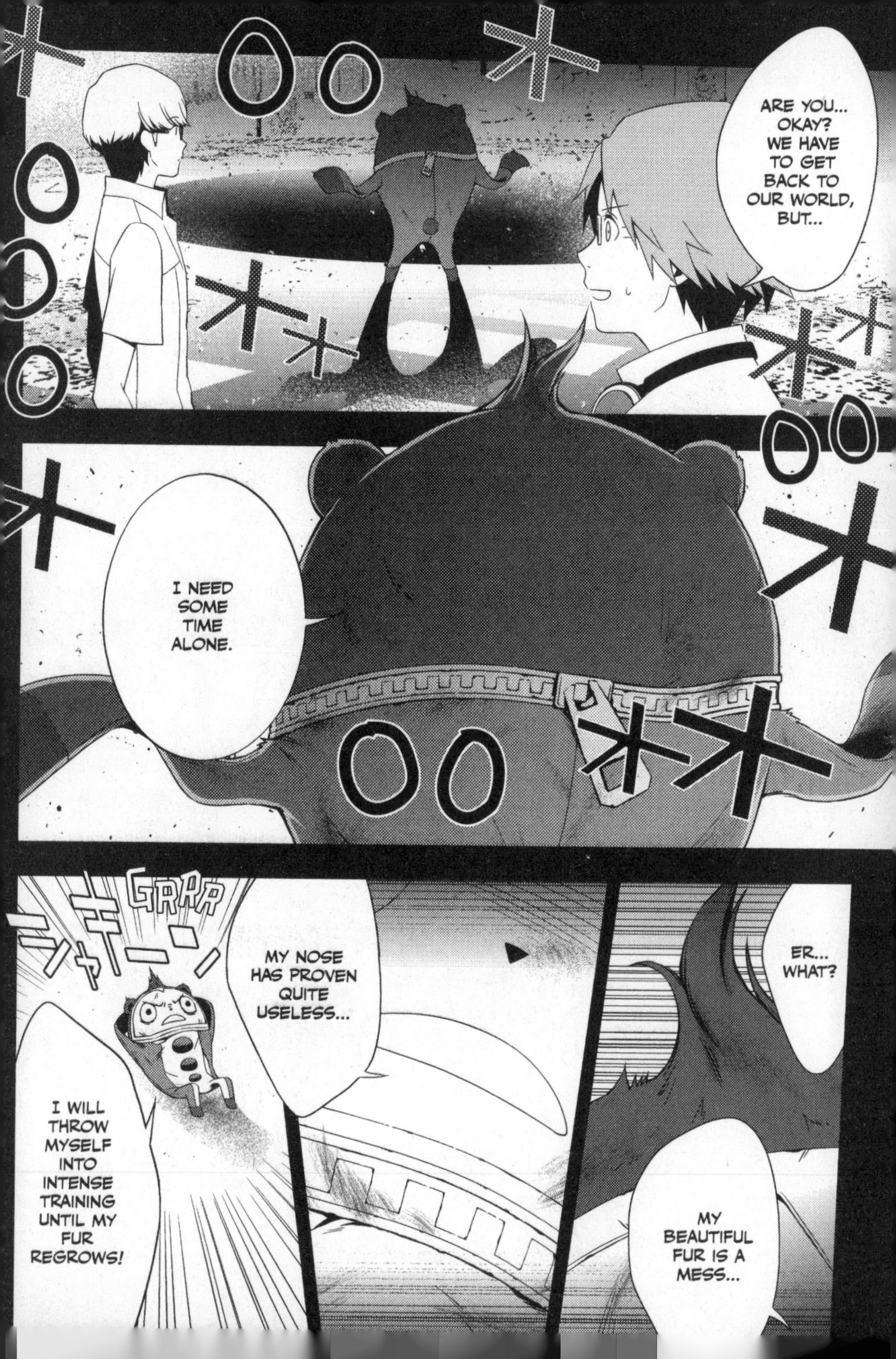
ARE YOU... OKAY? WE HAVE TO GET BACK TO OUR WORLD, BUT...
I NEED SOME TIME ALONE.
ER... WHAT?
MY BEAUTIFUL FUR IS A MESS...
MY NOSE HAS PROVEN QUITE USELESS...
GRRR
I WILL THROW MYSELF INTO INTENSE TRAINING UNTIL MY FUR REGROWS!

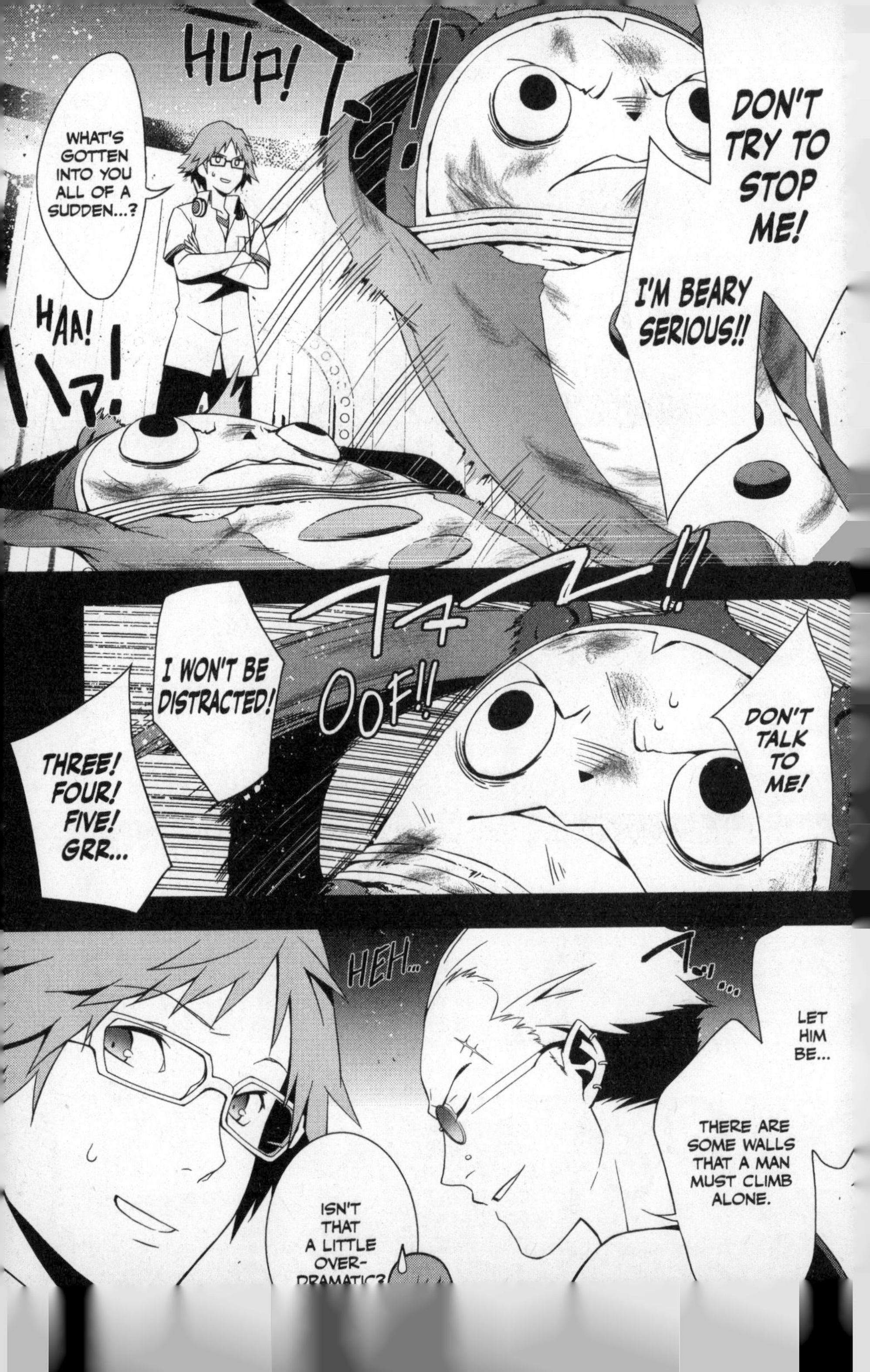
DON'T TRY TO STOP ME!
I'M BEARY SERIOUS!!
HUP!
WHAT'S GOTTEN INTO YOU ALL OF A SUDDEN...?
HAA!
DON'T TALK TO ME!
OOF!!
I WON'T BE DISTRACTED!
THREE! FOUR! FIVE! GRR...
LET HIM BE...
THERE ARE SOME WALLS THAT A MAN MUST CLIMB ALONE.
HEH...
ISN'T THAT A LITTLE OVER-DRAMATIC?

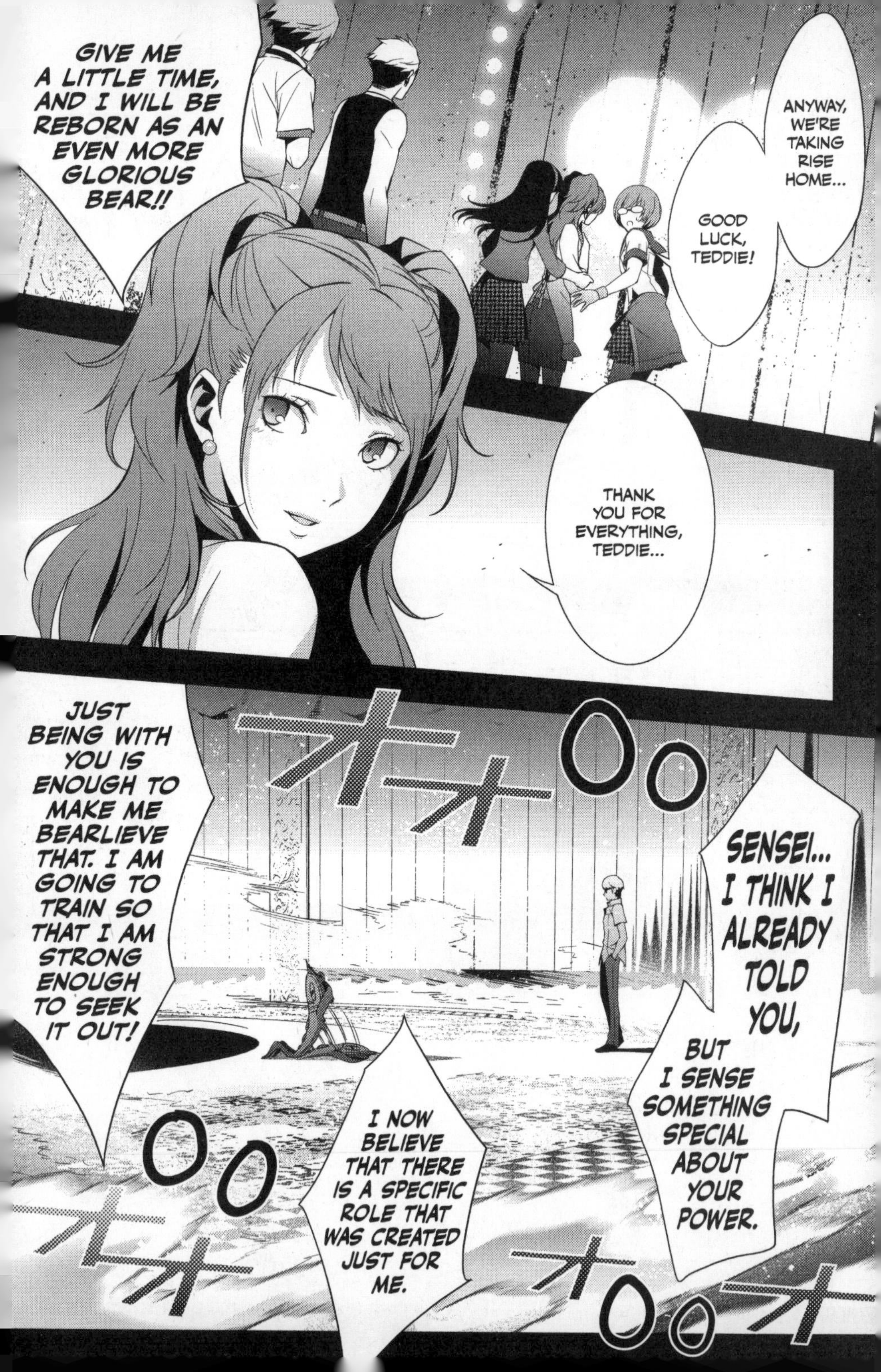
ANYWAY, WE'RE TAKING RISE HOME...
GOOD LUCK, TEDDIE!
GIVE ME A LITTLE TIME, AND I WILL BE REBORN AS AN EVEN MORE GLORIOUS BEAR!!
THANK YOU FOR EVERYTHING, TEDDIE...
SENSEI... I THINK I ALREADY TOLD YOU,
BUT I SENSE SOMETHING SPECIAL ABOUT YOUR POWER.
I NOW BELIEVE THAT THERE IS A SPECIFIC ROLE THAT WAS CREATED JUST FOR ME.
JUST BEING WITH YOU IS ENOUGH TO MAKE ME BEARLIEVE THAT. I AM GOING TO TRAIN SO THAT I AM STRONG ENOUGH TO SEEK IT OUT!

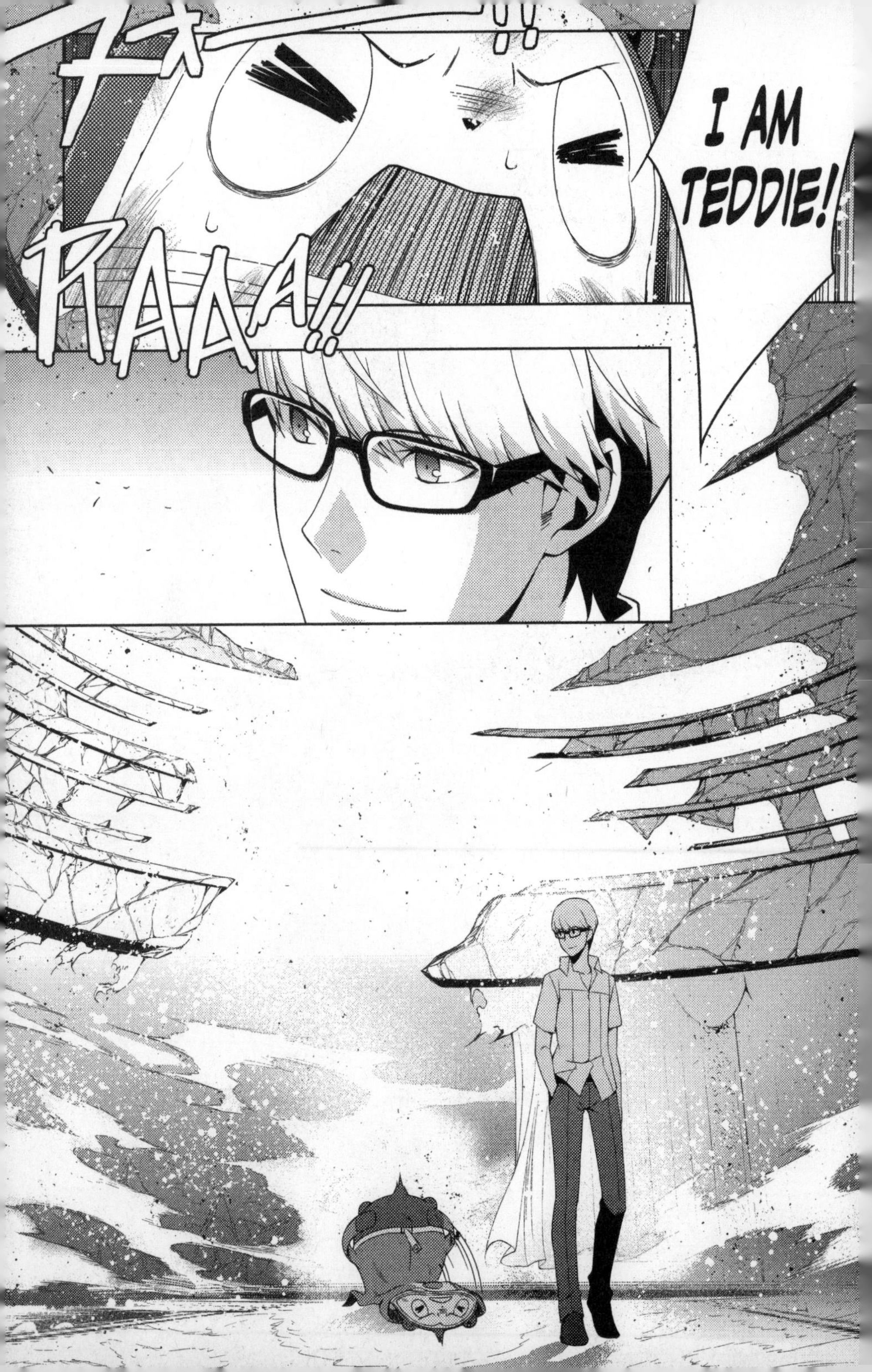
I AM TEDDIE!
RAAA!!

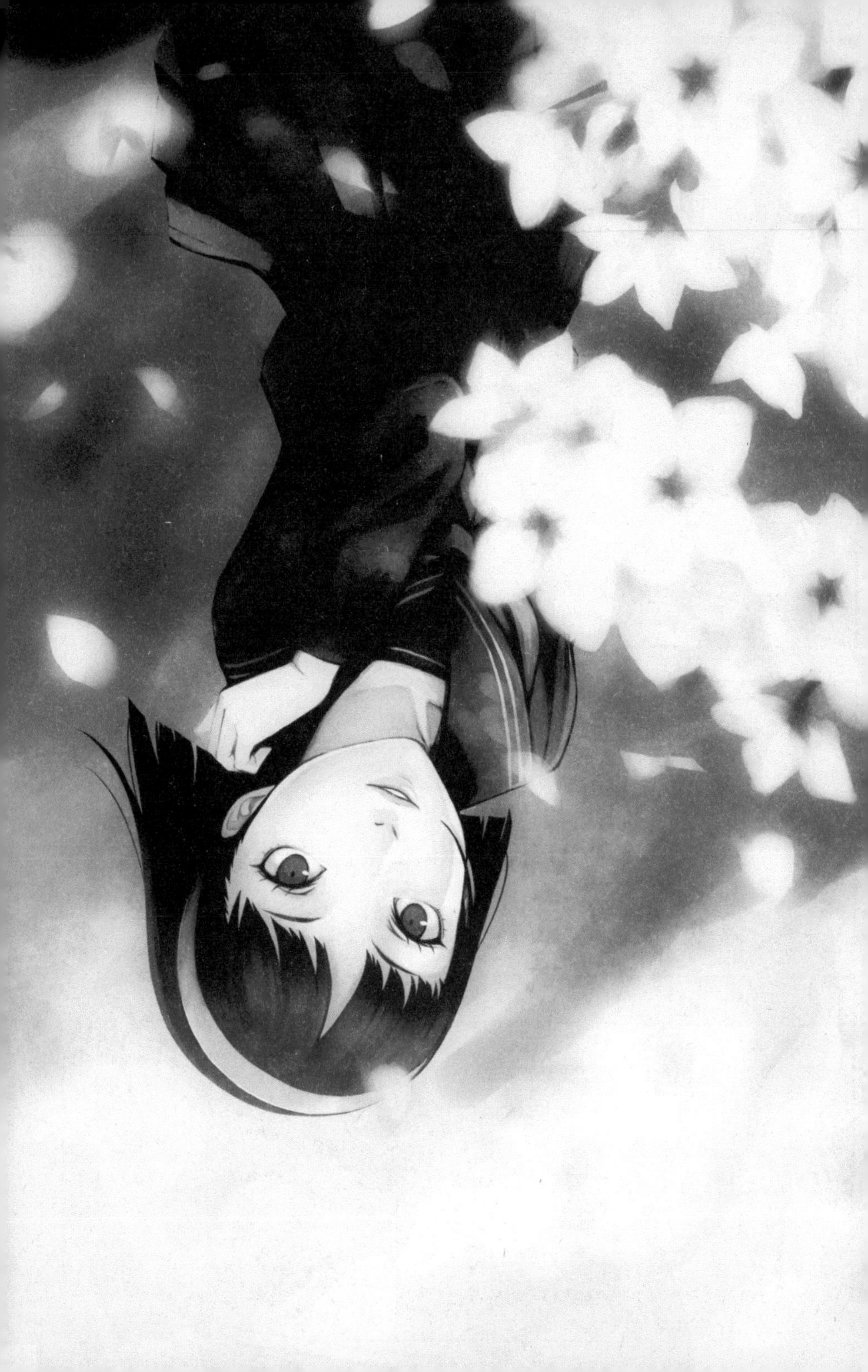

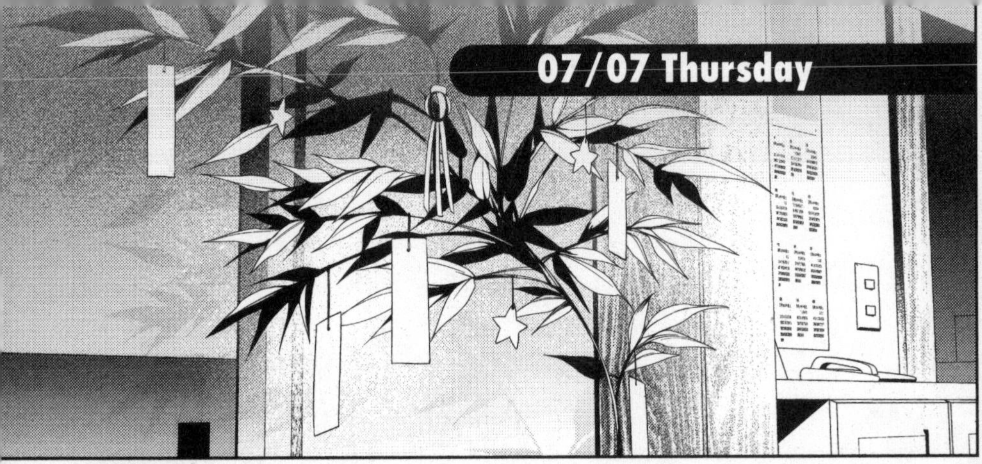
07/07 Thursday

#25 Stray

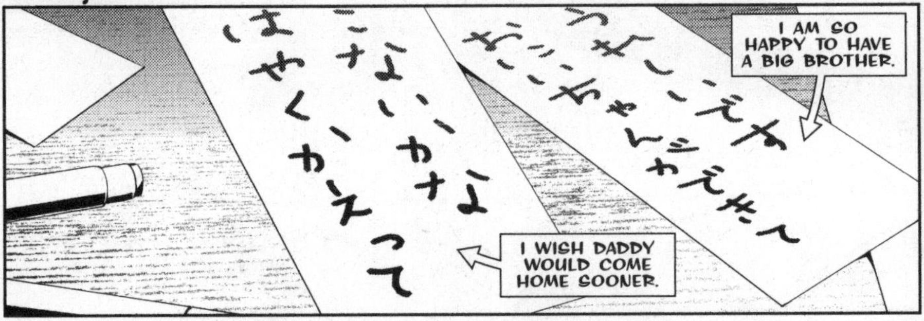
I AM SO HAPPY TO HAVE A BIG BROTHER.
はやくかえって
こないかな
I WISH DADDY WOULD COME HOME SOONER.

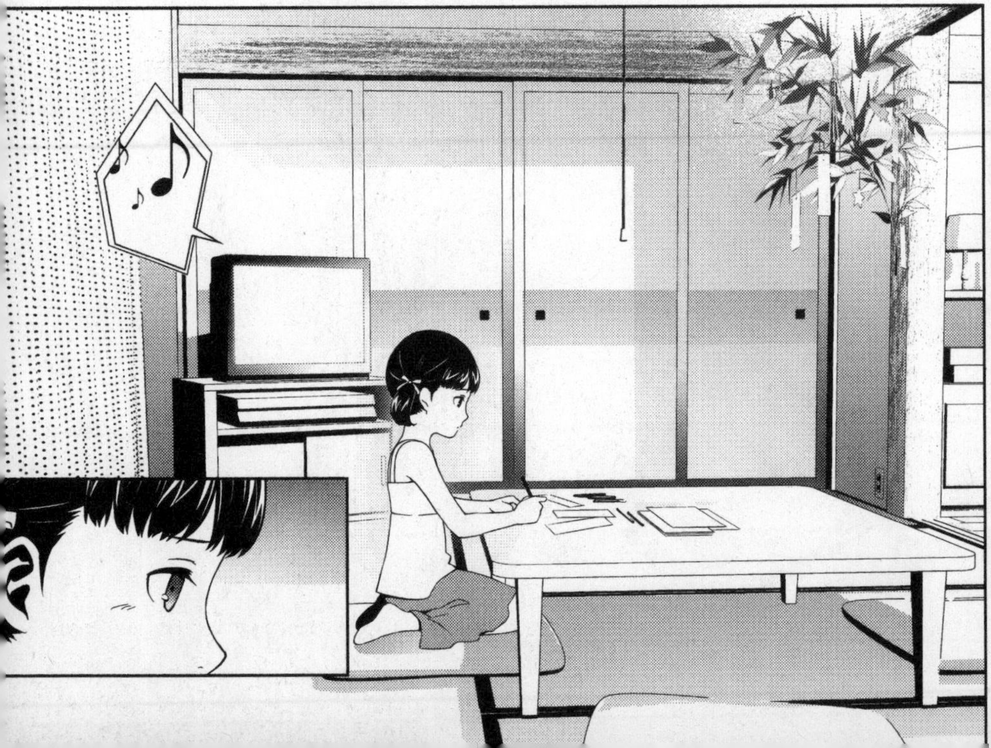

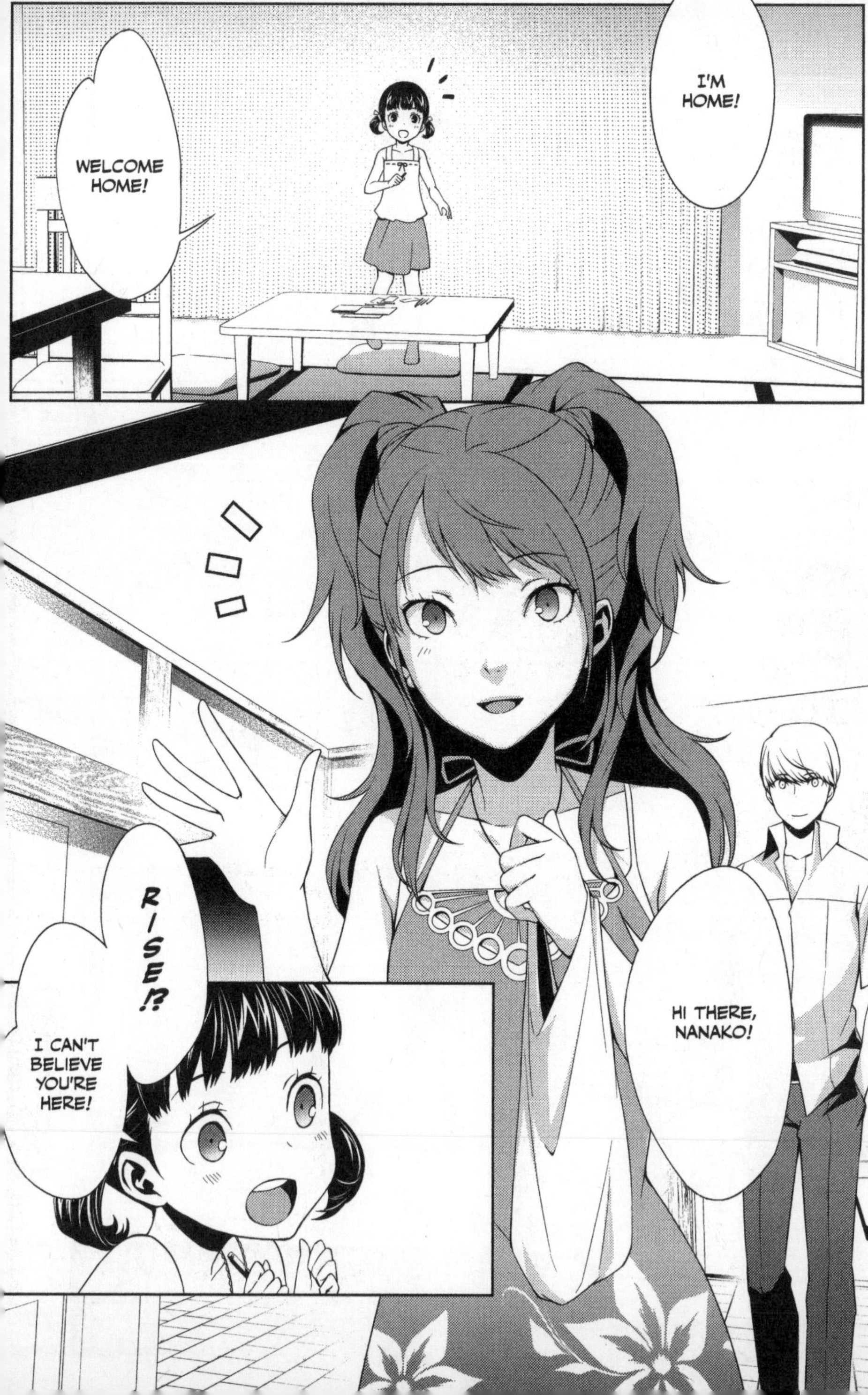
I'M HOME!
WELCOME HOME!
HI THERE, NANAKO!
RISE!?
I CAN'T BELIEVE YOU'RE HERE!

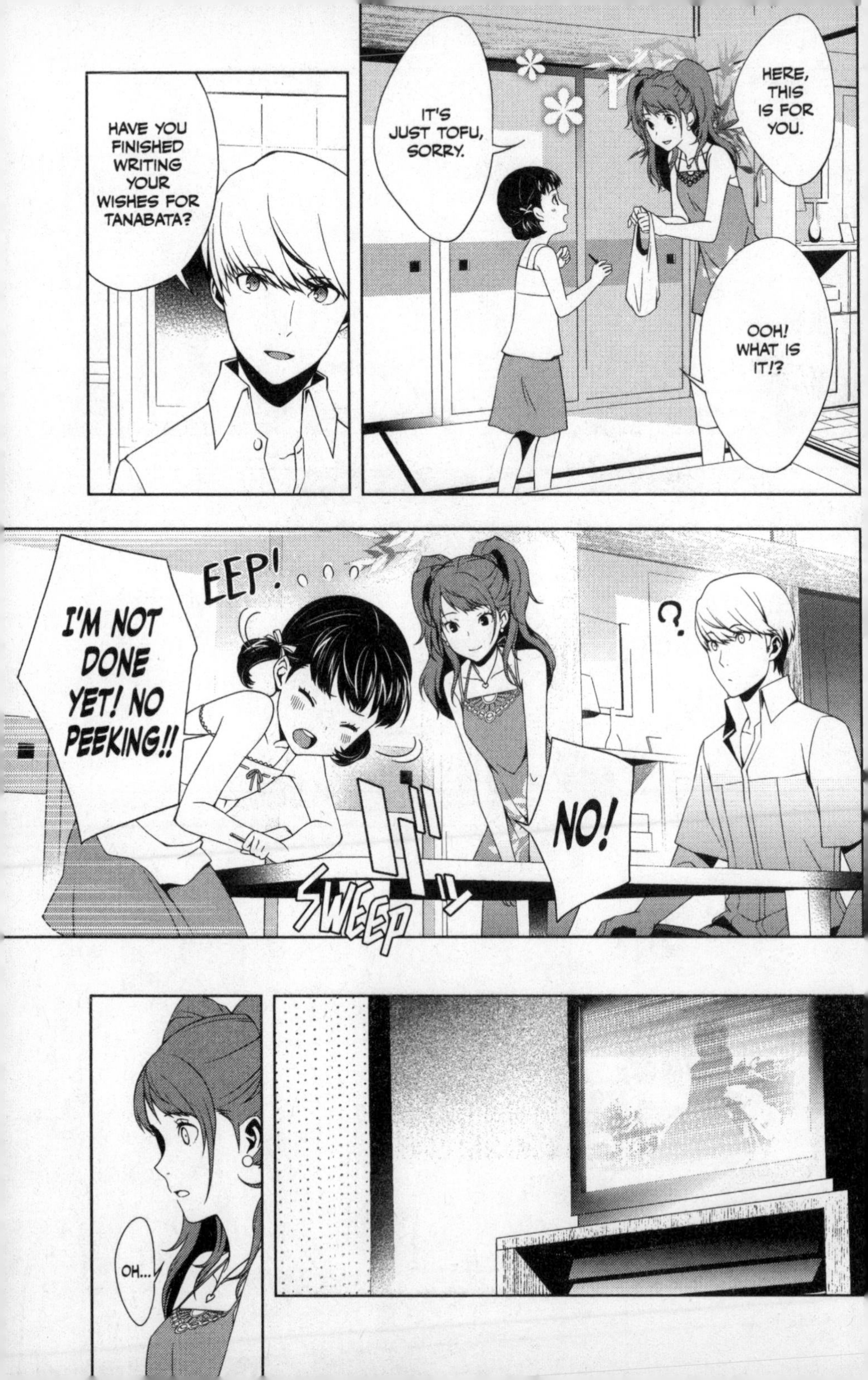
HERE, THIS IS FOR YOU.
OOH! WHAT IS IT!?
IT'S JUST TOFU, SORRY.
HAVE YOU FINISHED WRITING YOUR WISHES FOR TANABATA?
?
NO!
EEP!
I'M NOT DONE YET! NO PEEKING!!
SWEEP
OH...

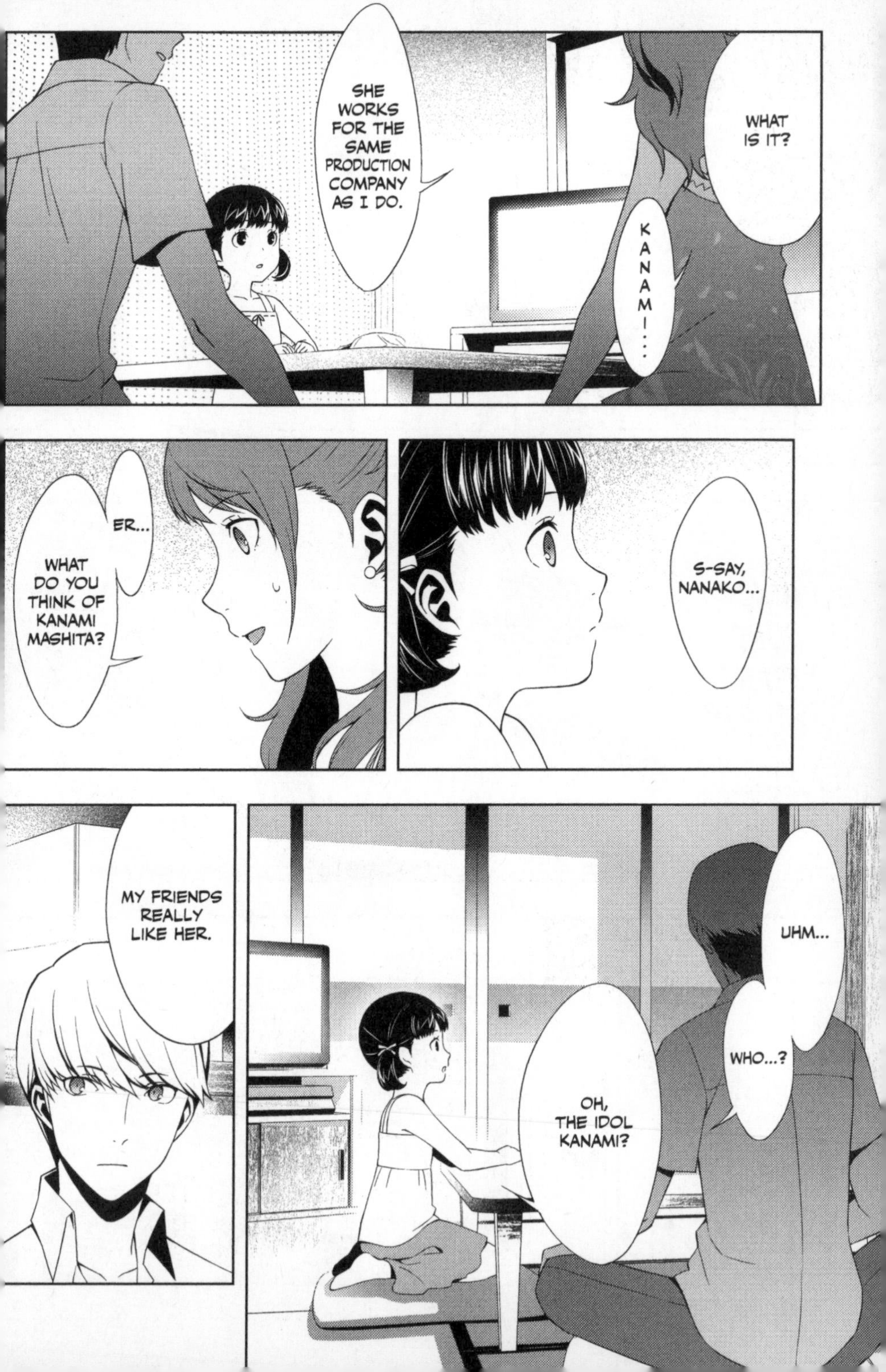
WHAT IS IT?
KANAMI!...
SHE WORKS FOR THE SAME PRODUCTION COMPANY AS I DO.
S-SAY, NANAKO...
ER...
WHAT DO YOU THINK OF KANAMI MASHITA?
UHM...
WHO...?
OH, THE IDOL KANAMI?
MY FRIENDS REALLY LIKE HER.

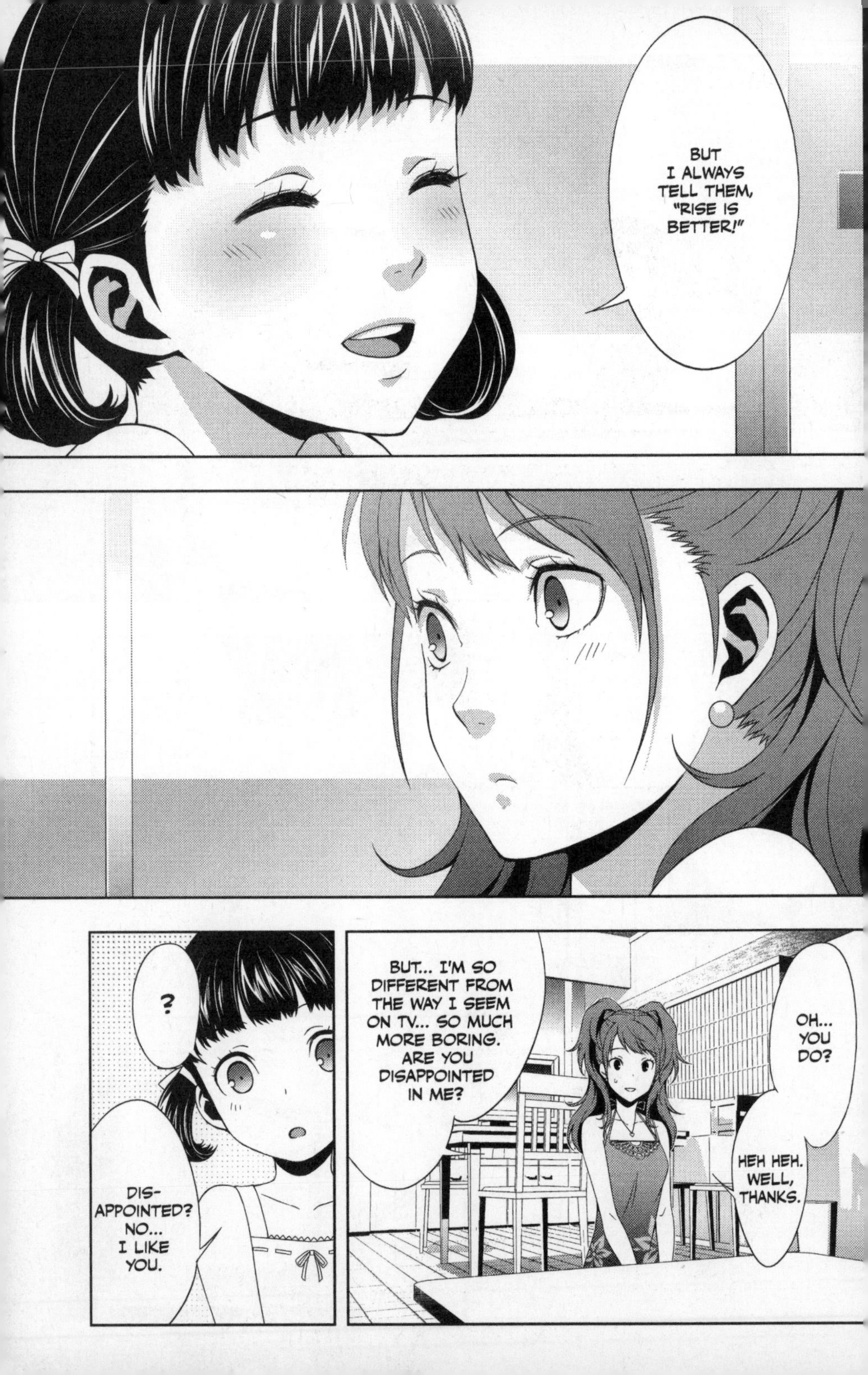
BUT I ALWAYS TELL THEM, "RISE IS BETTER!"
OH... YOU DO?
HEH HEH. WELL, THANKS.
BUT... I'M SO DIFFERENT FROM THE WAY I SEEM ON TV... SO MUCH MORE BORING. ARE YOU DISAPPOINTED IN ME?
?
DIS-APPOINTED? NO... I LIKE YOU.

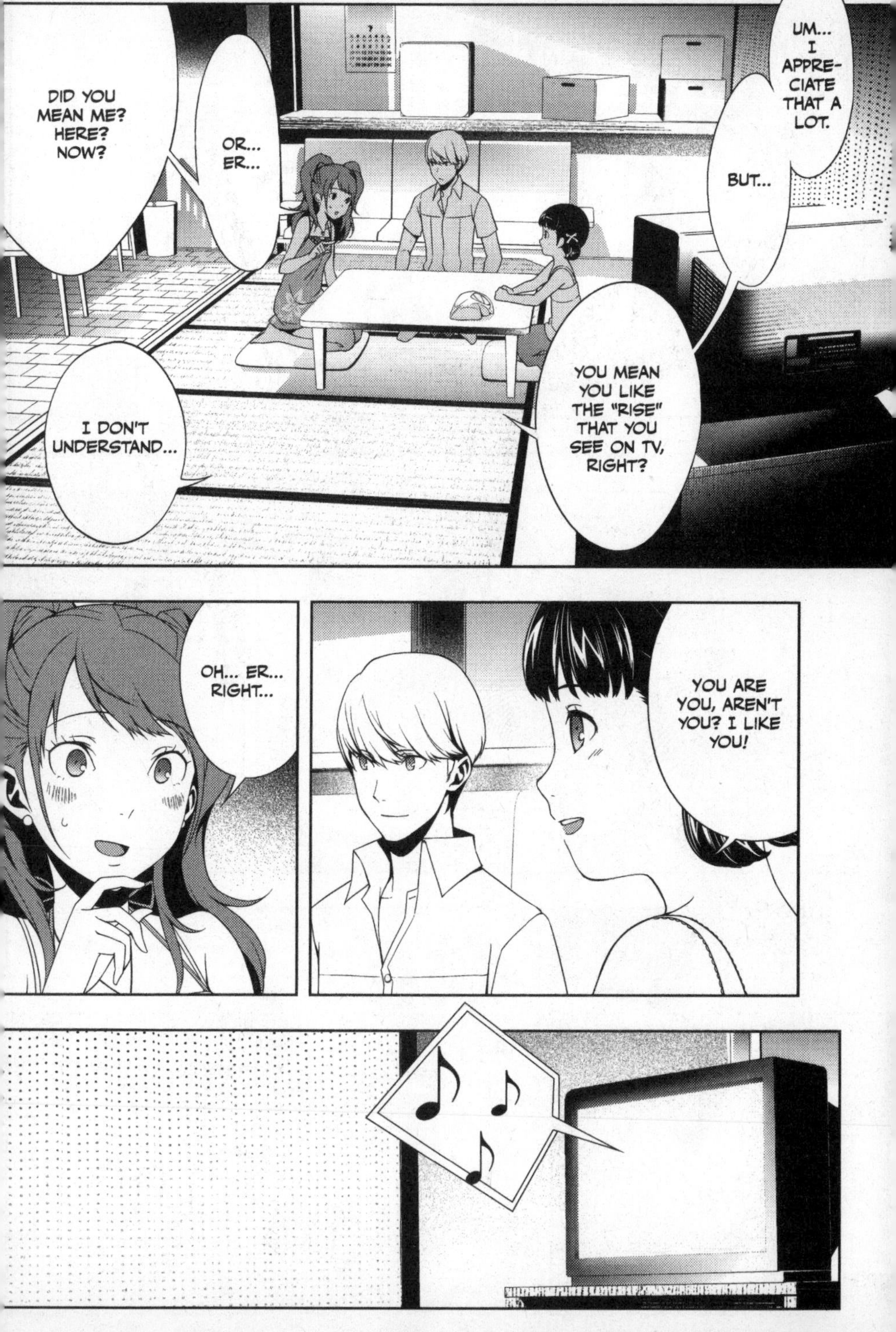
UM... I APPRE-CIATE THAT A LOT.
BUT...
YOU MEAN YOU LIKE THE "RISE" THAT YOU SEE ON TV, RIGHT?
OR... ER...
DID YOU MEAN ME? HERE? NOW?
I DON'T UNDERSTAND...
YOU ARE YOU, AREN'T YOU? I LIKE YOU!
OH... ER... RIGHT...

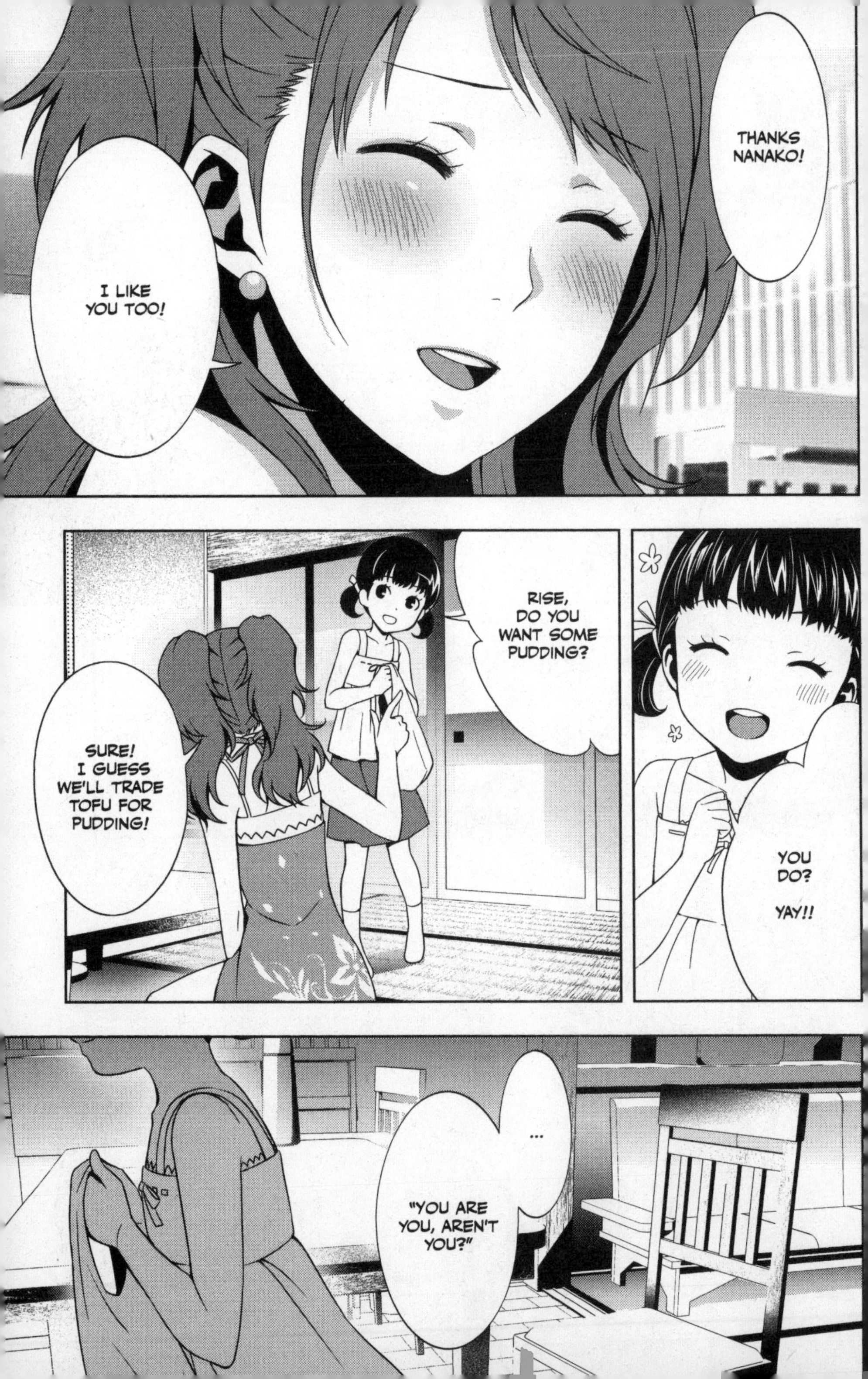
THANKS NANAKO!
I LIKE YOU TOO!
YOU DO?
YAY!!
RISE, DO YOU WANT SOME PUDDING?
SURE! I GUESS WE'LL TRADE TOFU FOR PUDDING!
...
"YOU ARE YOU, AREN'T YOU?"

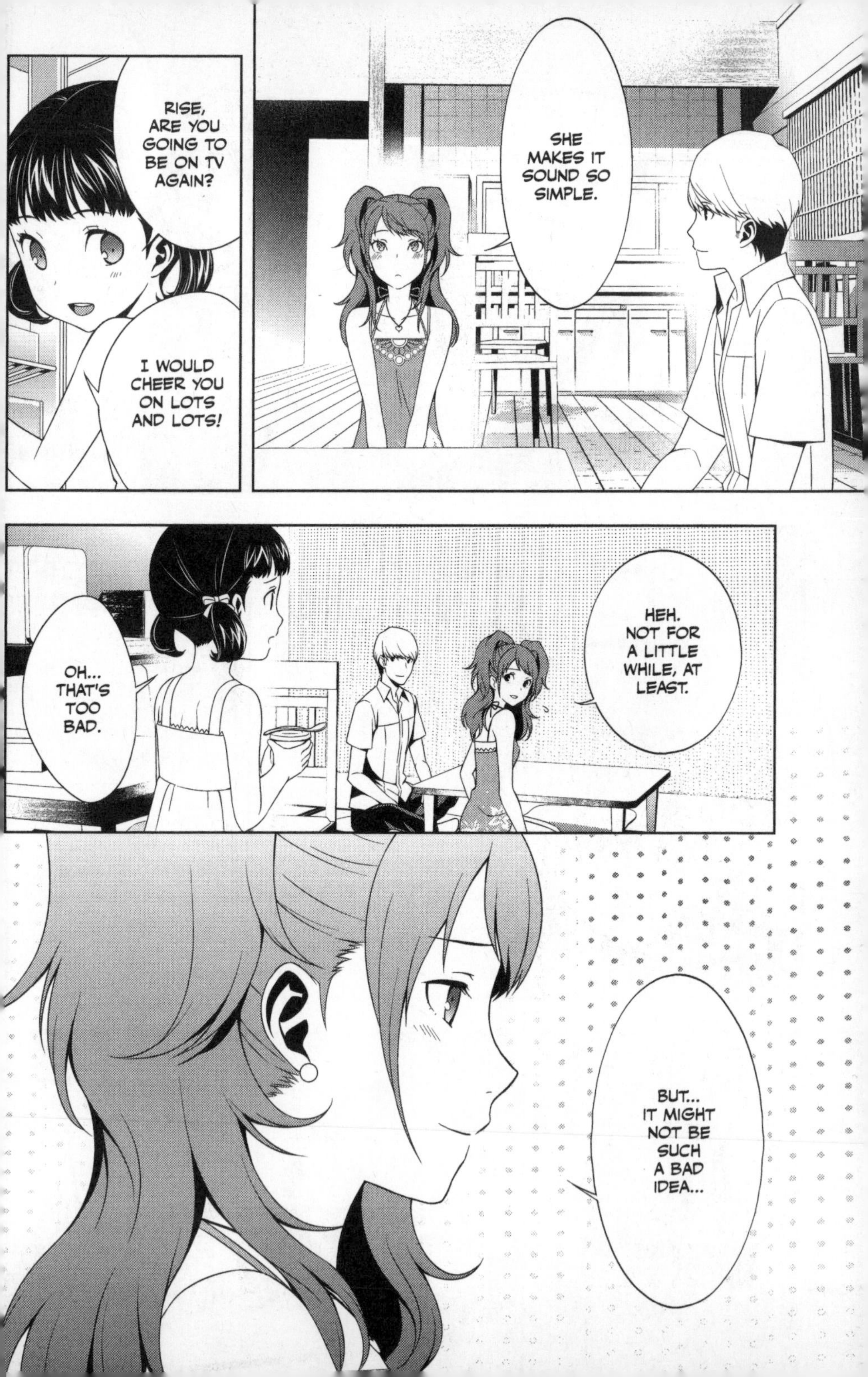
SHE MAKES IT SOUND SO SIMPLE.
RISE, ARE YOU GOING TO BE ON TV AGAIN?
I WOULD CHEER YOU ON LOTS AND LOTS!
HEH. NOT FOR A LITTLE WHILE, AT LEAST.
OH... THAT'S TOO BAD.
BUT... IT MIGHT NOT BE SUCH A BAD IDEA...

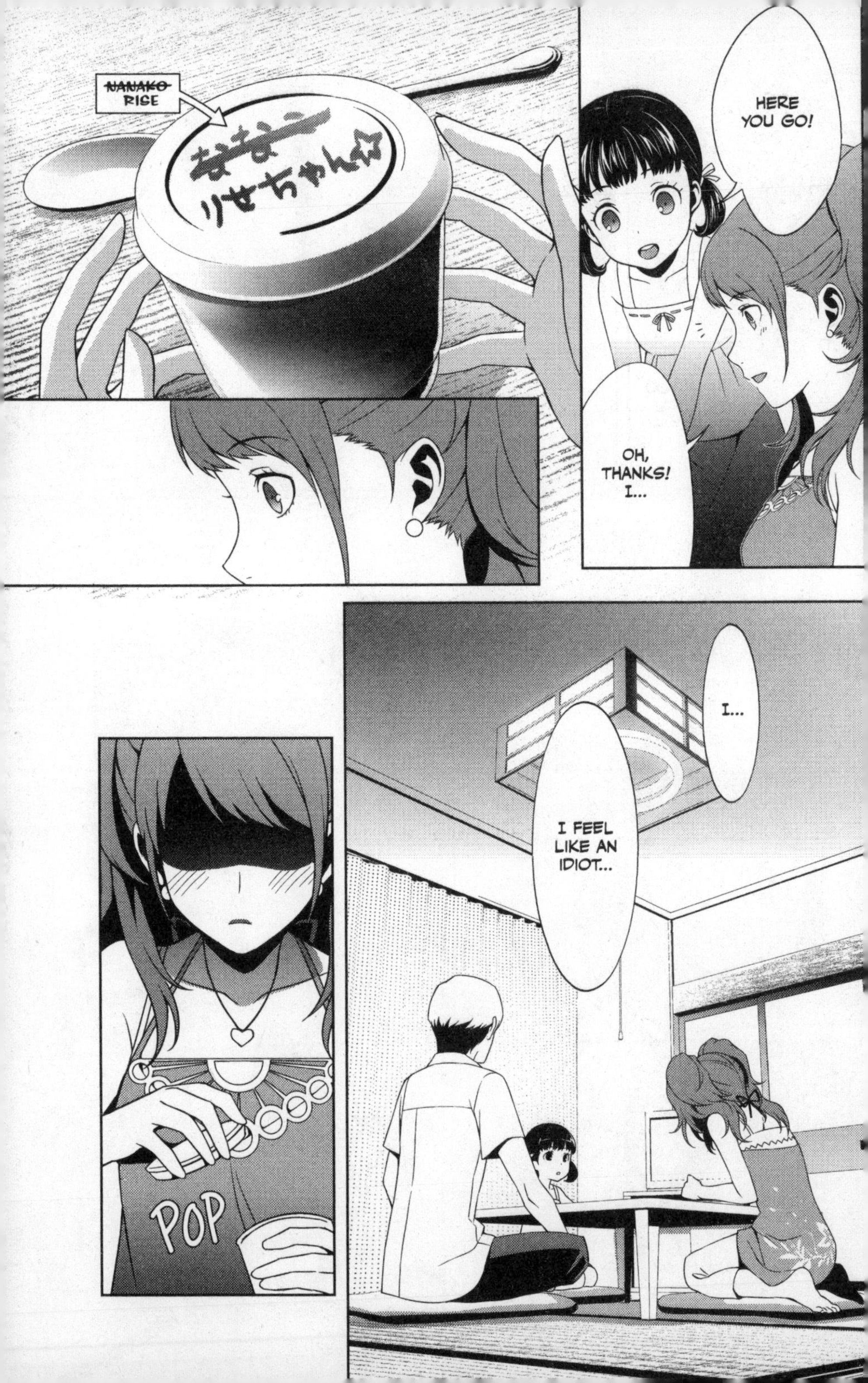
HERE YOU GO!
OH, THANKS! I...
NANAKO RISE
ななこ りせちゃん☆
I...
I FEEL LIKE AN IDIOT...
POP

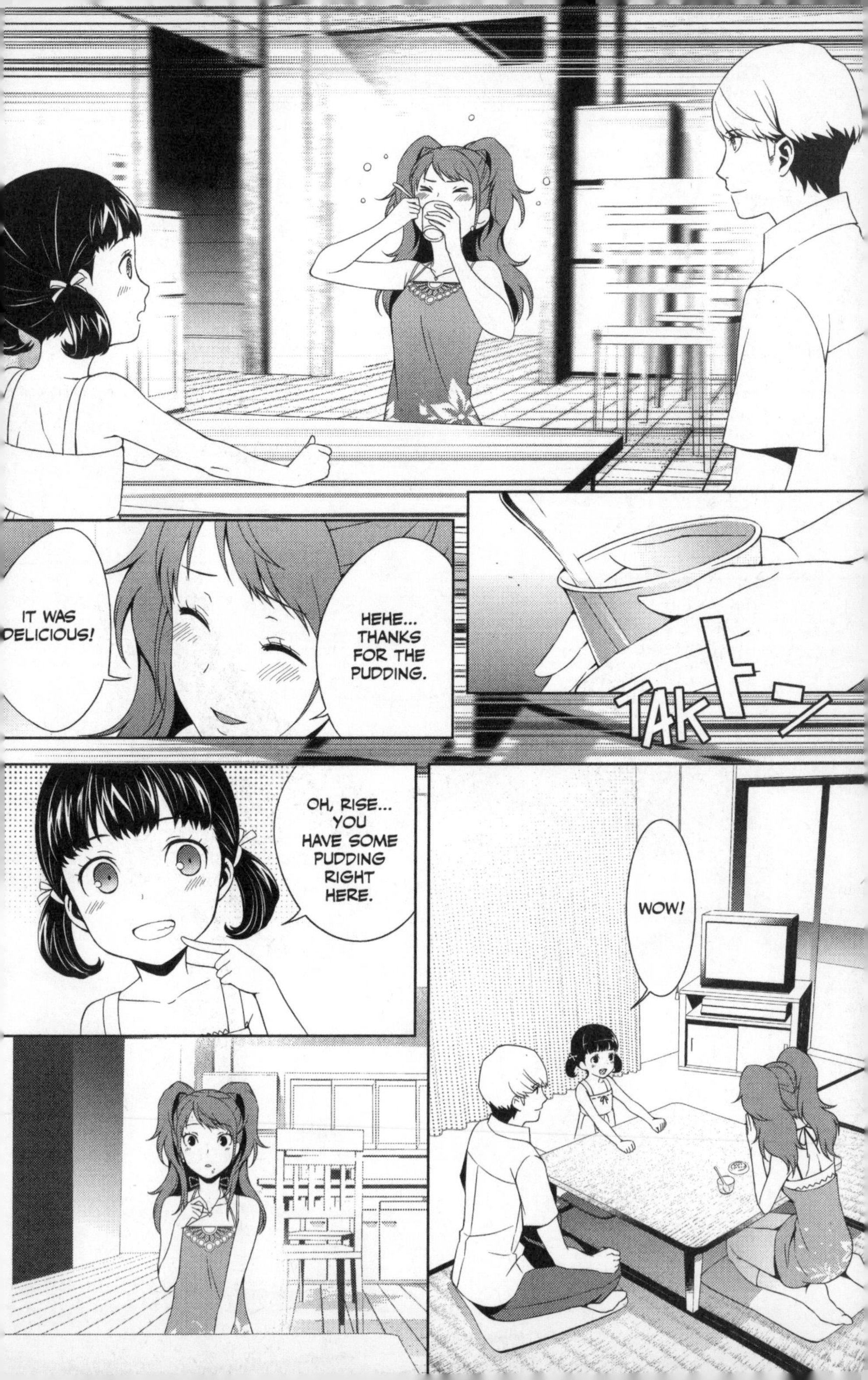
TAK
HEHE... THANKS FOR THE PUDDING.
IT WAS DELICIOUS!
WOW!
OH, RISE... YOU HAVE SOME PUDDING RIGHT HERE.

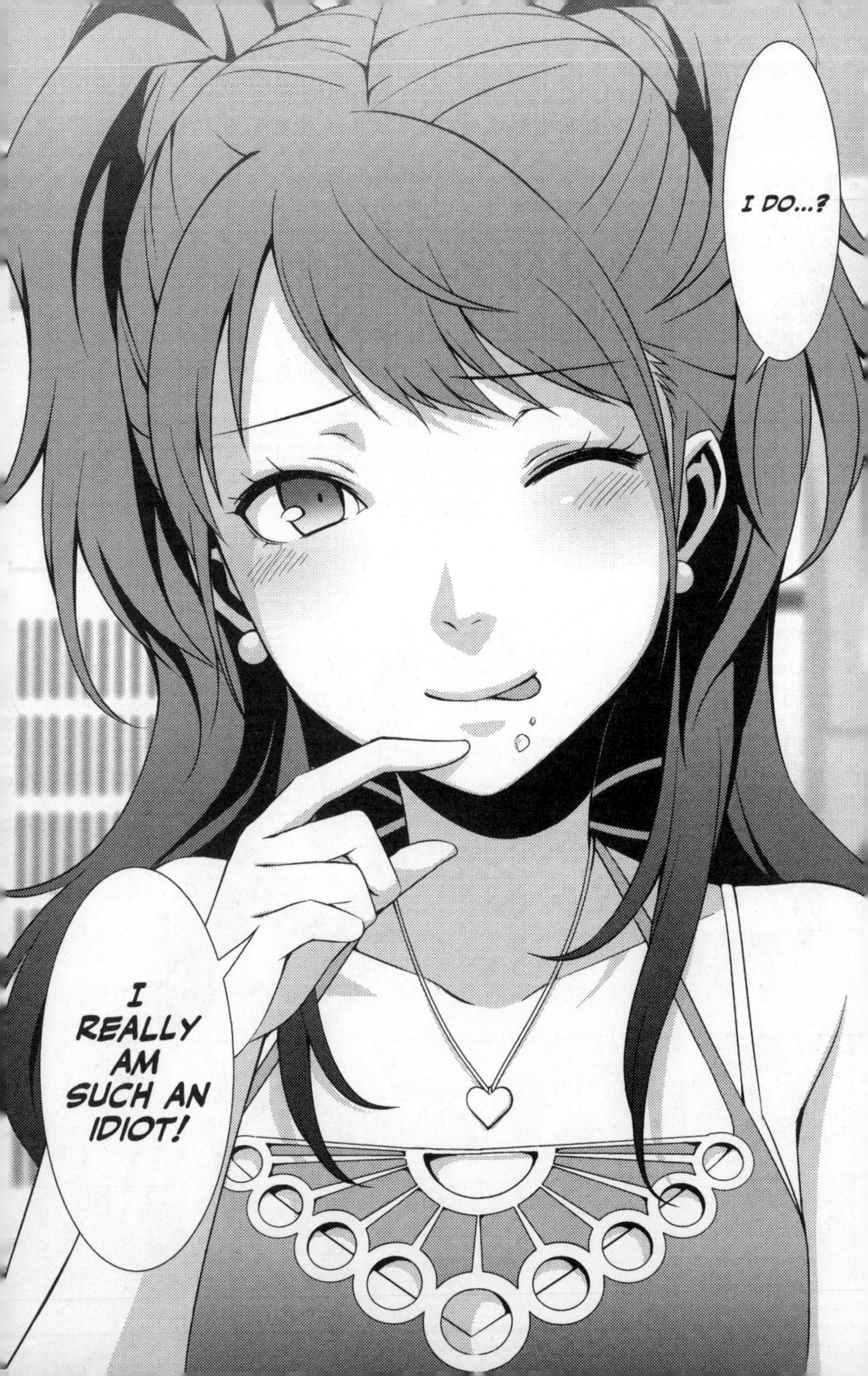
I DO...?
I REALLY AM SUCH AN IDIOT!

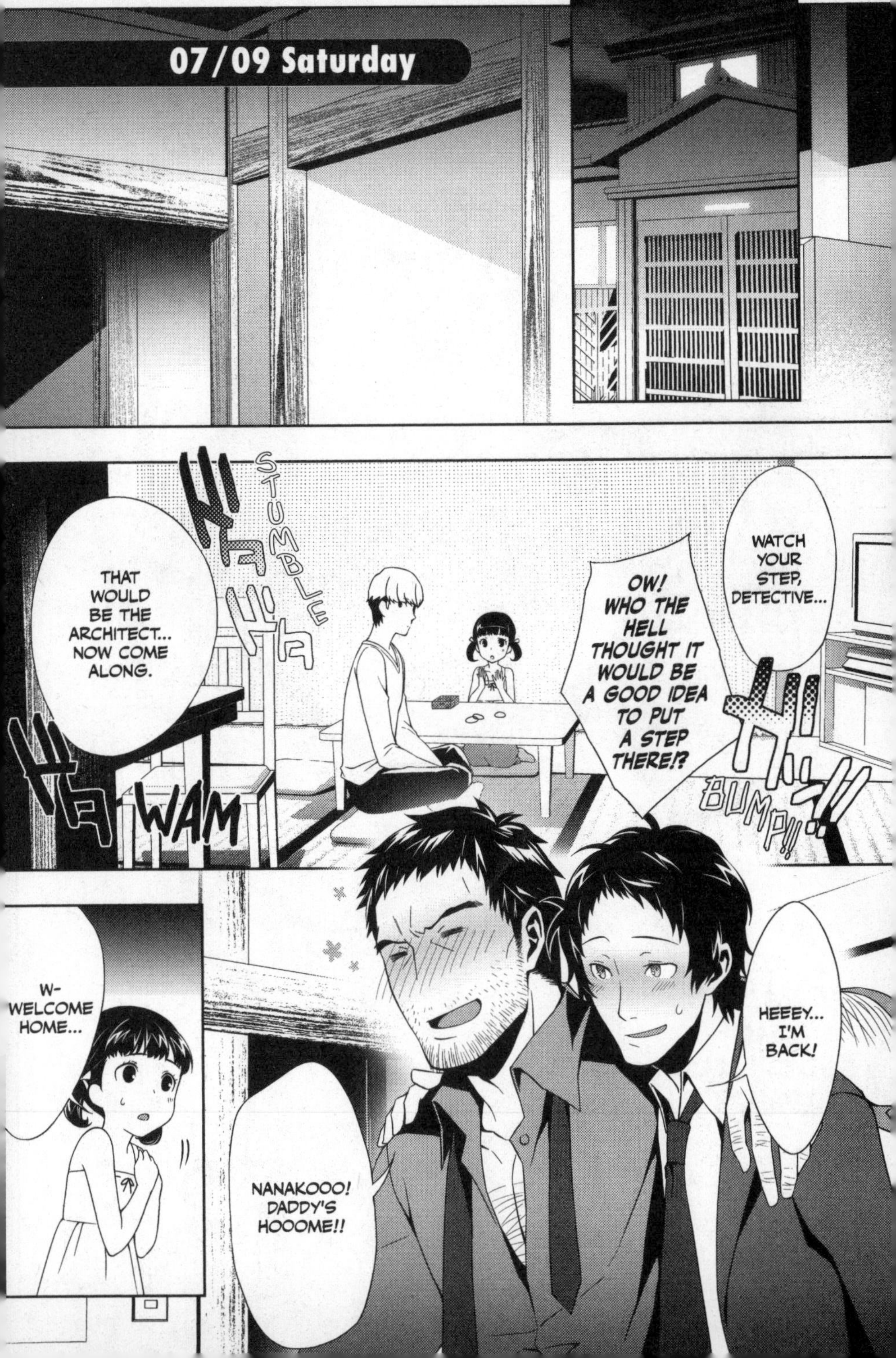
07/09 Saturday
BUMP!!
WATCH YOUR STEP, DETECTIVE...
OW! WHO THE HELL THOUGHT IT WOULD BE A GOOD IDEA TO PUT A STEP THERE!?
STUMBLE
THAT WOULD BE THE ARCHITECT... NOW COME ALONG.
WAM
HEEEY... I'M BACK!
NANAKOOO! DADDY'S HOOOME!!
W- WELCOME HOME...

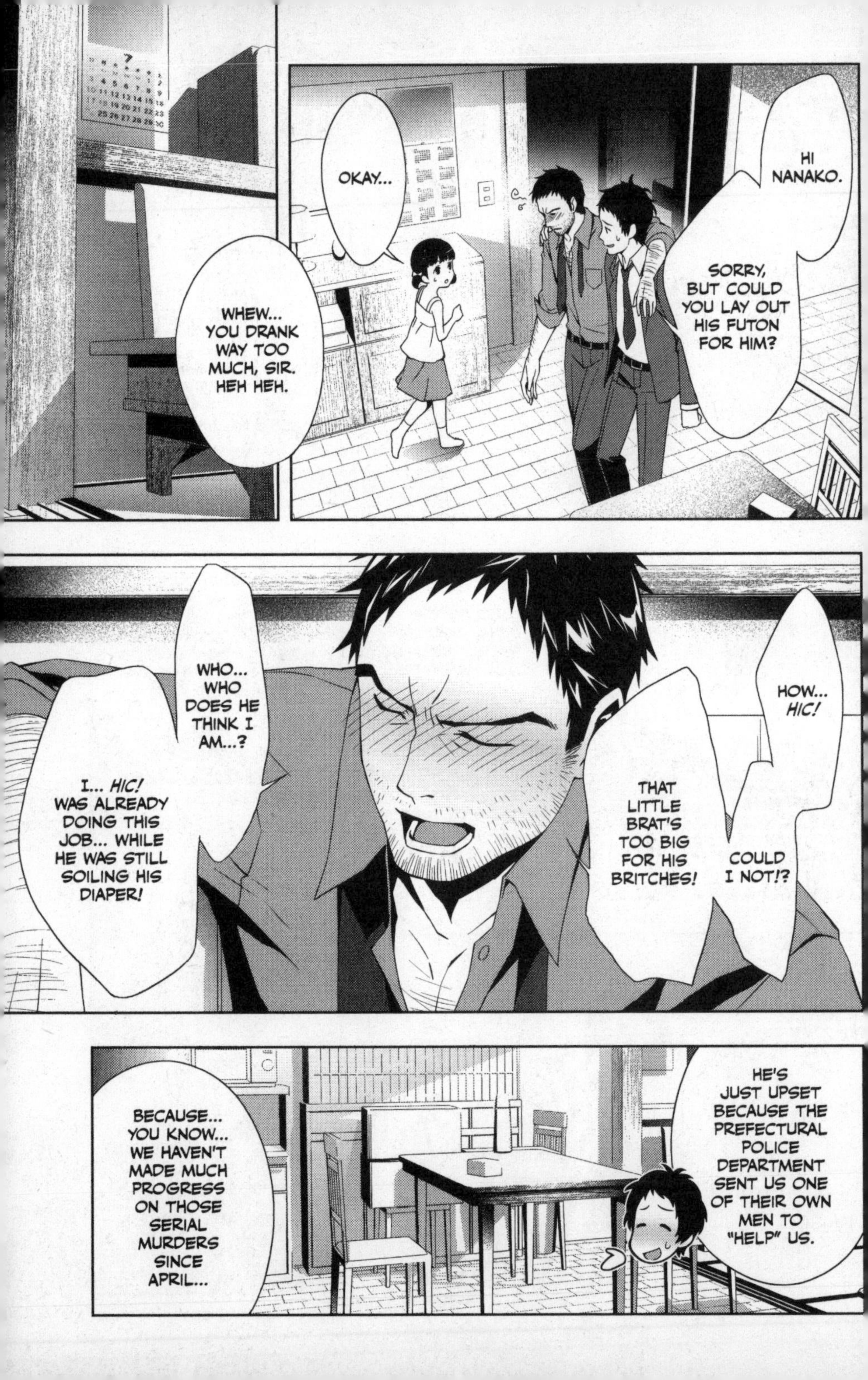
HI NANAKO.
SORRY, BUT COULD YOU LAY OUT HIS FUTON FOR HIM?
OKAY...
WHEW... YOU DRANK WAY TOO MUCH, SIR. HEH HEH.
HOW... HIC!
COULD I NOT!?
THAT LITTLE BRAT'S TOO BIG FOR HIS BRITCHES!
WHO... WHO DOES HE THINK I AM...?
I... HIC! WAS ALREADY DOING THIS JOB... WHILE HE WAS STILL SOILING HIS DIAPER!
HE'S JUST UPSET BECAUSE THE PREFECTURAL POLICE DEPARTMENT SENT US ONE OF THEIR OWN MEN TO "HELP" US.
BECAUSE... YOU KNOW... WE HAVEN'T MADE MUCH PROGRESS ON THOSE SERIAL MURDERS SINCE APRIL...

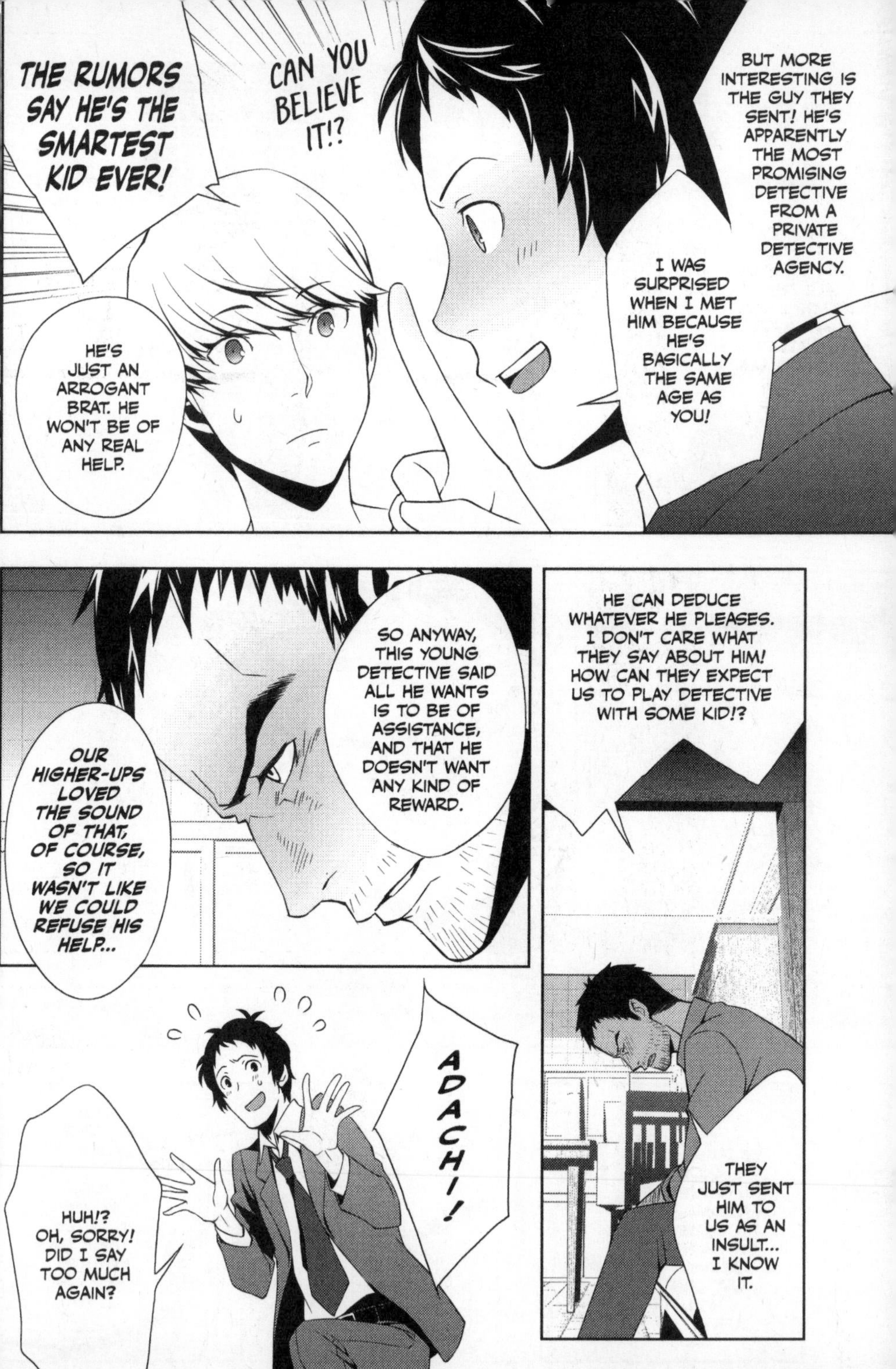
BUT MORE INTERESTING IS THE GUY THEY SENT! HE'S APPARENTLY THE MOST PROMISING DETECTIVE FROM A PRIVATE DETECTIVE AGENCY.
I WAS SURPRISED WHEN I MET HIM BECAUSE HE'S BASICALLY THE SAME AGE AS YOU!
CAN YOU BELIEVE IT!?
THE RUMORS SAY HE'S THE SMARTEST KID EVER!
HE'S JUST AN ARROGANT BRAT. HE WON'T BE OF ANY REAL HELP.
HE CAN DEDUCE WHATEVER HE PLEASES. I DON'T CARE WHAT THEY SAY ABOUT HIM! HOW CAN THEY EXPECT US TO PLAY DETECTIVE WITH SOME KID!?
THEY JUST SENT HIM TO US AS AN INSULT... I KNOW IT.
SO ANYWAY, THIS YOUNG DETECTIVE SAID ALL HE WANTS IS TO BE OF ASSISTANCE, AND THAT HE DOESN'T WANT ANY KIND OF REWARD.
OUR HIGHER-UPS LOVED THE SOUND OF THAT, OF COURSE, SO IT WASN'T LIKE WE COULD REFUSE HIS HELP...
ADACHI!
HUH!? OH, SORRY! DID I SAY TOO MUCH AGAIN?

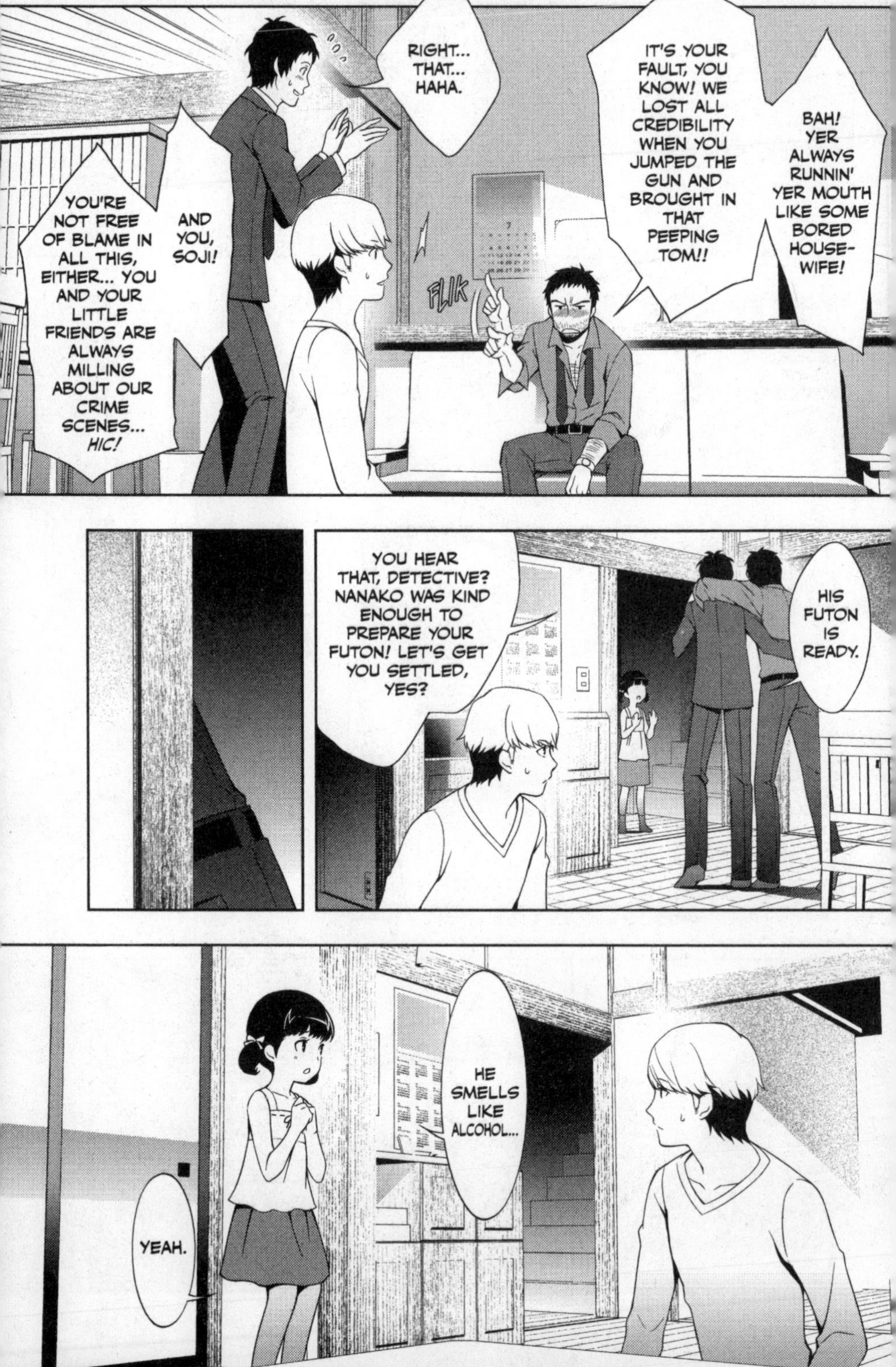
BAH! YER ALWAYS RUNNIN' YER MOUTH LIKE SOME BORED HOUSE-WIFE!
IT'S YOUR FAULT, YOU KNOW! WE LOST ALL CREDIBILITY WHEN YOU JUMPED THE GUN AND BROUGHT IN THAT PEEPING TOM!!
FLIK
RIGHT... THAT... HAHA.
AND YOU, SOJI!
YOU'RE NOT FREE OF BLAME IN ALL THIS, EITHER... YOU AND YOUR LITTLE FRIENDS ARE ALWAYS MILLING ABOUT OUR CRIME SCENES... HIC!
HIS FUTON IS READY.
YOU HEAR THAT, DETECTIVE? NANAKO WAS KIND ENOUGH TO PREPARE YOUR FUTON! LET'S GET YOU SETTLED, YES?
HE SMELLS LIKE ALCOHOL...
YEAH.

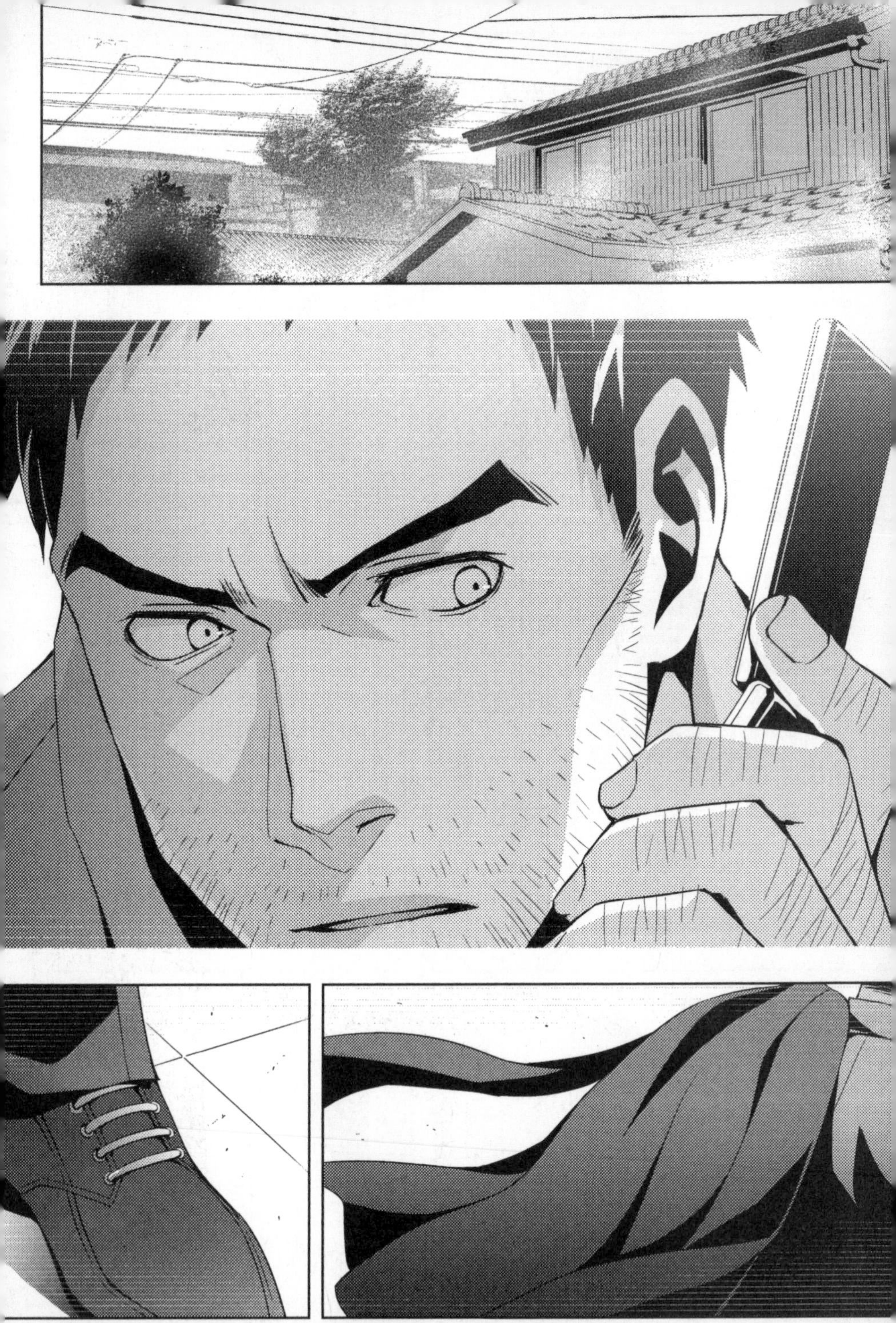

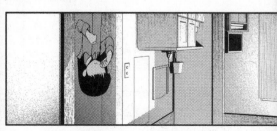

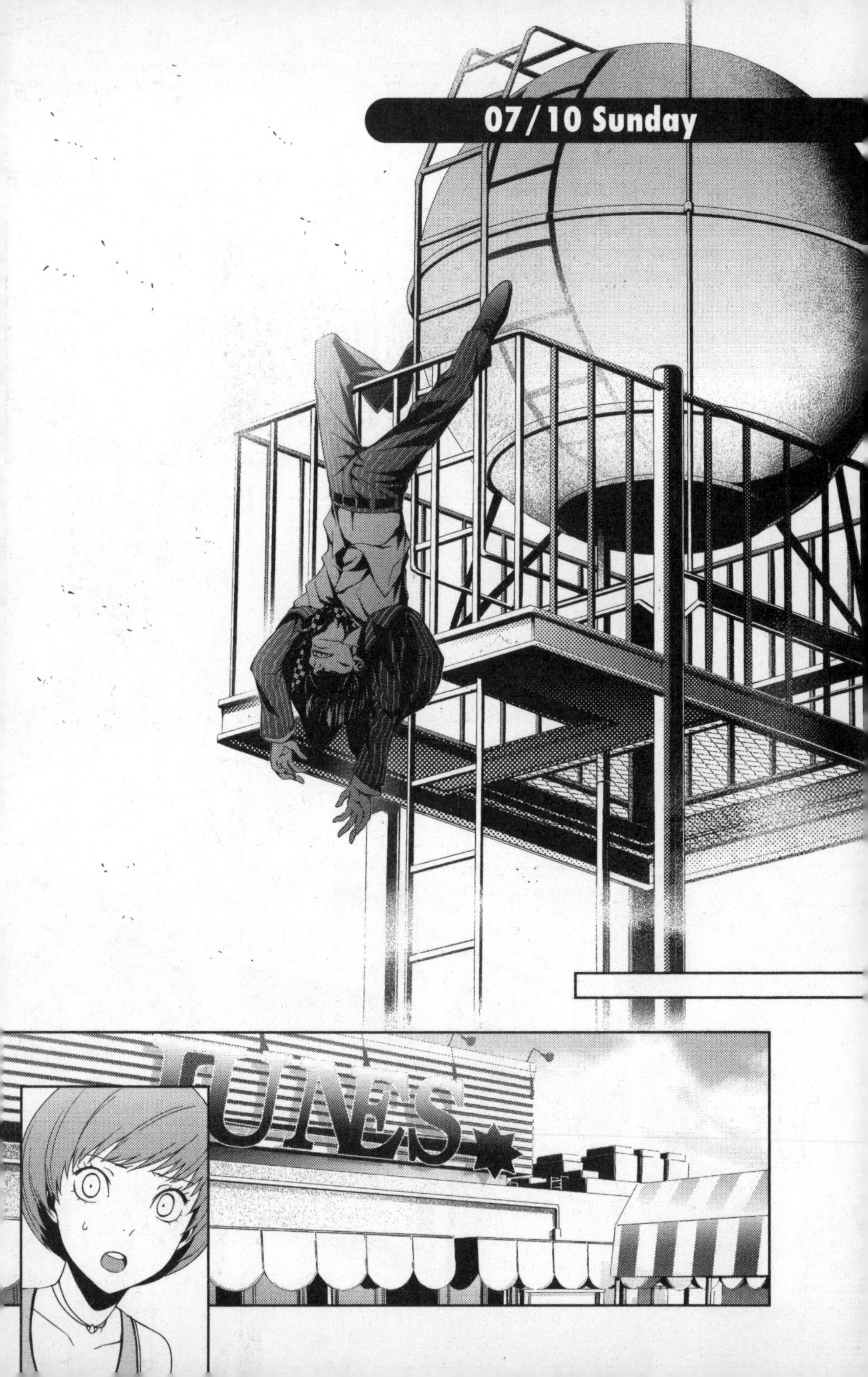
07/10 Sunday

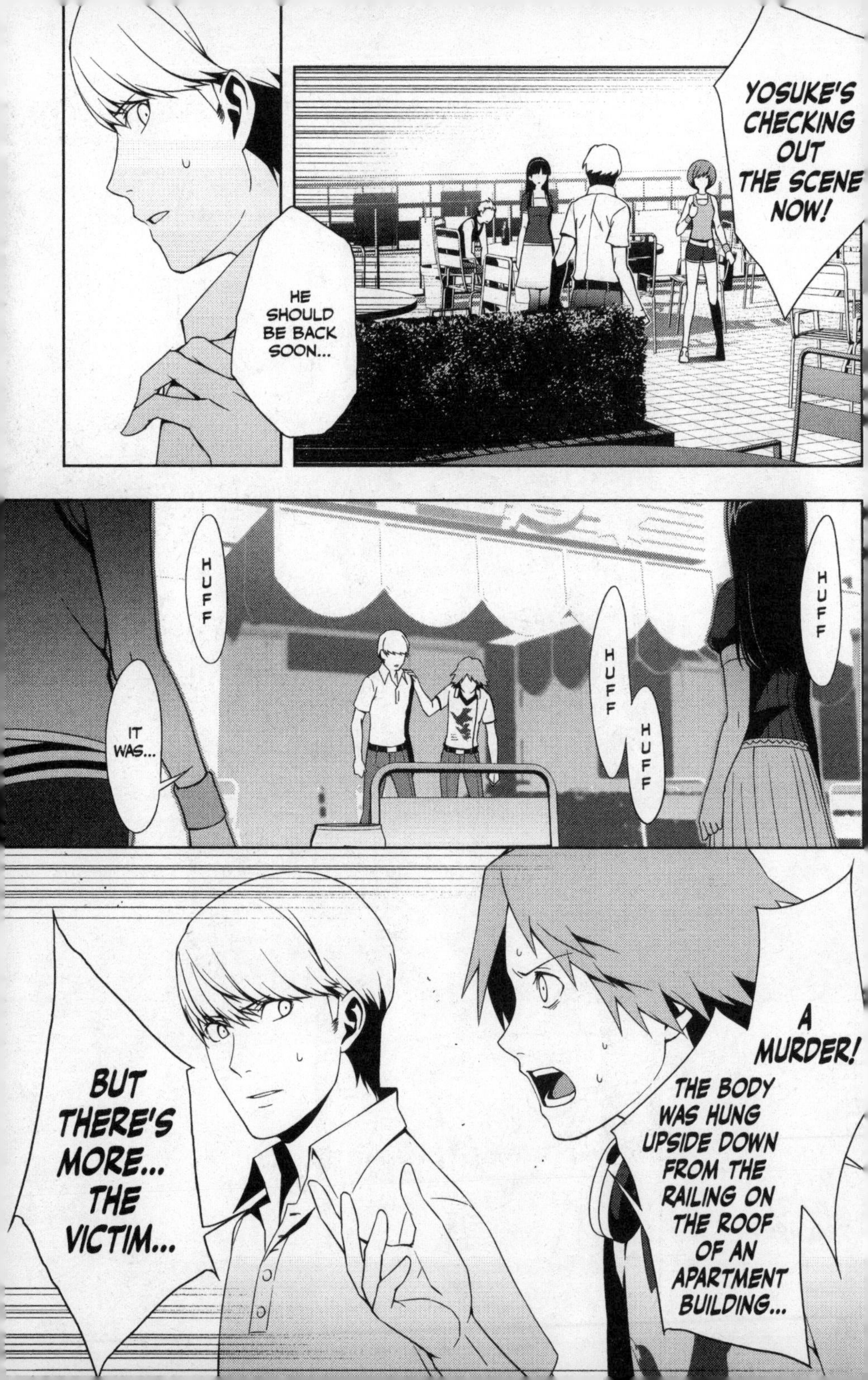
YOSUKE'S CHECKING OUT THE SCENE NOW!
HE SHOULD BE BACK SOON...
HUFF
HUFF
HUFF
HUFF
IT WAS...
A MURDER!
THE BODY WAS HUNG UPSIDE DOWN FROM THE RAILING ON THE ROOF OF AN APARTMENT BUILDING...
BUT THERE'S MORE... THE VICTIM...

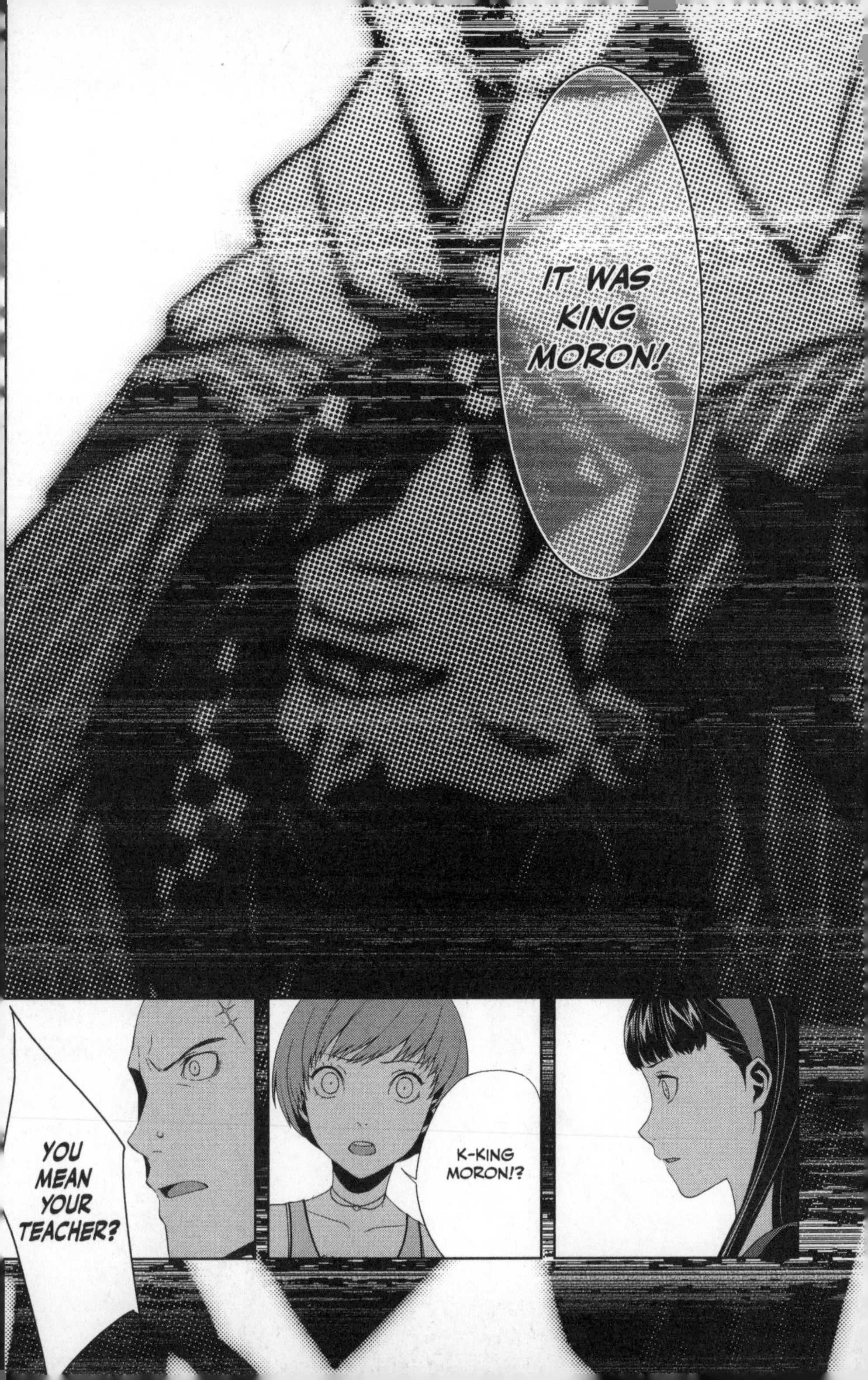
IT WAS KING MORON!
K-KING MORON!?
YOU MEAN YOUR TEACHER?

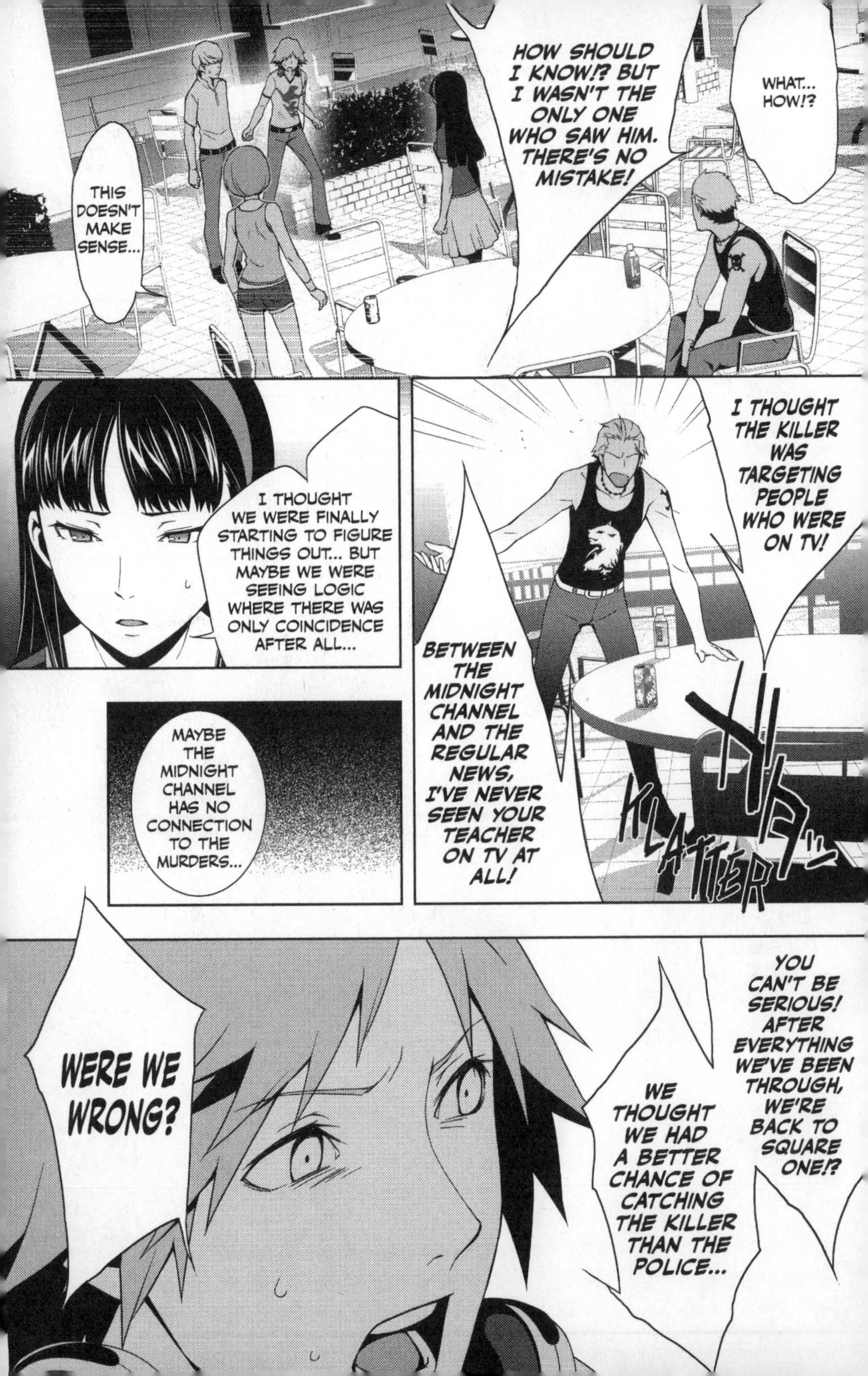
WHAT... HOW!?
HOW SHOULD I KNOW!? BUT I WASN'T THE ONLY ONE WHO SAW HIM. THERE'S NO MISTAKE!
THIS DOESN'T MAKE SENSE...
I THOUGHT THE KILLER WAS TARGETING PEOPLE WHO WERE ON TV!
BETWEEN THE MIDNIGHT CHANNEL AND THE REGULAR NEWS, I'VE NEVER SEEN YOUR TEACHER ON TV AT ALL!
KLATTER
I THOUGHT WE WERE FINALLY STARTING TO FIGURE THINGS OUT... BUT MAYBE WE WERE SEEING LOGIC WHERE THERE WAS ONLY COINCIDENCE AFTER ALL...
MAYBE THE MIDNIGHT CHANNEL HAS NO CONNECTION TO THE MURDERS...
YOU CAN'T BE SERIOUS! AFTER EVERYTHING WE'VE BEEN THROUGH, WE'RE BACK TO SQUARE ONE!?
WE THOUGHT WE HAD A BETTER CHANCE OF CATCHING THE KILLER THAN THE POLICE...
WERE WE WRONG?

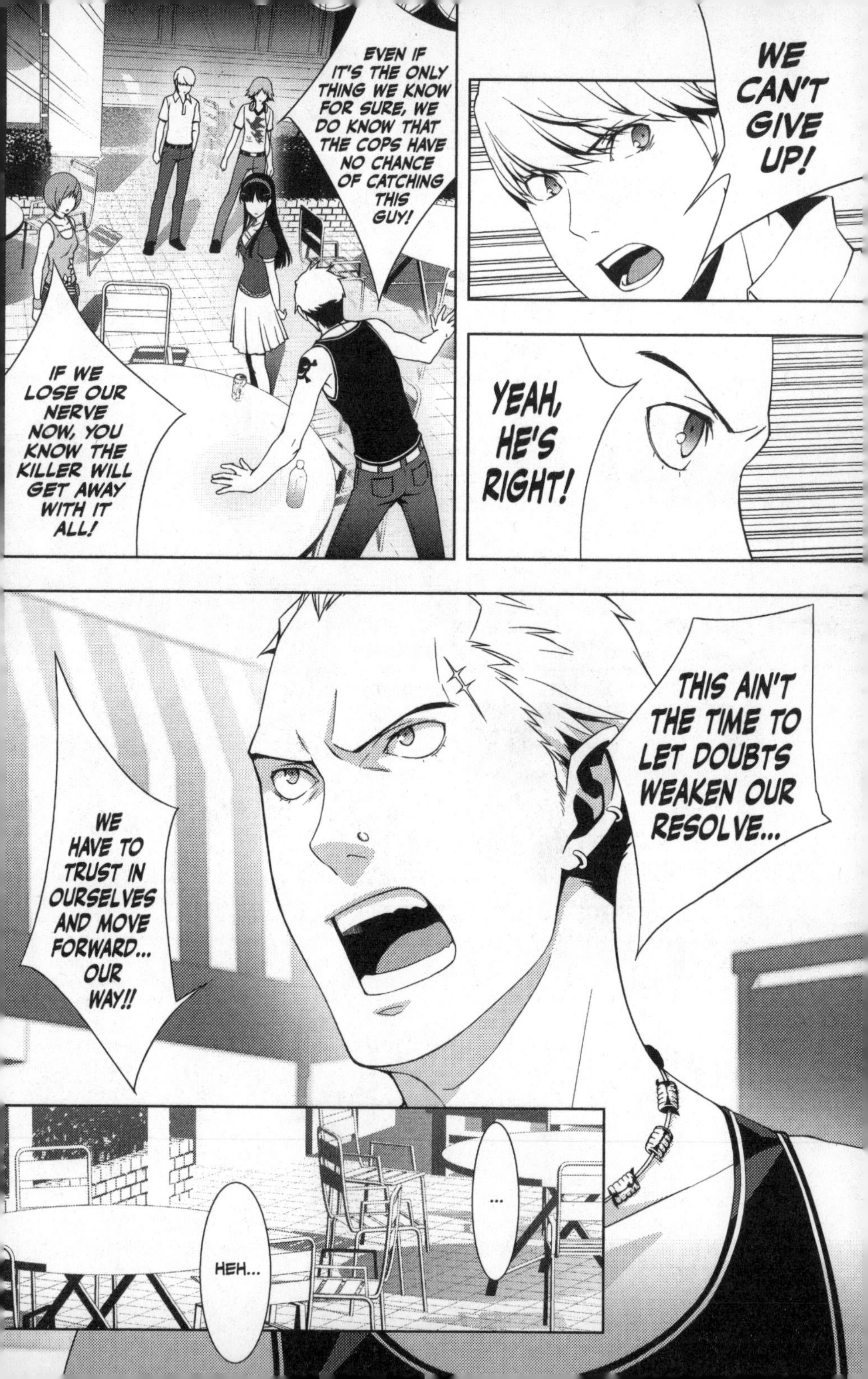
WE CAN'T GIVE UP!
EVEN IF IT'S THE ONLY THING WE KNOW FOR SURE, WE DO KNOW THAT THE COPS HAVE NO CHANCE OF CATCHING THIS GUY!
IF WE LOSE OUR NERVE NOW, YOU KNOW THE KILLER WILL GET AWAY WITH IT ALL!
YEAH, HE'S RIGHT!
THIS AIN'T THE TIME TO LET DOUBTS WEAKEN OUR RESOLVE...
WE HAVE TO TRUST IN OURSELVES AND MOVE FORWARD... OUR WAY!!
...
HEH...

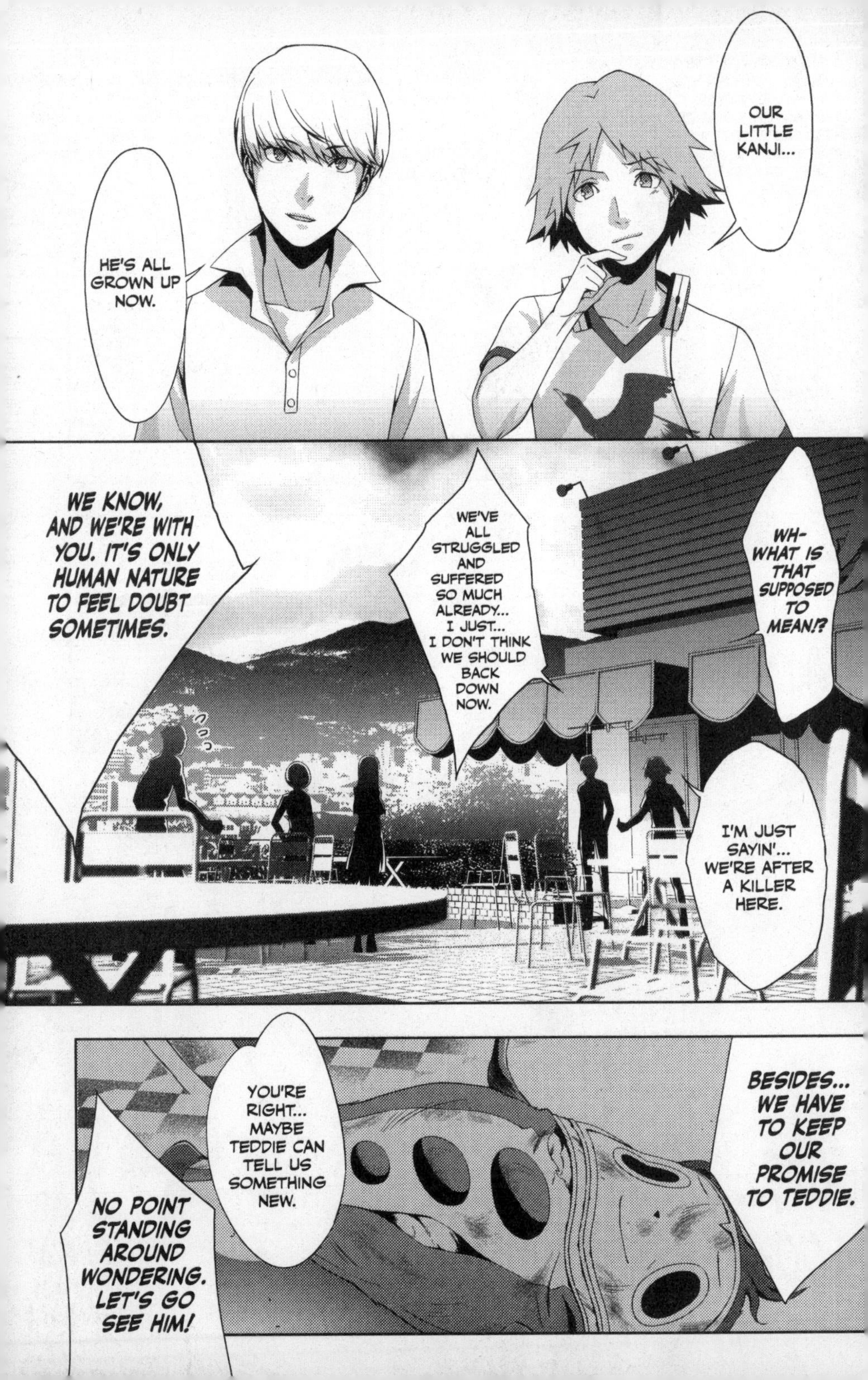
OUR LITTLE KANJI...
HE'S ALL GROWN UP NOW.
WH- WHAT IS THAT SUPPOSED TO MEAN!?
I'M JUST SAYIN'... WE'RE AFTER A KILLER HERE.
WE'VE ALL STRUGGLED AND SUFFERED SO MUCH ALREADY... I JUST... I DON'T THINK WE SHOULD BACK DOWN NOW.
WE KNOW, AND WE'RE WITH YOU. IT'S ONLY HUMAN NATURE TO FEEL DOUBT SOMETIMES.
BESIDES... WE HAVE TO KEEP OUR PROMISE TO TEDDIE.
YOU'RE RIGHT... MAYBE TEDDIE CAN TELL US SOMETHING NEW.
NO POINT STANDING AROUND WONDERING. LET'S GO SEE HIM!

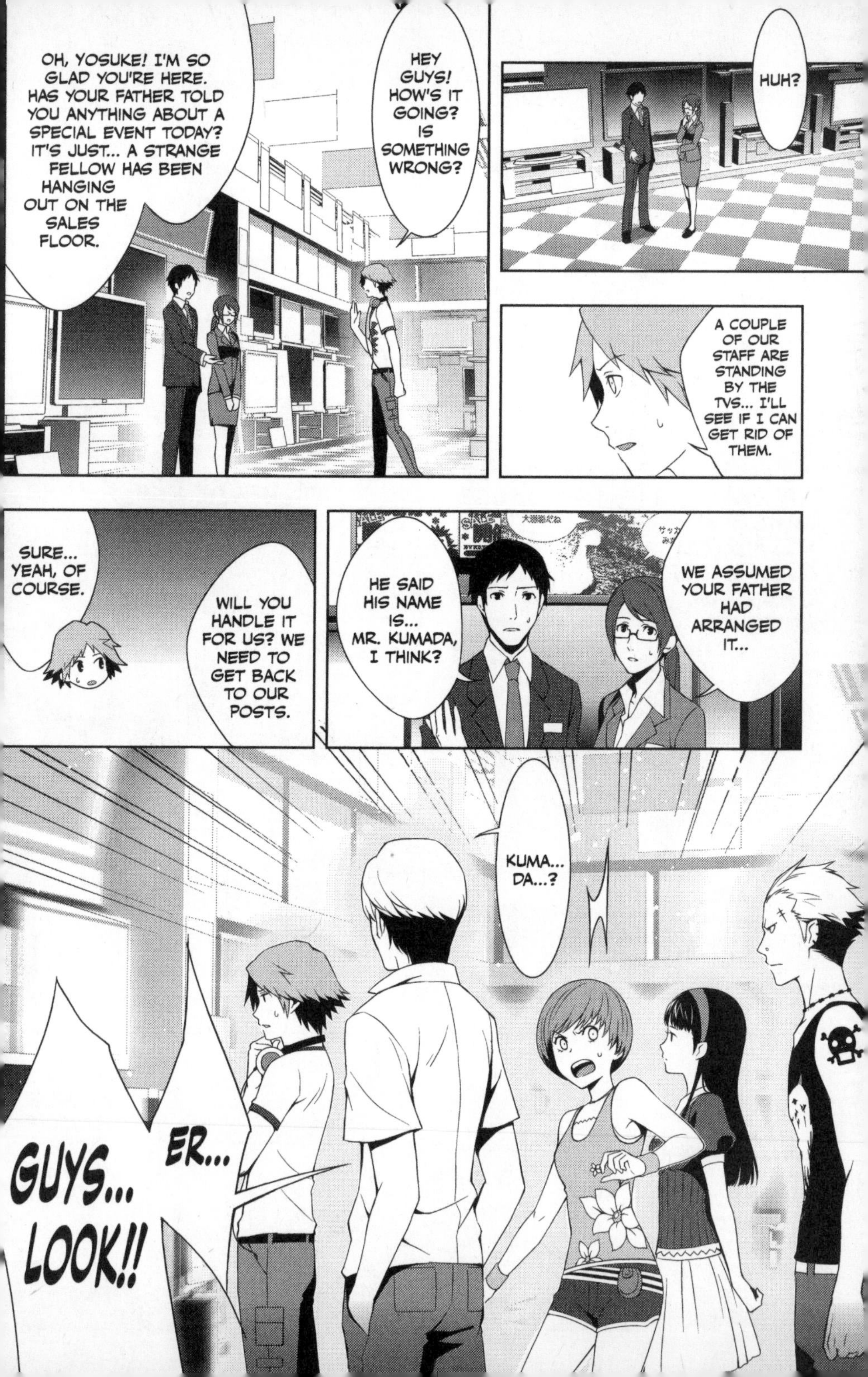
HUH?
A COUPLE OF OUR STAFF ARE STANDING BY THE TVS... I'LL SEE IF I CAN GET RID OF THEM.
HEY GUYS! HOW'S IT GOING? IS SOMETHING WRONG?
OH, YOSUKE! I'M SO GLAD YOU'RE HERE. HAS YOUR FATHER TOLD YOU ANYTHING ABOUT A SPECIAL EVENT TODAY? IT'S JUST... A STRANGE FELLOW HAS BEEN HANGING OUT ON THE SALES FLOOR.
WE ASSUMED YOUR FATHER HAD ARRANGED IT...
HE SAID HIS NAME IS... MR. KUMADA, I THINK?
WILL YOU HANDLE IT FOR US? WE NEED TO GET BACK TO OUR POSTS.
SURE... YEAH, OF COURSE.
KUMA... DA...?
ER...
GUYS... LOOK!!

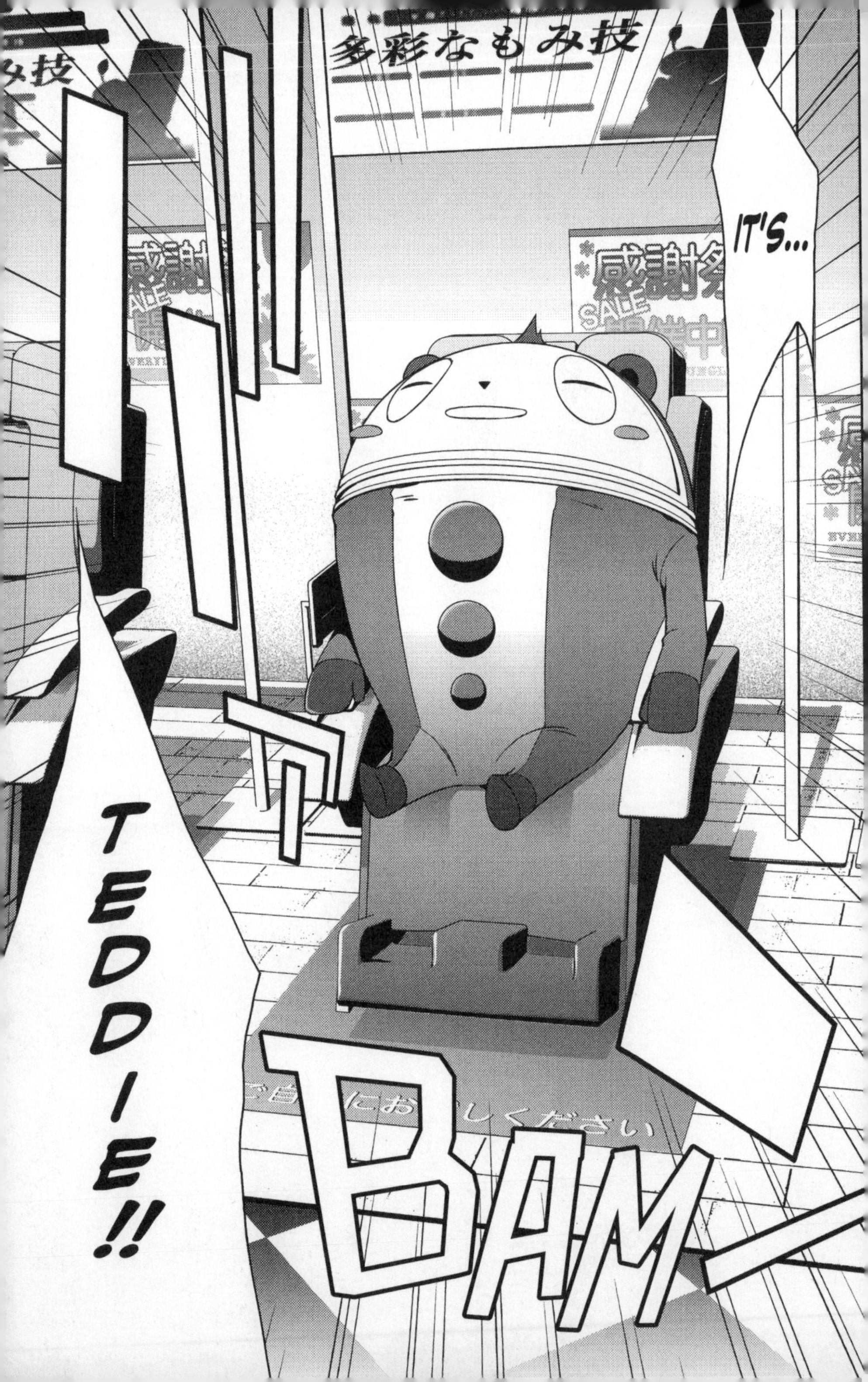
多彩なもみ技
感謝祭
SALE
IT'S...
TEDDIE!!
BAM

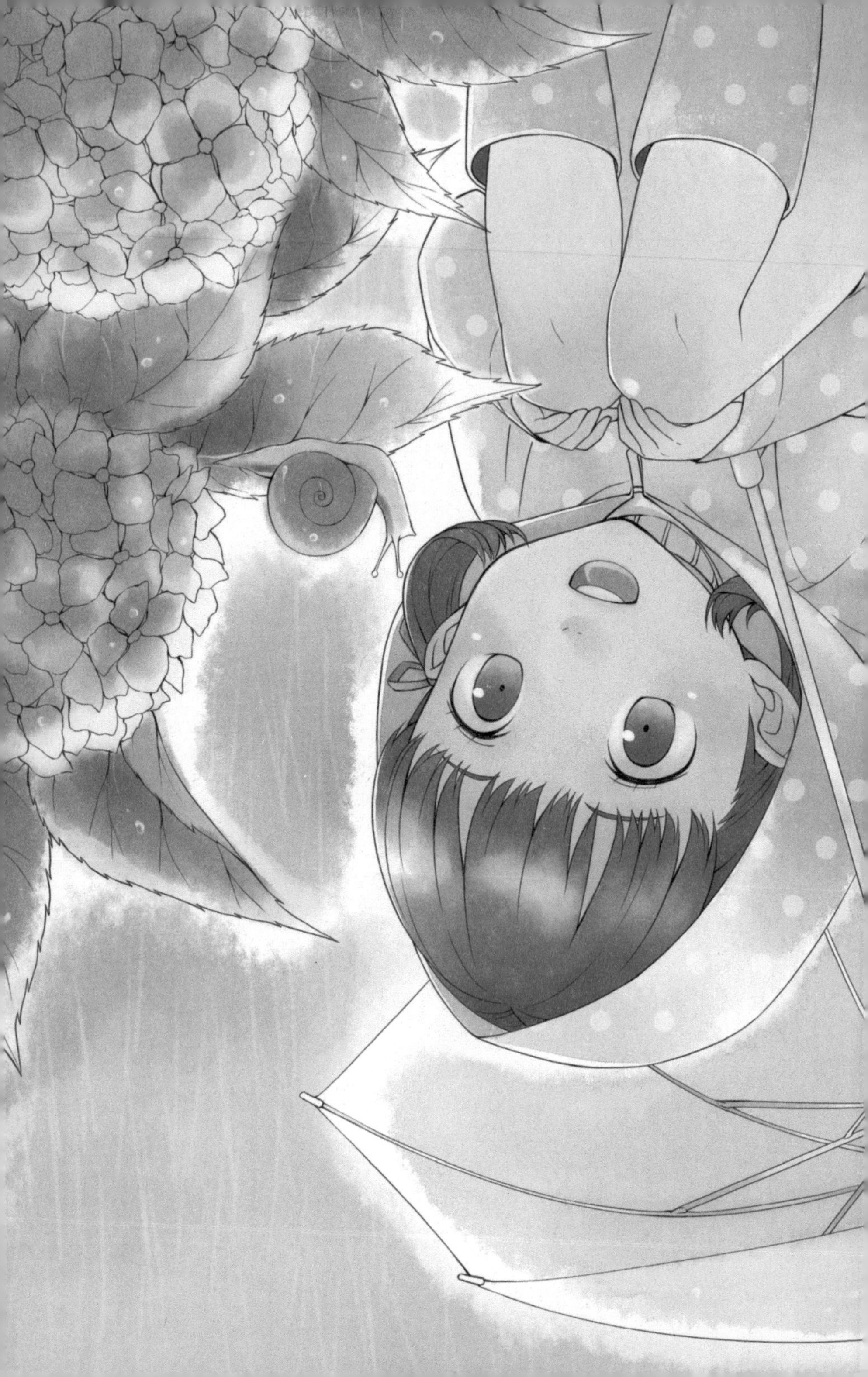

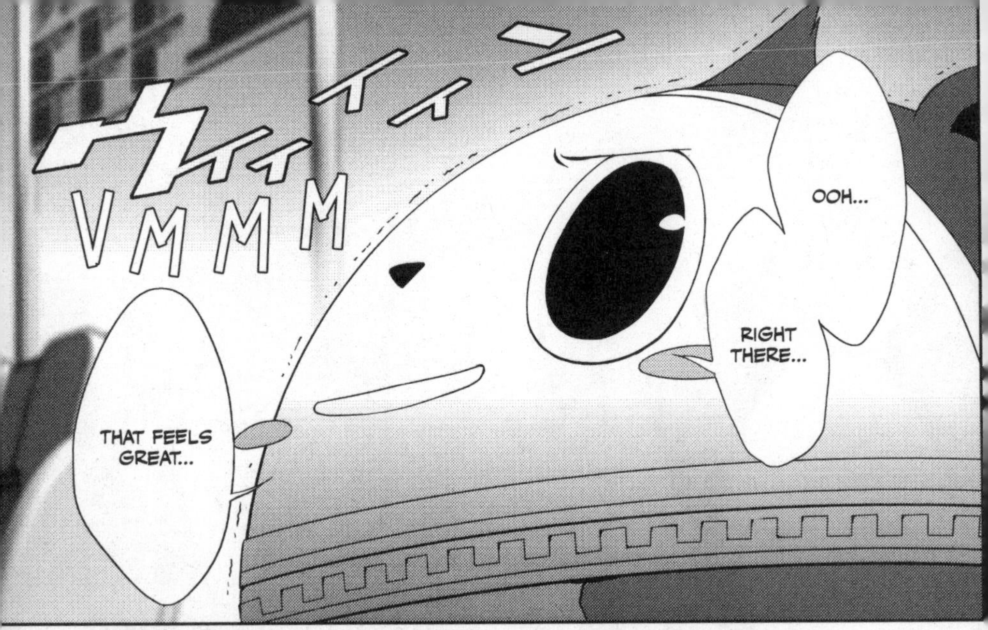
OOH...
RIGHT THERE...
VMMM
THAT FEELS GREAT...

#26 Next Phase

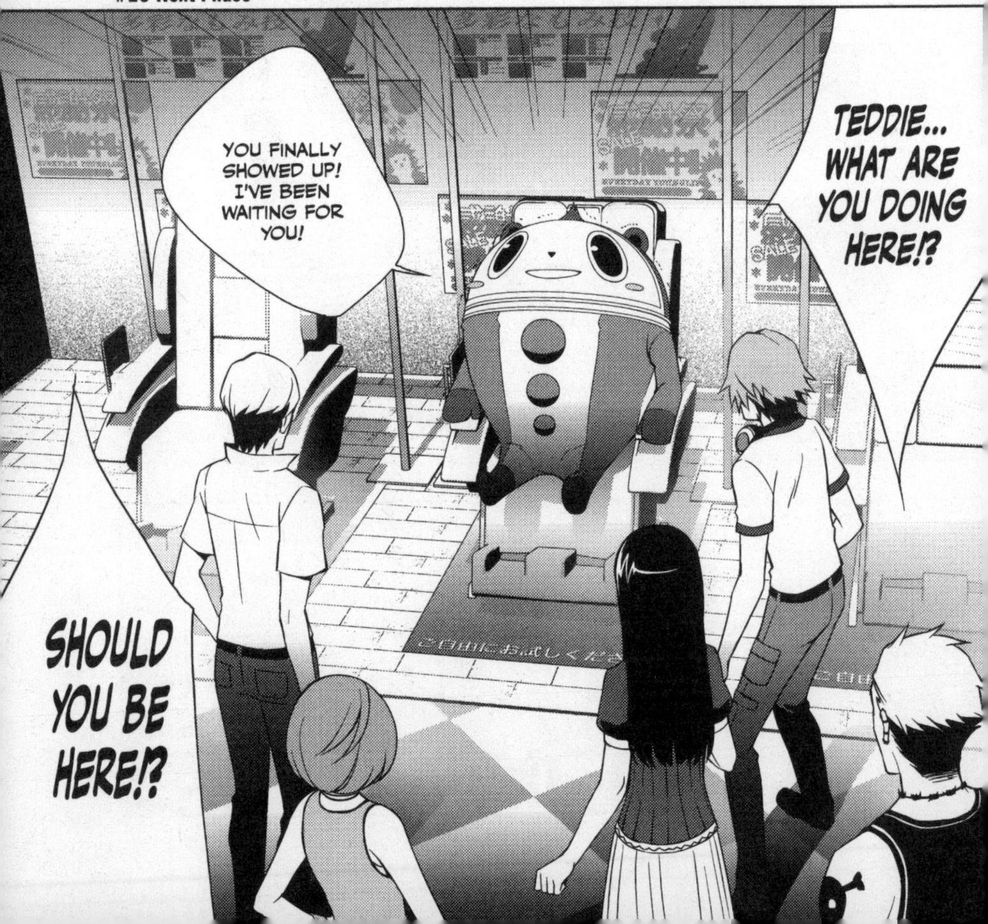
TEDDIE... WHAT ARE YOU DOING HERE!?
YOU FINALLY SHOWED UP! I'VE BEEN WAITING FOR YOU!
SHOULD YOU BE HERE!?

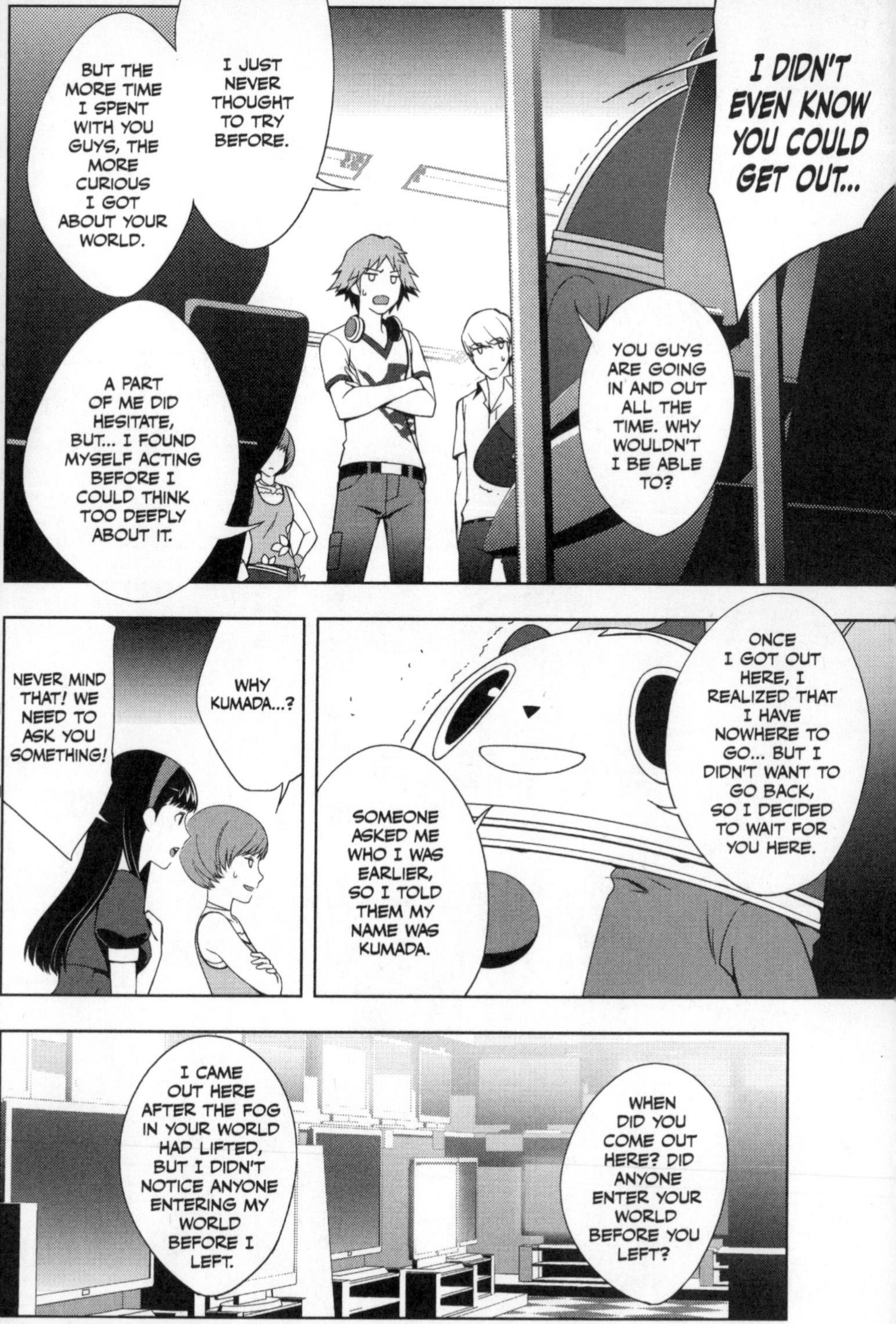
I DIDN'T EVEN KNOW YOU COULD GET OUT...
YOU GUYS ARE GOING IN AND OUT ALL THE TIME. WHY WOULDN'T I BE ABLE TO?
I JUST NEVER THOUGHT TO TRY BEFORE.
BUT THE MORE TIME I SPENT WITH YOU GUYS, THE MORE CURIOUS I GOT ABOUT YOUR WORLD.
A PART OF ME DID HESITATE, BUT... I FOUND MYSELF ACTING BEFORE I COULD THINK TOO DEEPLY ABOUT IT.
ONCE I GOT OUT HERE, I REALIZED THAT I HAVE NOWHERE TO GO... BUT I DIDN'T WANT TO GO BACK, SO I DECIDED TO WAIT FOR YOU HERE.
SOMEONE ASKED ME WHO I WAS EARLIER, SO I TOLD THEM MY NAME WAS KUMADA.
WHY KUMADA...?
NEVER MIND THAT! WE NEED TO ASK YOU SOMETHING!
WHEN DID YOU COME OUT HERE? DID ANYONE ENTER YOUR WORLD BEFORE YOU LEFT?
I CAME OUT HERE AFTER THE FOG IN YOUR WORLD HAD LIFTED, BUT I DIDN'T NOTICE ANYONE ENTERING MY WORLD BEFORE I LEFT.

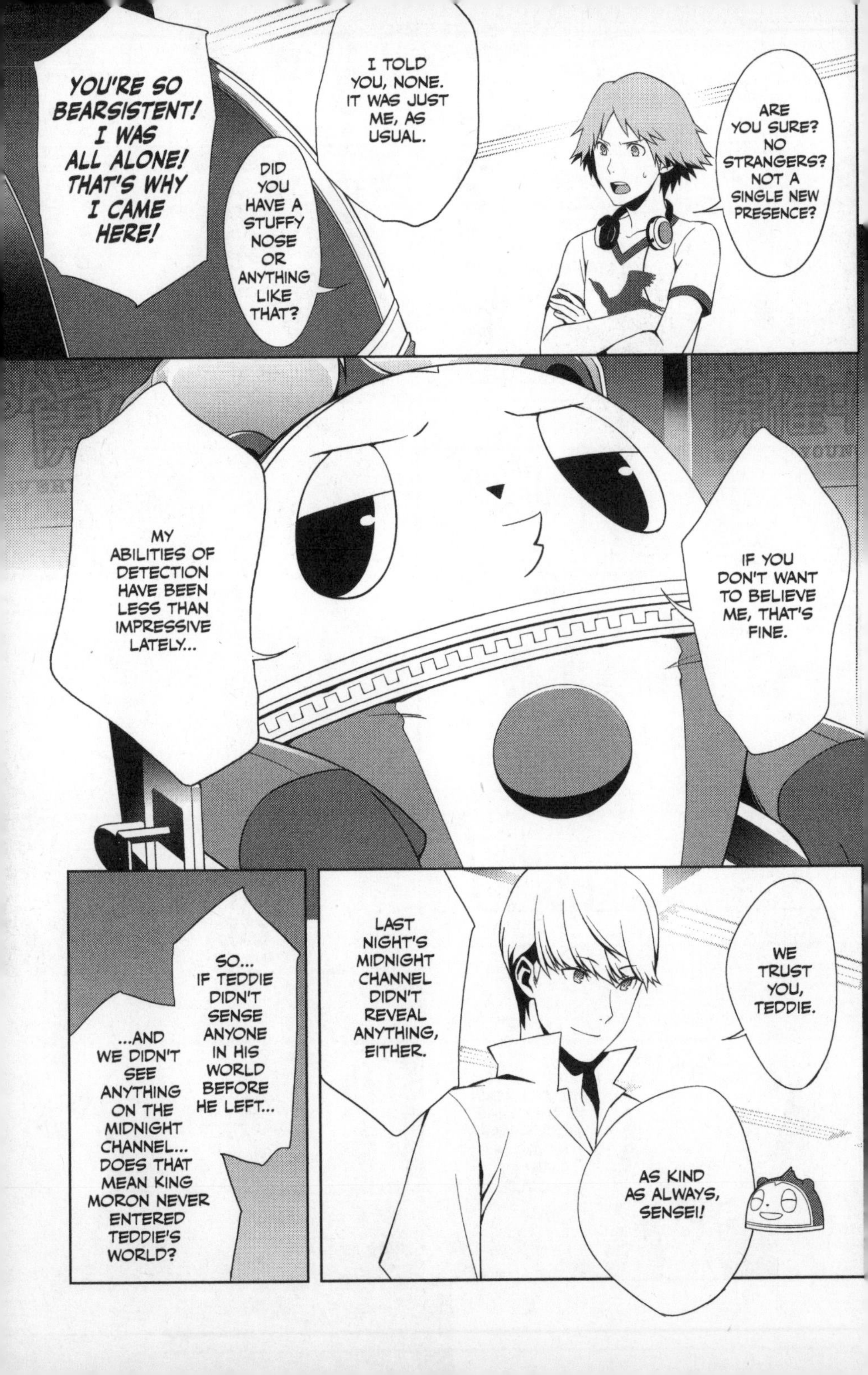
ARE YOU SURE? NO STRANGERS? NOT A SINGLE NEW PRESENCE?
I TOLD YOU, NONE. IT WAS JUST ME, AS USUAL.
DID YOU HAVE A STUFFY NOSE OR ANYTHING LIKE THAT?
YOU'RE SO BEARSISTENT! I WAS ALL ALONE! THAT'S WHY I CAME HERE!
IF YOU DON'T WANT TO BELIEVE ME, THAT'S FINE.
MY ABILITIES OF DETECTION HAVE BEEN LESS THAN IMPRESSIVE LATELY...
WE TRUST YOU, TEDDIE.
LAST NIGHT'S MIDNIGHT CHANNEL DIDN'T REVEAL ANYTHING, EITHER.
AS KIND AS ALWAYS, SENSEI!
SO... IF TEDDIE DIDN'T SENSE ANYONE IN HIS WORLD BEFORE HE LEFT...
...AND WE DIDN'T SEE ANYTHING ON THE MIDNIGHT CHANNEL... DOES THAT MEAN KING MORON NEVER ENTERED TEDDIE'S WORLD?

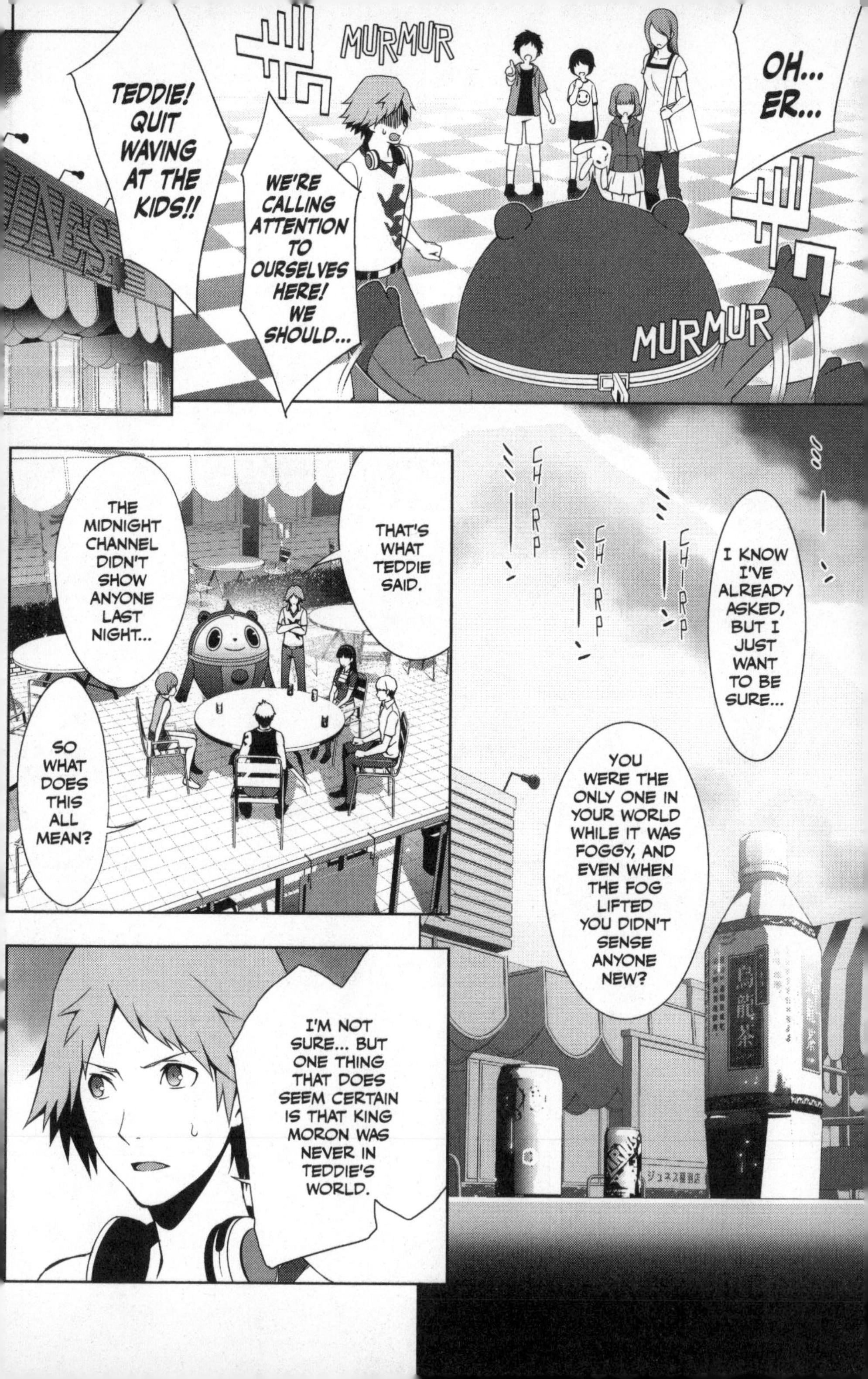
OH... ER...
MURMUR
TEDDIE! QUIT WAVING AT THE KIDS!!
WE'RE CALLING ATTENTION TO OURSELVES HERE! WE SHOULD...
MURMUR
...
CHIRP
CHIRP
CHIRP
I KNOW I'VE ALREADY ASKED, BUT I JUST WANT TO BE SURE...
YOU WERE THE ONLY ONE IN YOUR WORLD WHILE IT WAS FOGGY, AND EVEN WHEN THE FOG LIFTED YOU DIDN'T SENSE ANYONE NEW?
THE MIDNIGHT CHANNEL DIDN'T SHOW ANYONE LAST NIGHT...
THAT'S WHAT TEDDIE SAID.
SO WHAT DOES THIS ALL MEAN?
I'M NOT SURE... BUT ONE THING THAT DOES SEEM CERTAIN IS THAT KING MORON WAS NEVER IN TEDDIE'S WORLD.

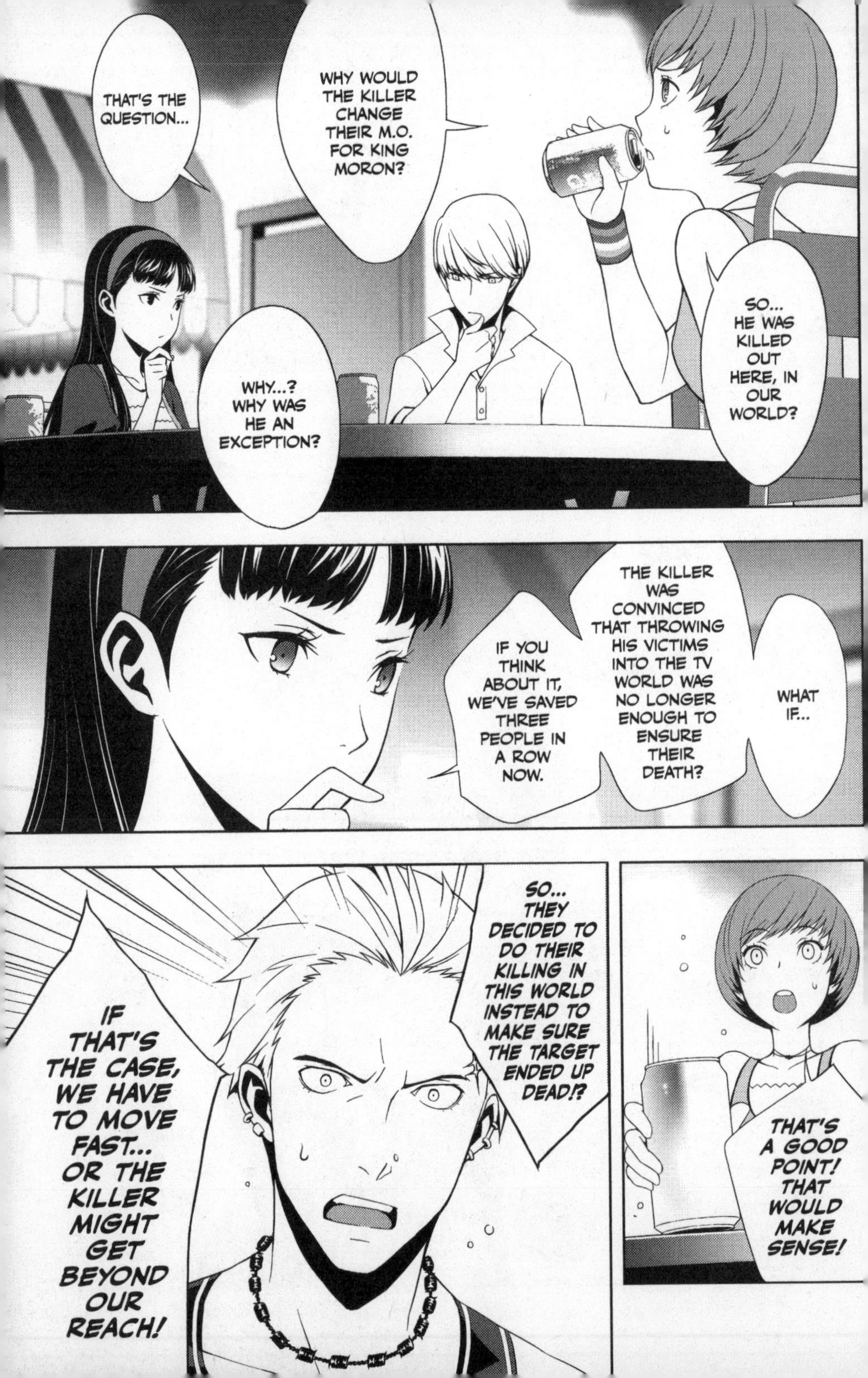
SO... HE WAS KILLED OUT HERE, IN OUR WORLD?
WHY WOULD THE KILLER CHANGE THEIR M.O. FOR KING MORON?
THAT'S THE QUESTION...
WHY...? WHY WAS HE AN EXCEPTION?
WHAT IF...
THE KILLER WAS CONVINCED THAT THROWING HIS VICTIMS INTO THE TV WORLD WAS NO LONGER ENOUGH TO ENSURE THEIR DEATH?
IF YOU THINK ABOUT IT, WE'VE SAVED THREE PEOPLE IN A ROW NOW.
THAT'S A GOOD POINT! THAT WOULD MAKE SENSE!
SO... THEY DECIDED TO DO THEIR KILLING IN THIS WORLD INSTEAD TO MAKE SURE THE TARGET ENDED UP DEAD!?
IF THAT'S THE CASE, WE HAVE TO MOVE FAST... OR THE KILLER MIGHT GET BEYOND OUR REACH!

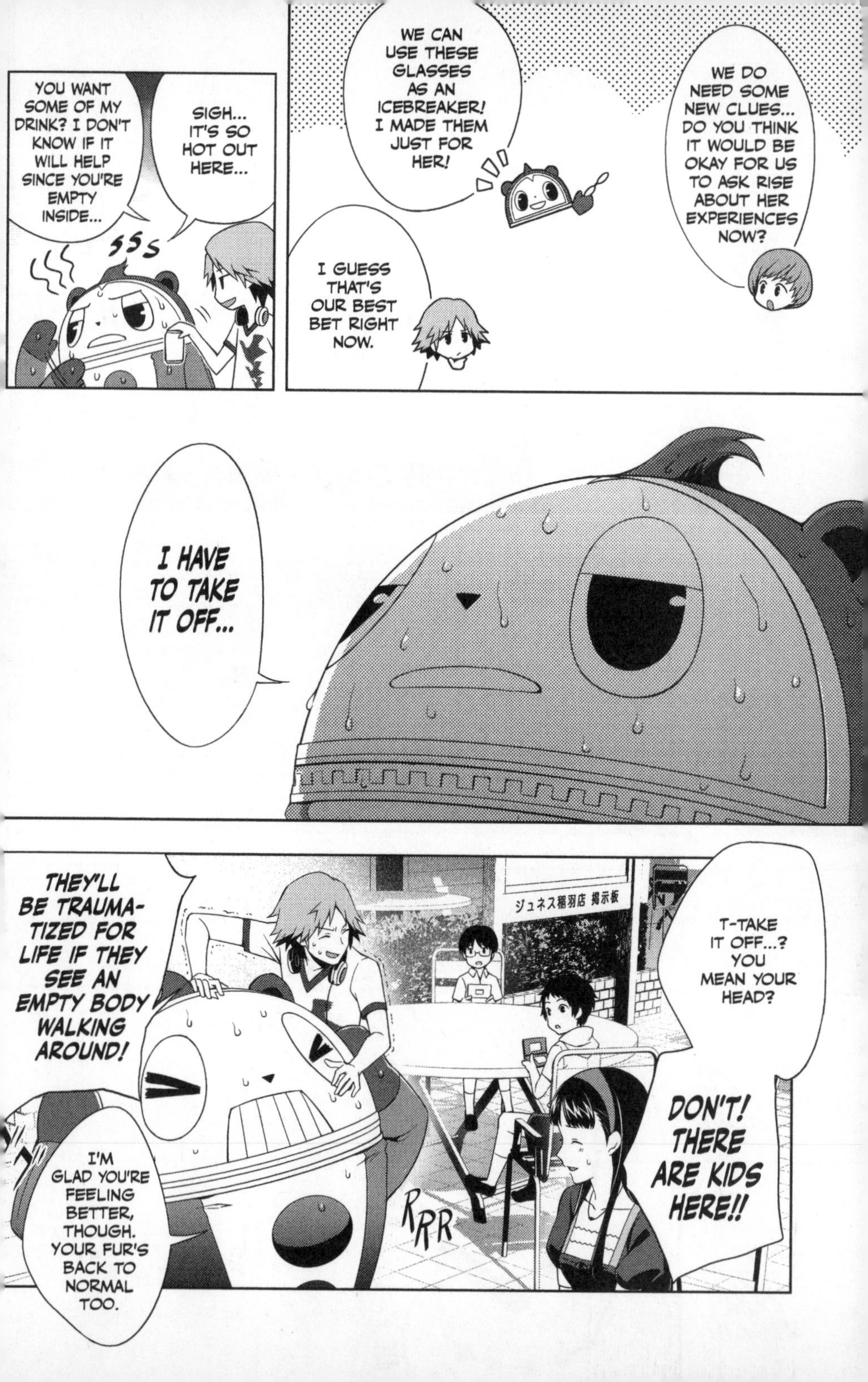
WE DO NEED SOME NEW CLUES... DO YOU THINK IT WOULD BE OKAY FOR US TO ASK RISE ABOUT HER EXPERIENCES NOW?
WE CAN USE THESE GLASSES AS AN ICEBREAKER! I MADE THEM JUST FOR HER!
I GUESS THAT'S OUR BEST BET RIGHT NOW.
SIGH... IT'S SO HOT OUT HERE...
YOU WANT SOME OF MY DRINK? I DON'T KNOW IF IT WILL HELP SINCE YOU'RE EMPTY INSIDE...
I HAVE TO TAKE IT OFF...
T-TAKE IT OFF...? YOU MEAN YOUR HEAD?
DON'T! THERE ARE KIDS HERE!!
ジュネス稲羽店 掲示板
RRR
THEY'LL BE TRAUMATIZED FOR LIFE IF THEY SEE AN EMPTY BODY WALKING AROUND!
I'M GLAD YOU'RE FEELING BETTER, THOUGH. YOUR FUR'S BACK TO NORMAL TOO.

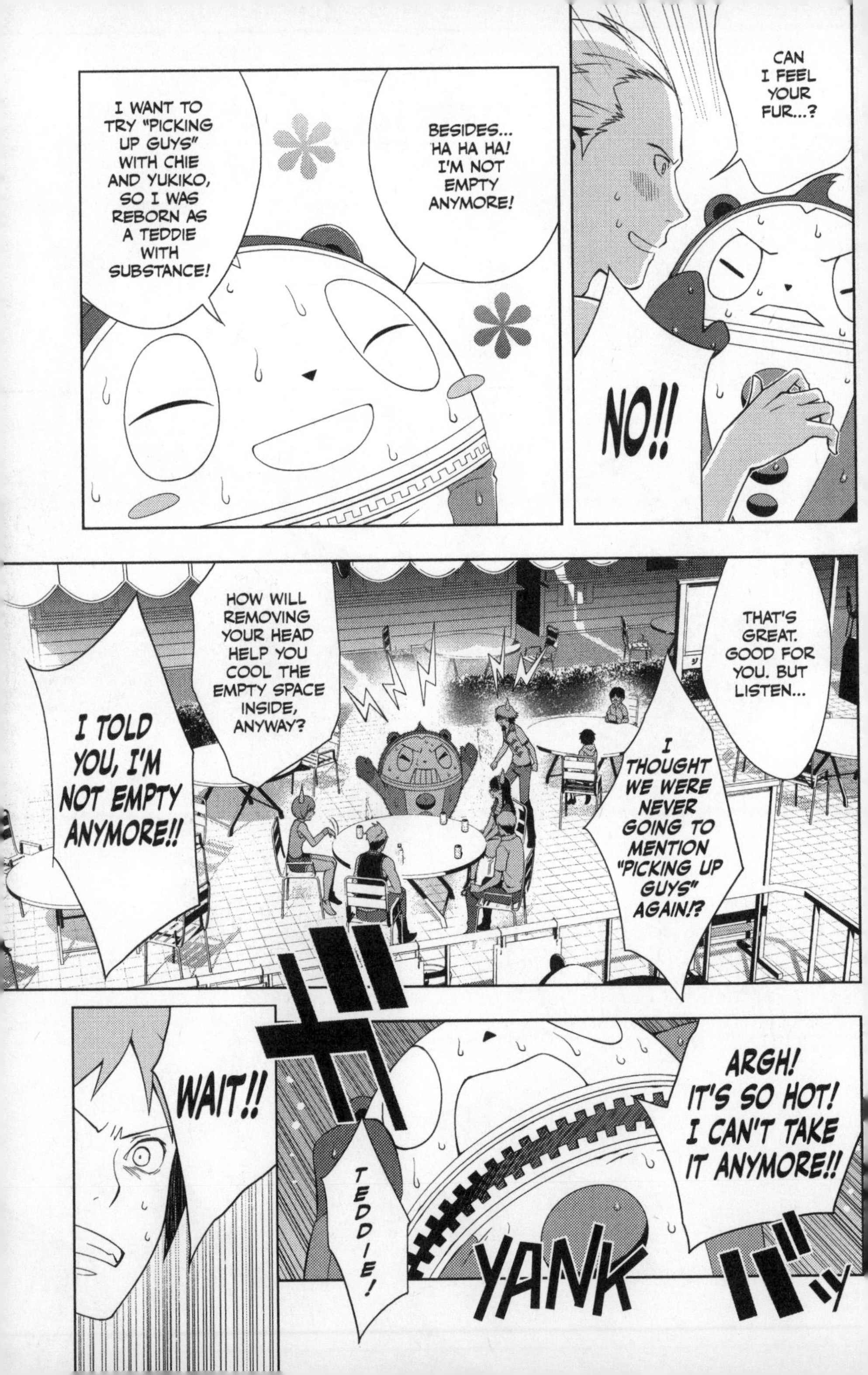
CAN I FEEL YOUR FUR...?
NO!!
I WANT TO TRY "PICKING UP GUYS" WITH CHIE AND YUKIKO, SO I WAS REBORN AS A TEDDIE WITH SUBSTANCE!
BESIDES... HA HA HA! I'M NOT EMPTY ANYMORE!
THAT'S GREAT. GOOD FOR YOU. BUT LISTEN...
I THOUGHT WE WERE NEVER GOING TO MENTION "PICKING UP GUYS" AGAIN!?
HOW WILL REMOVING YOUR HEAD HELP YOU COOL THE EMPTY SPACE INSIDE, ANYWAY?
I TOLD YOU, I'M NOT EMPTY ANYMORE!!
ARGH! IT'S SO HOT! I CAN'T TAKE IT ANYMORE!!
YANK
TEDDIE!
WAIT!!

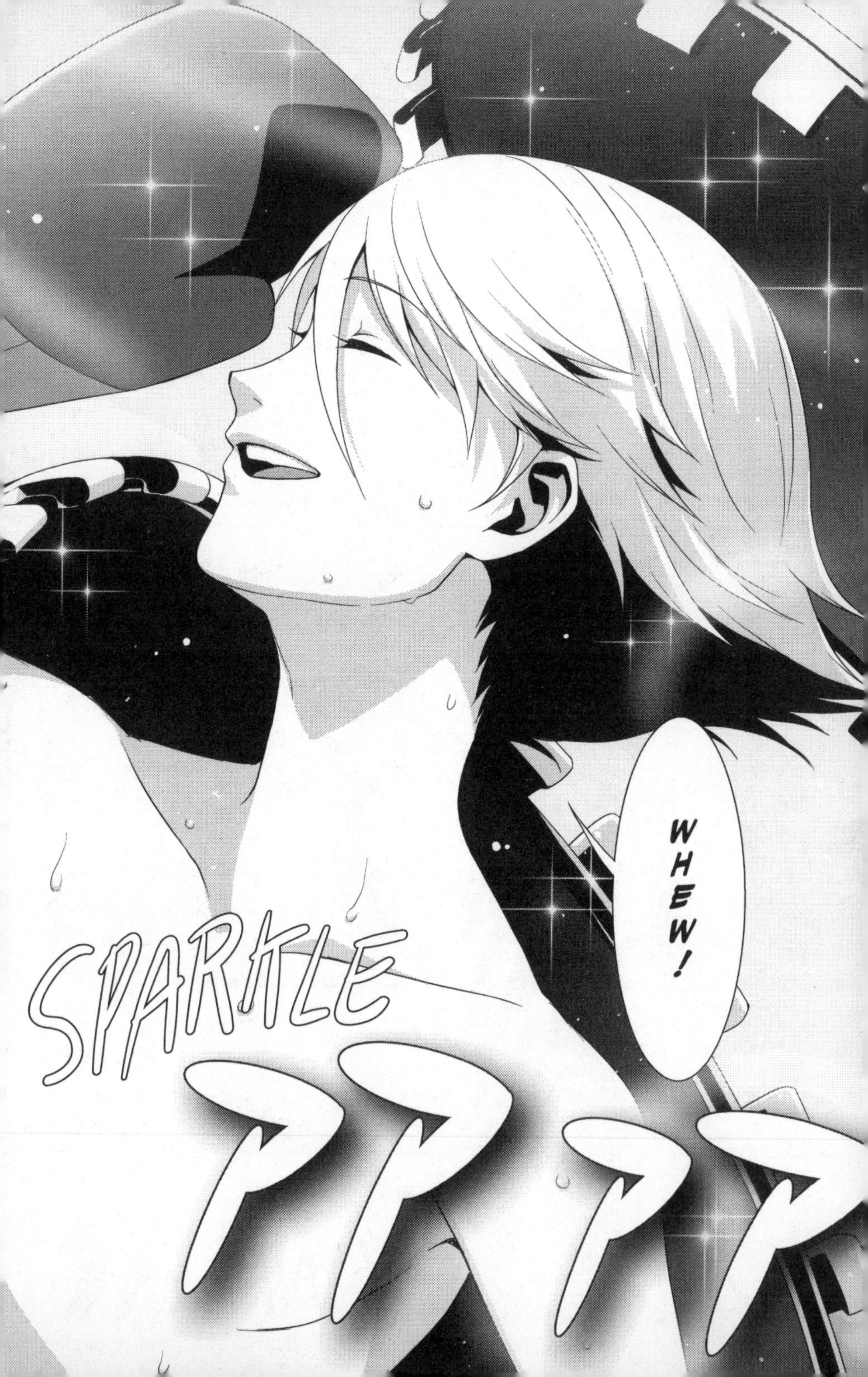
WHEW!
SPARKLE

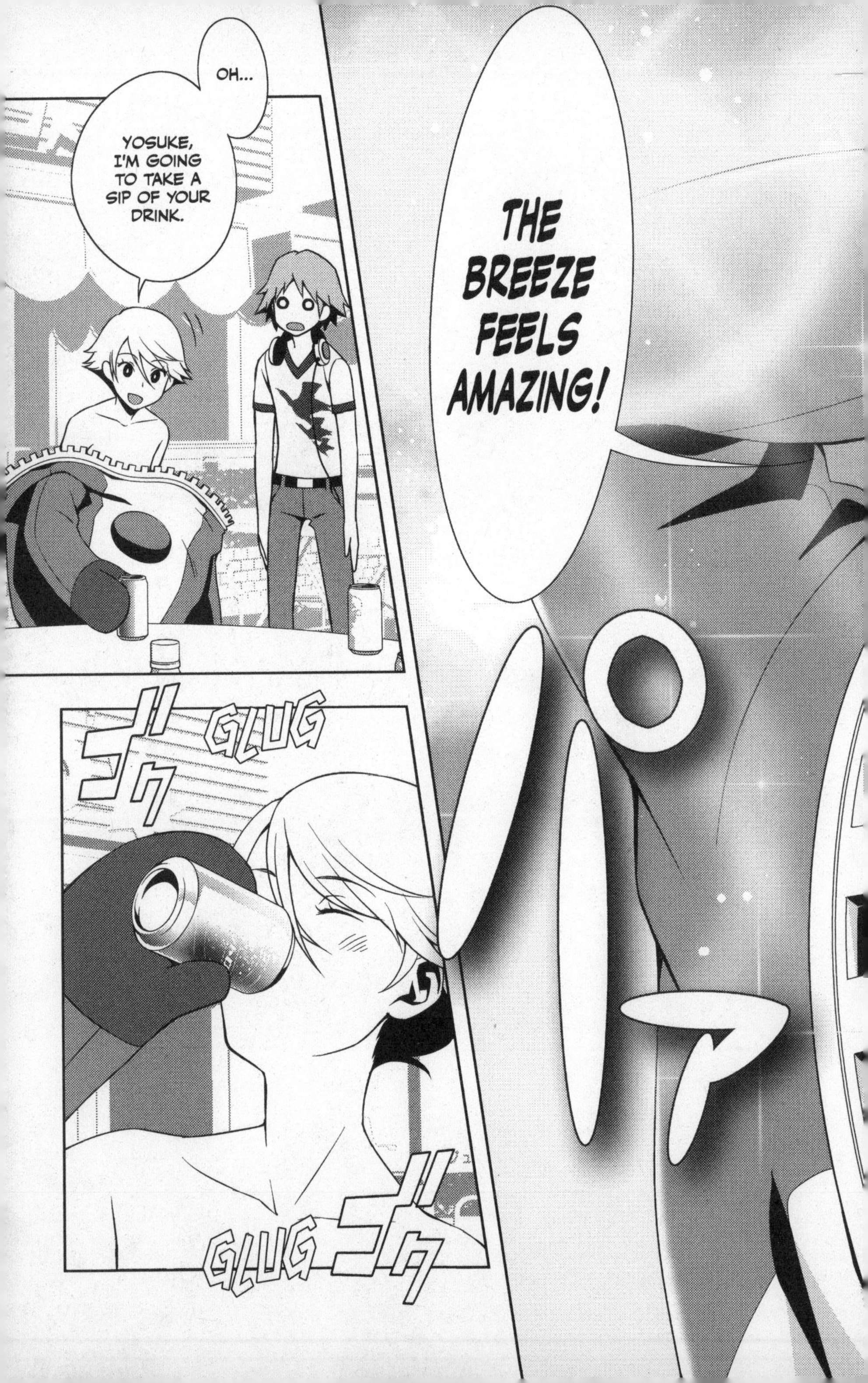
THE BREEZE FEELS AMAZING!
OH...
YOSUKE, I'M GOING TO TAKE A SIP OF YOUR DRINK.
GLUG
GLUG

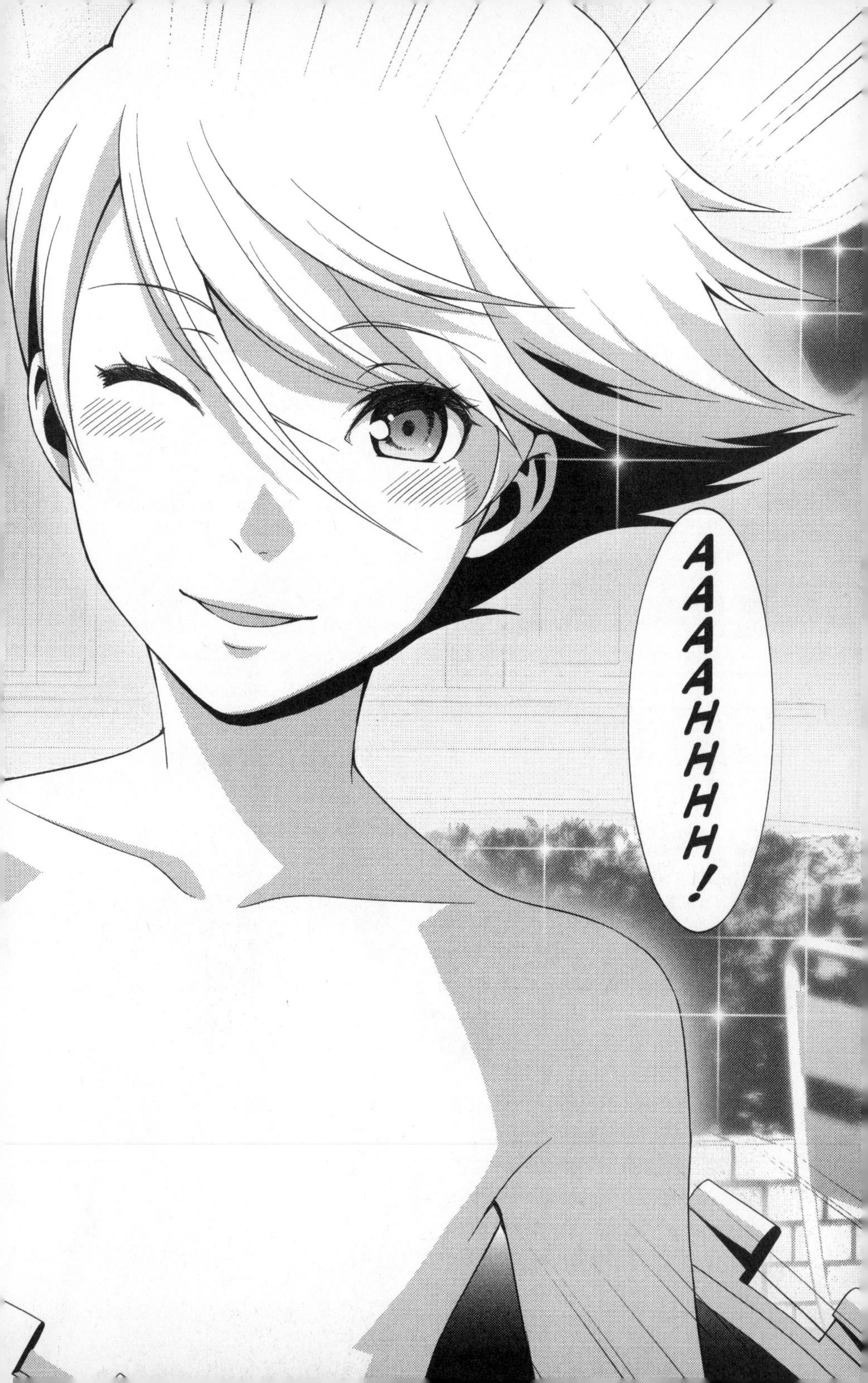
AAAAHHHHH!

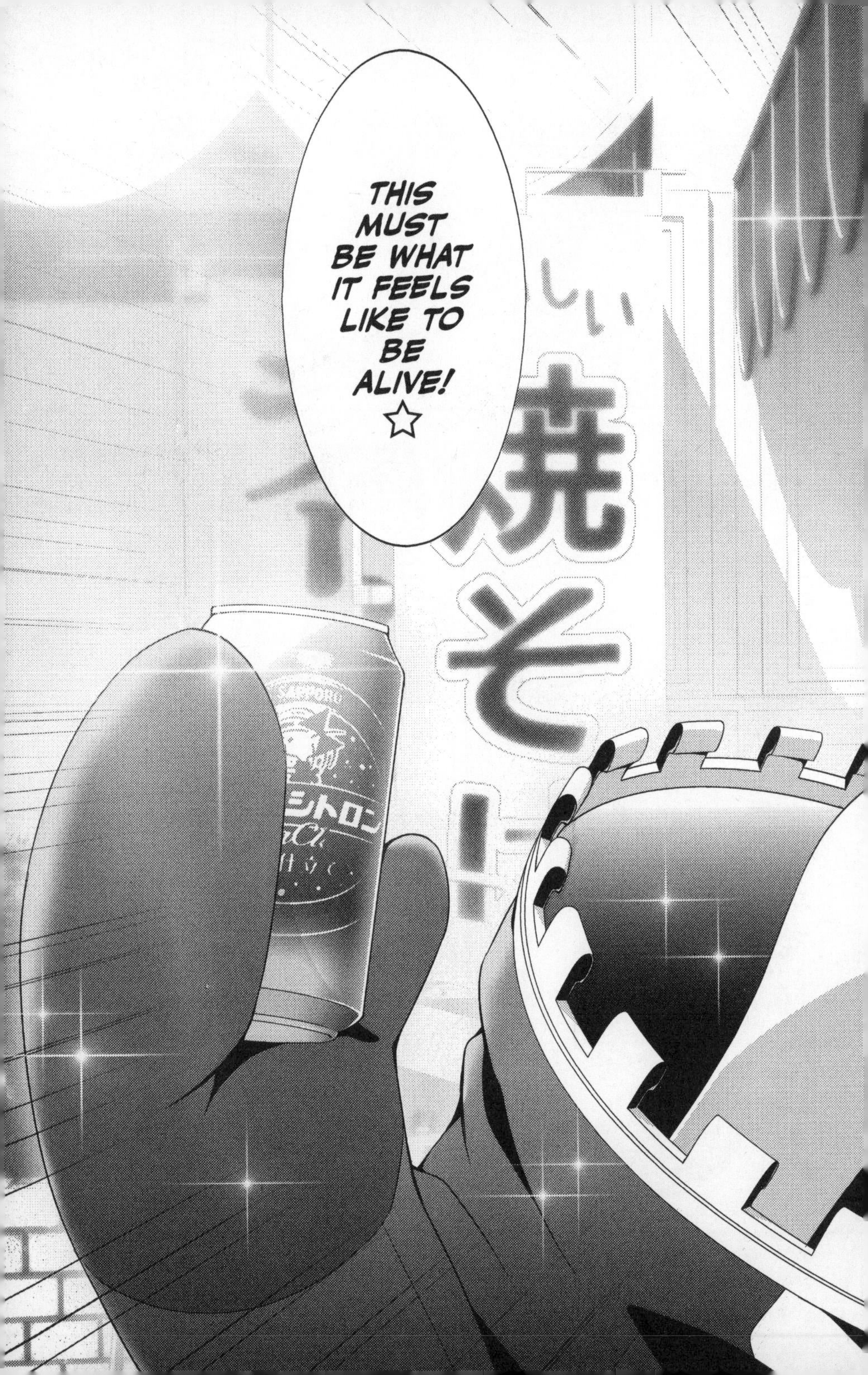
THIS MUST BE WHAT IT FEELS LIKE TO BE ALIVE! ☆

ジュネス稲羽店 掲示板
WHAT...?
HOW...?

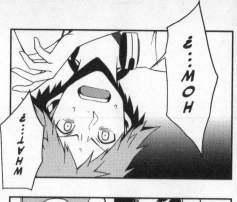

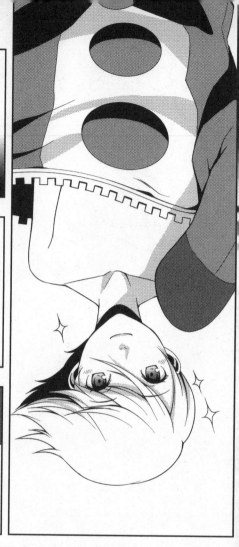

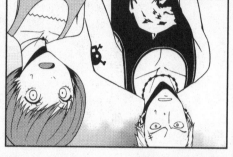

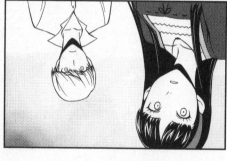

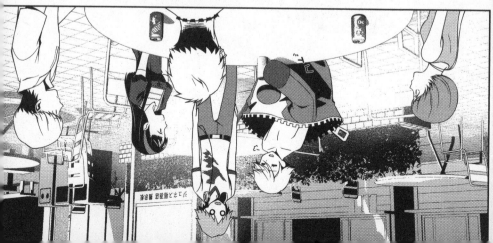

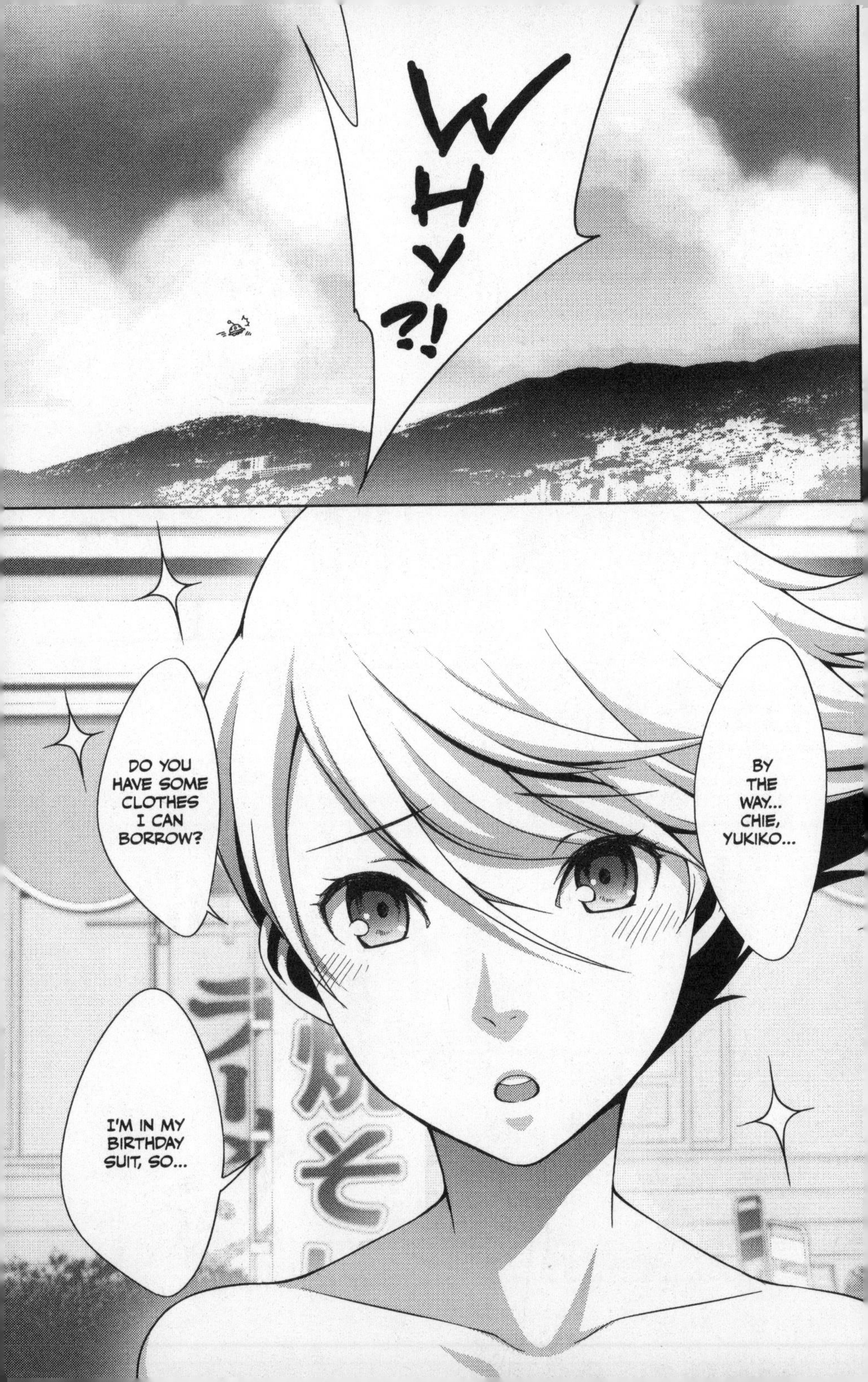
WHY?!
BY THE WAY... CHIE, YUKIKO...
DO YOU HAVE SOME CLOTHES I CAN BORROW?
I'M IN MY BIRTHDAY SUIT, SO...

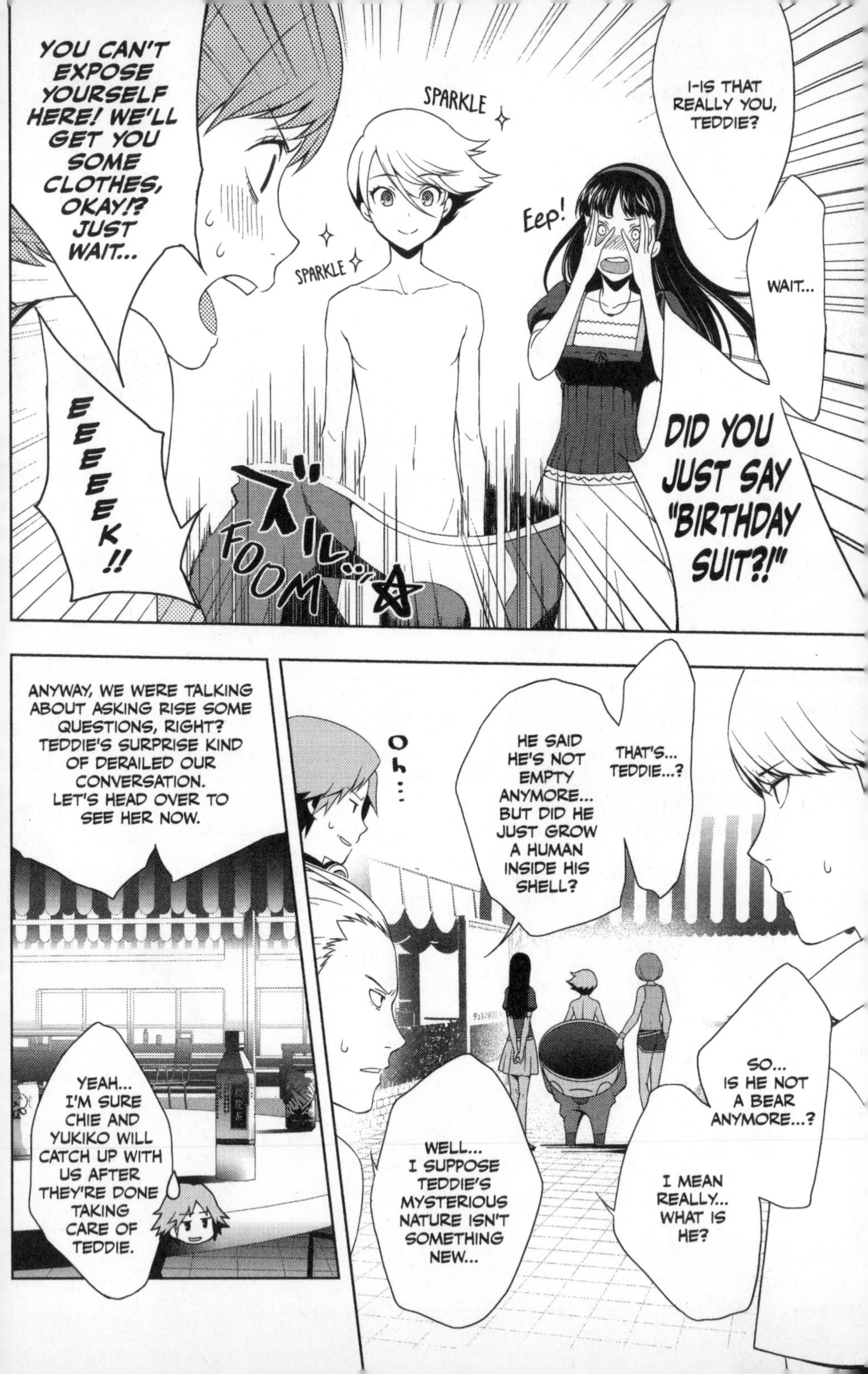
I-IS THAT REALLY YOU, TEDDIE?
WAIT...
DID YOU JUST SAY "BIRTHDAY SUIT?!"
Eep!
SPARKLE
SPARKLE
YOU CAN'T EXPOSE YOURSELF HERE! WE'LL GET YOU SOME CLOTHES, OKAY!? JUST WAIT...
EEEEEK!!
FOOM
THAT'S... TEDDIE...?
HE SAID HE'S NOT EMPTY ANYMORE... BUT DID HE JUST GROW A HUMAN INSIDE HIS SHELL?
Oh...
SO... IS HE NOT A BEAR ANYMORE...?
I MEAN REALLY... WHAT IS HE?
WELL... I SUPPOSE TEDDIE'S MYSTERIOUS NATURE ISN'T SOMETHING NEW...
ANYWAY, WE WERE TALKING ABOUT ASKING RISE SOME QUESTIONS, RIGHT? TEDDIE'S SURPRISE KIND OF DERAILED OUR CONVERSATION. LET'S HEAD OVER TO SEE HER NOW.
YEAH... I'M SURE CHIE AND YUKIKO WILL CATCH UP WITH US AFTER THEY'RE DONE TAKING CARE OF TEDDIE.

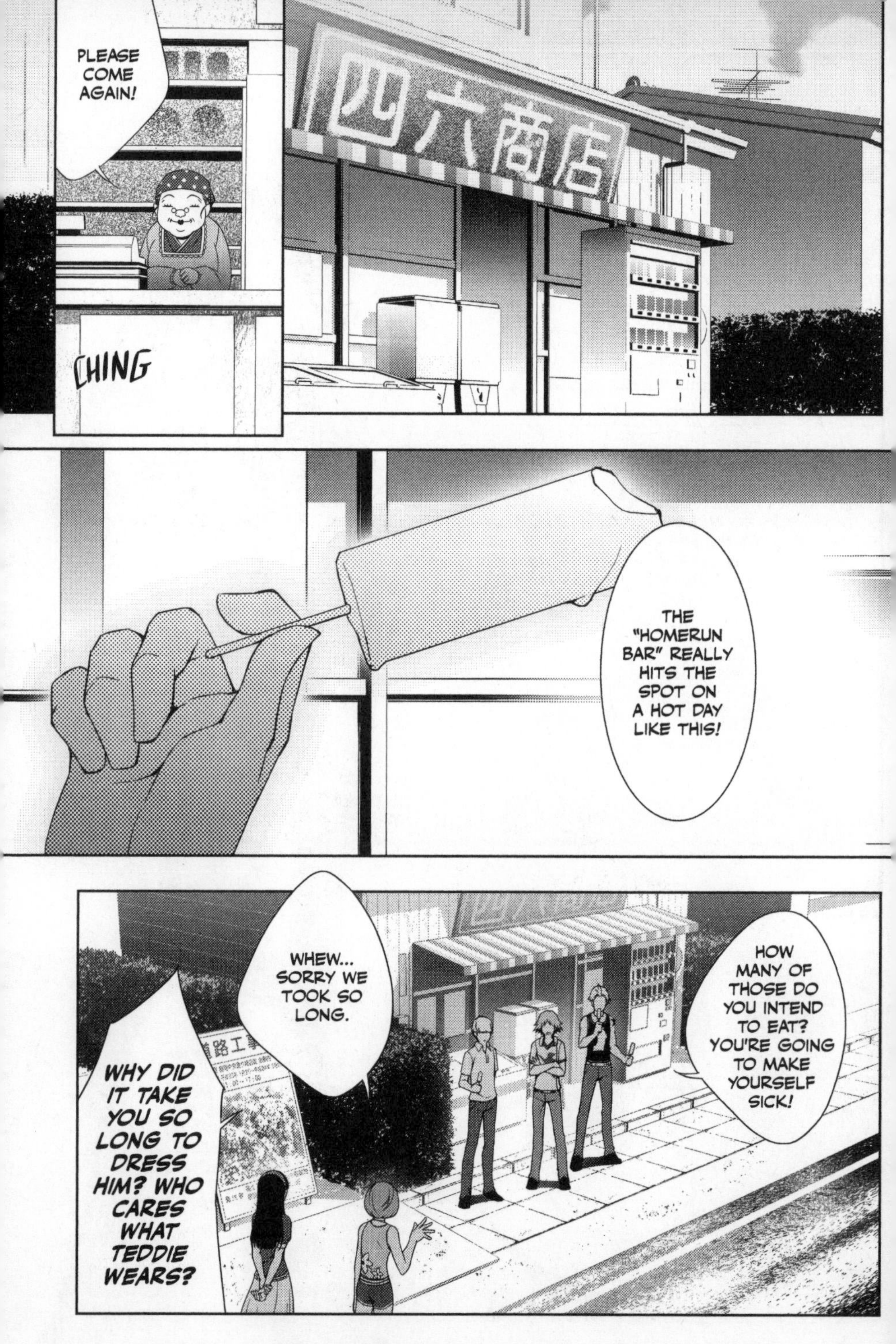
四六商店
PLEASE COME AGAIN!
CHING
THE "HOMERUN BAR" REALLY HITS THE SPOT ON A HOT DAY LIKE THIS!
HOW MANY OF THOSE DO YOU INTEND TO EAT? YOU'RE GOING TO MAKE YOURSELF SICK!
WHEW... SORRY WE TOOK SO LONG.
WHY DID IT TAKE YOU SO LONG TO DRESS HIM? WHO CARES WHAT TEDDIE WEARS?

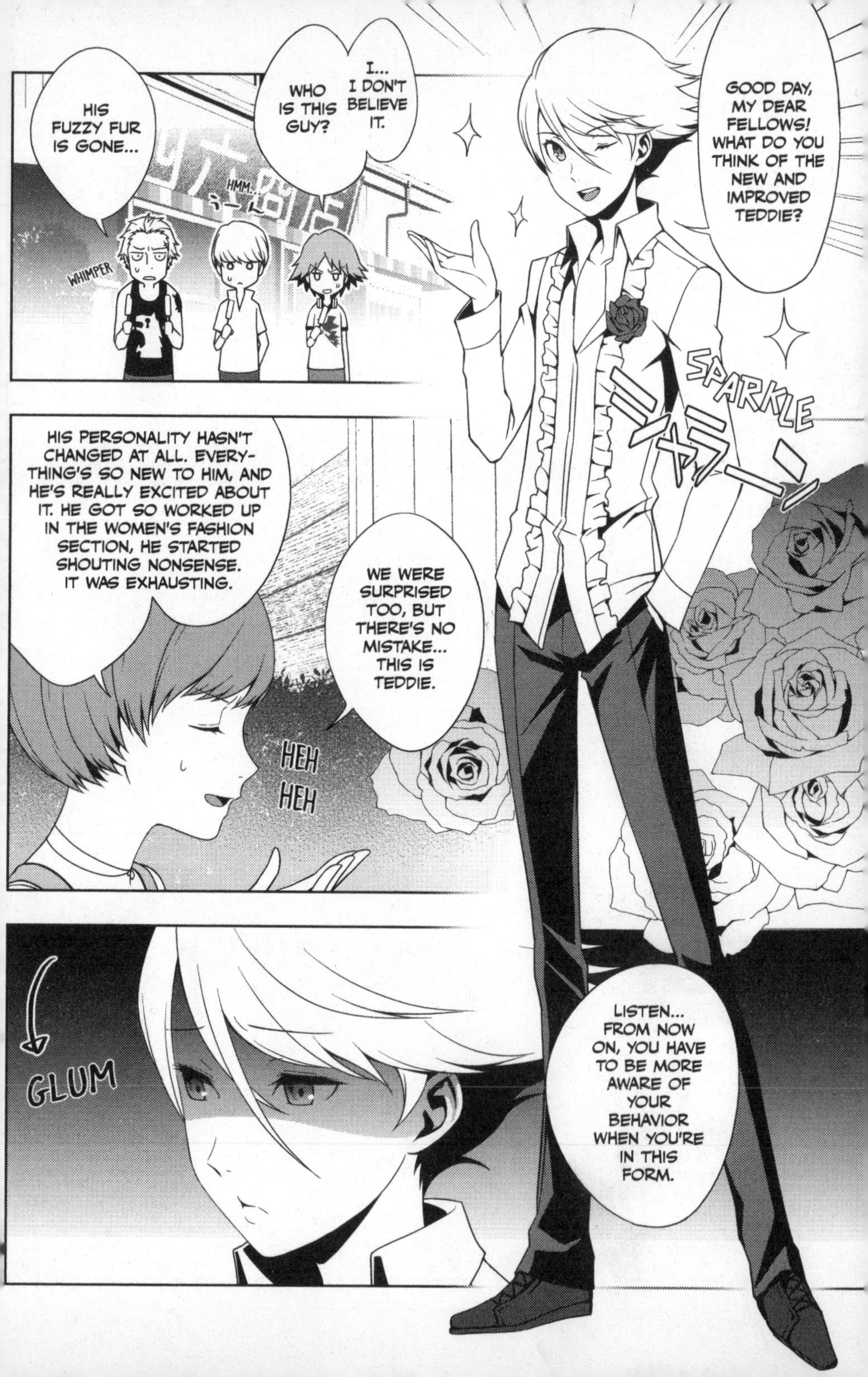
GOOD DAY, MY DEAR FELLOWS! WHAT DO YOU THINK OF THE NEW AND IMPROVED TEDDIE?
SPARKLE
シャラーン
I... I DON'T BELIEVE IT.
WHO IS THIS GUY?
HMM...
HIS FUZZY FUR IS GONE...
WHIMPER
HIS PERSONALITY HASN'T CHANGED AT ALL. EVERY-THING'S SO NEW TO HIM, AND HE'S REALLY EXCITED ABOUT IT. HE GOT SO WORKED UP IN THE WOMEN'S FASHION SECTION, HE STARTED SHOUTING NONSENSE. IT WAS EXHAUSTING.
WE WERE SURPRISED TOO, BUT THERE'S NO MISTAKE... THIS IS TEDDIE.
HEH HEH
LISTEN... FROM NOW ON, YOU HAVE TO BE MORE AWARE OF YOUR BEHAVIOR WHEN YOU'RE IN THIS FORM.
GLUM

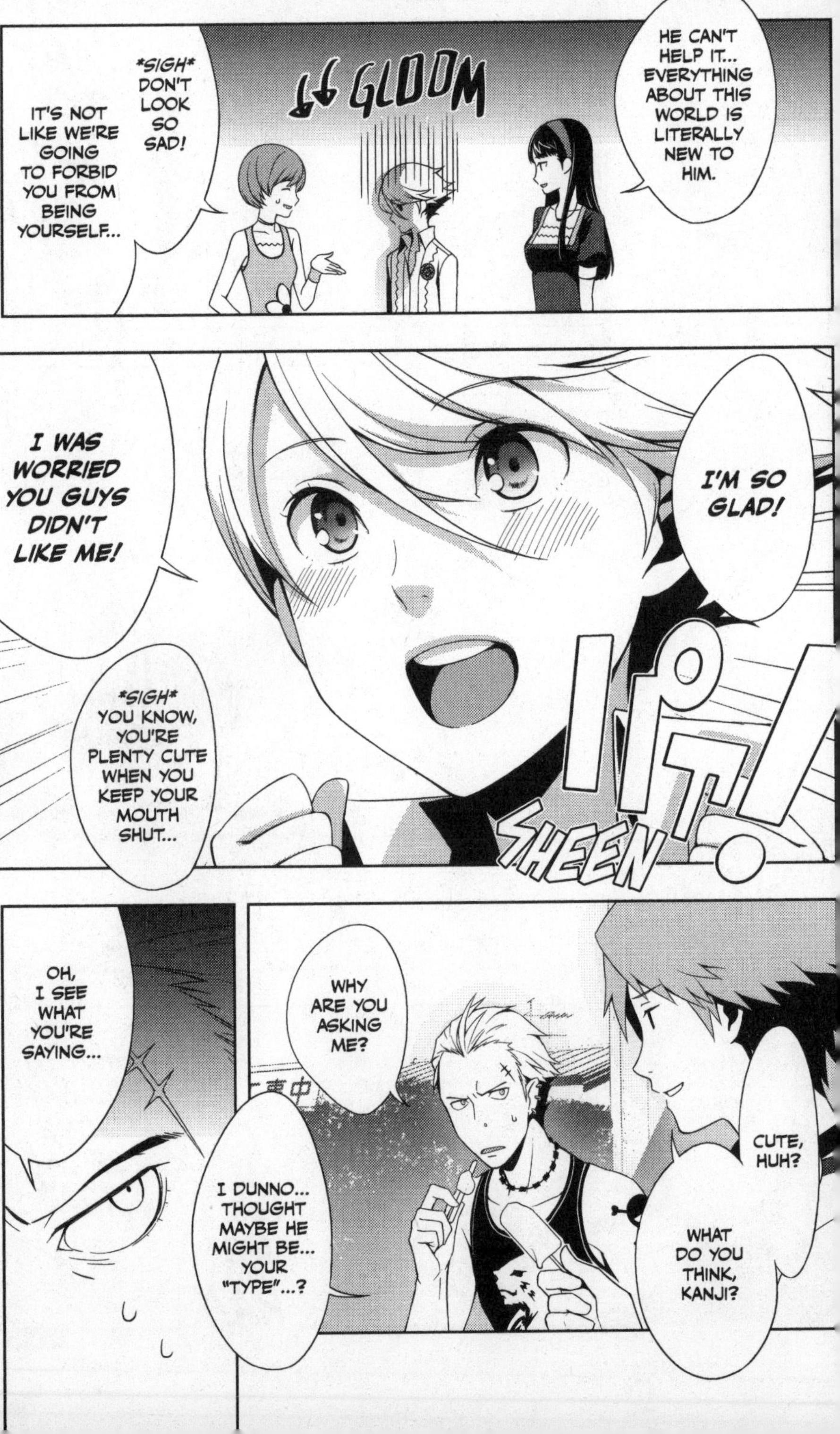
HE CAN'T HELP IT... EVERYTHING ABOUT THIS WORLD IS LITERALLY NEW TO HIM.
GLOOM
SIGH DON'T LOOK SO SAD!
IT'S NOT LIKE WE'RE GOING TO FORBID YOU FROM BEING YOURSELF...
I'M SO GLAD!
I WAS WORRIED YOU GUYS DIDN'T LIKE ME!
SHEEN
SIGH YOU KNOW, YOU'RE PLENTY CUTE WHEN YOU KEEP YOUR MOUTH SHUT...
CUTE, HUH?
WHAT DO YOU THINK, KANJI?
WHY ARE YOU ASKING ME?
I DUNNO... THOUGHT MAYBE HE MIGHT BE... YOUR "TYPE"...?
OH, I SEE WHAT YOU'RE SAYING...

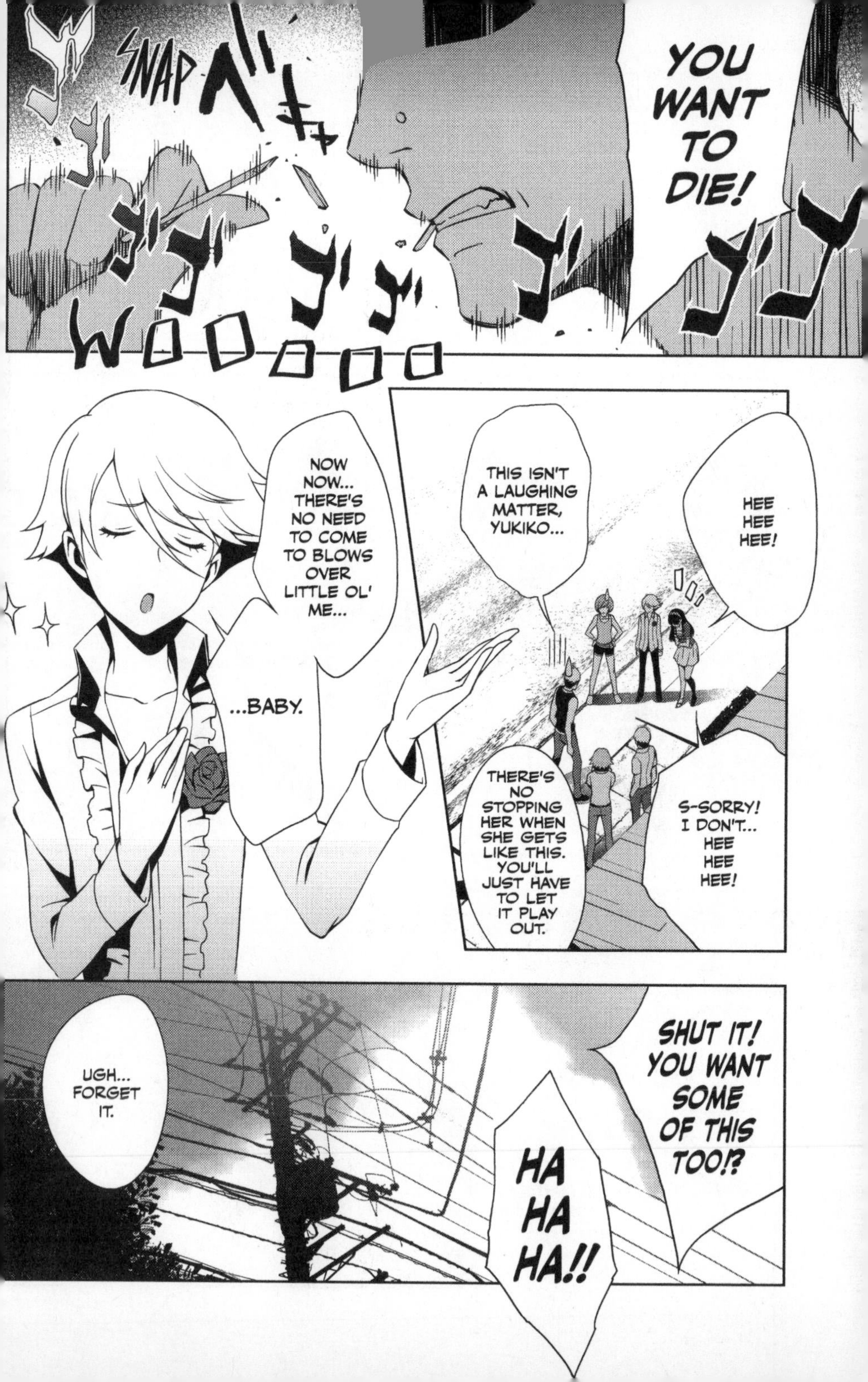
YOU WANT TO DIE!
SNAP
WOOOOOO
HEE HEE HEE!
THIS ISN'T A LAUGHING MATTER, YUKIKO...
S-SORRY! I DON'T... HEE HEE HEE!
THERE'S NO STOPPING HER WHEN SHE GETS LIKE THIS. YOU'LL JUST HAVE TO LET IT PLAY OUT.
NOW NOW... THERE'S NO NEED TO COME TO BLOWS OVER LITTLE OL' ME...
...BABY.
SHUT IT! YOU WANT SOME OF THIS TOO!?
HA HA HA HA!!
UGH... FORGET IT.

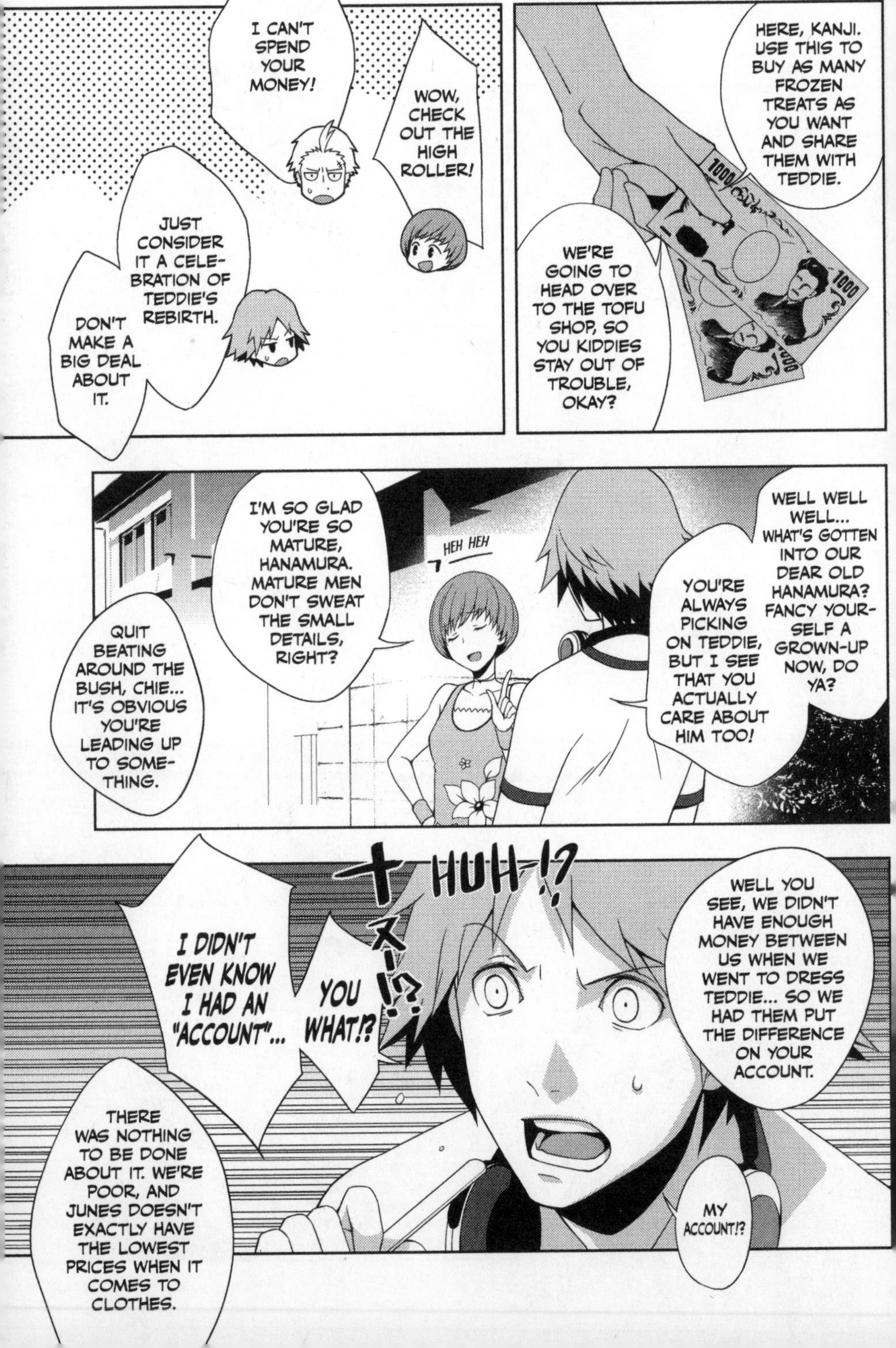
HERE, KANJI. USE THIS TO BUY AS MANY FROZEN TREATS AS YOU WANT AND SHARE THEM WITH TEDDIE.
WE'RE GOING TO HEAD OVER TO THE TOFU SHOP, SO YOU KIDDIES STAY OUT OF TROUBLE, OKAY?
1000
I CAN'T SPEND YOUR MONEY!
WOW, CHECK OUT THE HIGH ROLLER!
JUST CONSIDER IT A CELE-BRATION OF TEDDIE'S REBIRTH.
DON'T MAKE A BIG DEAL ABOUT IT.
WELL WELL WELL... WHAT'S GOTTEN INTO OUR DEAR OLD HANAMURA? FANCY YOUR-SELF A GROWN-UP NOW, DO YA?
YOU'RE ALWAYS PICKING ON TEDDIE, BUT I SEE THAT YOU ACTUALLY CARE ABOUT HIM TOO!
HEH HEH
I'M SO GLAD YOU'RE SO MATURE, HANAMURA. MATURE MEN DON'T SWEAT THE SMALL DETAILS, RIGHT?
QUIT BEATING AROUND THE BUSH, CHIE... IT'S OBVIOUS YOU'RE LEADING UP TO SOME-THING.
WELL YOU SEE, WE DIDN'T HAVE ENOUGH MONEY BETWEEN US WHEN WE WENT TO DRESS TEDDIE... SO WE HAD THEM PUT THE DIFFERENCE ON YOUR ACCOUNT.
HUH-!?
YOU WHAT!?
I DIDN'T EVEN KNOW I HAD AN "ACCOUNT"...
MY ACCOUNT!?
THERE WAS NOTHING TO BE DONE ABOUT IT. WE'RE POOR, AND JUNES DOESN'T EXACTLY HAVE THE LOWEST PRICES WHEN IT COMES TO CLOTHES.

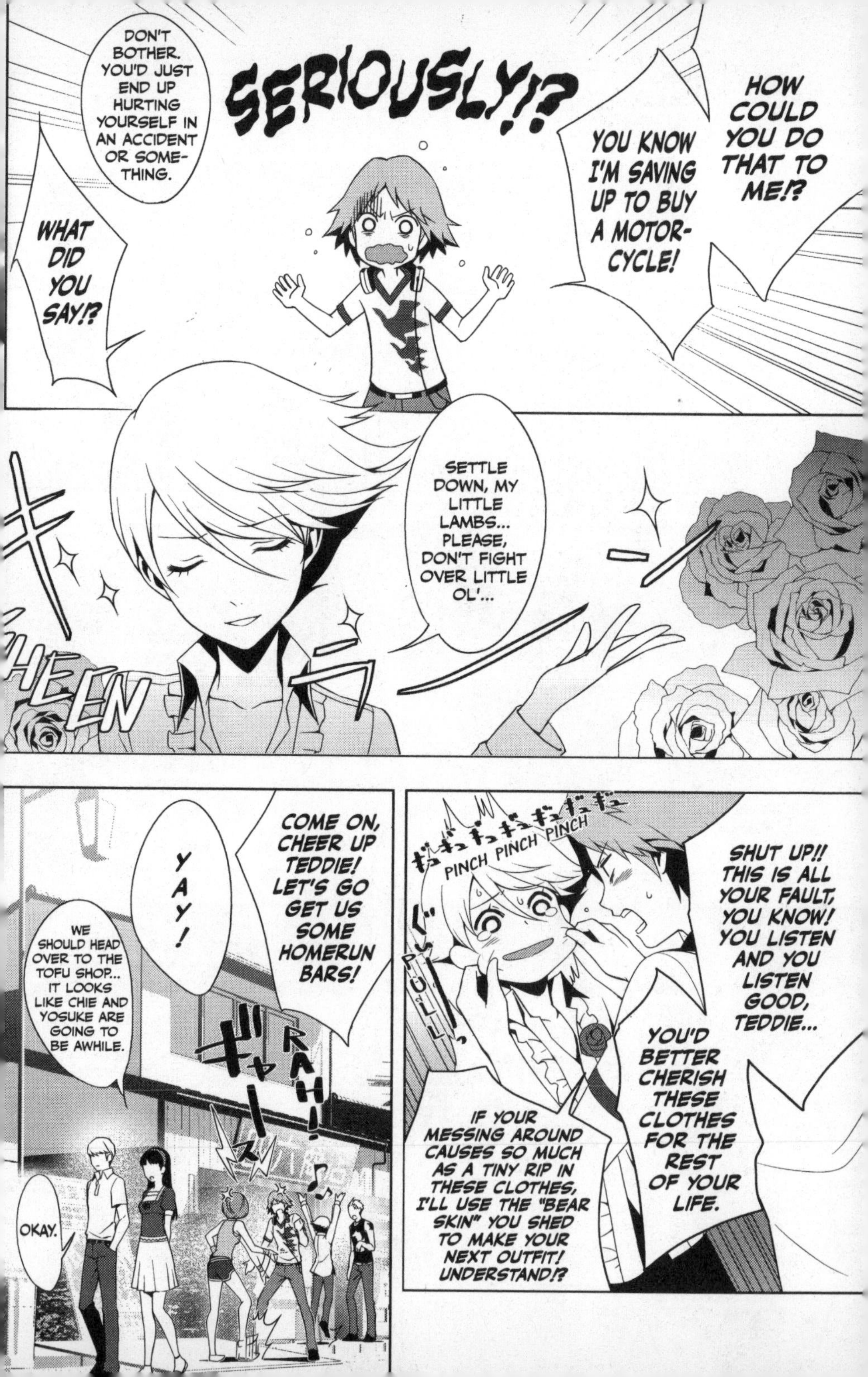
HOW COULD YOU DO THAT TO ME!?
YOU KNOW I'M SAVING UP TO BUY A MOTOR-CYCLE!
SERIOUSLY!?
DON'T BOTHER. YOU'D JUST END UP HURTING YOURSELF IN AN ACCIDENT OR SOME-THING.
WHAT DID YOU SAY!?
SETTLE DOWN, MY LITTLE LAMBS... PLEASE, DON'T FIGHT OVER LITTLE OL'...
SHEEN
SHUT UP!! THIS IS ALL YOUR FAULT, YOU KNOW! YOU LISTEN AND YOU LISTEN GOOD, TEDDIE...
PINCH PINCH PINCH
PULL
YOU'D BETTER CHERISH THESE CLOTHES FOR THE REST OF YOUR LIFE.
IF YOUR MESSING AROUND CAUSES SO MUCH AS A TINY RIP IN THESE CLOTHES, I'LL USE THE "BEAR SKIN" YOU SHED TO MAKE YOUR NEXT OUTFIT! UNDERSTAND!?
COME ON, CHEER UP TEDDIE! LET'S GO GET US SOME HOMERUN BARS!
YAY!
RAH!
WE SHOULD HEAD OVER TO THE TOFU SHOP... IT LOOKS LIKE CHIE AND YOSUKE ARE GOING TO BE AWHILE.
OKAY.

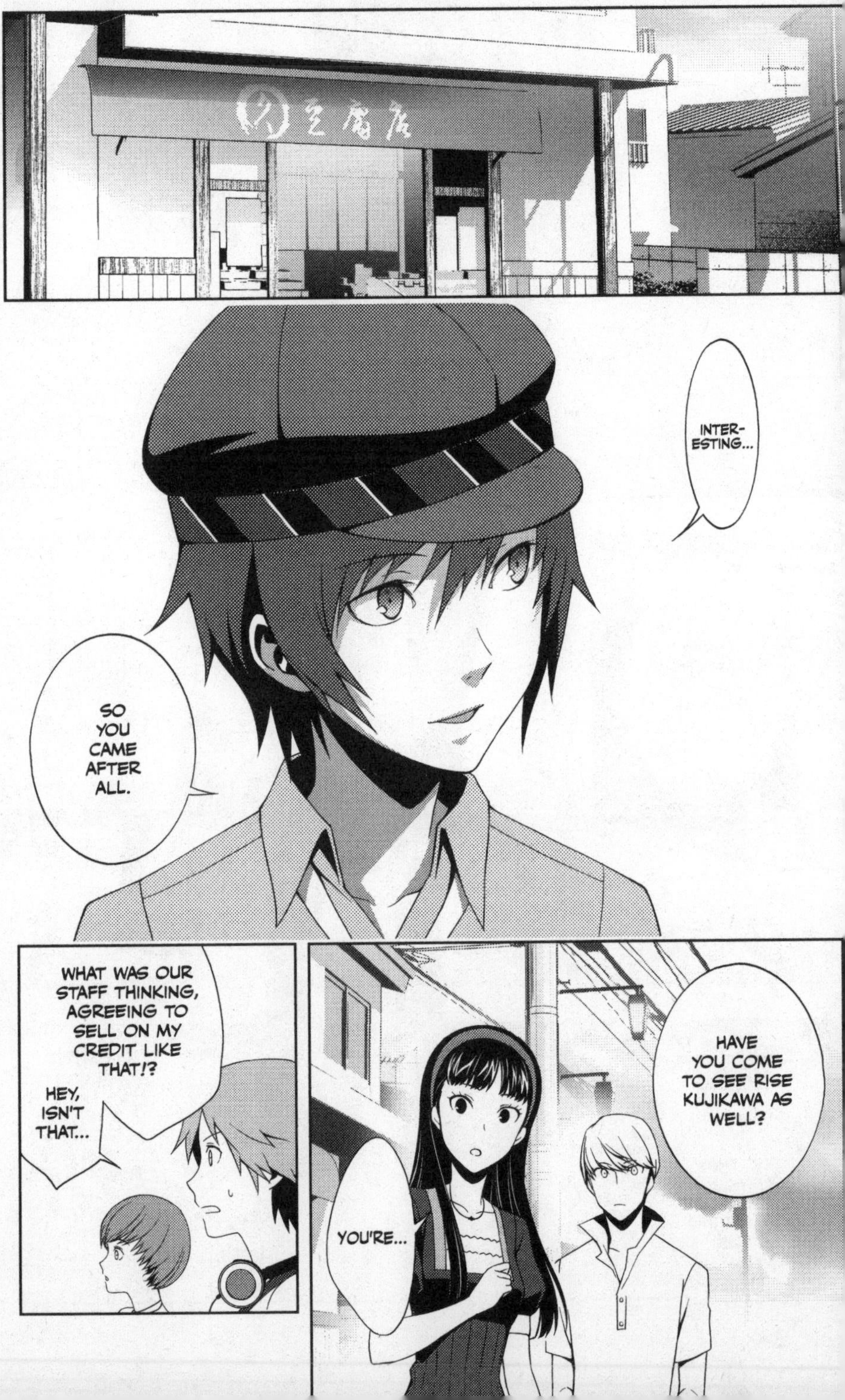
INTER-ESTING...
SO YOU CAME AFTER ALL.
HAVE YOU COME TO SEE RISE KUJIKAWA AS WELL?
YOU'RE...
WHAT WAS OUR STAFF THINKING, AGREEING TO SELL ON MY CREDIT LIKE THAT!?
HEY, ISN'T THAT...

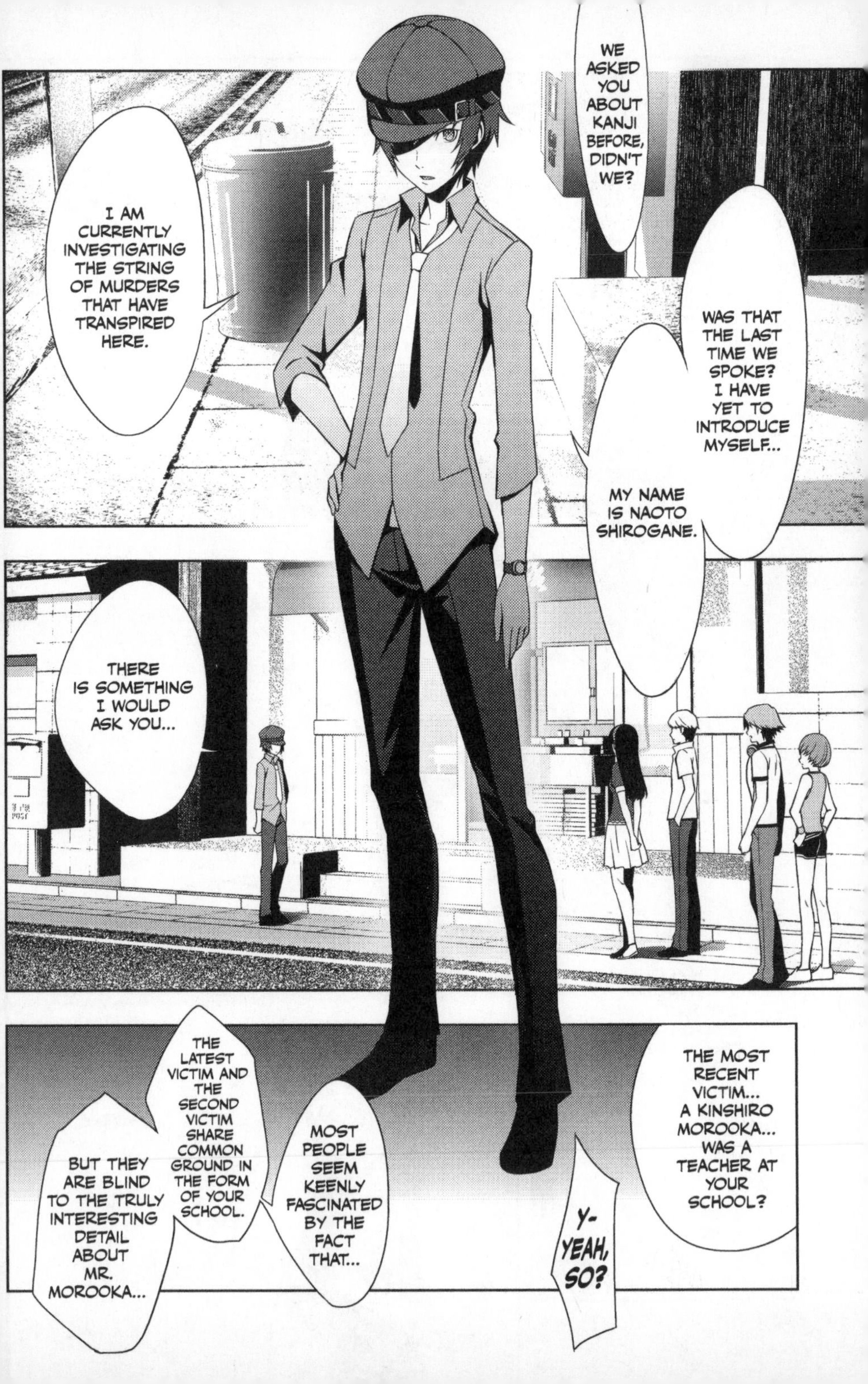
WE ASKED YOU ABOUT KANJI BEFORE, DIDN'T WE?
WAS THAT THE LAST TIME WE SPOKE? I HAVE YET TO INTRODUCE MYSELF...
MY NAME IS NAOTO SHIROGANE.
I AM CURRENTLY INVESTIGATING THE STRING OF MURDERS THAT HAVE TRANSPIRED HERE.
THERE IS SOMETHING I WOULD ASK YOU...
POST
THE MOST RECENT VICTIM... A KINSHIRO MOROOKA... WAS A TEACHER AT YOUR SCHOOL?
Y-YEAH, SO?
MOST PEOPLE SEEM KEENLY FASCINATED BY THE FACT THAT...
THE LATEST VICTIM AND THE SECOND VICTIM SHARE COMMON GROUND IN THE FORM OF YOUR SCHOOL.
BUT THEY ARE BLIND TO THE TRULY INTERESTING DETAIL ABOUT MR. MOROOKA...

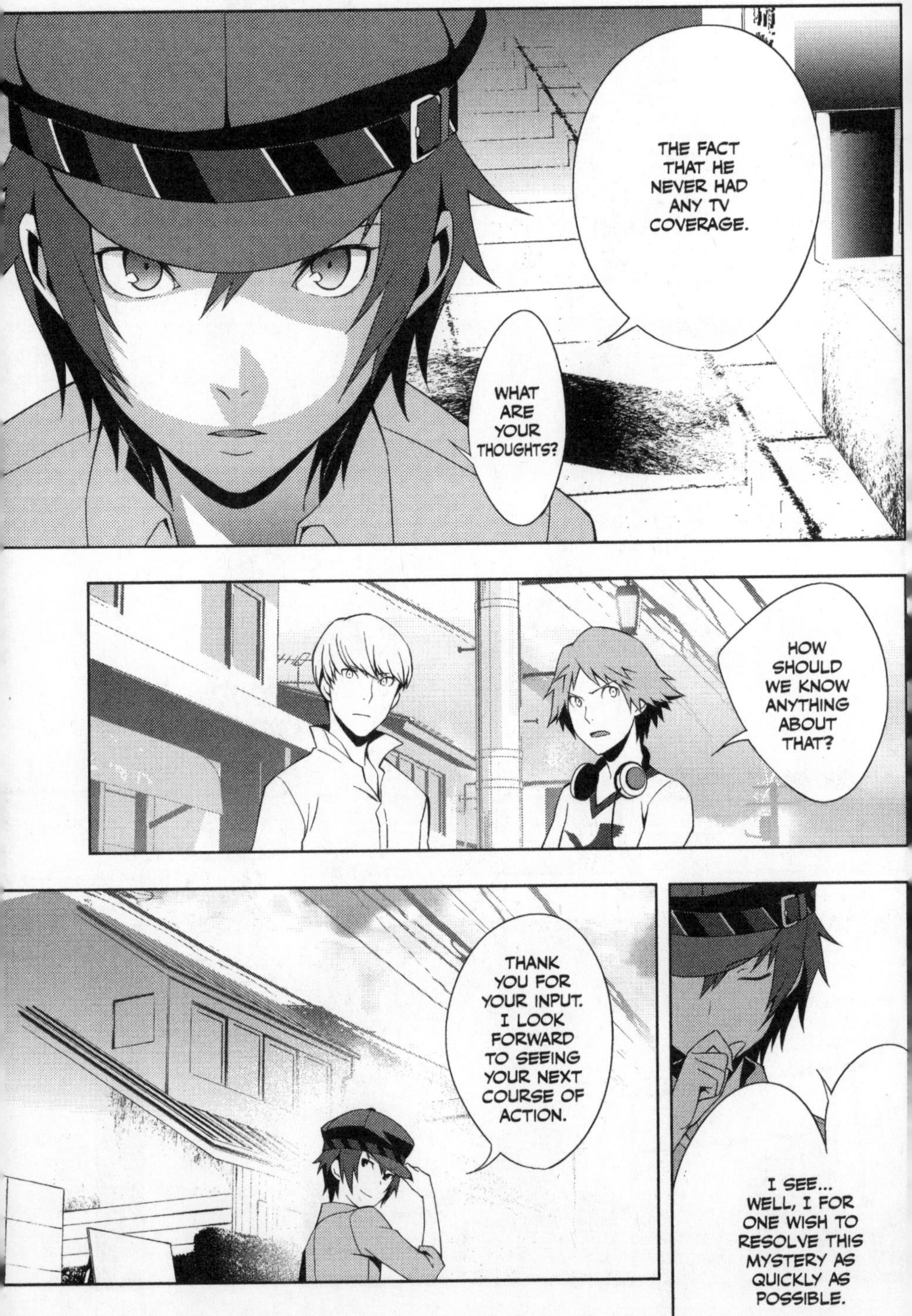
THE FACT THAT HE NEVER HAD ANY TV COVERAGE.
WHAT ARE YOUR THOUGHTS?
HOW SHOULD WE KNOW ANYTHING ABOUT THAT?
I SEE... WELL, I FOR ONE WISH TO RESOLVE THIS MYSTERY AS QUICKLY AS POSSIBLE.
THANK YOU FOR YOUR INPUT. I LOOK FORWARD TO SEEING YOUR NEXT COURSE OF ACTION.

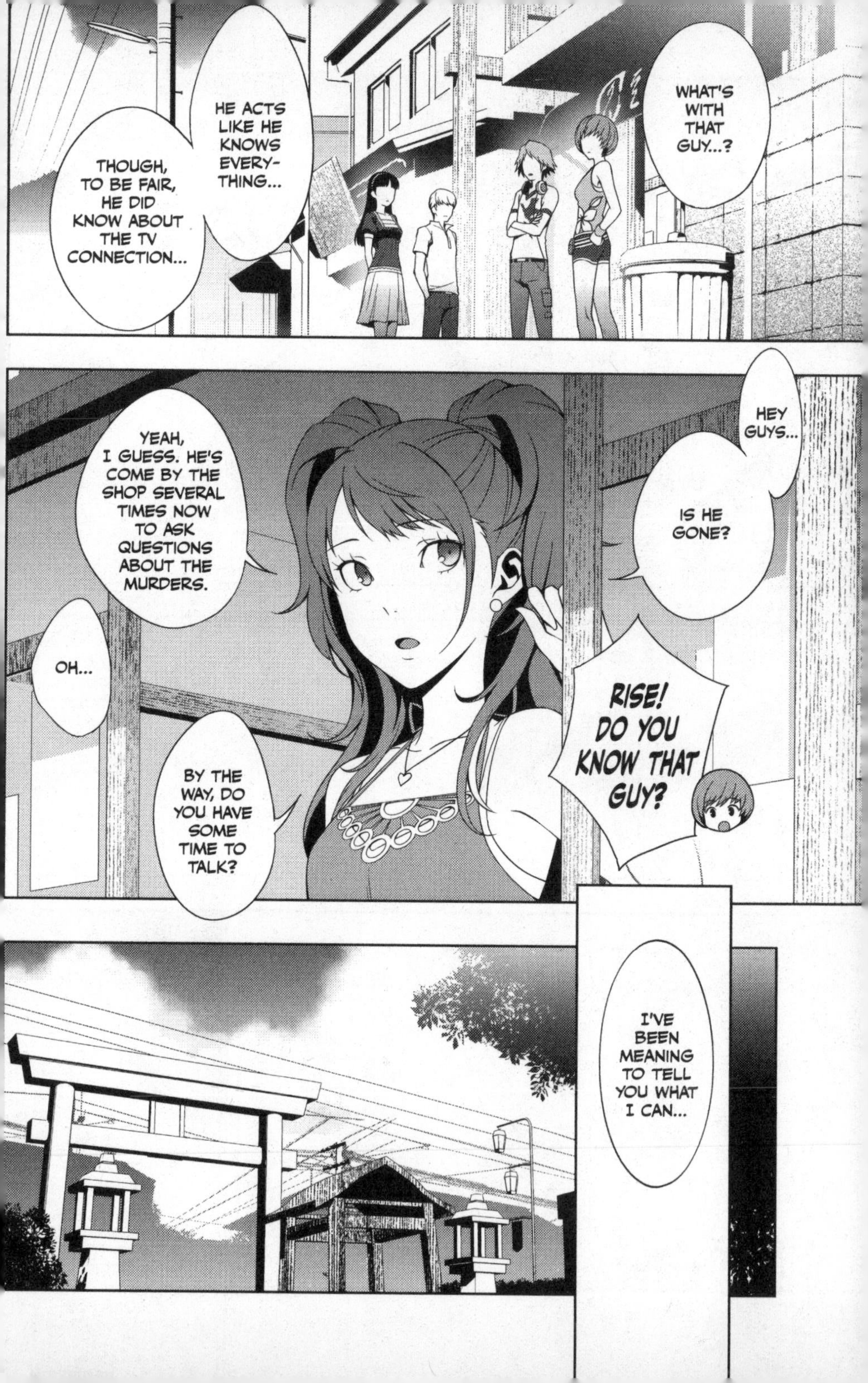
WHAT'S WITH THAT GUY...?
HE ACTS LIKE HE KNOWS EVERY-THING...
THOUGH, TO BE FAIR, HE DID KNOW ABOUT THE TV CONNECTION...
HEY GUYS...
IS HE GONE?
RISE! DO YOU KNOW THAT GUY?
YEAH, I GUESS. HE'S COME BY THE SHOP SEVERAL TIMES NOW TO ASK QUESTIONS ABOUT THE MURDERS.
OH...
BY THE WAY, DO YOU HAVE SOME TIME TO TALK?
I'VE BEEN MEANING TO TELL YOU WHAT I CAN...

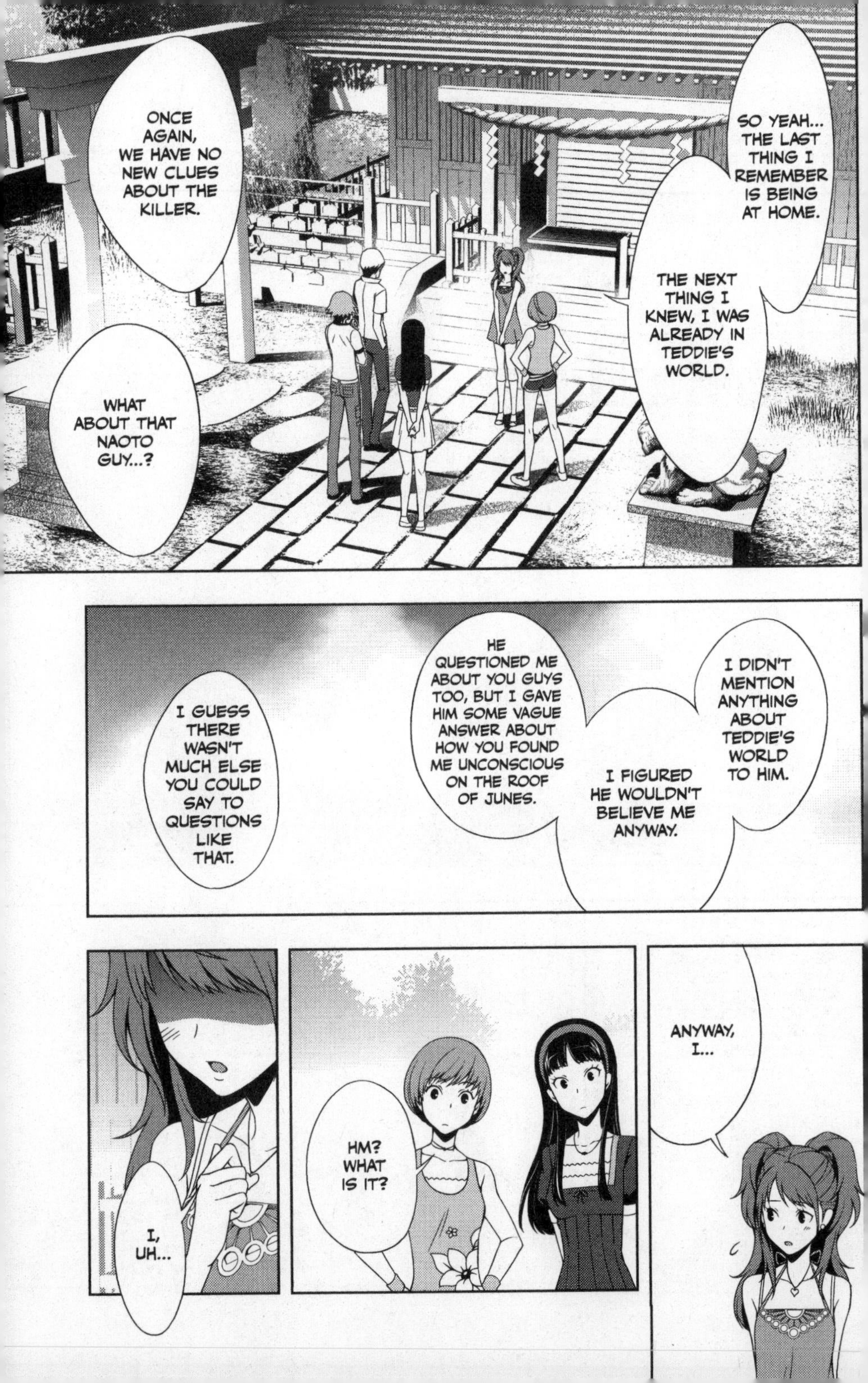
SO YEAH... THE LAST THING I REMEMBER IS BEING AT HOME.
THE NEXT THING I KNEW, I WAS ALREADY IN TEDDIE'S WORLD.
ONCE AGAIN, WE HAVE NO NEW CLUES ABOUT THE KILLER.
WHAT ABOUT THAT NAOTO GUY...?
I DIDN'T MENTION ANYTHING ABOUT TEDDIE'S WORLD TO HIM.
I FIGURED HE WOULDN'T BELIEVE ME ANYWAY.
HE QUESTIONED ME ABOUT YOU GUYS TOO, BUT I GAVE HIM SOME VAGUE ANSWER ABOUT HOW YOU FOUND ME UNCONSCIOUS ON THE ROOF OF JUNES.
I GUESS THERE WASN'T MUCH ELSE YOU COULD SAY TO QUESTIONS LIKE THAT.
ANYWAY, I...
HM? WHAT IS IT?
I, UH...

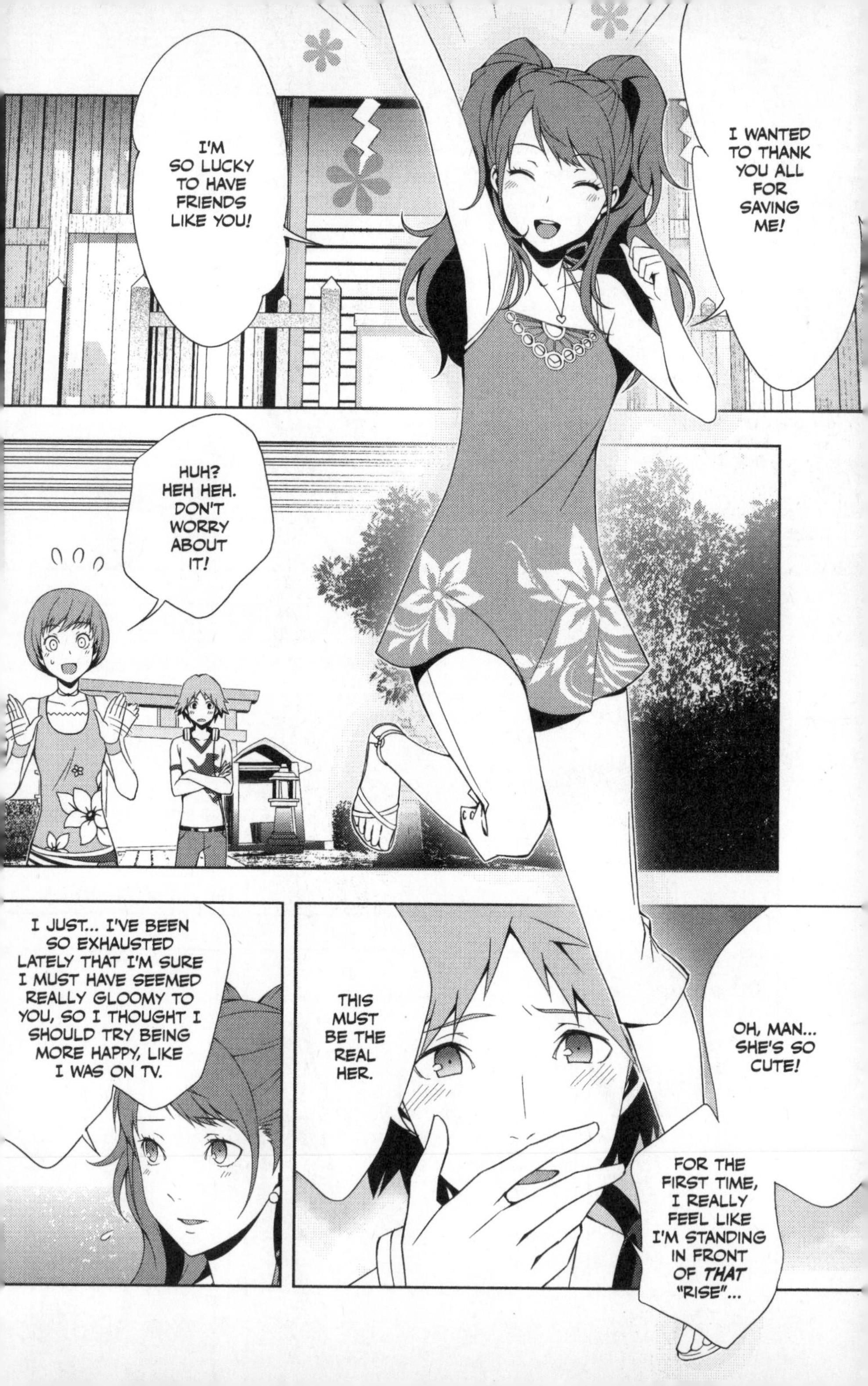
I WANTED TO THANK YOU ALL FOR SAVING ME!
I'M SO LUCKY TO HAVE FRIENDS LIKE YOU!
HUH? HEH HEH. DON'T WORRY ABOUT IT!
OH, MAN... SHE'S SO CUTE!
THIS MUST BE THE REAL HER.
FOR THE FIRST TIME, I REALLY FEEL LIKE I'M STANDING IN FRONT OF *THAT* "RISE"...
I JUST... I'VE BEEN SO EXHAUSTED LATELY THAT I'M SURE I MUST HAVE SEEMED REALLY GLOOMY TO YOU, SO I THOUGHT I SHOULD TRY BEING MORE HAPPY, LIKE I WAS ON TV.

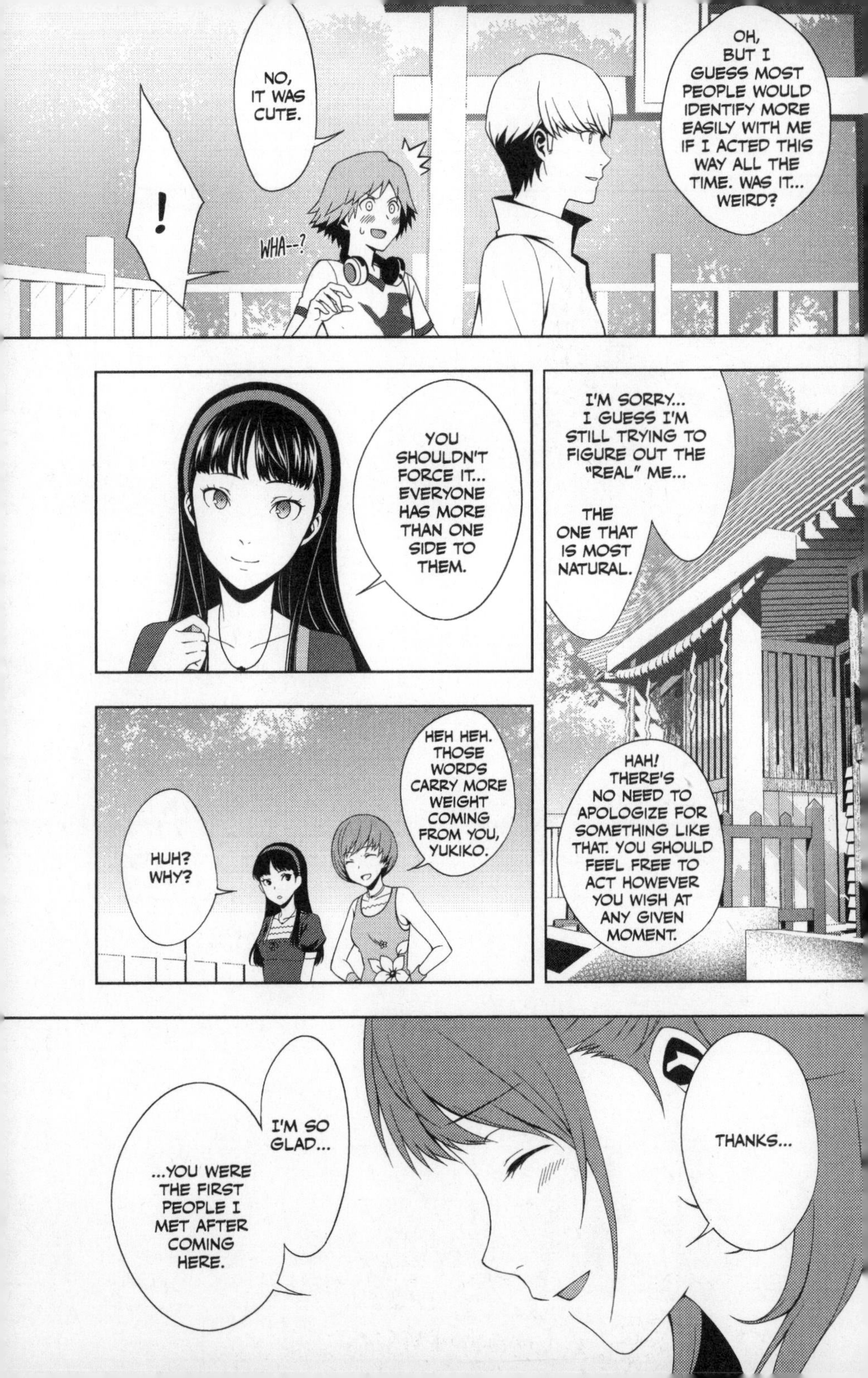
OH, BUT I GUESS MOST PEOPLE WOULD IDENTIFY MORE EASILY WITH ME IF I ACTED THIS WAY ALL THE TIME. WAS IT... WEIRD?
NO, IT WAS CUTE.
WHA--?
!
I'M SORRY... I GUESS I'M STILL TRYING TO FIGURE OUT THE "REAL" ME...
THE ONE THAT IS MOST NATURAL.
YOU SHOULDN'T FORCE IT... EVERYONE HAS MORE THAN ONE SIDE TO THEM.
HAH! THERE'S NO NEED TO APOLOGIZE FOR SOMETHING LIKE THAT. YOU SHOULD FEEL FREE TO ACT HOWEVER YOU WISH AT ANY GIVEN MOMENT.
HEH HEH. THOSE WORDS CARRY MORE WEIGHT COMING FROM YOU, YUKIKO.
HUH? WHY?
THANKS...
I'M SO GLAD...
...YOU WERE THE FIRST PEOPLE I MET AFTER COMING HERE.

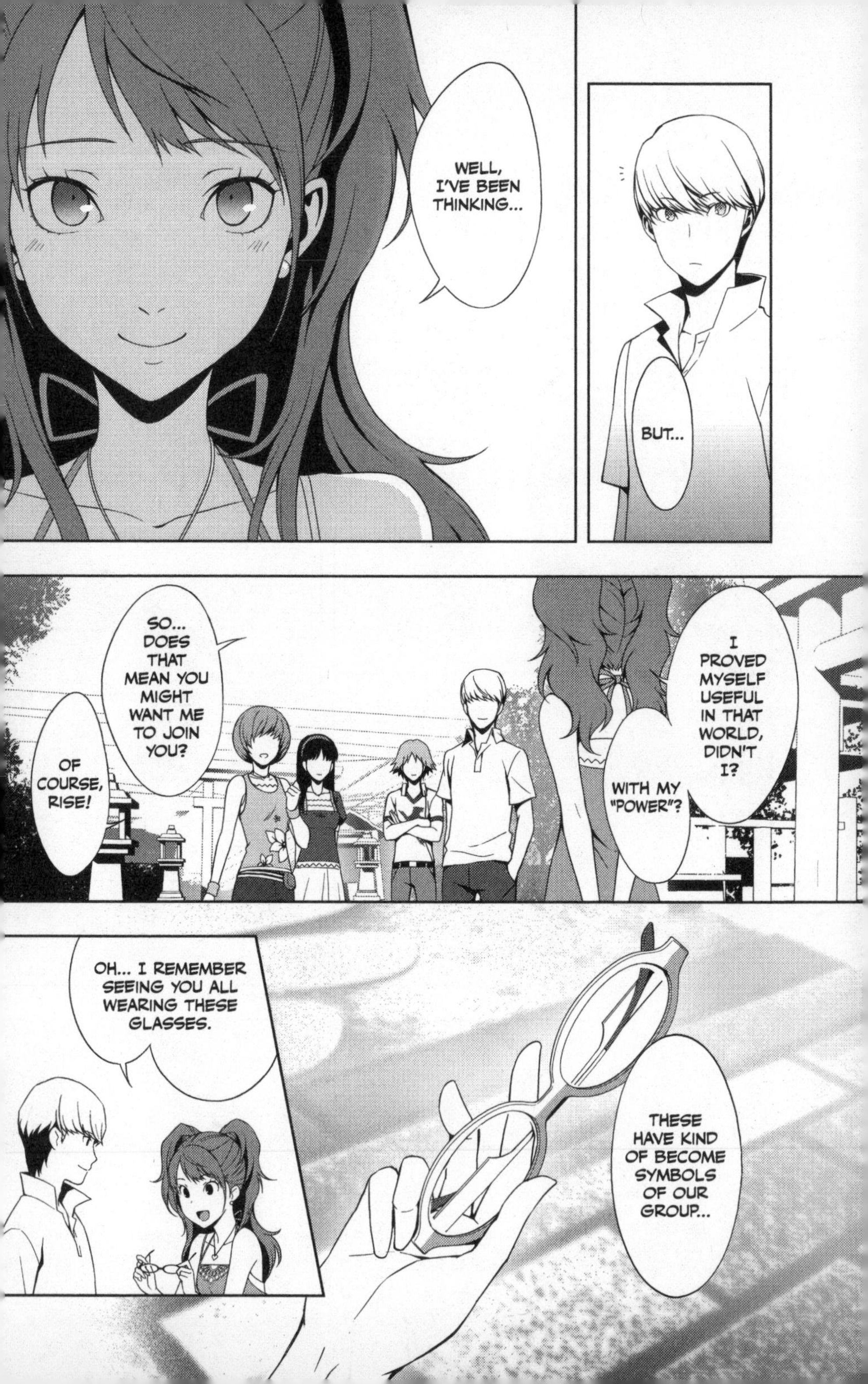
BUT...
WELL, I'VE BEEN THINKING...
I PROVED MYSELF USEFUL IN THAT WORLD, DIDN'T I?
WITH MY "POWER"?
SO... DOES THAT MEAN YOU MIGHT WANT ME TO JOIN YOU?
OF COURSE, RISE!
THESE HAVE KIND OF BECOME SYMBOLS OF OUR GROUP...
OH... I REMEMBER SEEING YOU ALL WEARING THESE GLASSES.

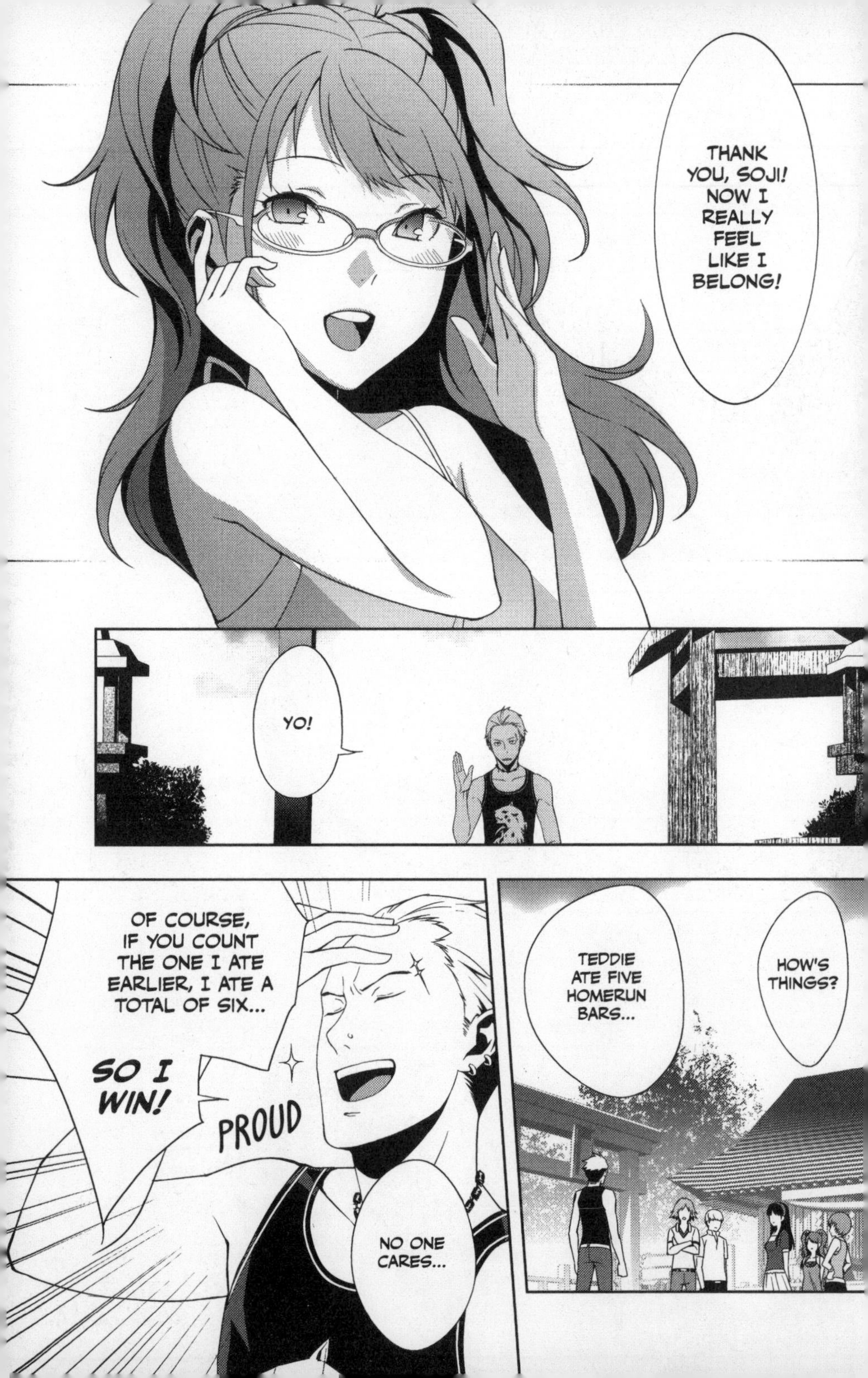
THANK YOU, SOJI! NOW I REALLY FEEL LIKE I BELONG!
YO!
HOW'S THINGS?
TEDDIE ATE FIVE HOMERUN BARS...
OF COURSE, IF YOU COUNT THE ONE I ATE EARLIER, I ATE A TOTAL OF SIX...
SO I WIN!
PROUD
NO ONE CARES...

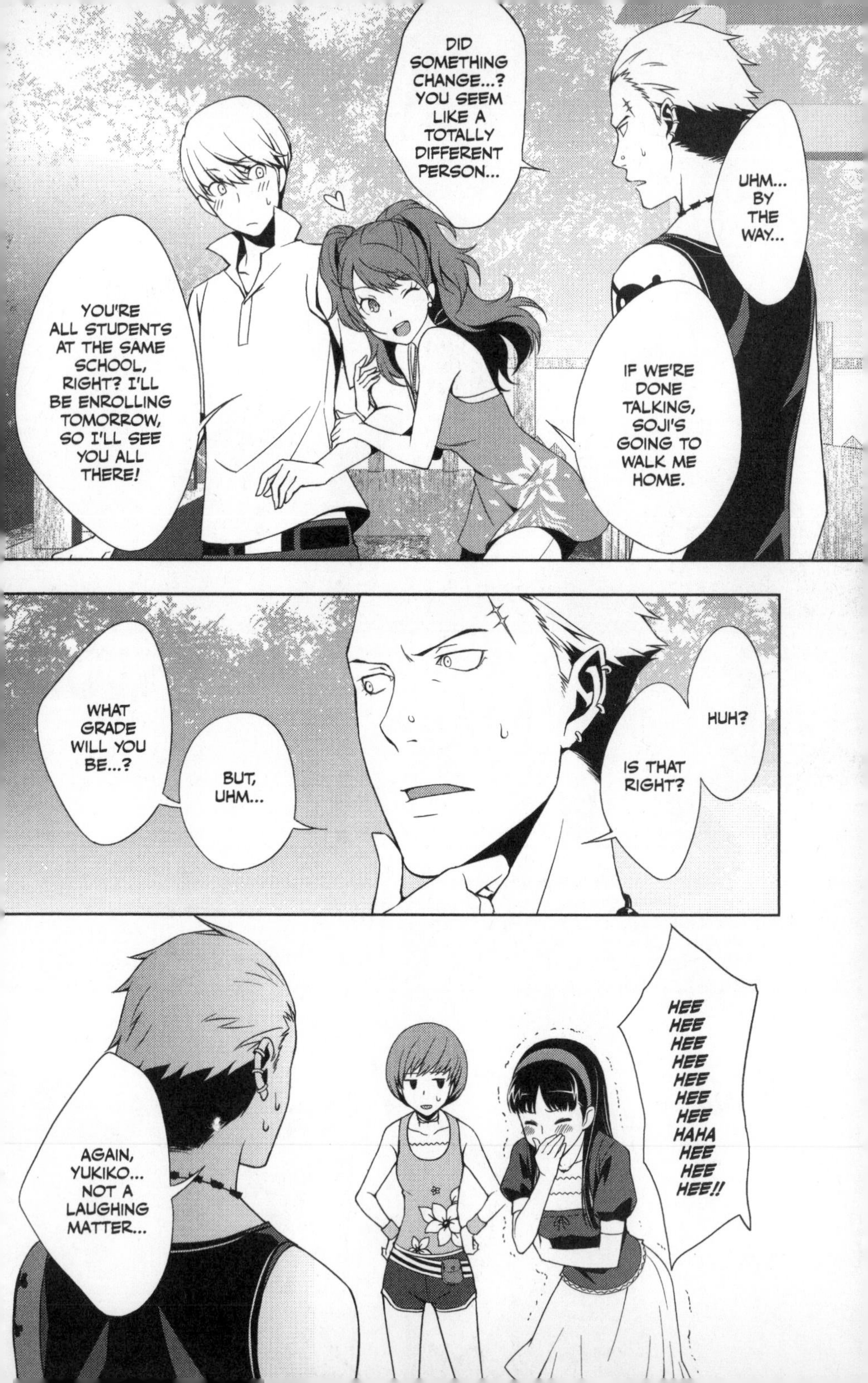
UHM... BY THE WAY...
DID SOMETHING CHANGE...? YOU SEEM LIKE A TOTALLY DIFFERENT PERSON...
IF WE'RE DONE TALKING, SOJI'S GOING TO WALK ME HOME.
YOU'RE ALL STUDENTS AT THE SAME SCHOOL, RIGHT? I'LL BE ENROLLING TOMORROW, SO I'LL SEE YOU ALL THERE!
HUH?
IS THAT RIGHT?
BUT, UHM...
WHAT GRADE WILL YOU BE...?
HEE HEE HEE HEE HEE HEE HEE HAHA HEE HEE HEE!!
AGAIN, YUKIKO... NOT A LAUGHING MATTER...

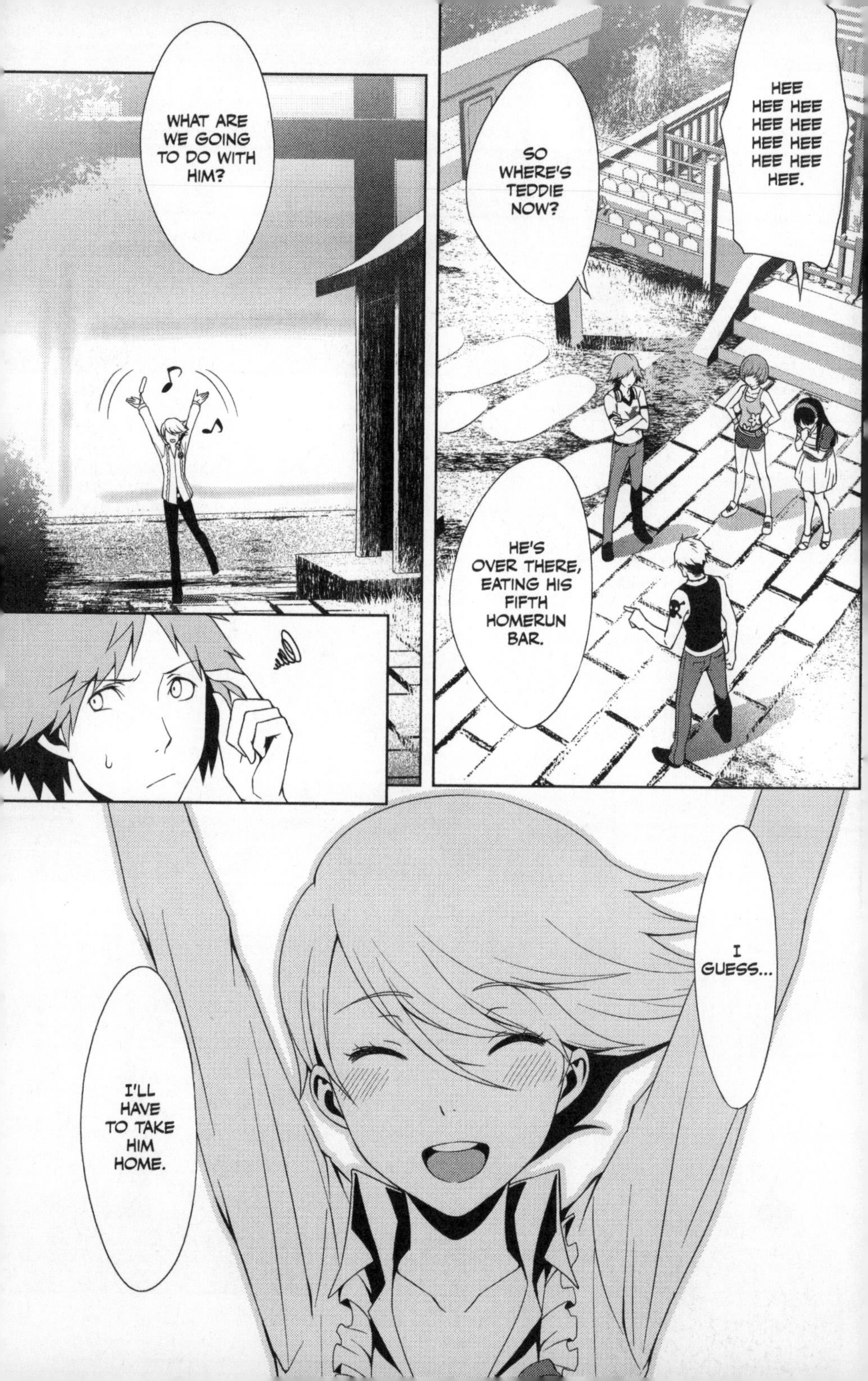
HEE HEE HEE HEE HEE HEE HEE HEE HEE HEE.
SO WHERE'S TEDDIE NOW?
HE'S OVER THERE, EATING HIS FIFTH HOMERUN BAR.
WHAT ARE WE GOING TO DO WITH HIM?
I GUESS...
I'LL HAVE TO TAKE HIM HOME.

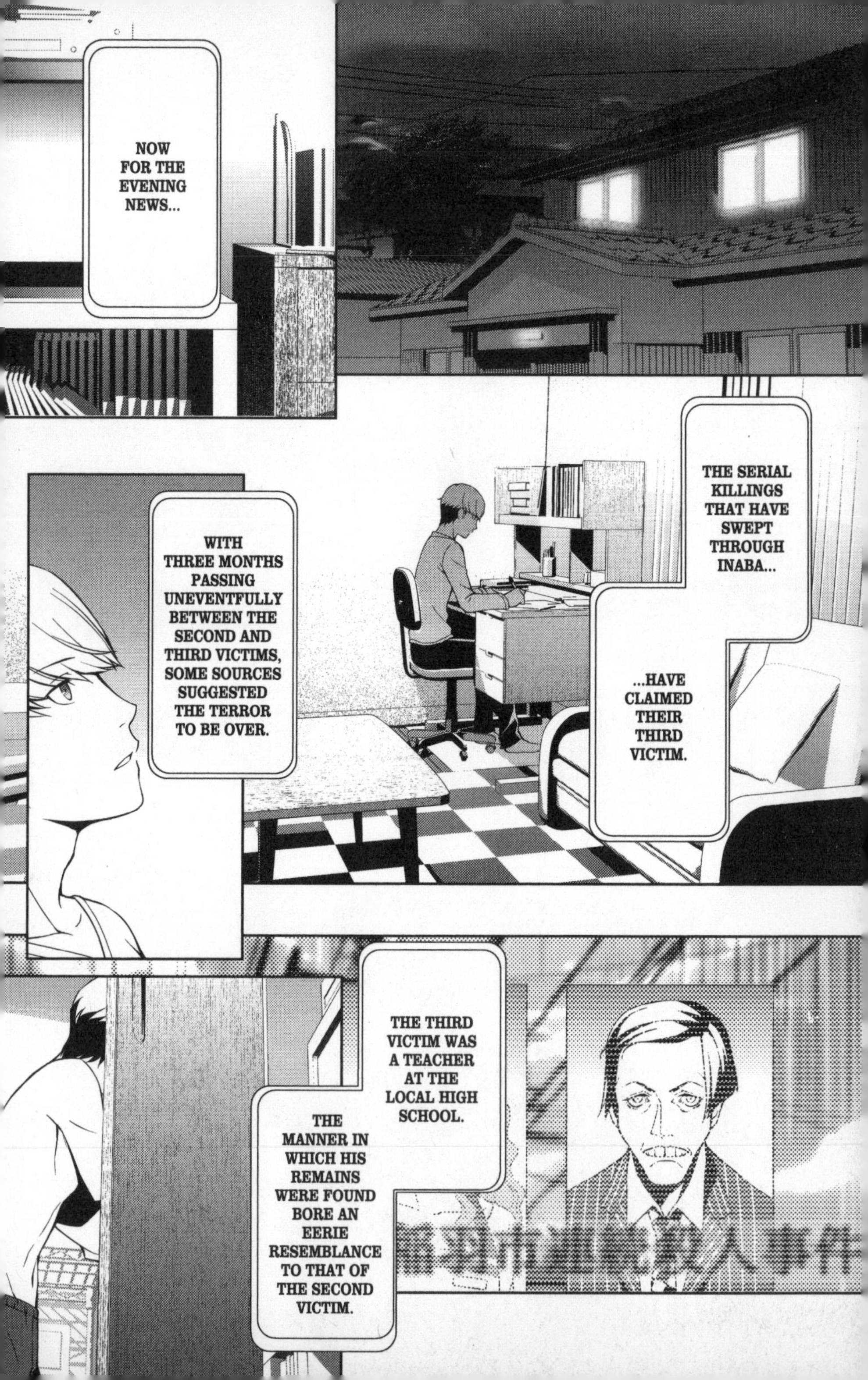
NOW FOR THE EVENING NEWS...
THE SERIAL KILLINGS THAT HAVE SWEPT THROUGH INABA...
...HAVE CLAIMED THEIR THIRD VICTIM.
WITH THREE MONTHS PASSING UNEVENTFULLY BETWEEN THE SECOND AND THIRD VICTIMS, SOME SOURCES SUGGESTED THE TERROR TO BE OVER.
THE THIRD VICTIM WAS A TEACHER AT THE LOCAL HIGH SCHOOL.
THE MANNER IN WHICH HIS REMAINS WERE FOUND BORE AN EERIE RESEMBLANCE TO THAT OF THE SECOND VICTIM.

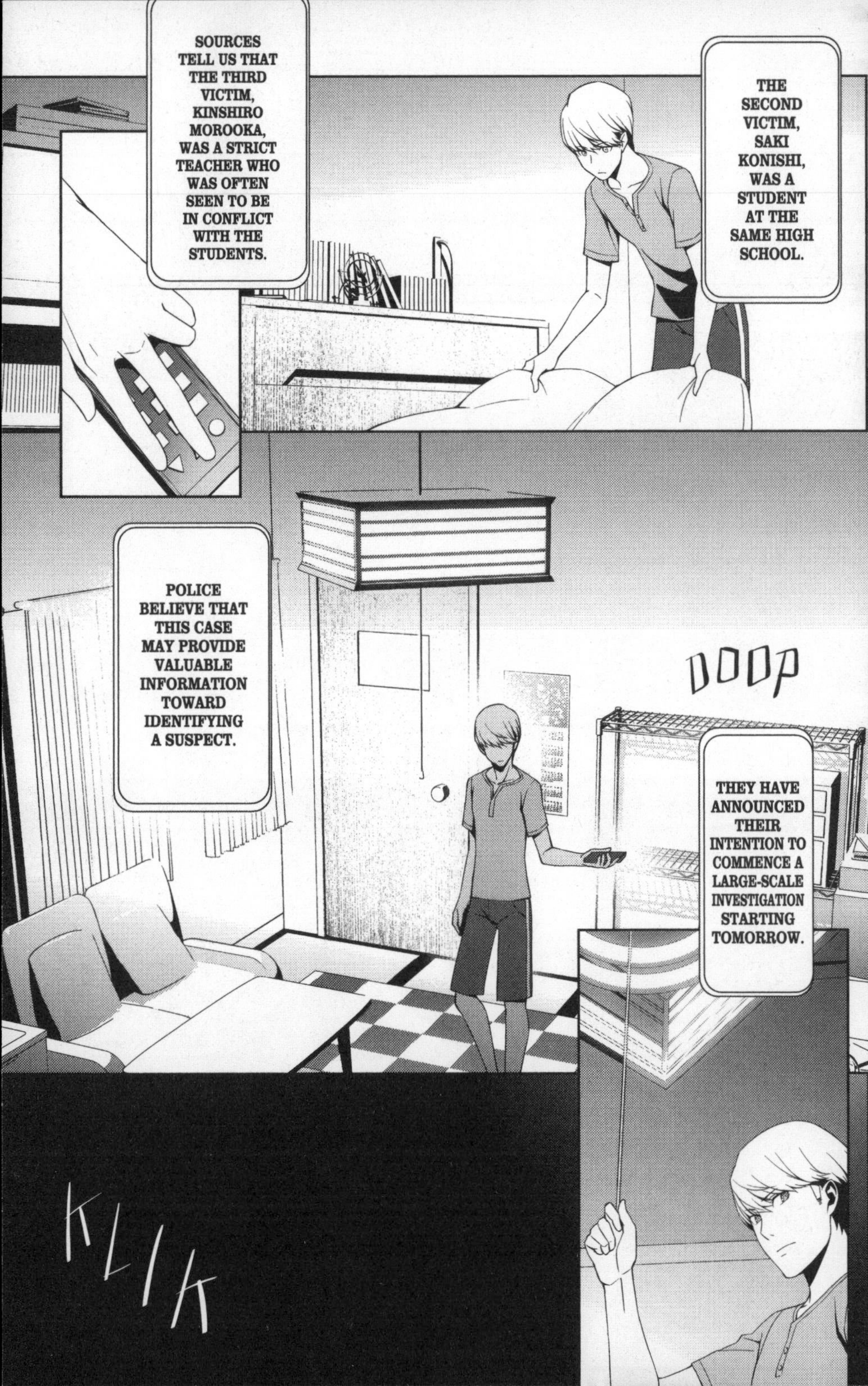
THE SECOND VICTIM, SAKI KONISHI, WAS A STUDENT AT THE SAME HIGH SCHOOL.
SOURCES TELL US THAT THE THIRD VICTIM, KINSHIRO MOROOKA, WAS A STRICT TEACHER WHO WAS OFTEN SEEN TO BE IN CONFLICT WITH THE STUDENTS.
THEY HAVE ANNOUNCED THEIR INTENTION TO COMMENCE A LARGE-SCALE INVESTIGATION STARTING TOMORROW.
DOOP
POLICE BELIEVE THAT THIS CASE MAY PROVIDE VALUABLE INFORMATION TOWARD IDENTIFYING A SUSPECT.
KLIK

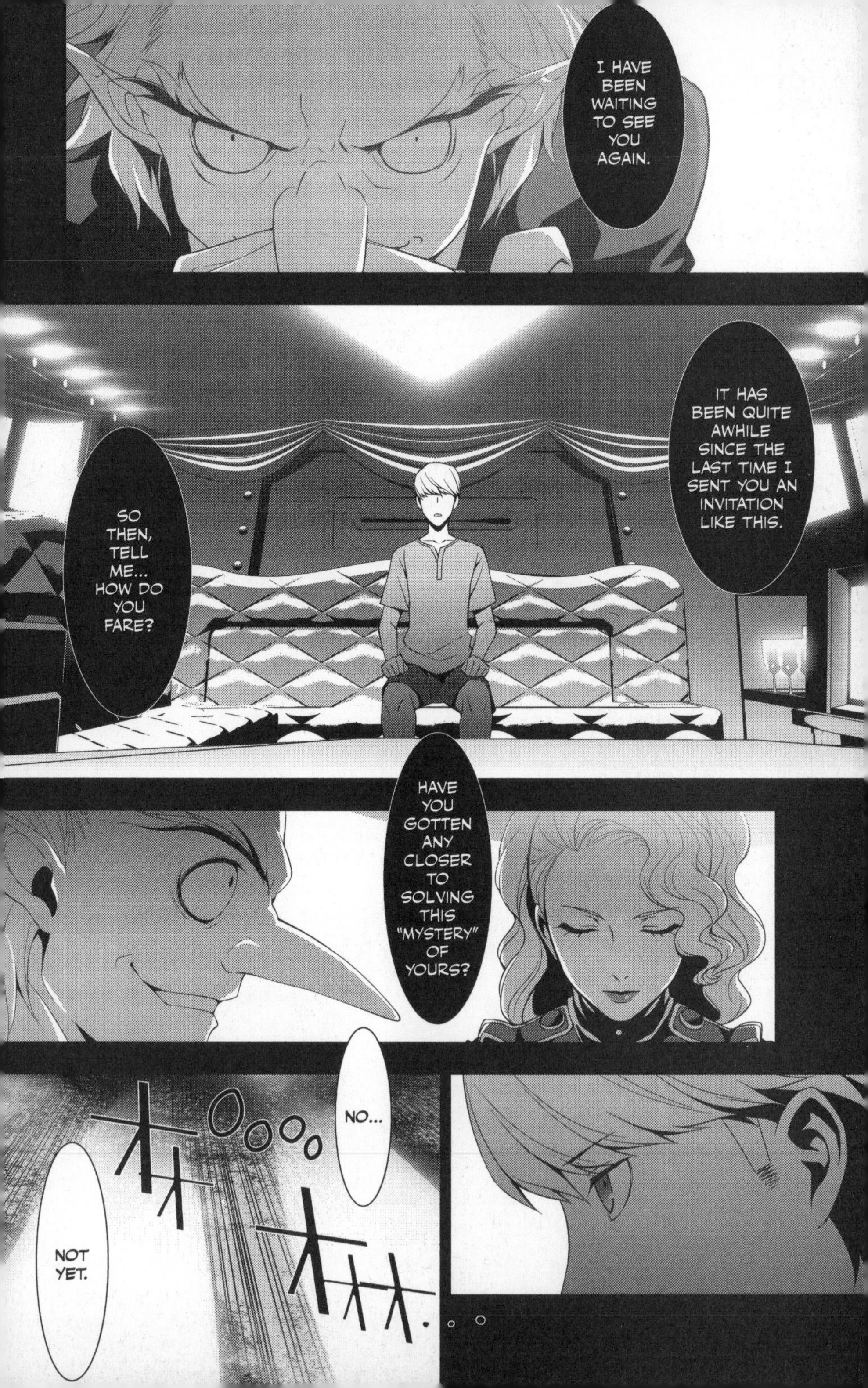
I HAVE BEEN WAITING TO SEE YOU AGAIN.
IT HAS BEEN QUITE AWHILE SINCE THE LAST TIME I SENT YOU AN INVITATION LIKE THIS.
SO THEN, TELL ME... HOW DO YOU FARE?
HAVE YOU GOTTEN ANY CLOSER TO SOLVING THIS "MYSTERY" OF YOURS?
NO...
NOT YET.

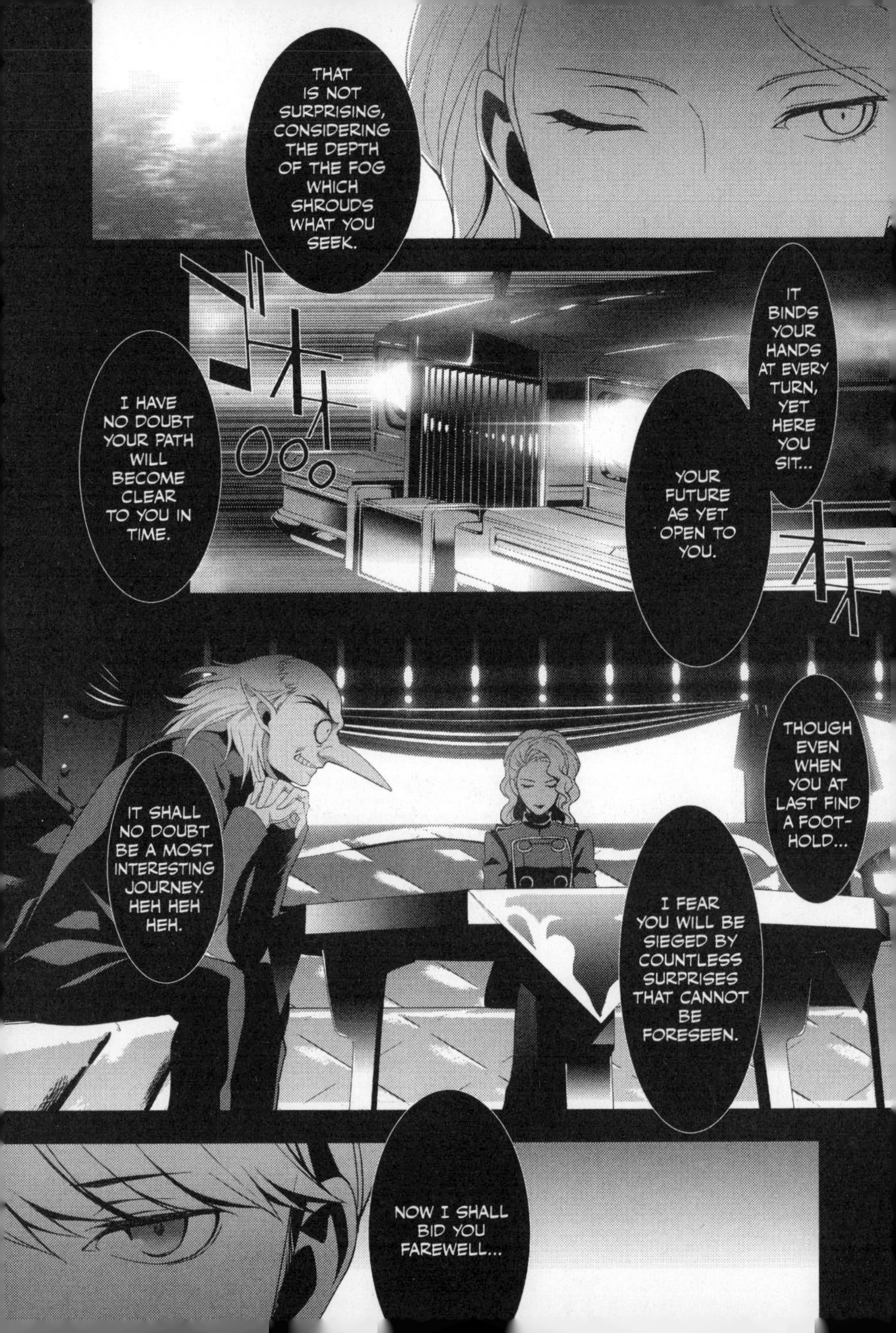
THAT IS NOT SURPRISING, CONSIDERING THE DEPTH OF THE FOG WHICH SHROUDS WHAT YOU SEEK.
IT BINDS YOUR HANDS AT EVERY TURN, YET HERE YOU SIT...
YOUR FUTURE AS YET OPEN TO YOU.
I HAVE NO DOUBT YOUR PATH WILL BECOME CLEAR TO YOU IN TIME.
THOUGH EVEN WHEN YOU AT LAST FIND A FOOT-HOLD...
I FEAR YOU WILL BE SIEGED BY COUNTLESS SURPRISES THAT CANNOT BE FORESEEN.
IT SHALL NO DOUBT BE A MOST INTERESTING JOURNEY. HEH HEH HEH.
NOW I SHALL BID YOU FAREWELL...

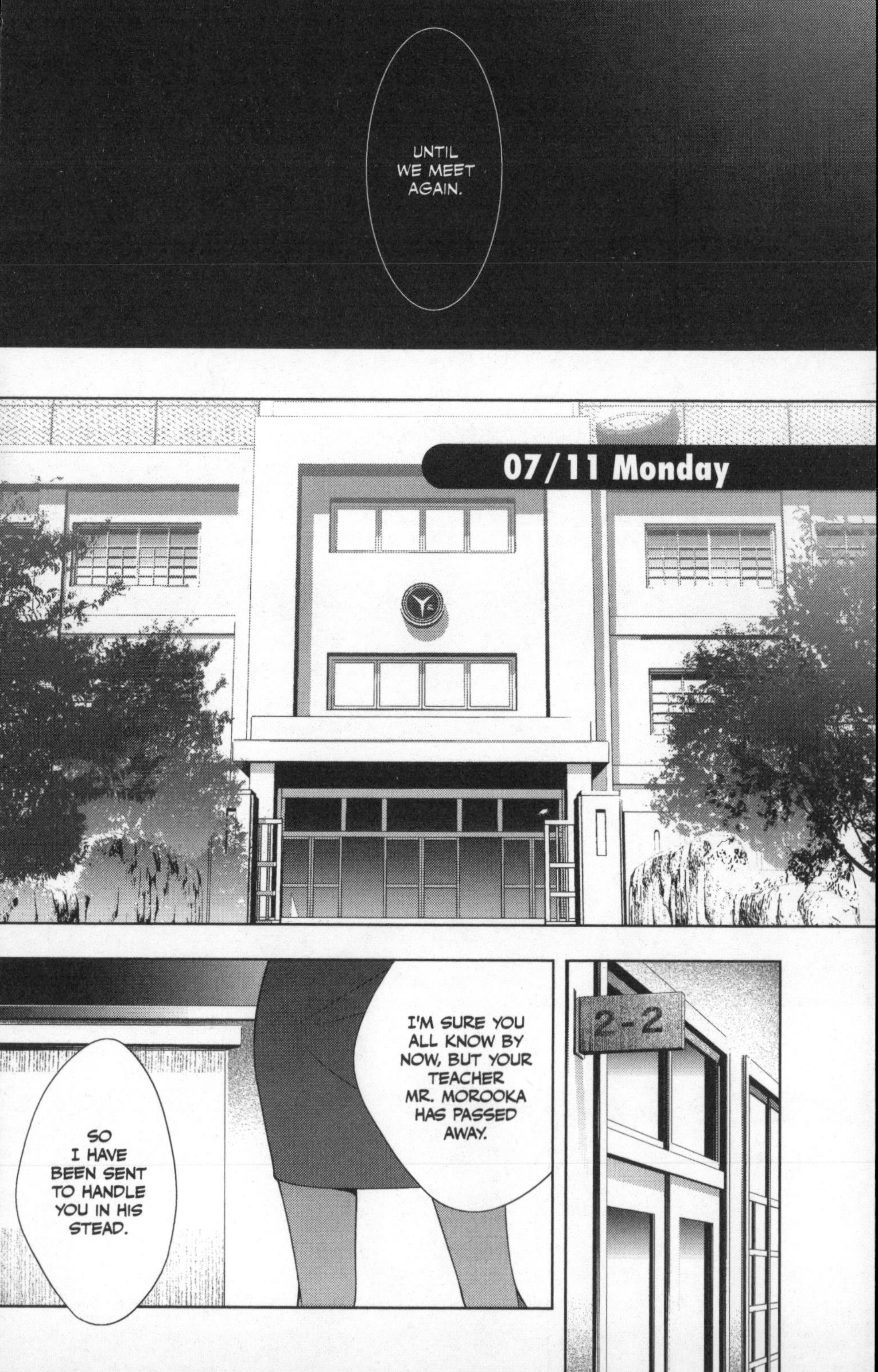
UNTIL WE MEET AGAIN.
07/11 Monday
2-2
I'M SURE YOU ALL KNOW BY NOW, BUT YOUR TEACHER MR. MOROOKA HAS PASSED AWAY.
SO I HAVE BEEN SENT TO HANDLE YOU IN HIS STEAD.

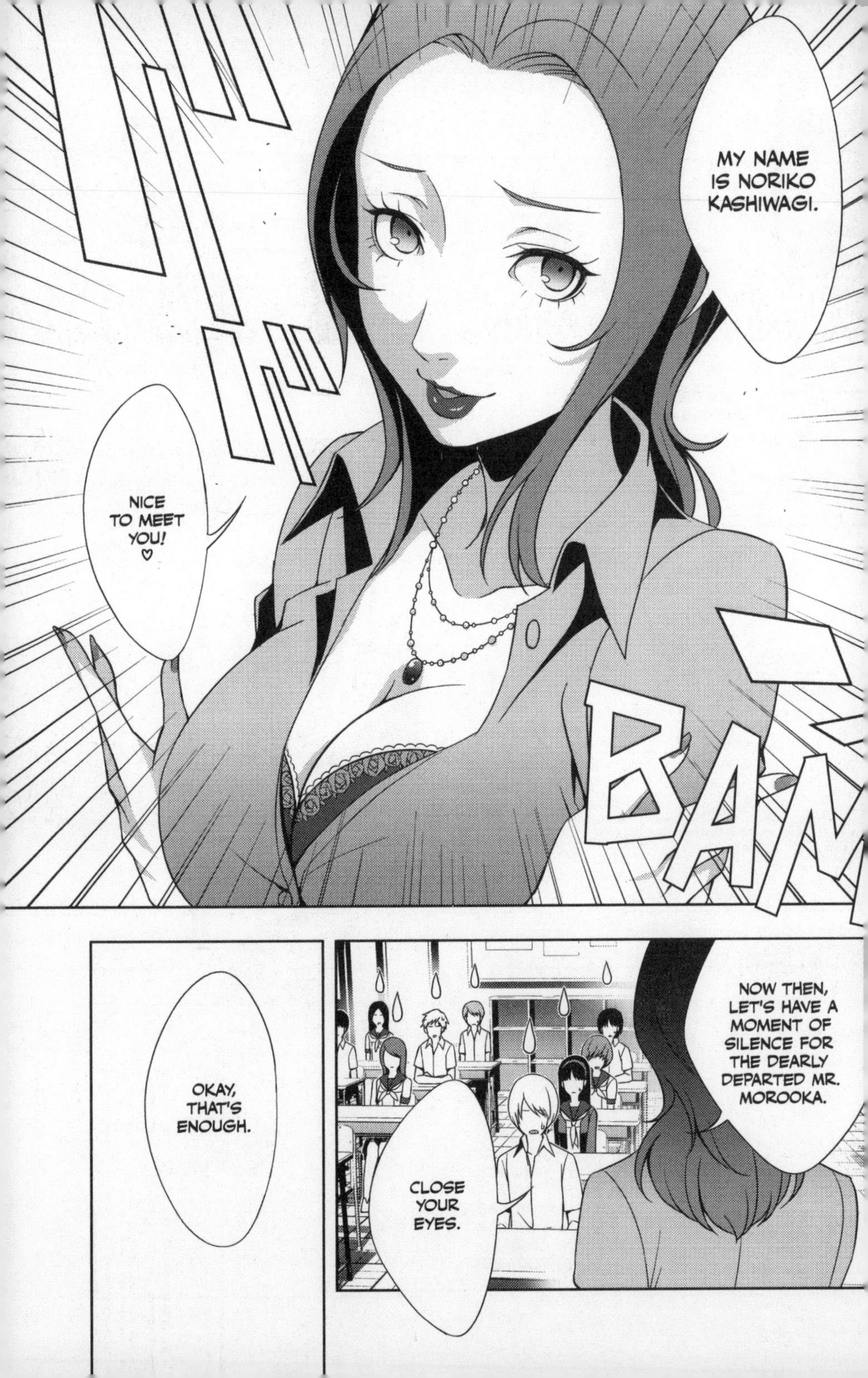
MY NAME IS NORIKO KASHIWAGI.
NICE TO MEET YOU! ♡
BAM
NOW THEN, LET'S HAVE A MOMENT OF SILENCE FOR THE DEARLY DEPARTED MR. MOROOKA.
CLOSE YOUR EYES.
OKAY, THAT'S ENOUGH.

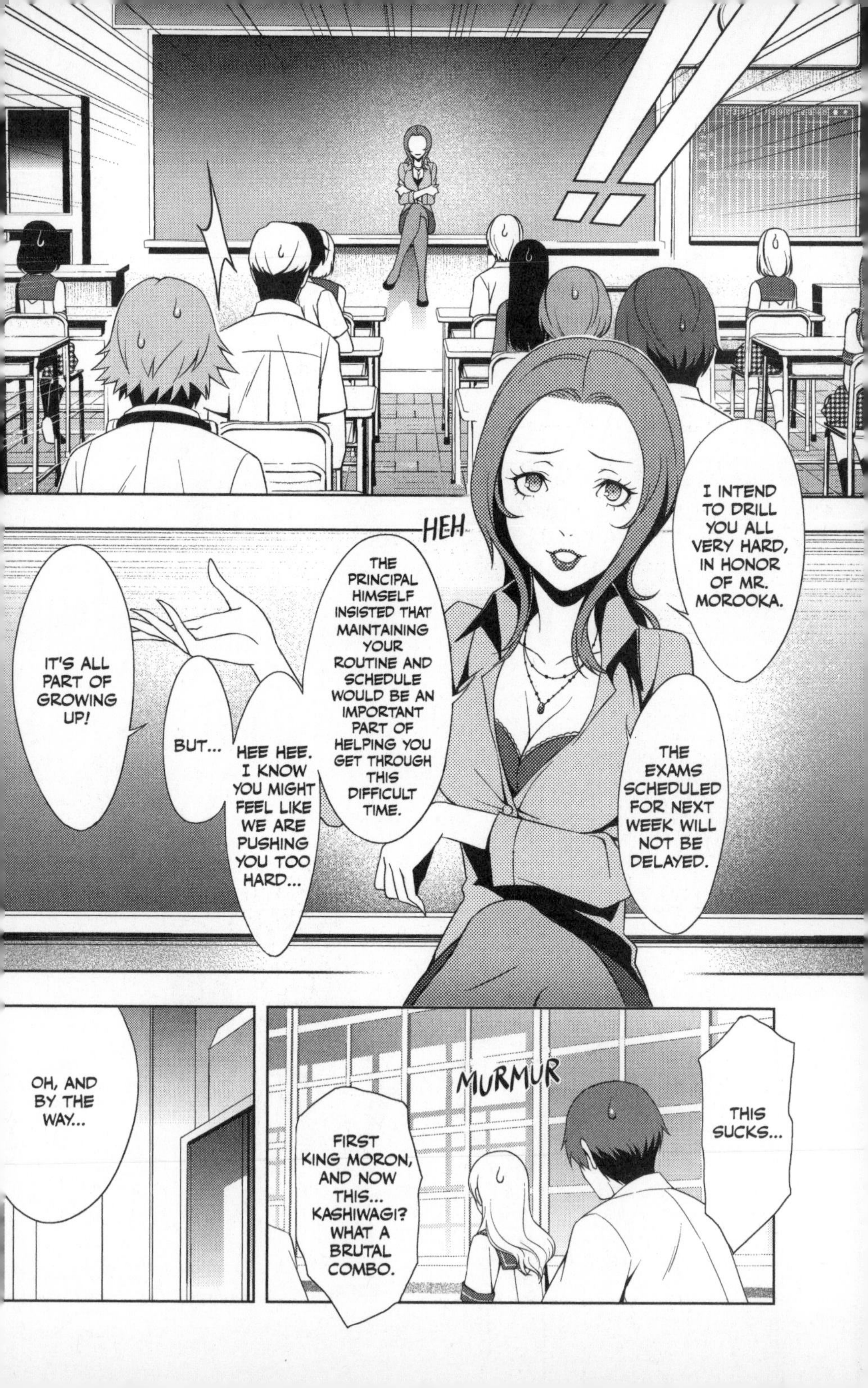
I INTEND TO DRILL YOU ALL VERY HARD, IN HONOR OF MR. MOROOKA.
THE EXAMS SCHEDULED FOR NEXT WEEK WILL NOT BE DELAYED.
HEH
THE PRINCIPAL HIMSELF INSISTED THAT MAINTAINING YOUR ROUTINE AND SCHEDULE WOULD BE AN IMPORTANT PART OF HELPING YOU GET THROUGH THIS DIFFICULT TIME.
HEE HEE. I KNOW YOU MIGHT FEEL LIKE WE ARE PUSHING YOU TOO HARD...
BUT...
IT'S ALL PART OF GROWING UP!
THIS SUCKS...
MURMUR
FIRST KING MORON, AND NOW THIS... KASHIWAGI? WHAT A BRUTAL COMBO.
OH, AND BY THE WAY...

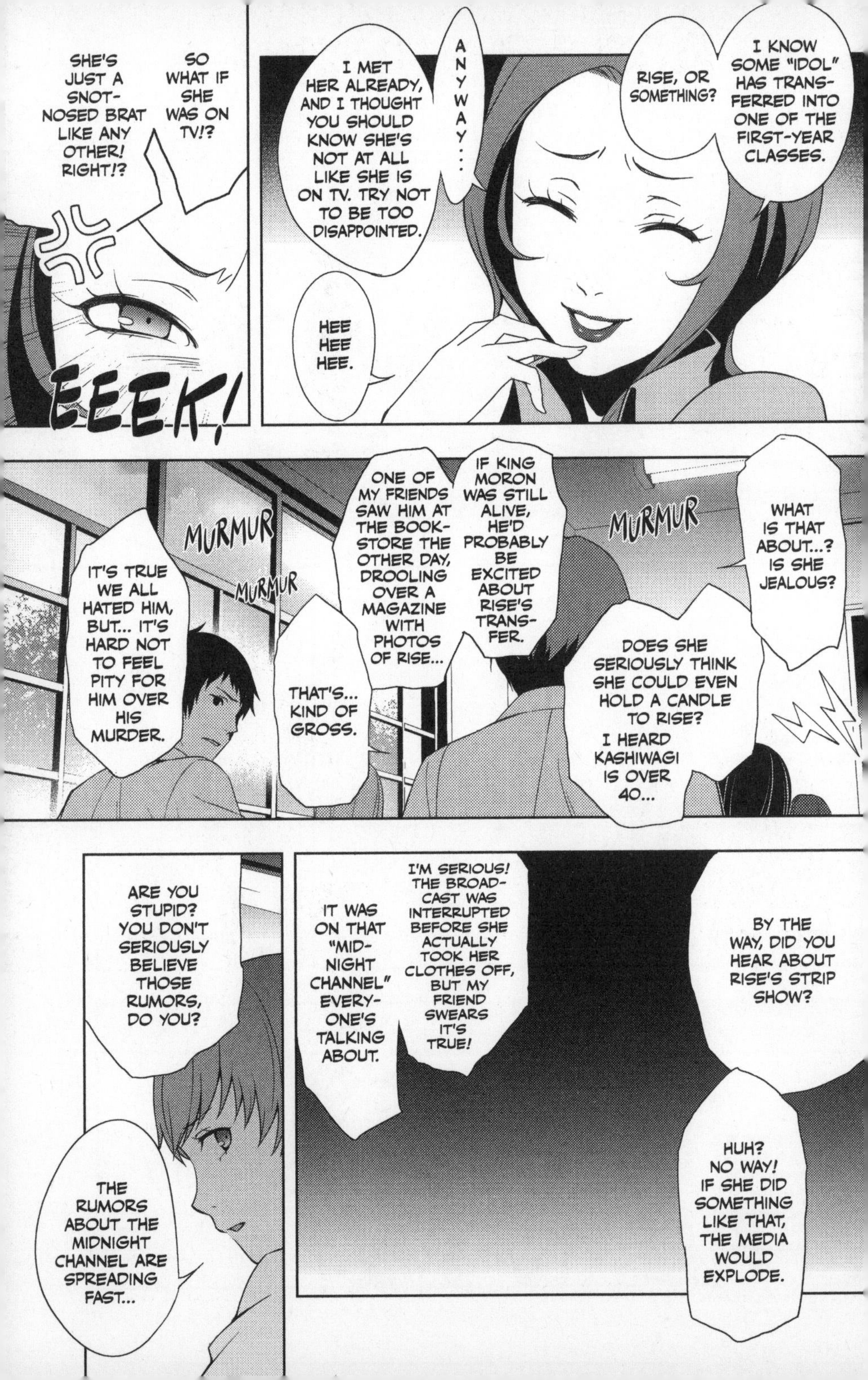
I KNOW SOME "IDOL" HAS TRANSFERRED INTO ONE OF THE FIRST-YEAR CLASSES.
RISE, OR SOMETHING?
ANYWAY...
I MET HER ALREADY, AND I THOUGHT YOU SHOULD KNOW SHE'S NOT AT ALL LIKE SHE IS ON TV. TRY NOT TO BE TOO DISAPPOINTED.
HEE HEE HEE.
SO WHAT IF SHE WAS ON TV!?
SHE'S JUST A SNOT-NOSED BRAT LIKE ANY OTHER! RIGHT!?
EEEK!
WHAT IS THAT ABOUT...? IS SHE JEALOUS?
DOES SHE SERIOUSLY THINK SHE COULD EVEN HOLD A CANDLE TO RISE?
I HEARD KASHIWAGI IS OVER 40...
MURMUR
IF KING MORON WAS STILL ALIVE, HE'D PROBABLY BE EXCITED ABOUT RISE'S TRANSFER.
ONE OF MY FRIENDS SAW HIM AT THE BOOKSTORE THE OTHER DAY, DROOLING OVER A MAGAZINE WITH PHOTOS OF RISE...
THAT'S... KIND OF GROSS.
MURMUR
MURMUR
IT'S TRUE WE ALL HATED HIM, BUT... IT'S HARD NOT TO FEEL PITY FOR HIM OVER HIS MURDER.
BY THE WAY, DID YOU HEAR ABOUT RISE'S STRIP SHOW?
HUH? NO WAY! IF SHE DID SOMETHING LIKE THAT, THE MEDIA WOULD EXPLODE.
I'M SERIOUS! THE BROADCAST WAS INTERRUPTED BEFORE SHE ACTUALLY TOOK HER CLOTHES OFF, BUT MY FRIEND SWEARS IT'S TRUE!
IT WAS ON THAT "MIDNIGHT CHANNEL" EVERYONE'S TALKING ABOUT.
ARE YOU STUPID? YOU DON'T SERIOUSLY BELIEVE THOSE RUMORS, DO YOU?
THE RUMORS ABOUT THE MIDNIGHT CHANNEL ARE SPREADING FAST...

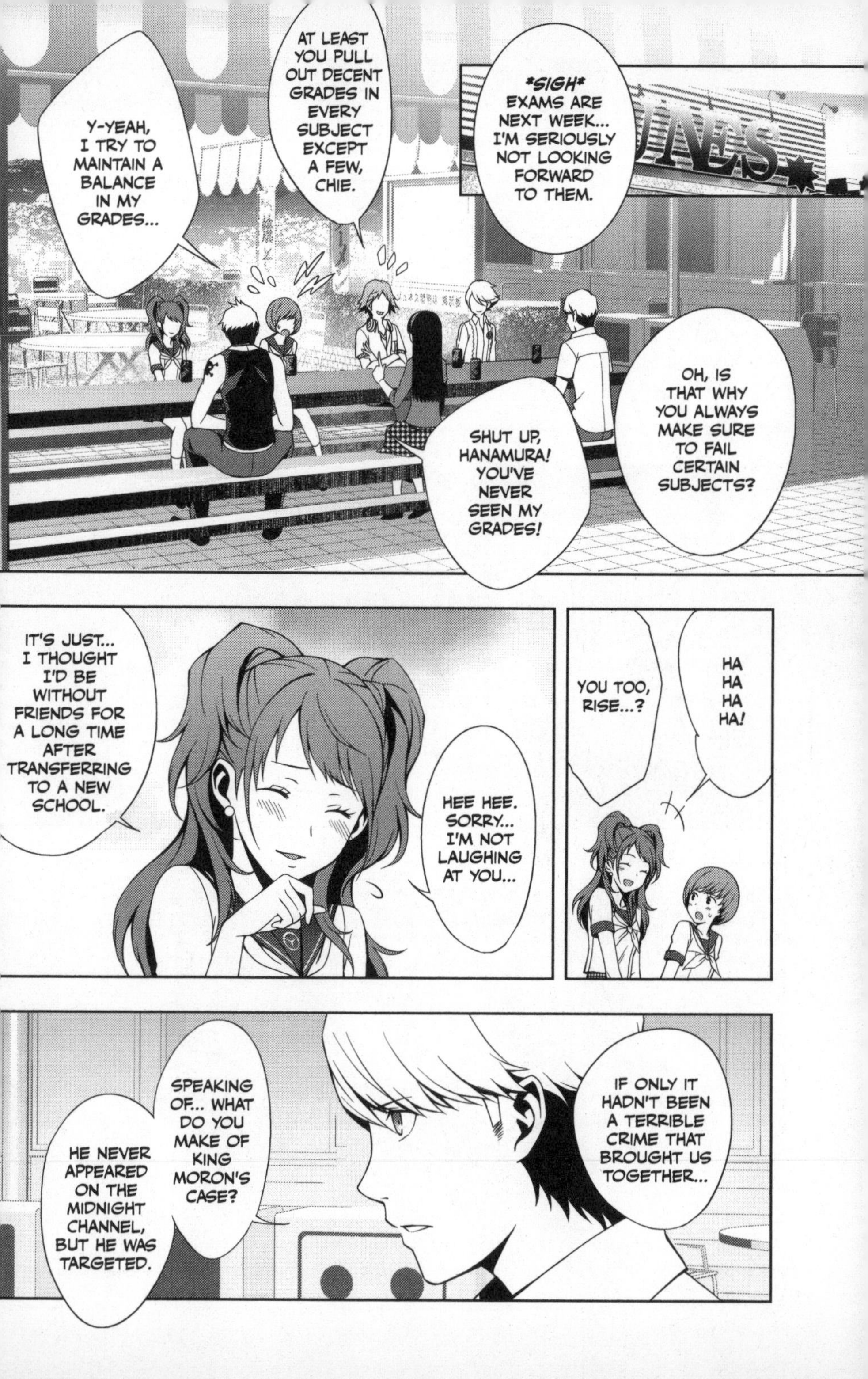
SIGH EXAMS ARE NEXT WEEK... I'M SERIOUSLY NOT LOOKING FORWARD TO THEM.
AT LEAST YOU PULL OUT DECENT GRADES IN EVERY SUBJECT EXCEPT A FEW, CHIE.
Y-YEAH, I TRY TO MAINTAIN A BALANCE IN MY GRADES...
OH, IS THAT WHY YOU ALWAYS MAKE SURE TO FAIL CERTAIN SUBJECTS?
SHUT UP, HANAMURA! YOU'VE NEVER SEEN MY GRADES!
HA HA HA HA!
YOU TOO, RISE...?
HEE HEE. SORRY... I'M NOT LAUGHING AT YOU...
IT'S JUST... I THOUGHT I'D BE WITHOUT FRIENDS FOR A LONG TIME AFTER TRANSFERRING TO A NEW SCHOOL.
IF ONLY IT HADN'T BEEN A TERRIBLE CRIME THAT BROUGHT US TOGETHER...
SPEAKING OF... WHAT DO YOU MAKE OF KING MORON'S CASE?
HE NEVER APPEARED ON THE MIDNIGHT CHANNEL, BUT HE WAS TARGETED.

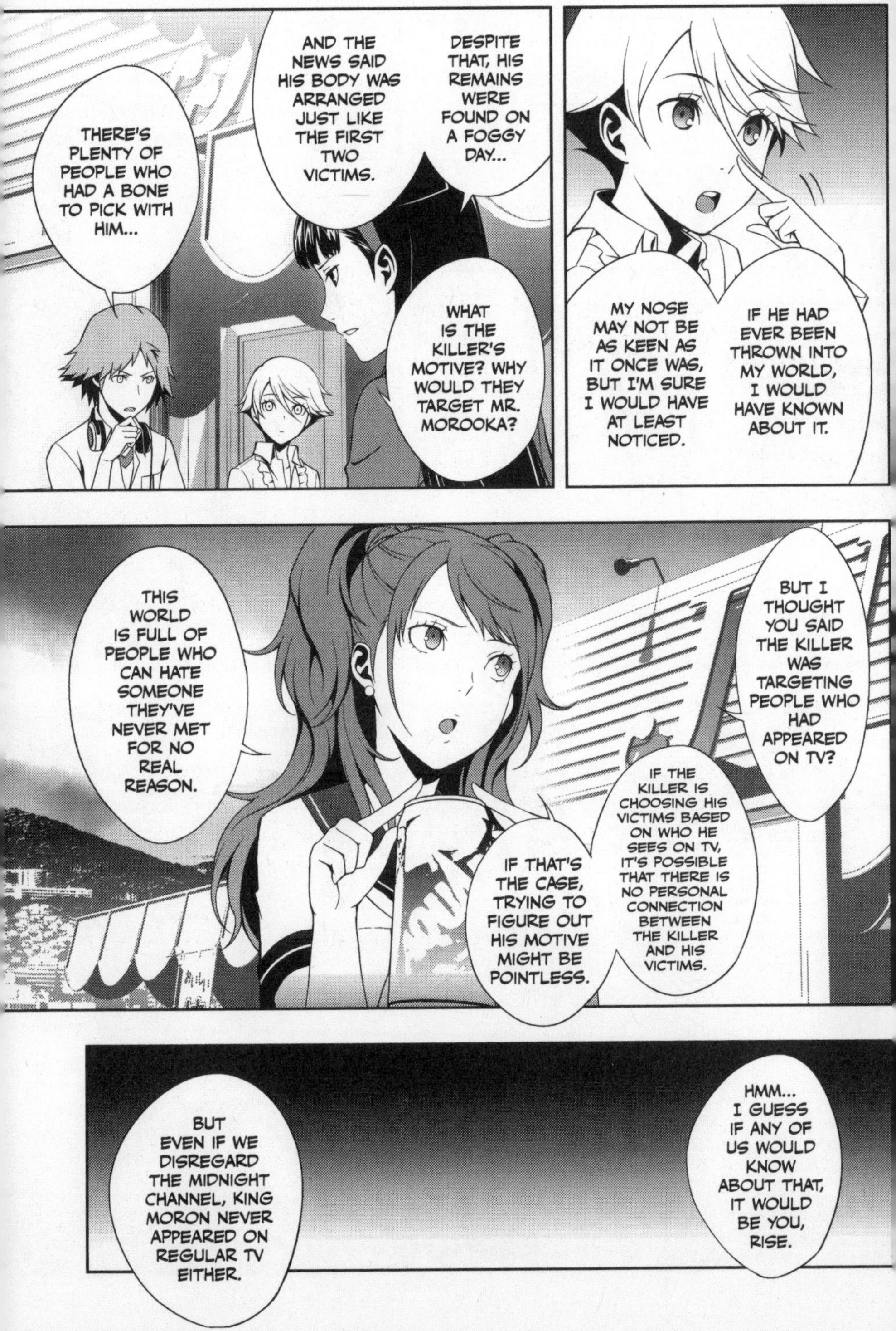
IF HE HAD EVER BEEN THROWN INTO MY WORLD, I WOULD HAVE KNOWN ABOUT IT.
MY NOSE MAY NOT BE AS KEEN AS IT ONCE WAS, BUT I'M SURE I WOULD HAVE AT LEAST NOTICED.
DESPITE THAT, HIS REMAINS WERE FOUND ON A FOGGY DAY...
AND THE NEWS SAID HIS BODY WAS ARRANGED JUST LIKE THE FIRST TWO VICTIMS.
THERE'S PLENTY OF PEOPLE WHO HAD A BONE TO PICK WITH HIM...
WHAT IS THE KILLER'S MOTIVE? WHY WOULD THEY TARGET MR. MOROOKA?
BUT I THOUGHT YOU SAID THE KILLER WAS TARGETING PEOPLE WHO HAD APPEARED ON TV?
IF THE KILLER IS CHOOSING HIS VICTIMS BASED ON WHO HE SEES ON TV, IT'S POSSIBLE THAT THERE IS NO PERSONAL CONNECTION BETWEEN THE KILLER AND HIS VICTIMS.
IF THAT'S THE CASE, TRYING TO FIGURE OUT HIS MOTIVE MIGHT BE POINTLESS.
THIS WORLD IS FULL OF PEOPLE WHO CAN HATE SOMEONE THEY'VE NEVER MET FOR NO REAL REASON.
HMM... I GUESS IF ANY OF US WOULD KNOW ABOUT THAT, IT WOULD BE YOU, RISE.
BUT EVEN IF WE DISREGARD THE MIDNIGHT CHANNEL, KING MORON NEVER APPEARED ON REGULAR TV EITHER.

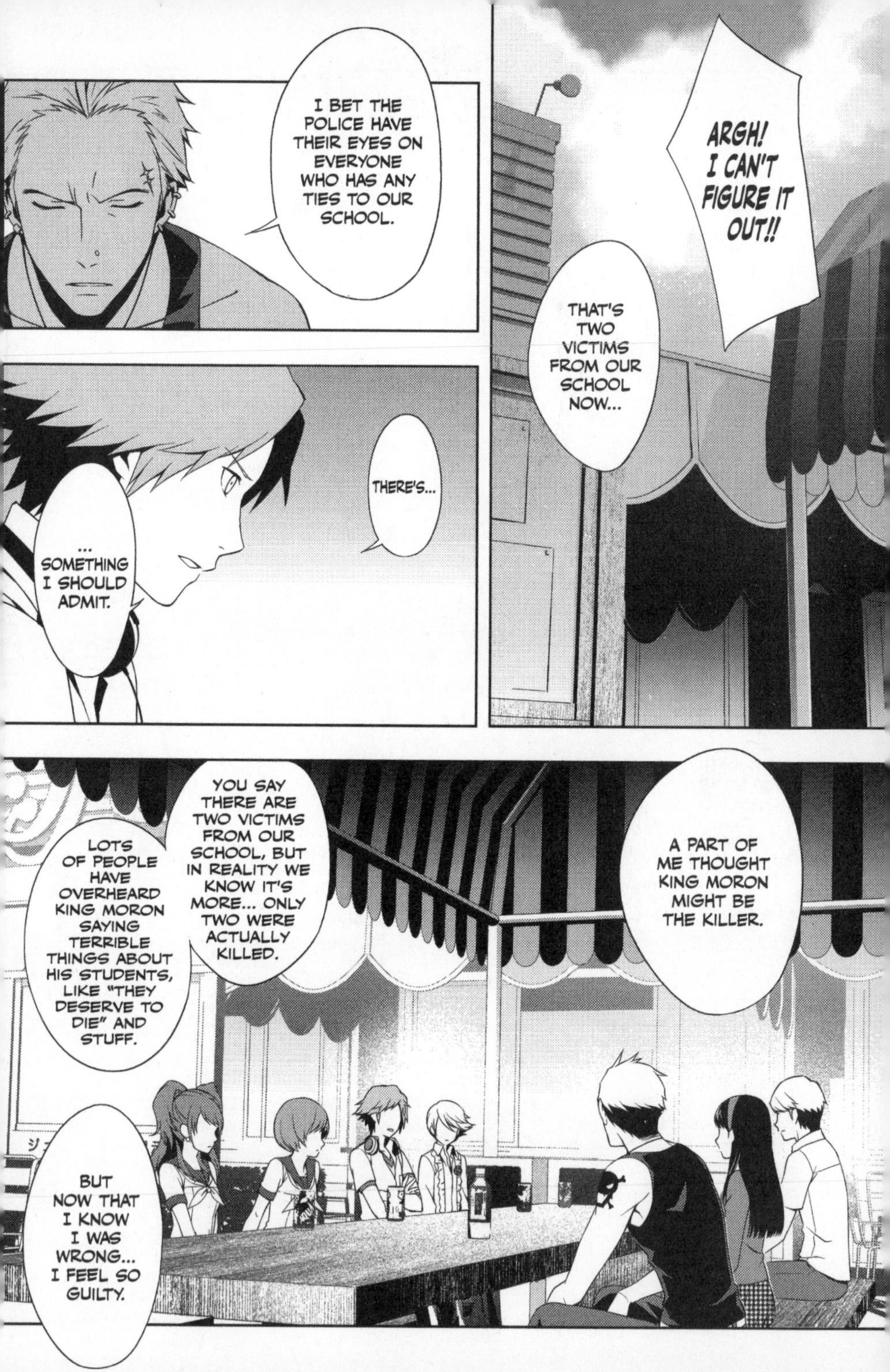
ARGH! I CAN'T FIGURE IT OUT!!
THAT'S TWO VICTIMS FROM OUR SCHOOL NOW...
I BET THE POLICE HAVE THEIR EYES ON EVERYONE WHO HAS ANY TIES TO OUR SCHOOL.
THERE'S...
... SOMETHING I SHOULD ADMIT.
A PART OF ME THOUGHT KING MORON MIGHT BE THE KILLER.
YOU SAY THERE ARE TWO VICTIMS FROM OUR SCHOOL, BUT IN REALITY WE KNOW IT'S MORE... ONLY TWO WERE ACTUALLY KILLED.
LOTS OF PEOPLE HAVE OVERHEARD KING MORON SAYING TERRIBLE THINGS ABOUT HIS STUDENTS, LIKE "THEY DESERVE TO DIE" AND STUFF.
BUT NOW THAT I KNOW I WAS WRONG... I FEEL SO GUILTY.

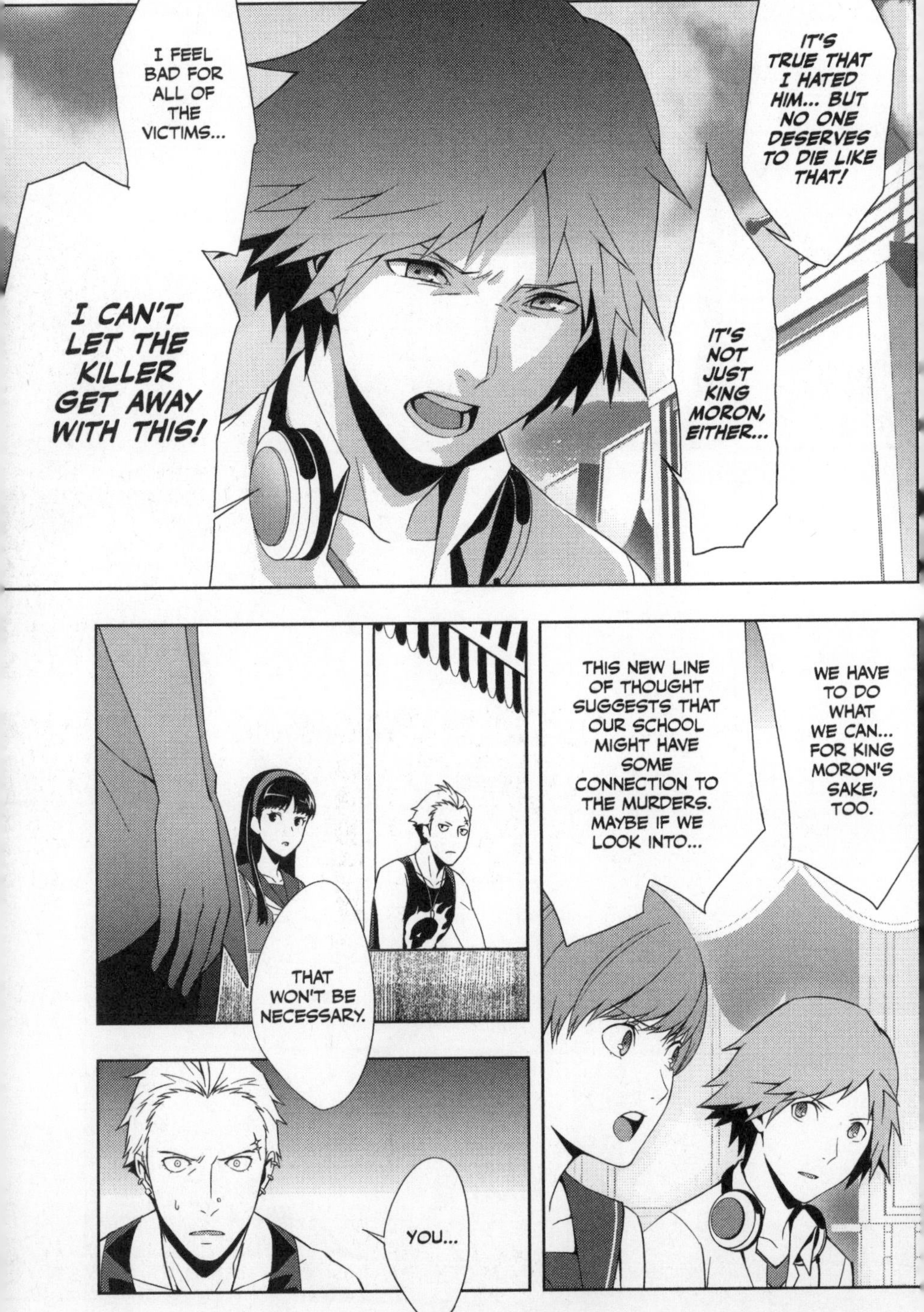
IT'S TRUE THAT I HATED HIM... BUT NO ONE DESERVES TO DIE LIKE THAT!
I FEEL BAD FOR ALL OF THE VICTIMS...
IT'S NOT JUST KING MORON, EITHER...
I CAN'T LET THE KILLER GET AWAY WITH THIS!
WE HAVE TO DO WHAT WE CAN... FOR KING MORON'S SAKE, TOO.
THIS NEW LINE OF THOUGHT SUGGESTS THAT OUR SCHOOL MIGHT HAVE SOME CONNECTION TO THE MURDERS. MAYBE IF WE LOOK INTO...
THAT WON'T BE NECESSARY.
YOU...

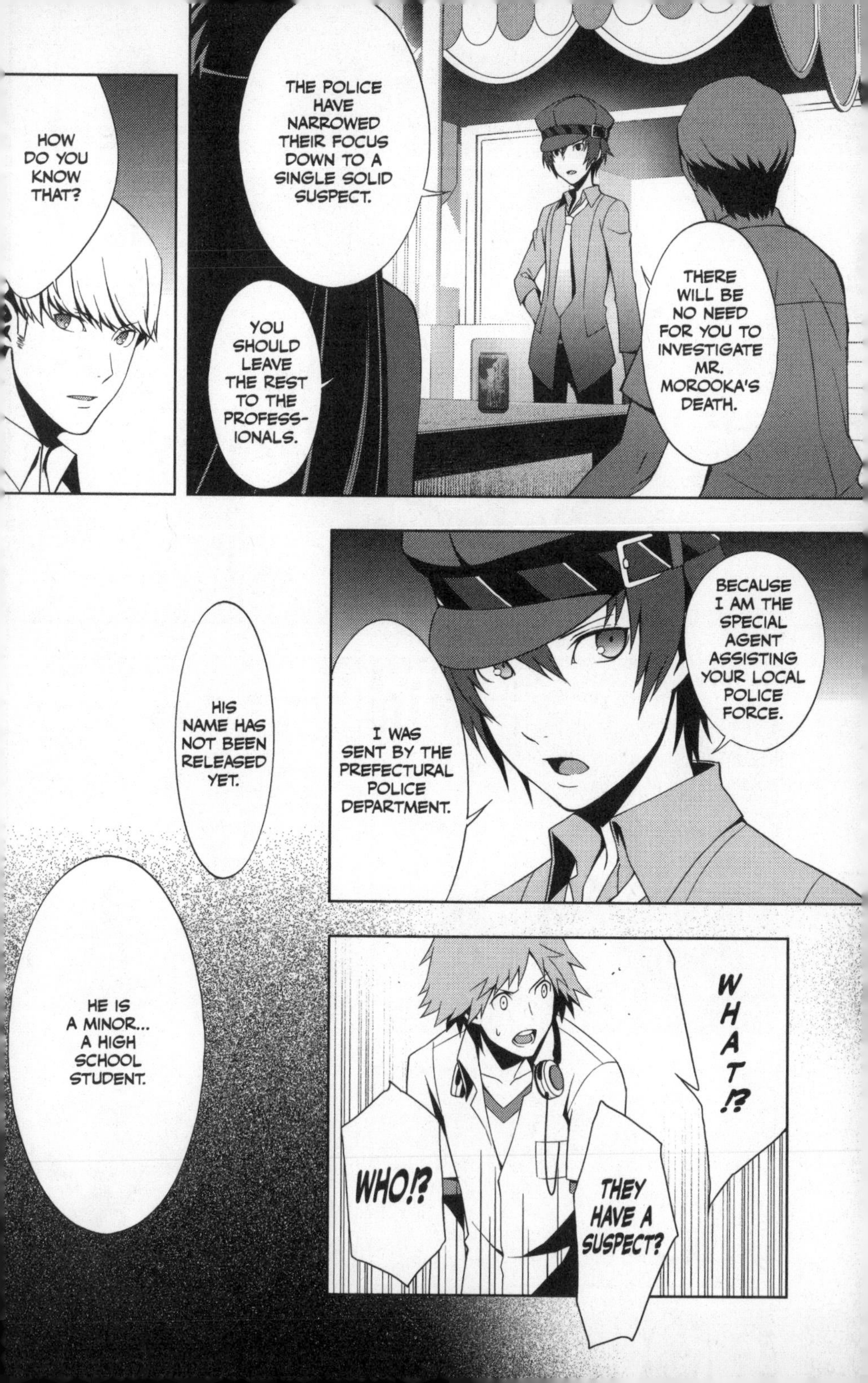
THERE WILL BE NO NEED FOR YOU TO INVESTIGATE MR. MOROOKA'S DEATH.
THE POLICE HAVE NARROWED THEIR FOCUS DOWN TO A SINGLE SOLID SUSPECT.
YOU SHOULD LEAVE THE REST TO THE PROFESS- IONALS.
HOW DO YOU KNOW THAT?
BECAUSE I AM THE SPECIAL AGENT ASSISTING YOUR LOCAL POLICE FORCE.
I WAS SENT BY THE PREFECTURAL POLICE DEPARTMENT.
HIS NAME HAS NOT BEEN RELEASED YET.
HE IS A MINOR... A HIGH SCHOOL STUDENT.
WHAT!?
THEY HAVE A SUSPECT?
WHO!?

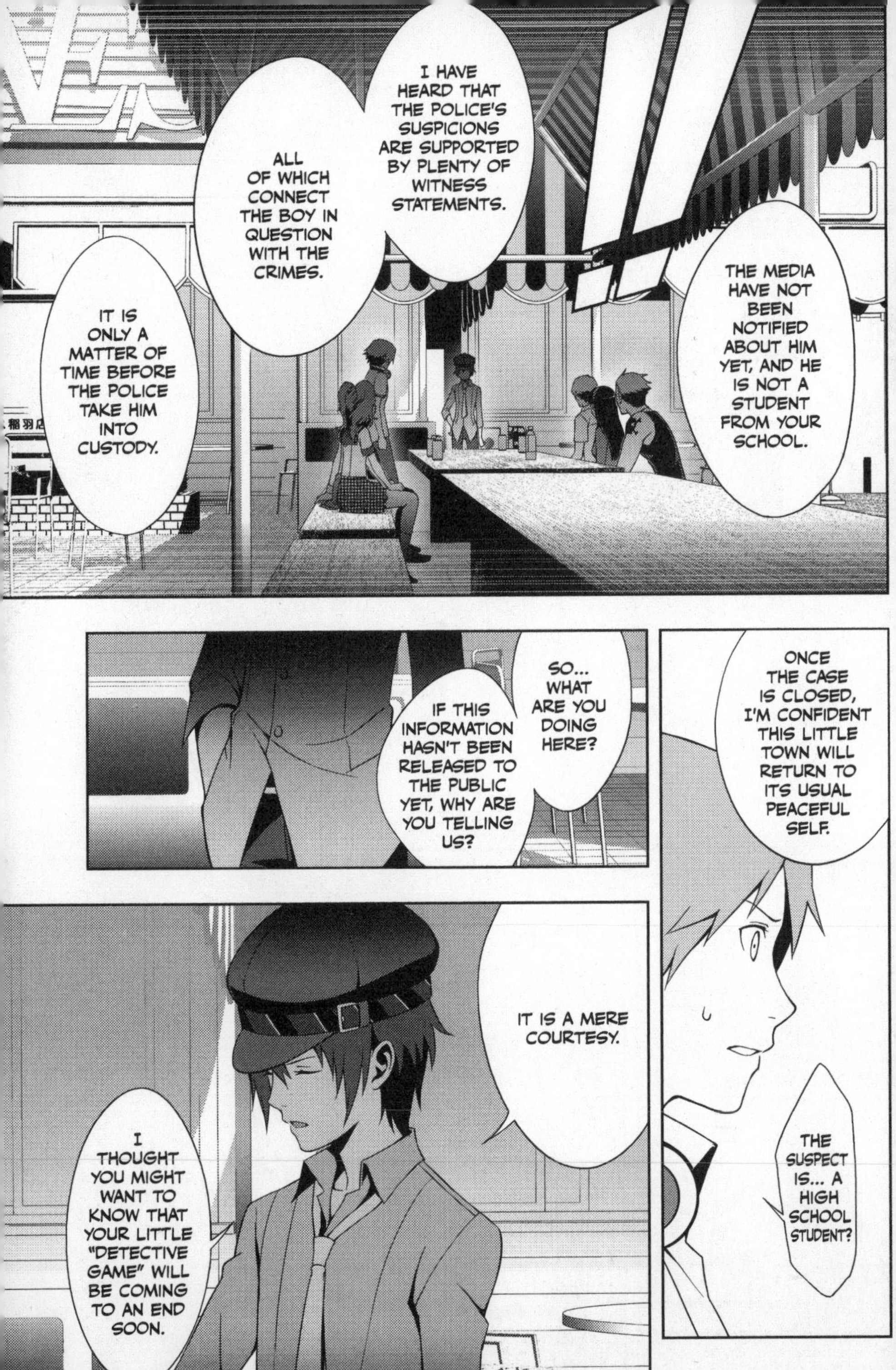
THE MEDIA HAVE NOT BEEN NOTIFIED ABOUT HIM YET, AND HE IS NOT A STUDENT FROM YOUR SCHOOL.
I HAVE HEARD THAT THE POLICE'S SUSPICIONS ARE SUPPORTED BY PLENTY OF WITNESS STATEMENTS.
ALL OF WHICH CONNECT THE BOY IN QUESTION WITH THE CRIMES.
IT IS ONLY A MATTER OF TIME BEFORE THE POLICE TAKE HIM INTO CUSTODY.
ONCE THE CASE IS CLOSED, I'M CONFIDENT THIS LITTLE TOWN WILL RETURN TO ITS USUAL PEACEFUL SELF.
THE SUSPECT IS... A HIGH SCHOOL STUDENT?
SO... WHAT ARE YOU DOING HERE?
IF THIS INFORMATION HASN'T BEEN RELEASED TO THE PUBLIC YET, WHY ARE YOU TELLING US?
IT IS A MERE COURTESY.
I THOUGHT YOU MIGHT WANT TO KNOW THAT YOUR LITTLE "DETECTIVE GAME" WILL BE COMING TO AN END SOON.

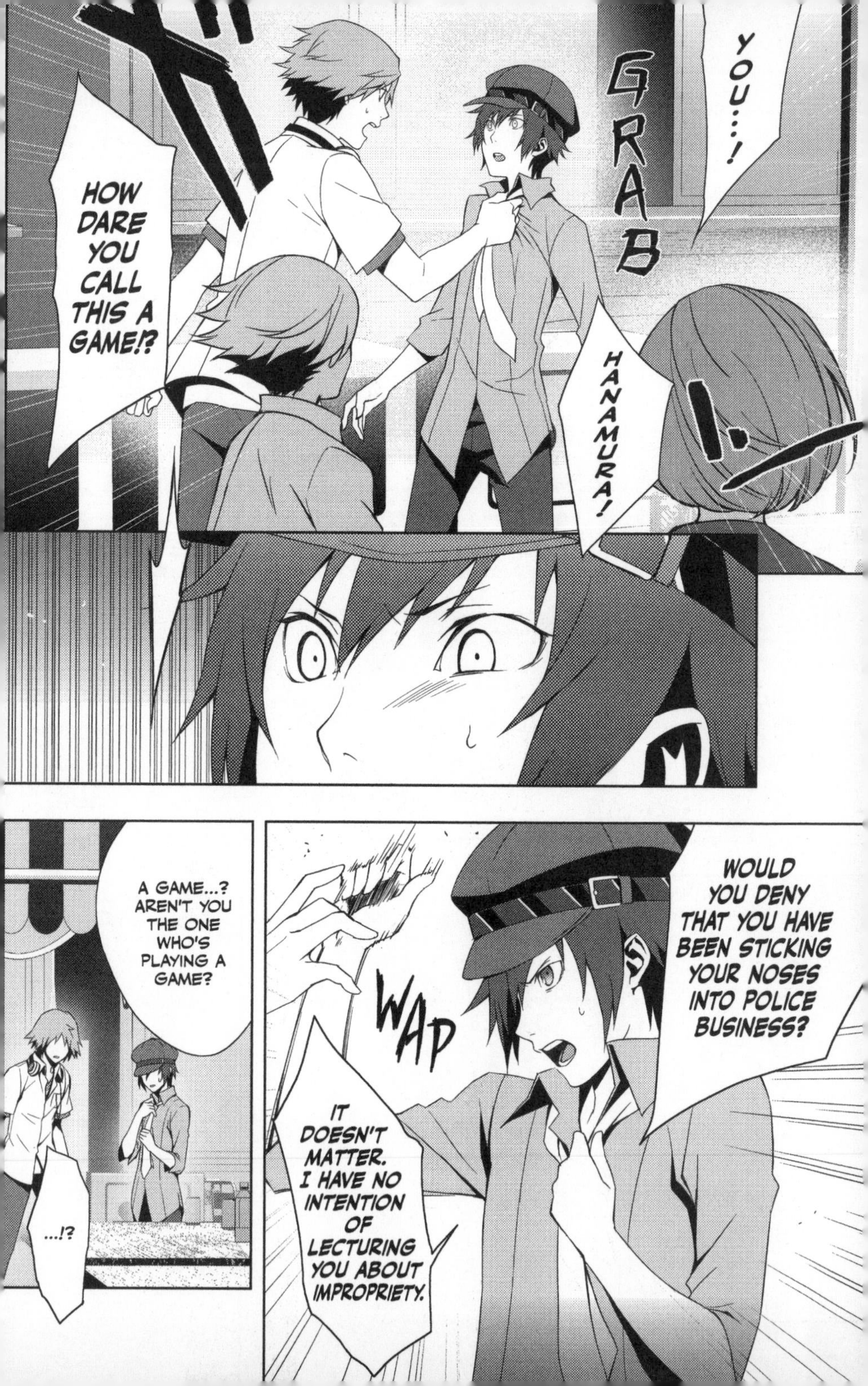
YOU...!
GRAB
HOW DARE YOU CALL THIS A GAME!?
HANAMURA!
!..
WOULD YOU DENY THAT YOU HAVE BEEN STICKING YOUR NOSES INTO POLICE BUSINESS?
WAP
IT DOESN'T MATTER. I HAVE NO INTENTION OF LECTURING YOU ABOUT IMPROPRIETY.
A GAME...? AREN'T YOU THE ONE WHO'S PLAYING A GAME?
...!?

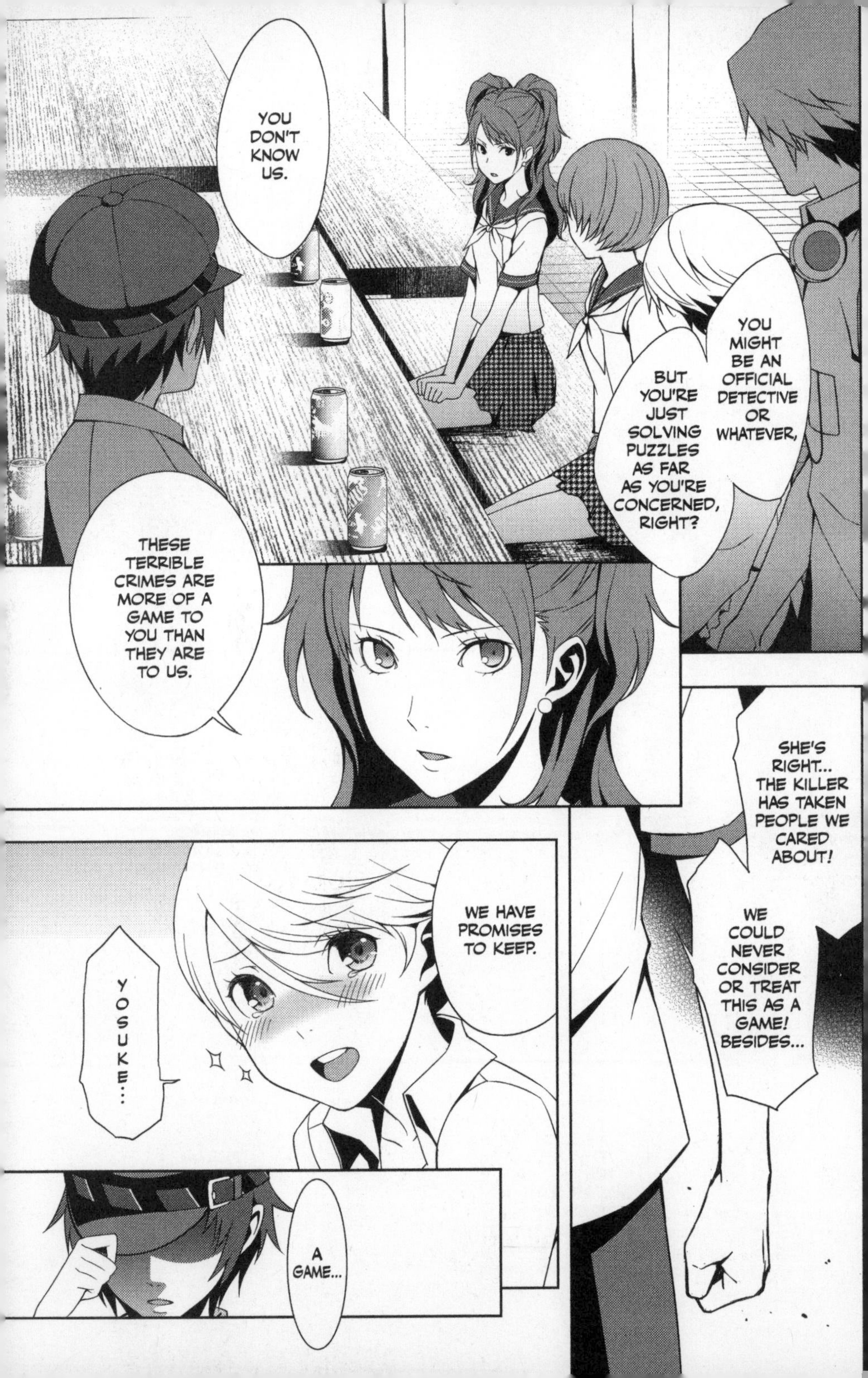
You might be an official detective or whatever,
But you're just solving puzzles as far as you're concerned, right?
You don't know us.
These terrible crimes are more of a game to you than they are to us.
She's right... the killer has taken people we cared about!
We could never consider or treat this as a game! Besides...
We have promises to keep.
Yosuke...
A game...

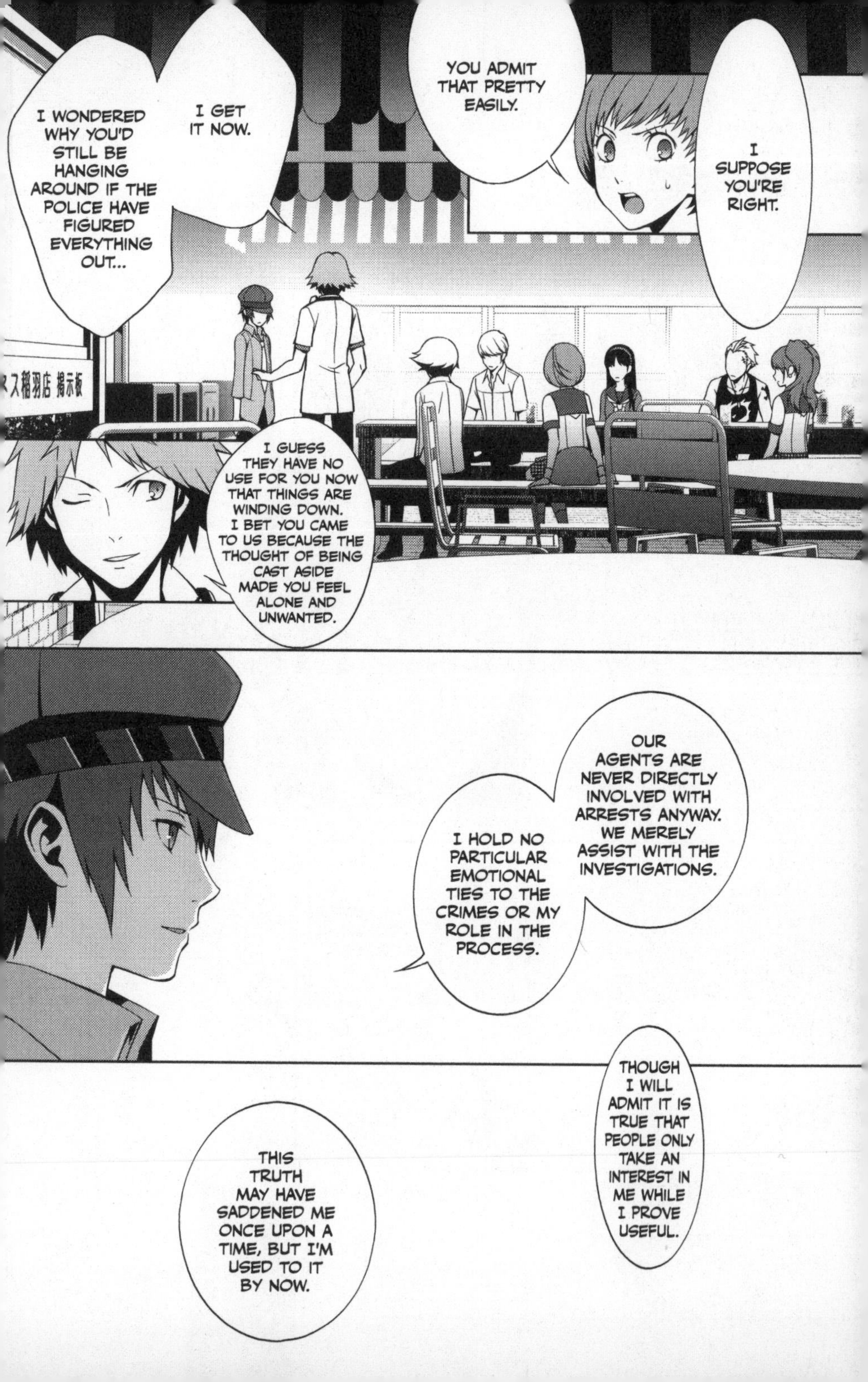
I SUPPOSE YOU'RE RIGHT.
YOU ADMIT THAT PRETTY EASILY.
I GET IT NOW.
I WONDERED WHY YOU'D STILL BE HANGING AROUND IF THE POLICE HAVE FIGURED EVERYTHING OUT...
ス稲羽店 掲示板
I GUESS THEY HAVE NO USE FOR YOU NOW THAT THINGS ARE WINDING DOWN. I BET YOU CAME TO US BECAUSE THE THOUGHT OF BEING CAST ASIDE MADE YOU FEEL ALONE AND UNWANTED.
OUR AGENTS ARE NEVER DIRECTLY INVOLVED WITH ARRESTS ANYWAY. WE MERELY ASSIST WITH THE INVESTIGATIONS.
I HOLD NO PARTICULAR EMOTIONAL TIES TO THE CRIMES OR MY ROLE IN THE PROCESS.
THOUGH I WILL ADMIT IT IS TRUE THAT PEOPLE ONLY TAKE AN INTEREST IN ME WHILE I PROVE USEFUL.
THIS TRUTH MAY HAVE SADDENED ME ONCE UPON A TIME, BUT I'M USED TO IT BY NOW.

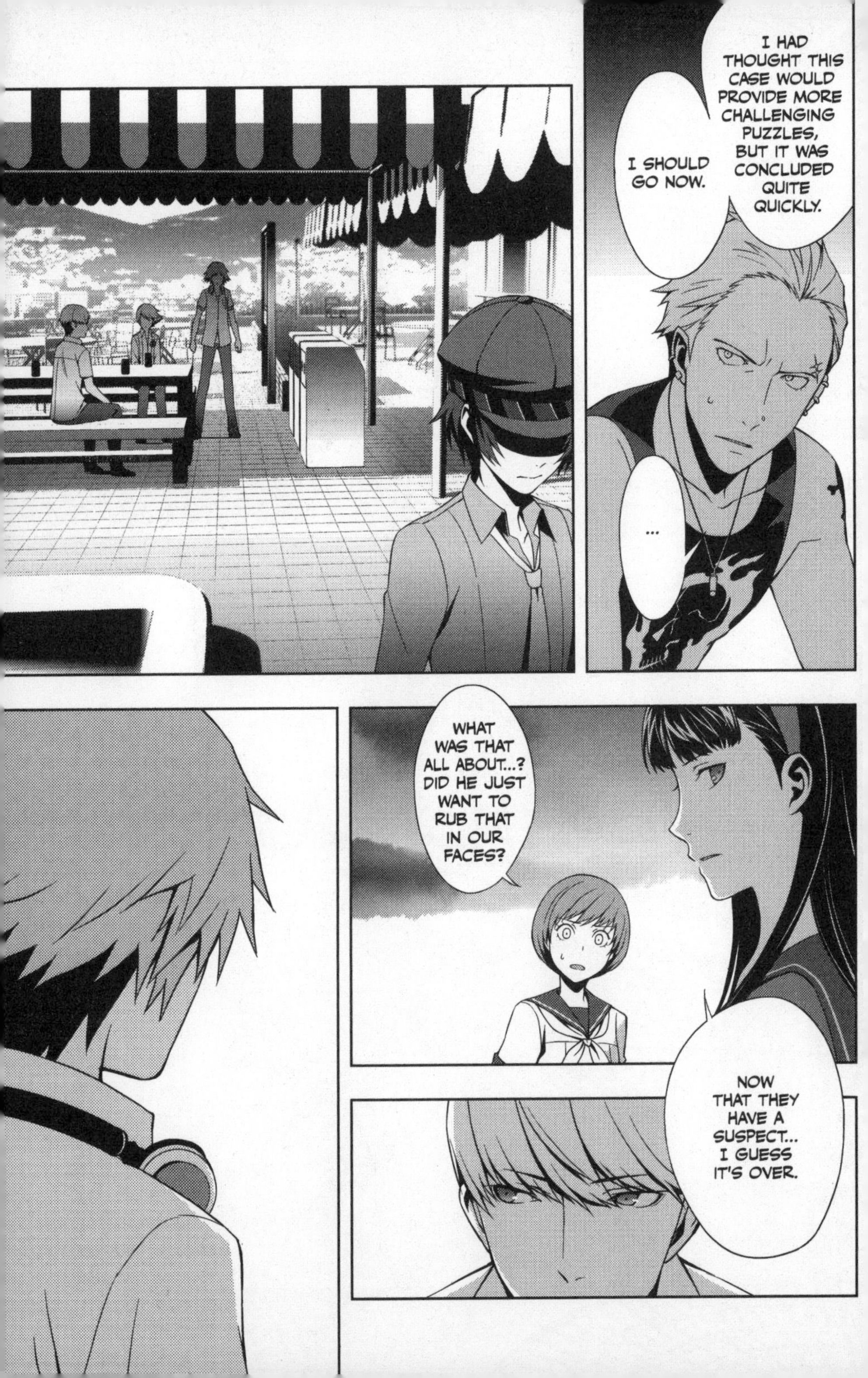
I HAD THOUGHT THIS CASE WOULD PROVIDE MORE CHALLENGING PUZZLES, BUT IT WAS CONCLUDED QUITE QUICKLY.
I SHOULD GO NOW.
...
WHAT WAS THAT ALL ABOUT...? DID HE JUST WANT TO RUB THAT IN OUR FACES?
NOW THAT THEY HAVE A SUSPECT... I GUESS IT'S OVER.

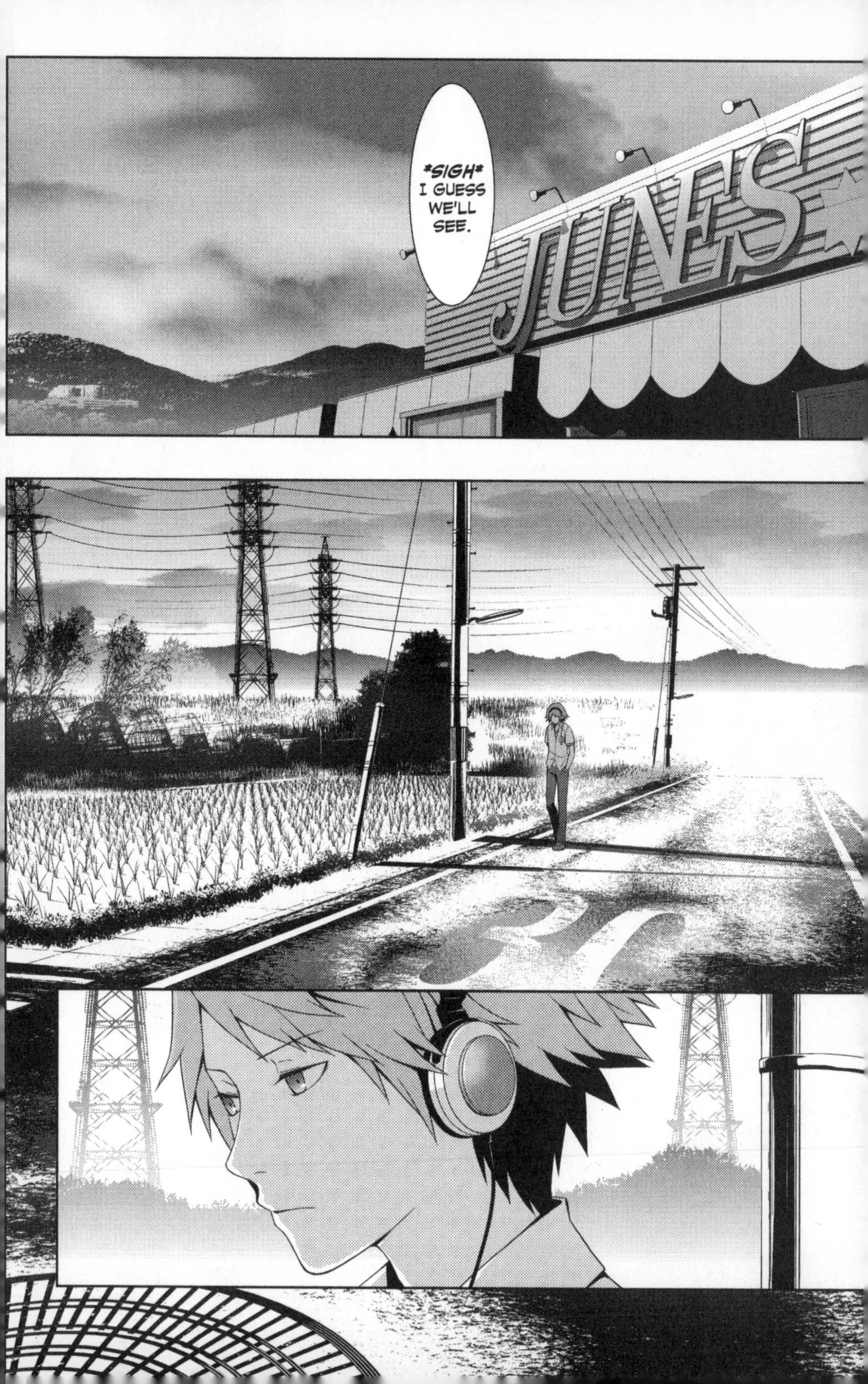
JUNES
SIGH I GUESS WE'LL SEE.

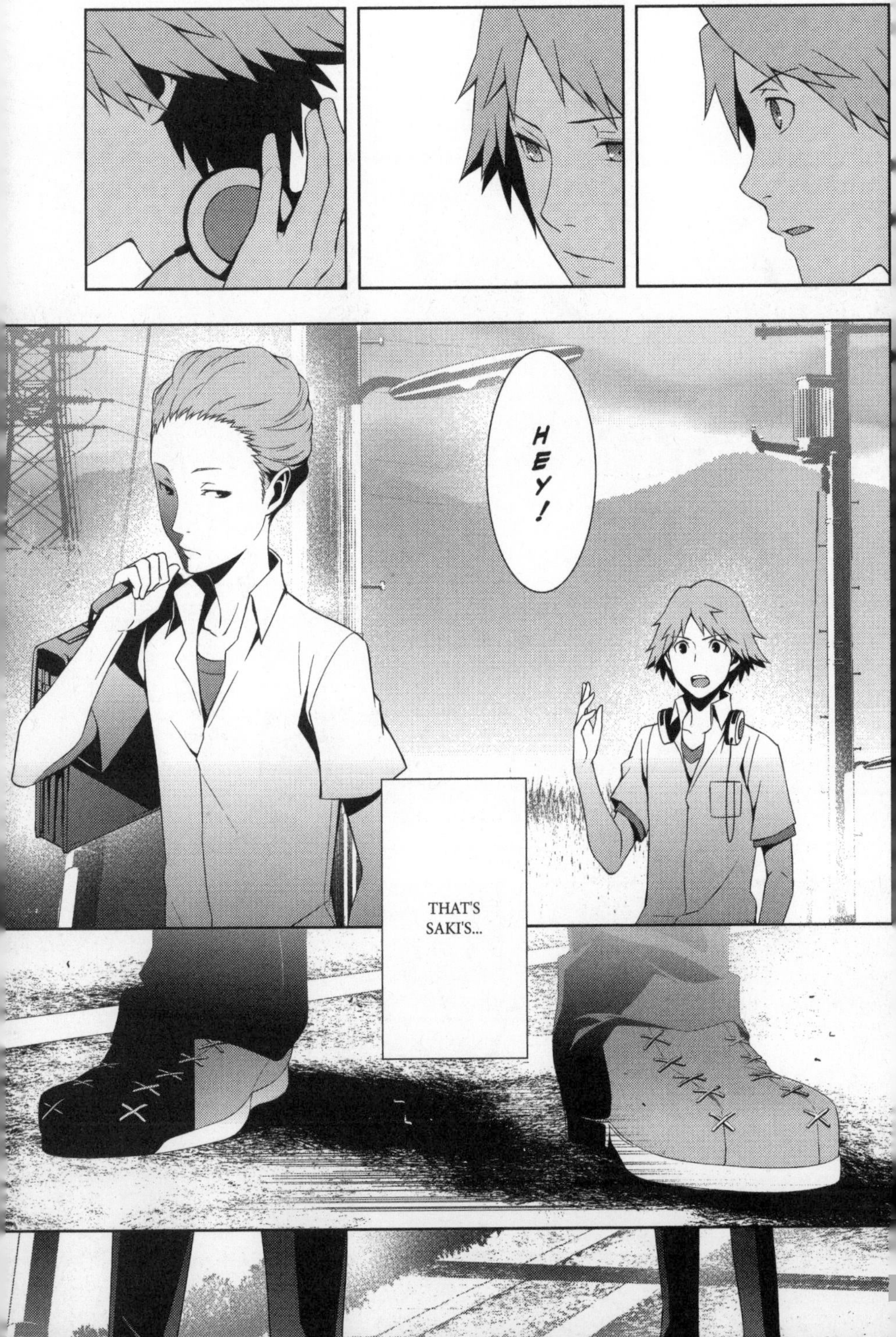
HEY!
THAT'S SAKI'S...

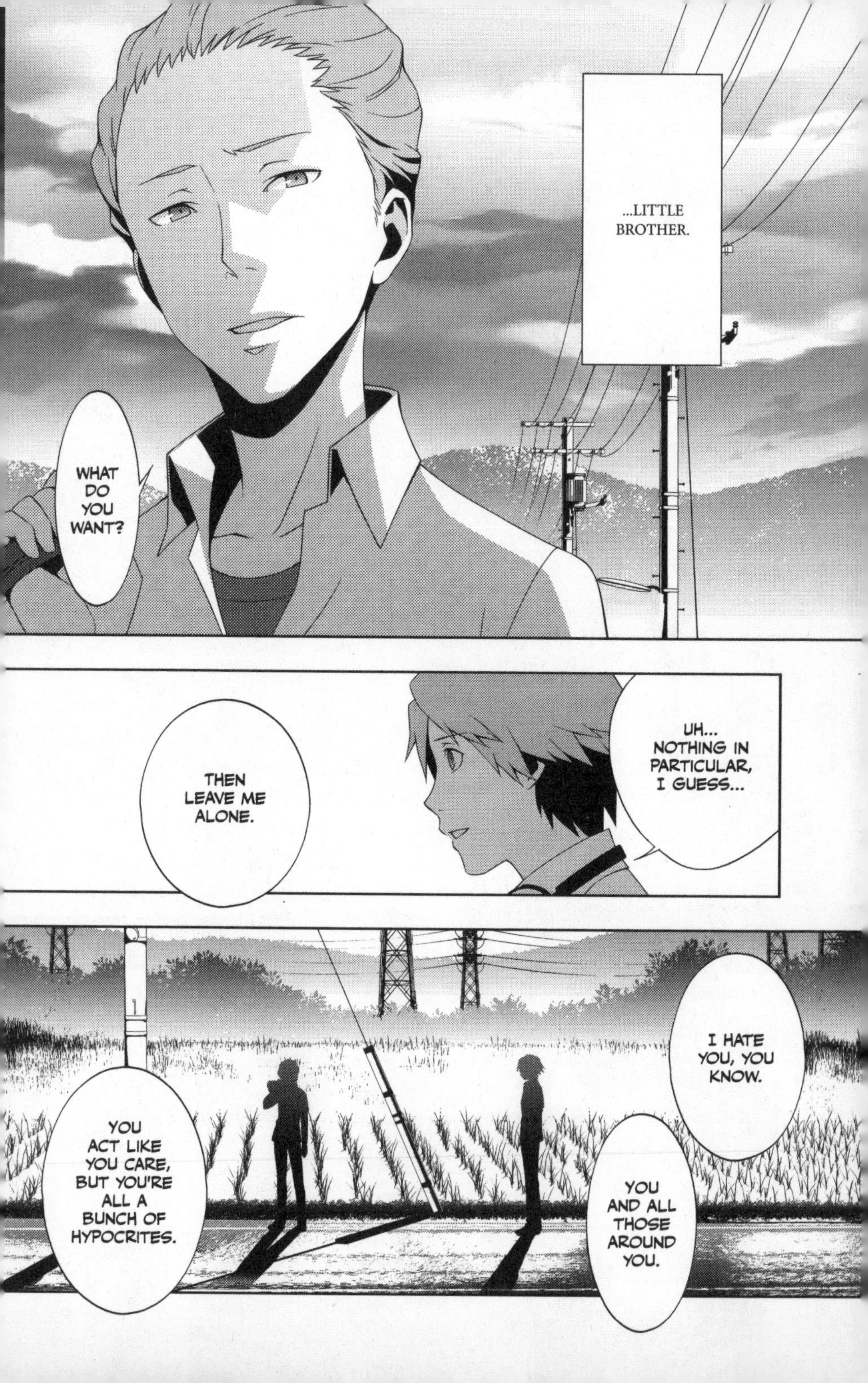
...LITTLE BROTHER.
WHAT DO YOU WANT?
UH... NOTHING IN PARTICULAR, I GUESS...
THEN LEAVE ME ALONE.
I HATE YOU, YOU KNOW.
YOU AND ALL THOSE AROUND YOU.
YOU ACT LIKE YOU CARE, BUT YOU'RE ALL A BUNCH OF HYPOCRITES.

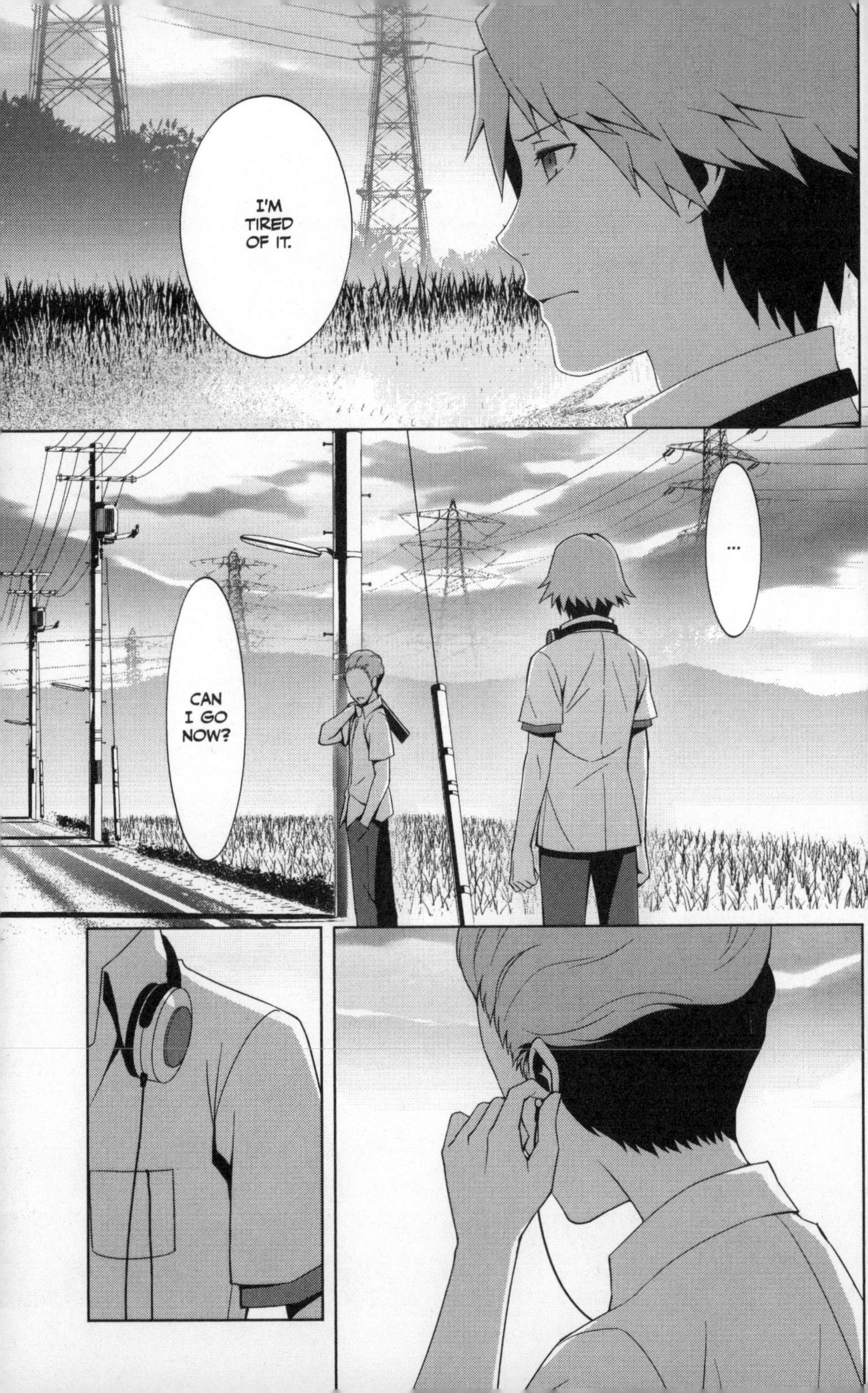
I'M TIRED OF IT.
...
CAN I GO NOW?

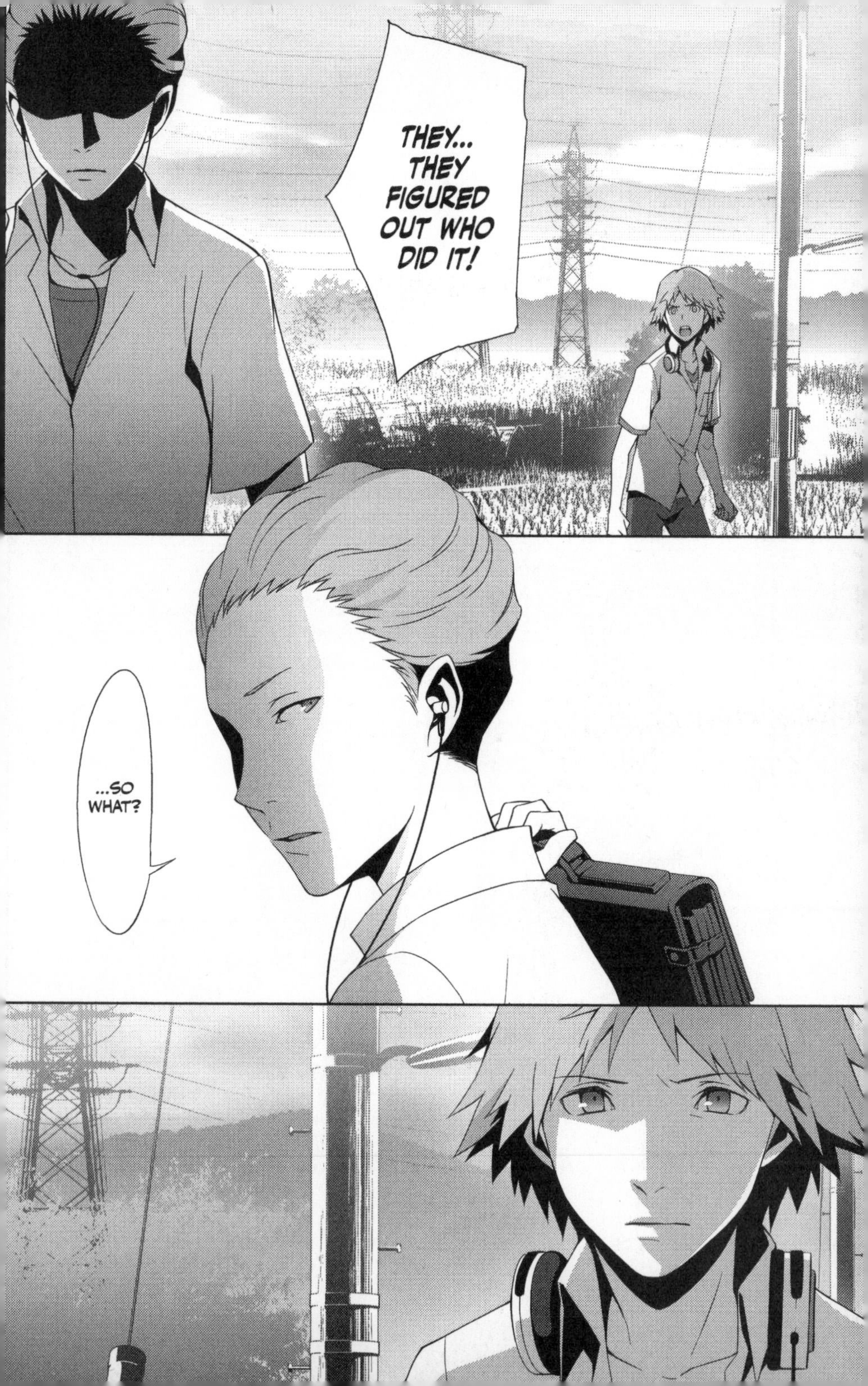
THEY... THEY FIGURED OUT WHO DID IT!
...SO WHAT?

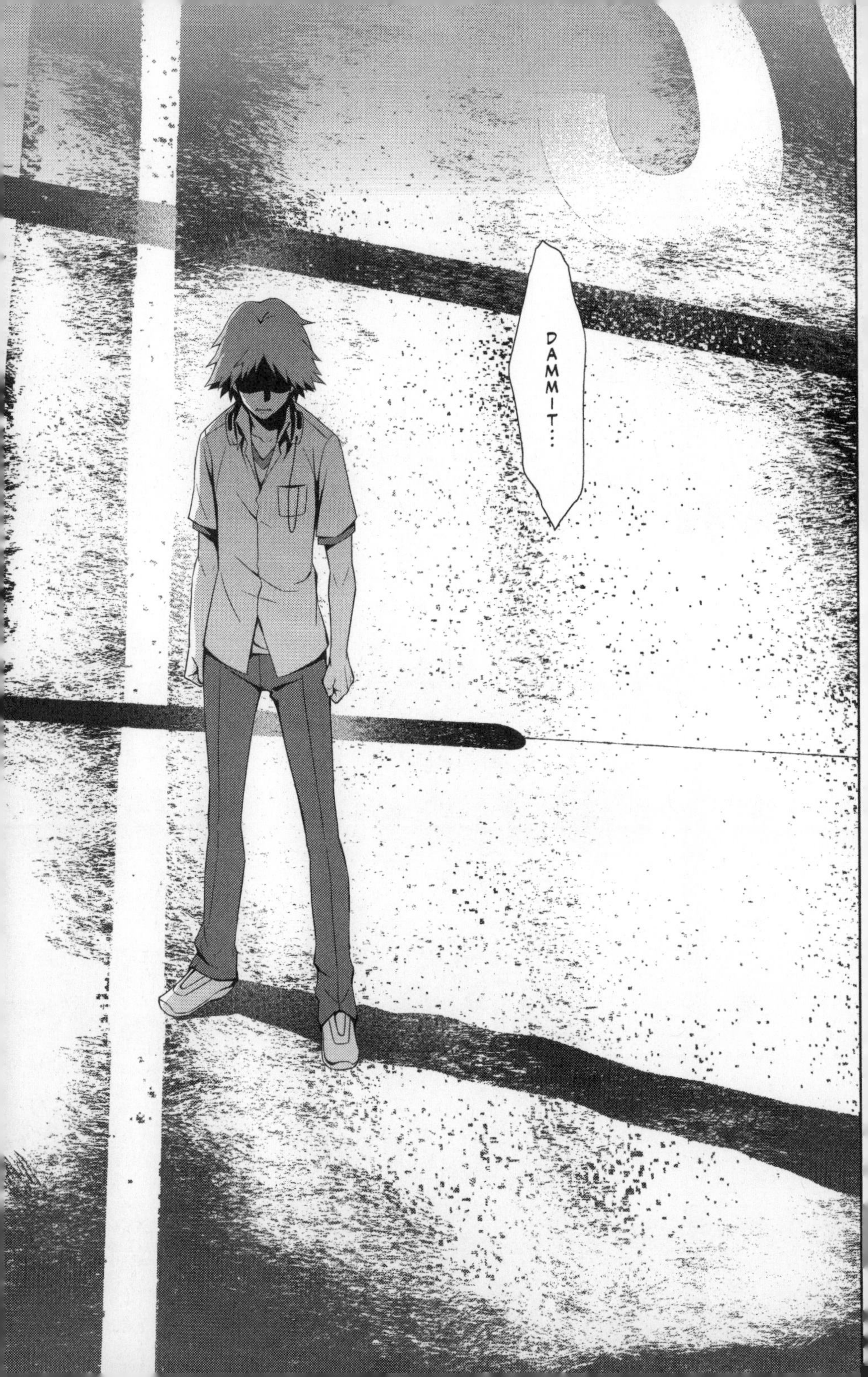
DAMMIT...

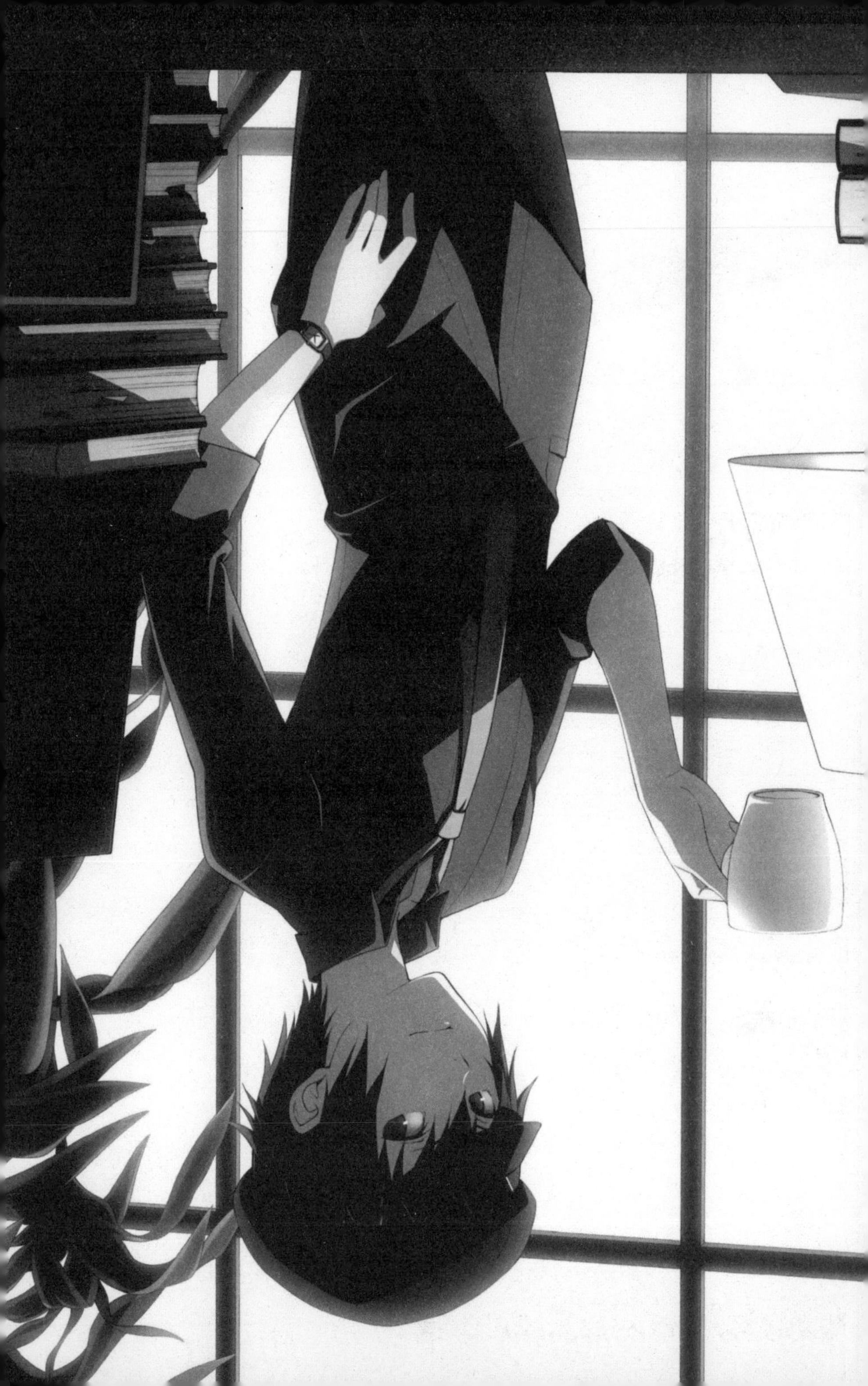

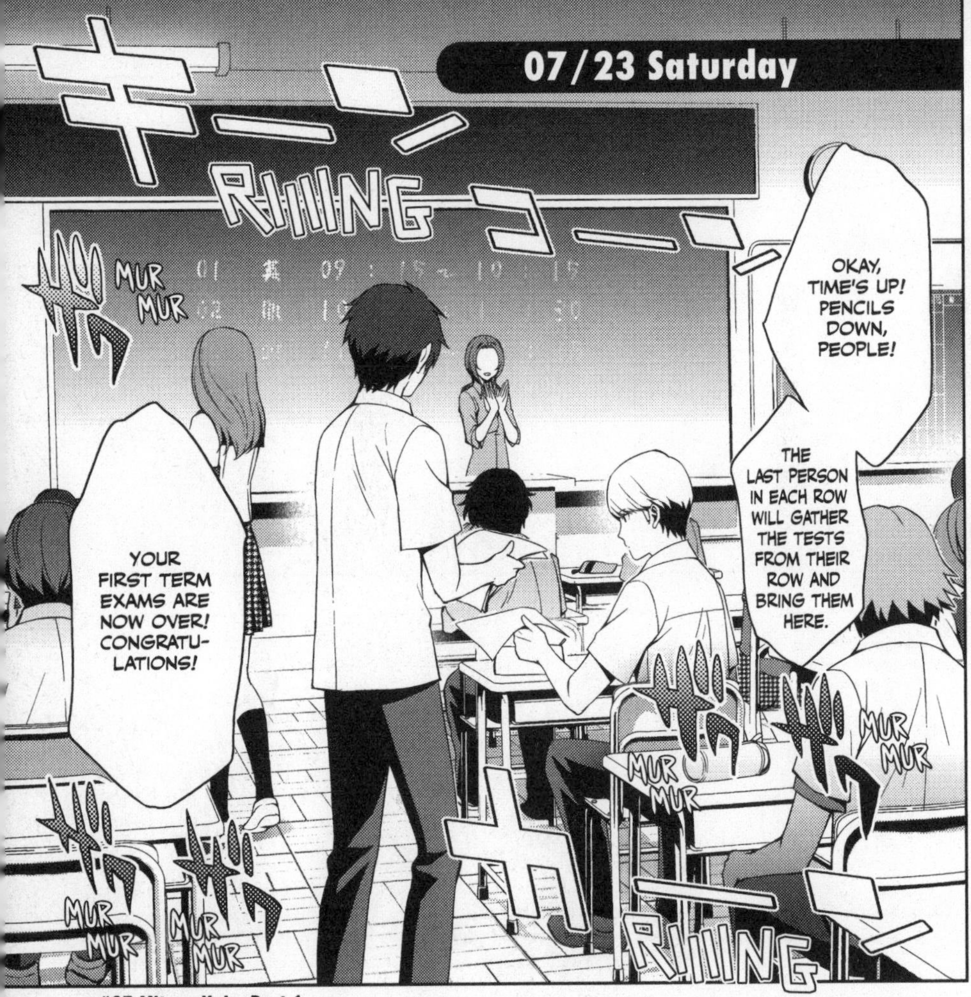
07/23 Saturday
RIIIING
OKAY, TIME'S UP! PENCILS DOWN, PEOPLE!
MUR MUR
THE LAST PERSON IN EACH ROW WILL GATHER THE TESTS FROM THEIR ROW AND BRING THEM HERE.
YOUR FIRST TERM EXAMS ARE NOW OVER! CONGRATULATIONS!
MUR MUR
MUR MUR
RIIIING
MUR MUR
MUR MUR

#27 Mitsuo Kubo Part 1

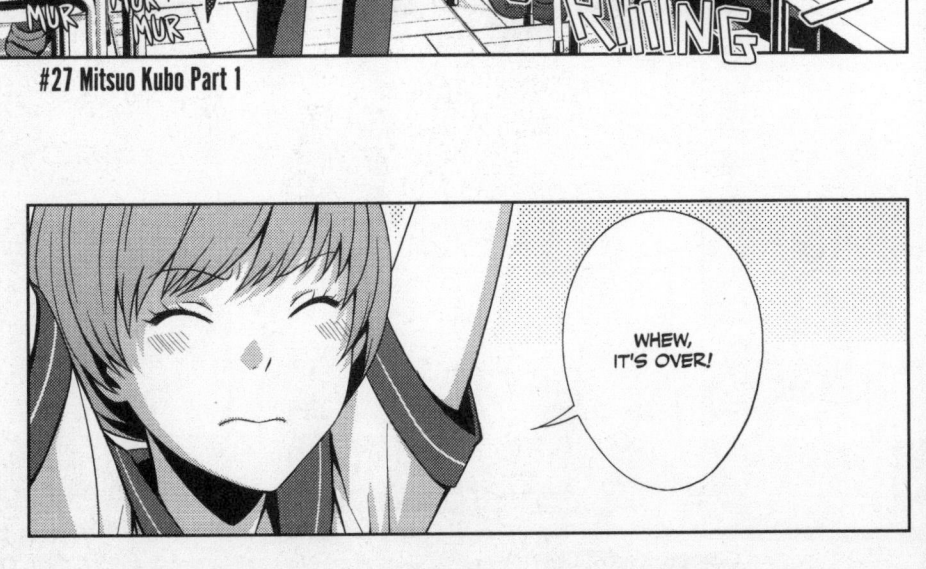

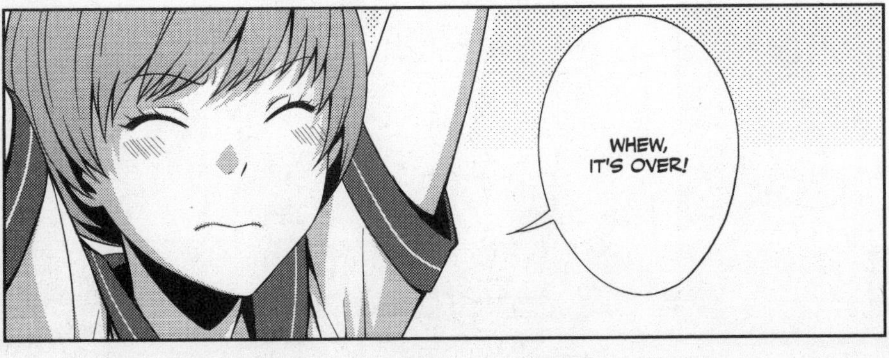
WHEW, IT'S OVER!

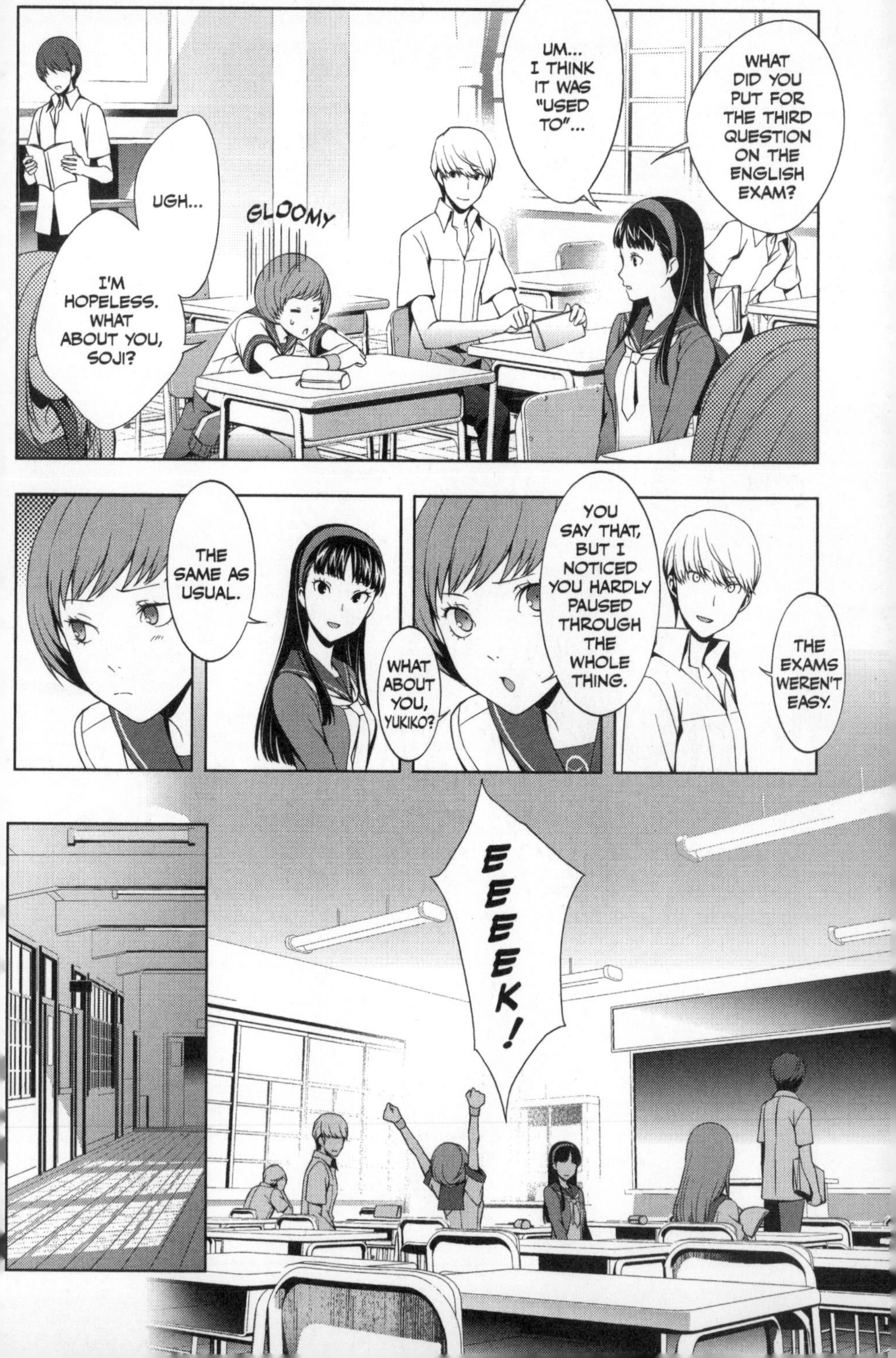
WHAT DID YOU PUT FOR THE THIRD QUESTION ON THE ENGLISH EXAM?
UM... I THINK IT WAS "USED TO"...
GLOOMY
UGH...
I'M HOPELESS. WHAT ABOUT YOU, SOJI?
THE EXAMS WEREN'T EASY.
YOU SAY THAT, BUT I NOTICED YOU HARDLY PAUSED THROUGH THE WHOLE THING.
WHAT ABOUT YOU, YUKIKO?
THE SAME AS USUAL.
EEEEK!

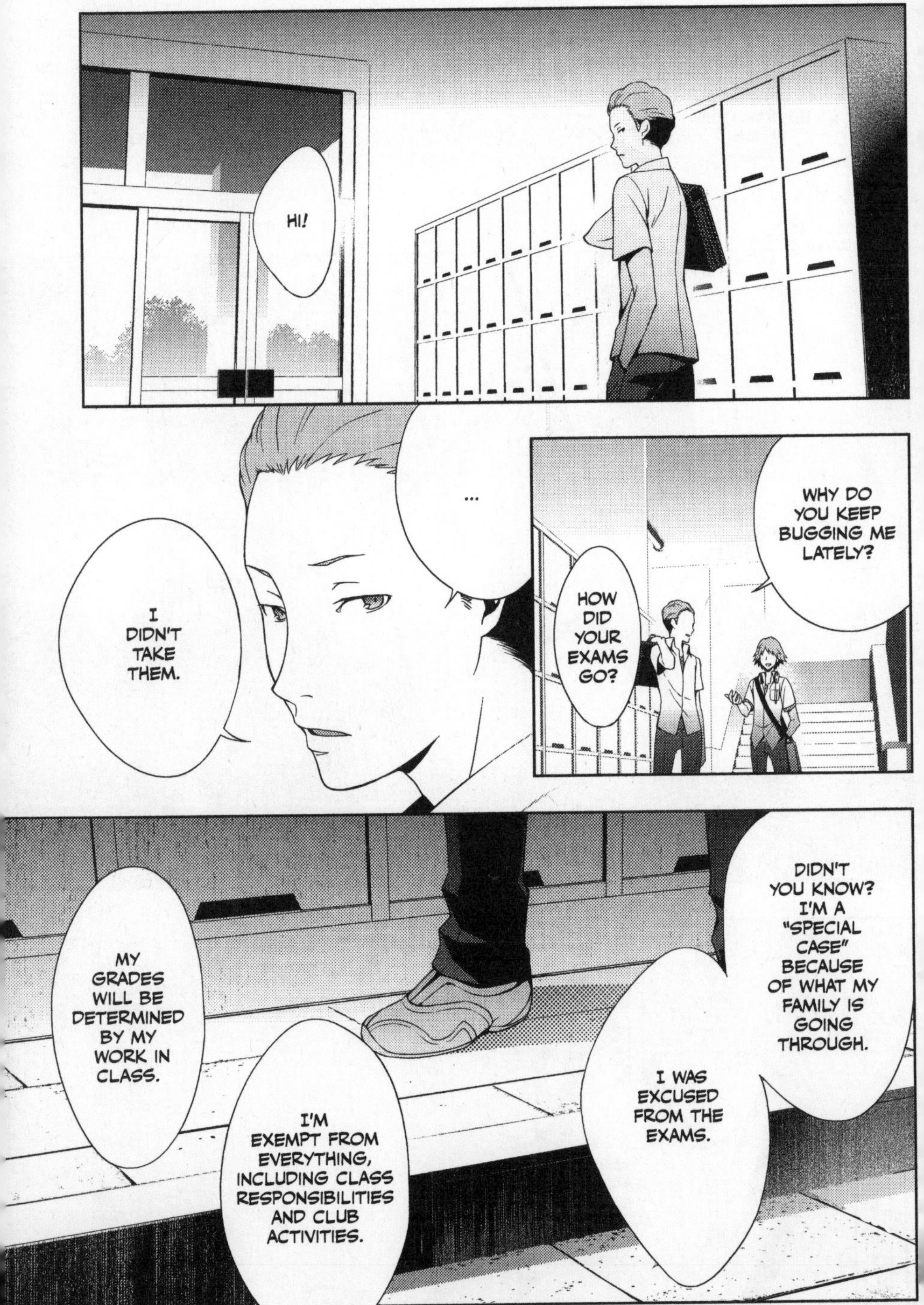
HI!
WHY DO YOU KEEP BUGGING ME LATELY?
HOW DID YOUR EXAMS GO?
...
I DIDN'T TAKE THEM.
DIDN'T YOU KNOW? I'M A "SPECIAL CASE" BECAUSE OF WHAT MY FAMILY IS GOING THROUGH.
I WAS EXCUSED FROM THE EXAMS.
I'M EXEMPT FROM EVERYTHING, INCLUDING CLASS RESPONSIBILITIES AND CLUB ACTIVITIES.
MY GRADES WILL BE DETERMINED BY MY WORK IN CLASS.

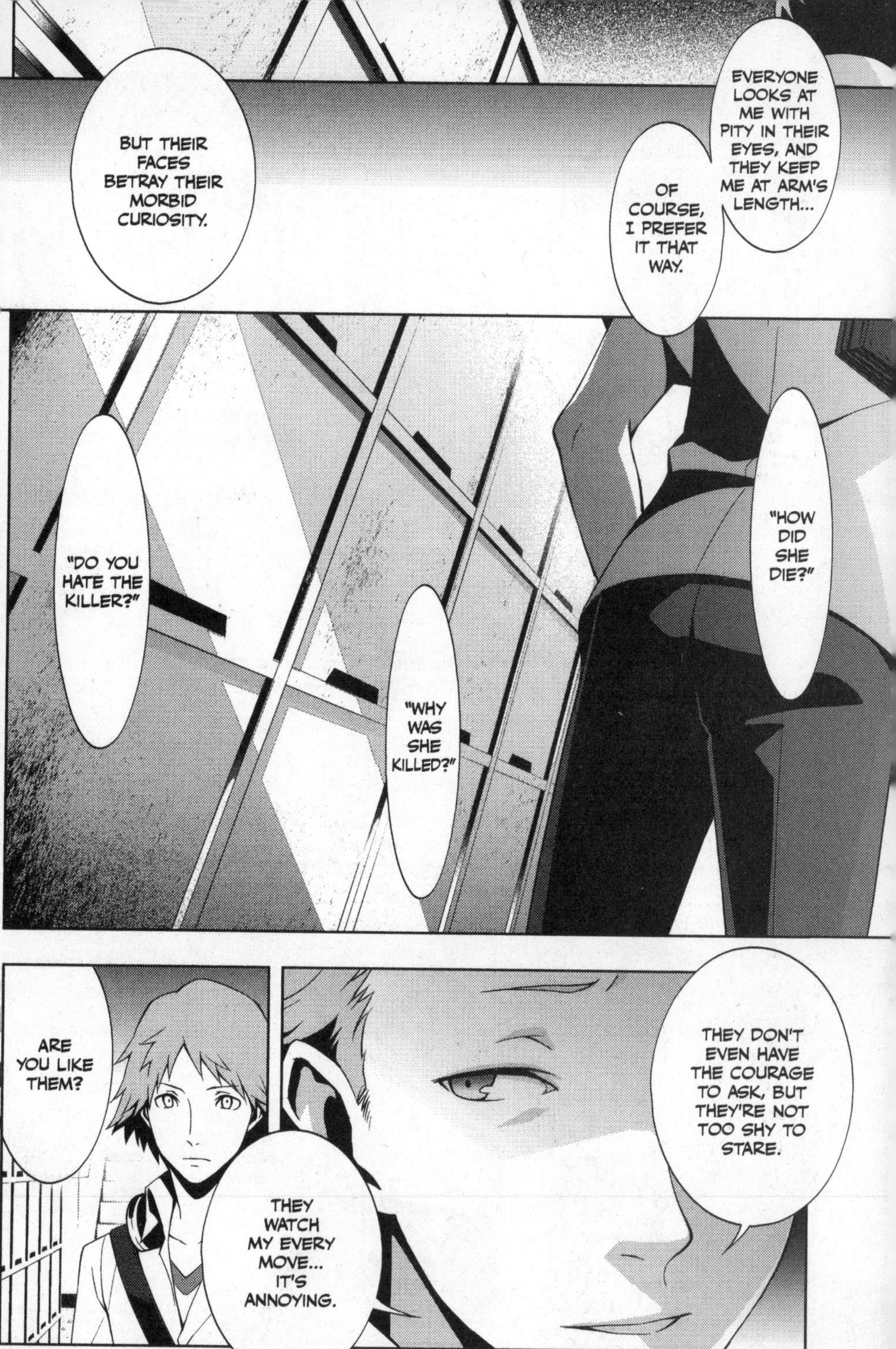
EVERYONE LOOKS AT ME WITH PITY IN THEIR EYES, AND THEY KEEP ME AT ARM'S LENGTH...
OF COURSE, I PREFER IT THAT WAY.
BUT THEIR FACES BETRAY THEIR MORBID CURIOSITY.
"HOW DID SHE DIE?"
"WHY WAS SHE KILLED?"
"DO YOU HATE THE KILLER?"
THEY DON'T EVEN HAVE THE COURAGE TO ASK, BUT THEY'RE NOT TOO SHY TO STARE.
THEY WATCH MY EVERY MOVE... IT'S ANNOYING.
ARE YOU LIKE THEM?

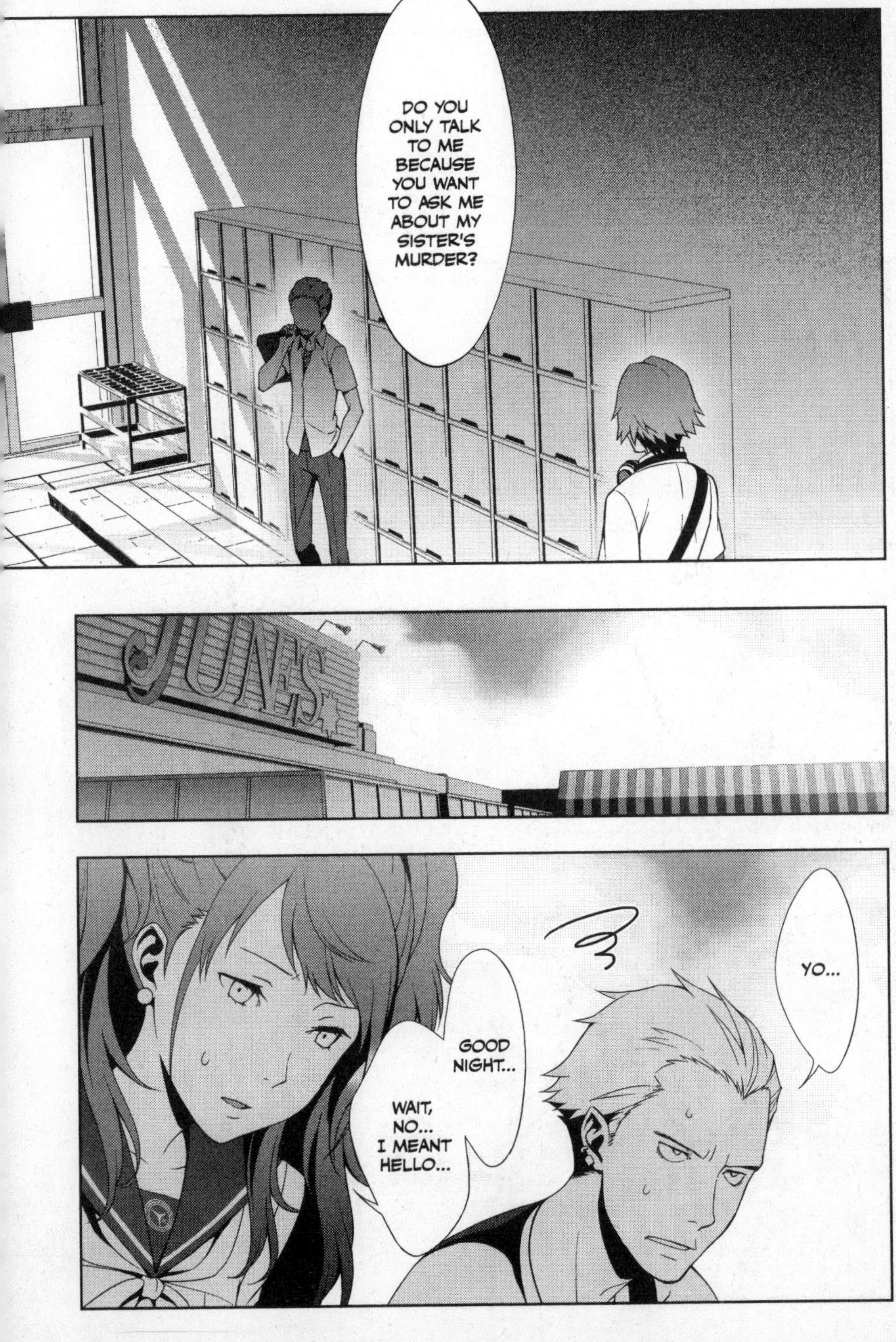
DO YOU ONLY TALK TO ME BECAUSE YOU WANT TO ASK ME ABOUT MY SISTER'S MURDER?
JUNES
YO...
GOOD NIGHT...
WAIT, NO... I MEANT HELLO...

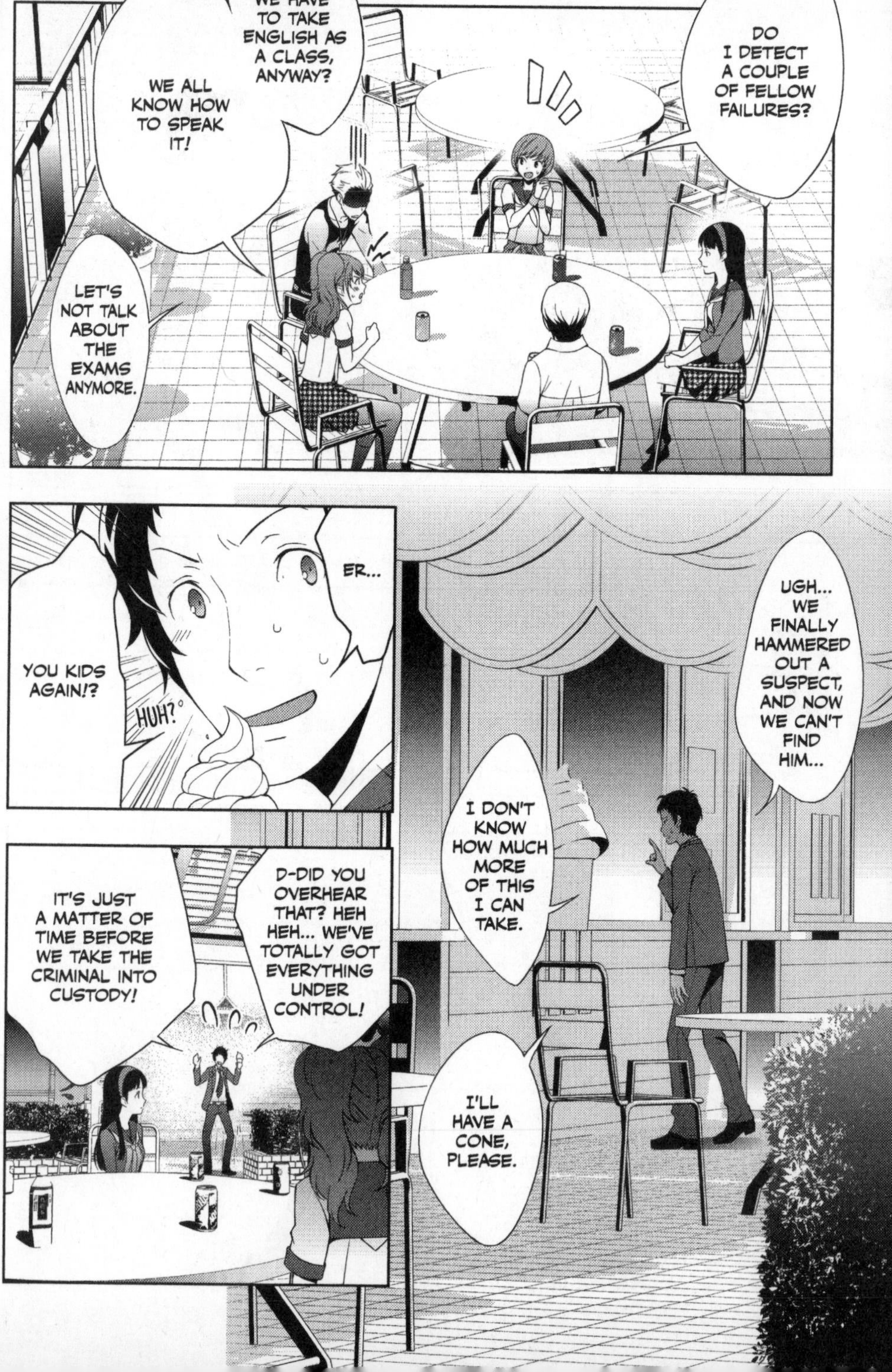
DO I DETECT A COUPLE OF FELLOW FAILURES?
WHY DO WE HAVE TO TAKE ENGLISH AS A CLASS, ANYWAY?
WE ALL KNOW HOW TO SPEAK IT!
LET'S NOT TALK ABOUT THE EXAMS ANYMORE.
UGH... WE FINALLY HAMMERED OUT A SUSPECT, AND NOW WE CAN'T FIND HIM...
I DON'T KNOW HOW MUCH MORE OF THIS I CAN TAKE.
I'LL HAVE A CONE, PLEASE.
ER...
HUH?
YOU KIDS AGAIN!?
D-DID YOU OVERHEAR THAT? HEH HEH... WE'VE TOTALLY GOT EVERYTHING UNDER CONTROL!
IT'S JUST A MATTER OF TIME BEFORE WE TAKE THE CRIMINAL INTO CUSTODY!

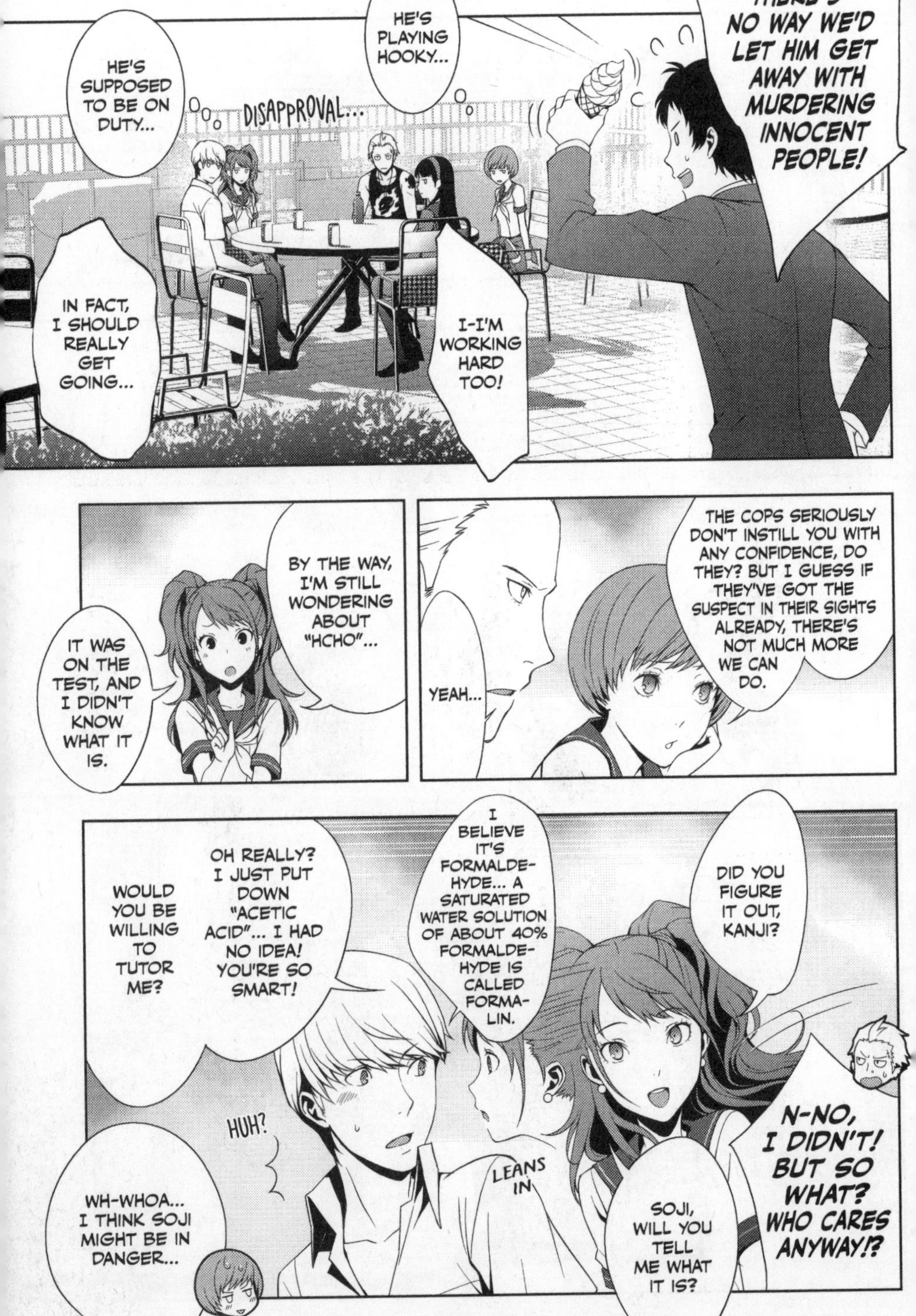
THERE'S NO WAY WE'D LET HIM GET AWAY WITH MURDERING INNOCENT PEOPLE!
HE'S PLAYING HOOKY...
HE'S SUPPOSED TO BE ON DUTY...
DISAPPROVAL...
I-I'M WORKING HARD TOO!
IN FACT, I SHOULD REALLY GET GOING...
THE COPS SERIOUSLY DON'T INSTILL YOU WITH ANY CONFIDENCE, DO THEY? BUT I GUESS IF THEY'VE GOT THE SUSPECT IN THEIR SIGHTS ALREADY, THERE'S NOT MUCH MORE WE CAN DO.
YEAH...
BY THE WAY, I'M STILL WONDERING ABOUT "HCHO"...
IT WAS ON THE TEST, AND I DIDN'T KNOW WHAT IT IS.
DID YOU FIGURE IT OUT, KANJI?
N-NO, I DIDN'T! BUT SO WHAT? WHO CARES ANYWAY!?
SOJI, WILL YOU TELL ME WHAT IT IS?
LEANS IN
I BELIEVE IT'S FORMALDE-HYDE... A SATURATED WATER SOLUTION OF ABOUT 40% FORMALDE-HYDE IS CALLED FORMA-LIN.
OH REALLY? I JUST PUT DOWN "ACETIC ACID"... I HAD NO IDEA! YOU'RE SO SMART!
WOULD YOU BE WILLING TO TUTOR ME?
HUH?
WH-WHOA... I THINK SOJI MIGHT BE IN DANGER...

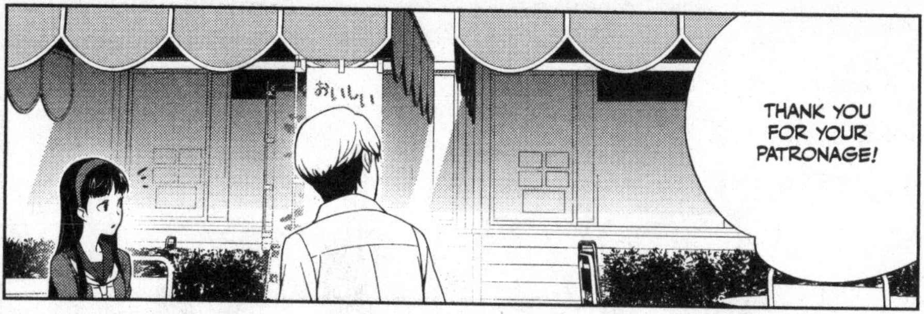
THANK YOU FOR YOUR PATRONAGE!
おいしい

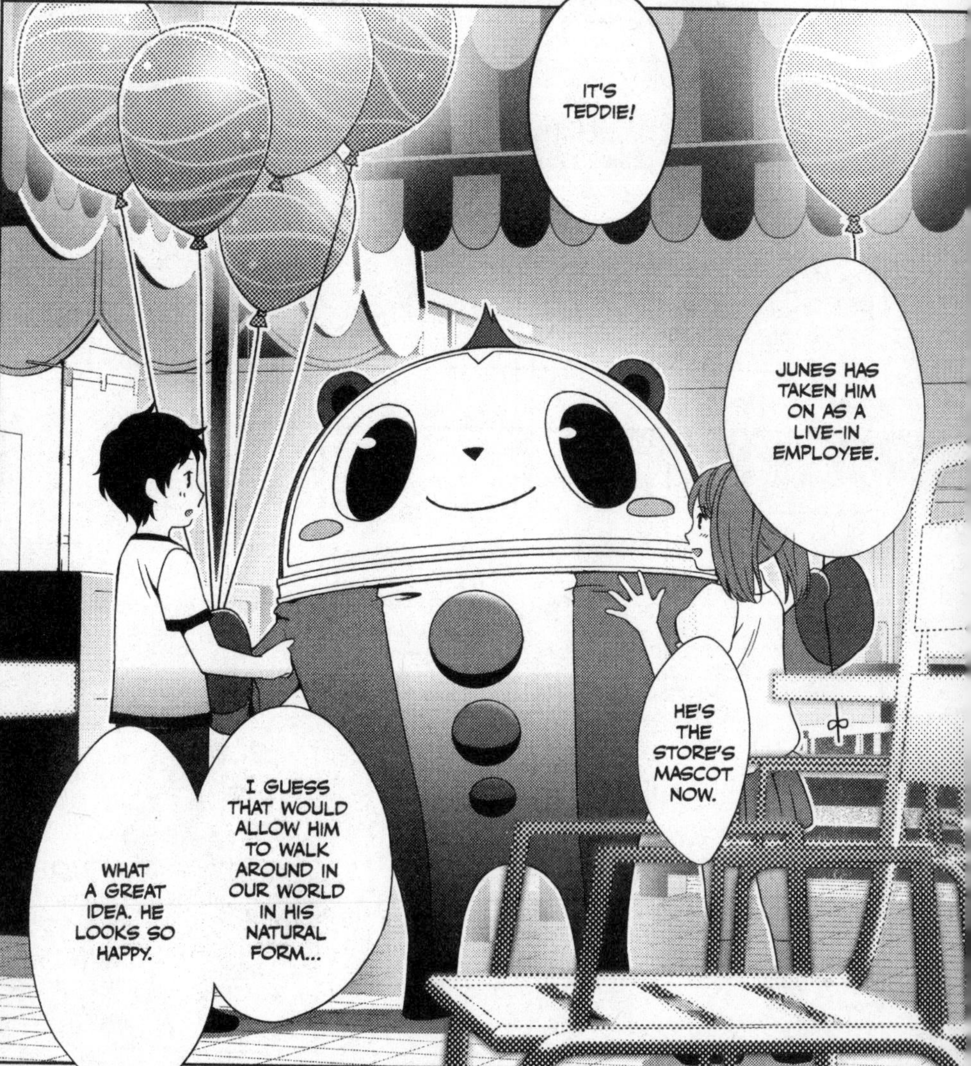
IT'S TEDDIE!
JUNES HAS TAKEN HIM ON AS A LIVE-IN EMPLOYEE.
HE'S THE STORE'S MASCOT NOW.
I GUESS THAT WOULD ALLOW HIM TO WALK AROUND IN OUR WORLD IN HIS NATURAL FORM...
WHAT A GREAT IDEA. HE LOOKS SO HAPPY.

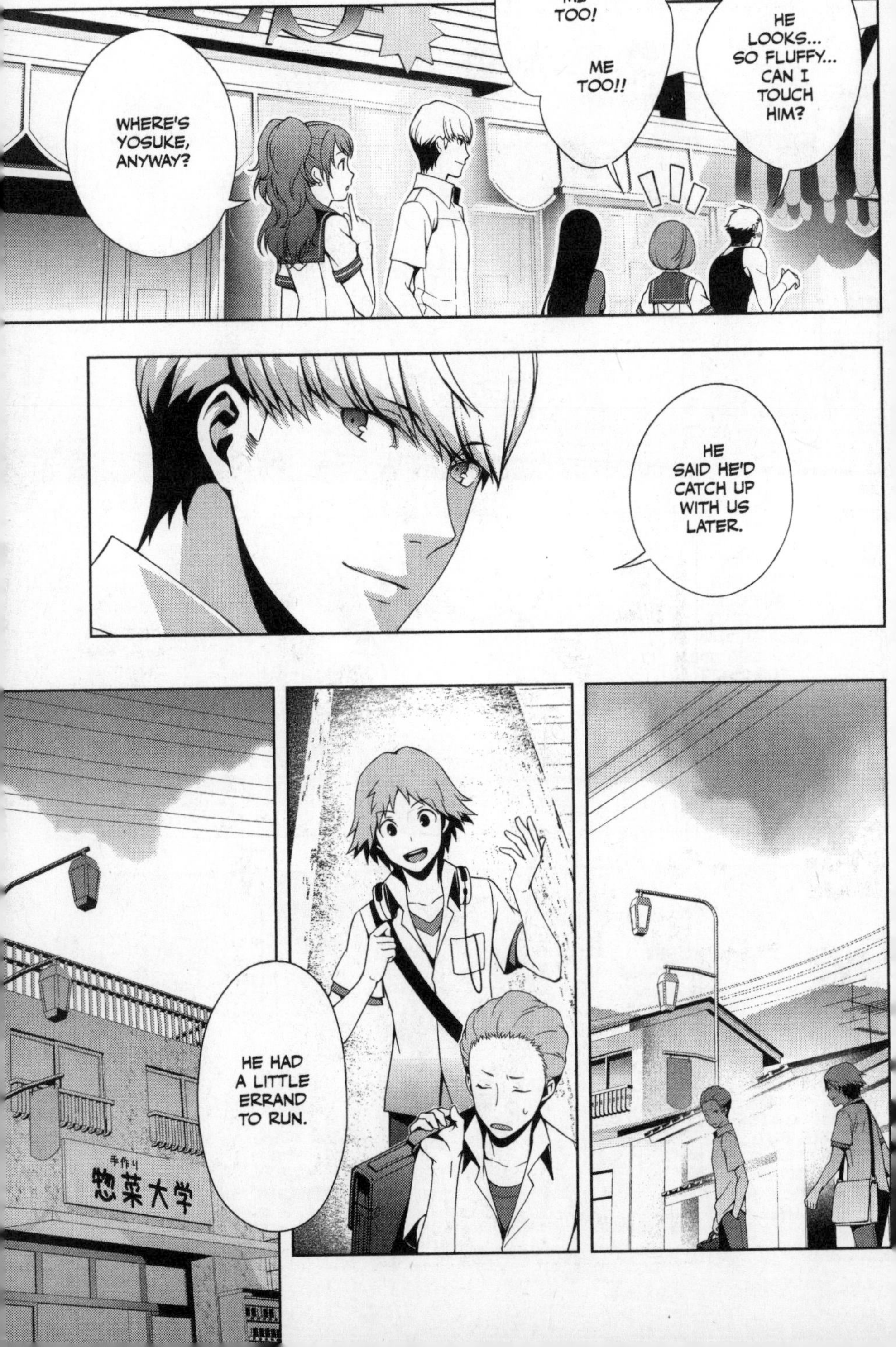
HE LOOKS... SO FLUFFY... CAN I TOUCH HIM?
ME TOO!
ME TOO!!
WHERE'S YOSUKE, ANYWAY?
HE SAID HE'D CATCH UP WITH US LATER.
HE HAD A LITTLE ERRAND TO RUN.
手作り
惣菜大学

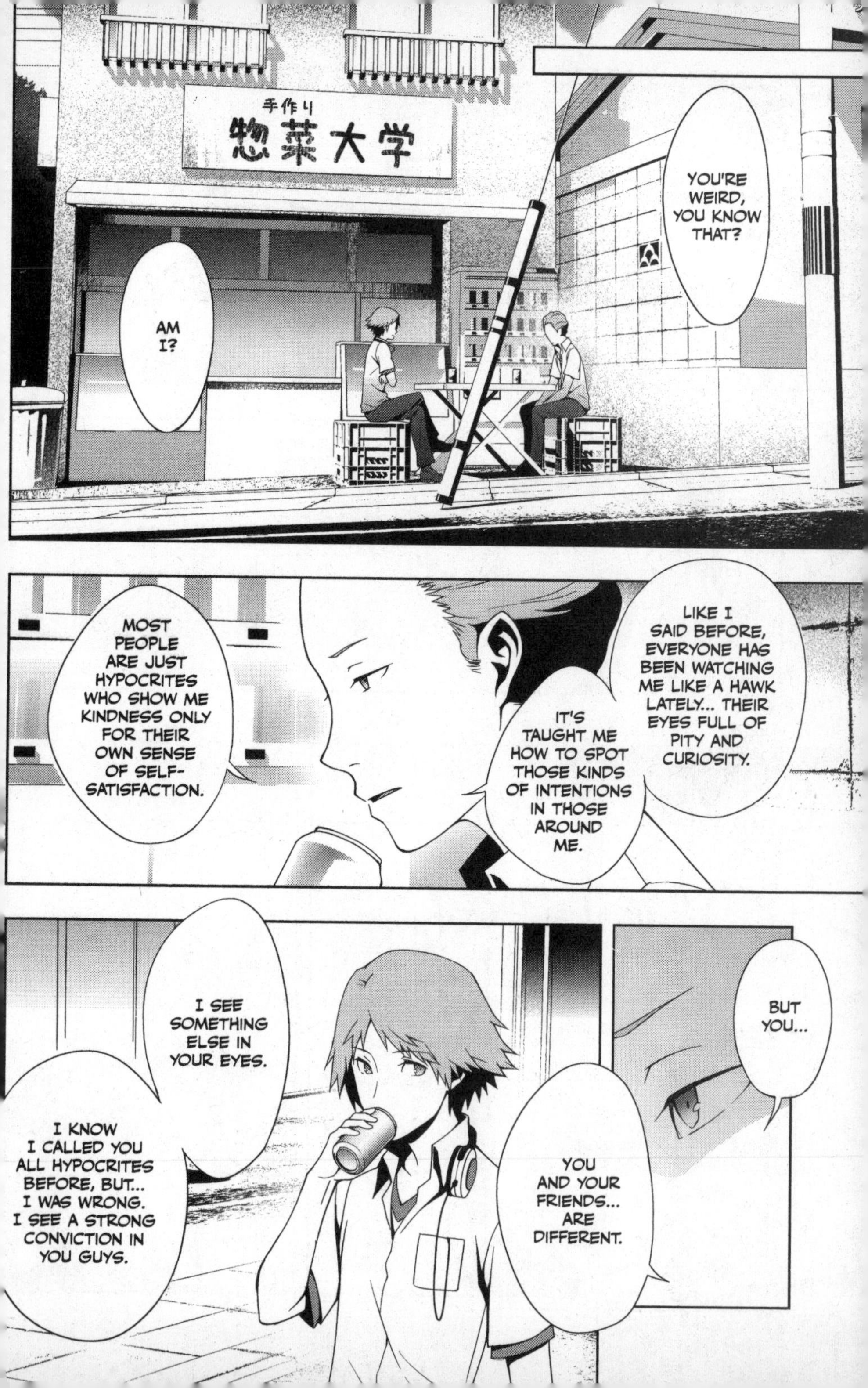

手作り
惣菜大学
YOU'RE WEIRD, YOU KNOW THAT?
AM I?
LIKE I SAID BEFORE, EVERYONE HAS BEEN WATCHING ME LIKE A HAWK LATELY... THEIR EYES FULL OF PITY AND CURIOSITY.
IT'S TAUGHT ME HOW TO SPOT THOSE KINDS OF INTENTIONS IN THOSE AROUND ME.
MOST PEOPLE ARE JUST HYPOCRITES WHO SHOW ME KINDNESS ONLY FOR THEIR OWN SENSE OF SELF-SATISFACTION.
BUT YOU...
YOU AND YOUR FRIENDS... ARE DIFFERENT.
I SEE SOMETHING ELSE IN YOUR EYES.
I KNOW I CALLED YOU ALL HYPOCRITES BEFORE, BUT... I WAS WRONG. I SEE A STRONG CONVICTION IN YOU GUYS.

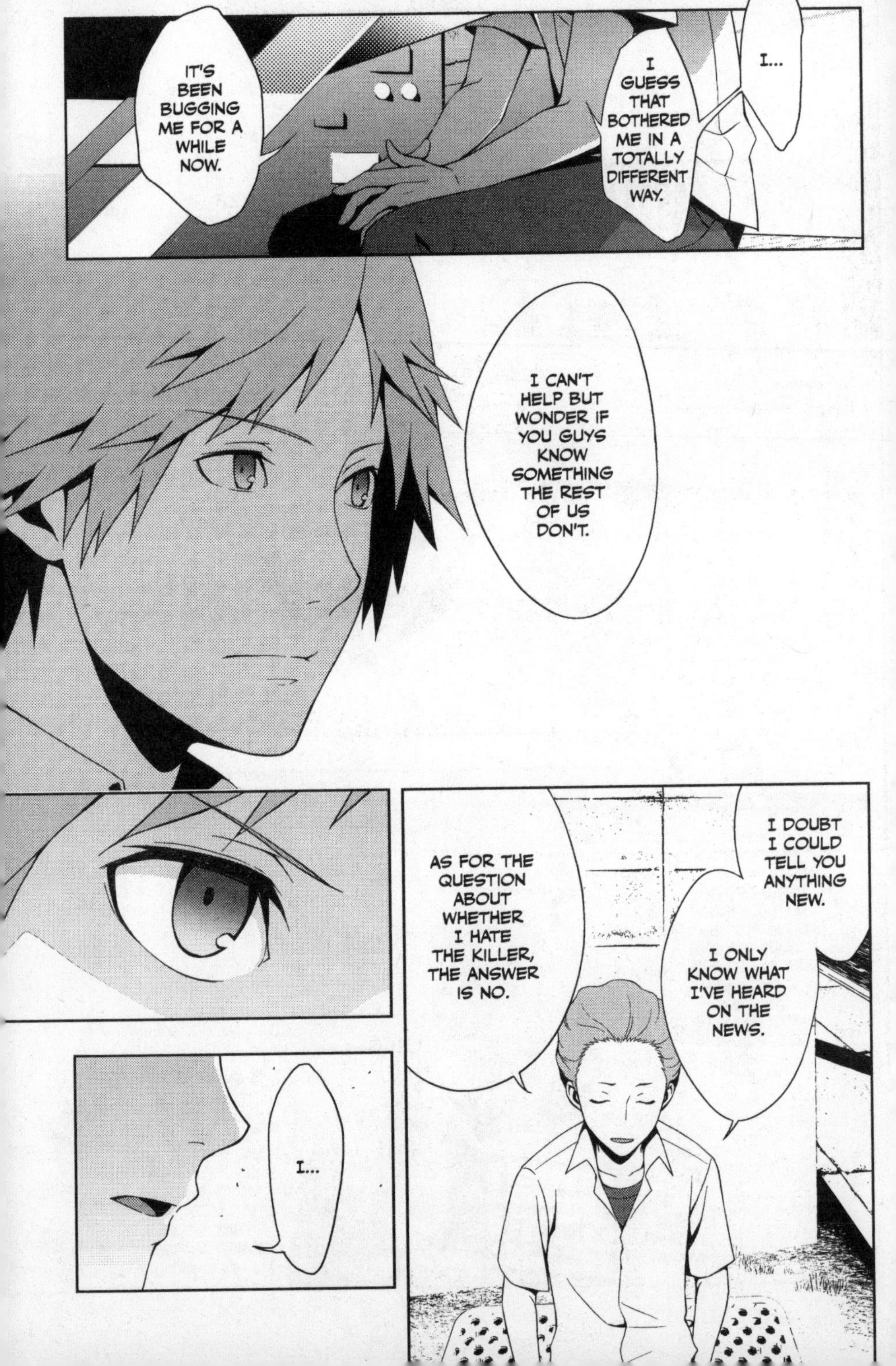
I...
I GUESS THAT BOTHERED ME IN A TOTALLY DIFFERENT WAY.
IT'S BEEN BUGGING ME FOR A WHILE NOW.
I CAN'T HELP BUT WONDER IF YOU GUYS KNOW SOMETHING THE REST OF US DON'T.
I DOUBT I COULD TELL YOU ANYTHING NEW.
I ONLY KNOW WHAT I'VE HEARD ON THE NEWS.
AS FOR THE QUESTION ABOUT WHETHER I HATE THE KILLER, THE ANSWER IS NO.
I...

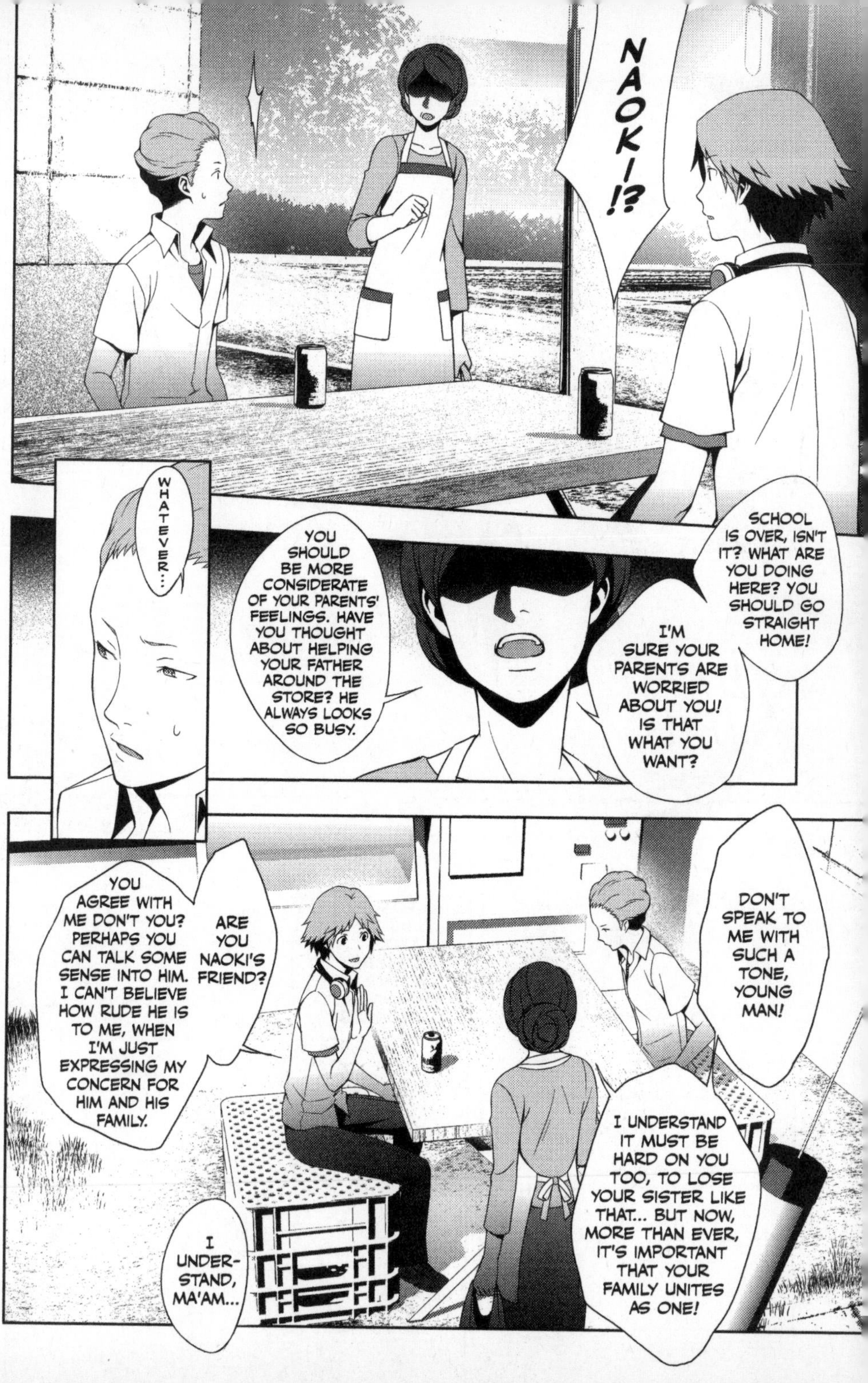
NAOKI!?
SCHOOL IS OVER, ISN'T IT? WHAT ARE YOU DOING HERE? YOU SHOULD GO STRAIGHT HOME!
I'M SURE YOUR PARENTS ARE WORRIED ABOUT YOU! IS THAT WHAT YOU WANT?
YOU SHOULD BE MORE CONSIDERATE OF YOUR PARENTS' FEELINGS. HAVE YOU THOUGHT ABOUT HELPING YOUR FATHER AROUND THE STORE? HE ALWAYS LOOKS SO BUSY.
WHATEVER...
DON'T SPEAK TO ME WITH SUCH A TONE, YOUNG MAN!
I UNDERSTAND IT MUST BE HARD ON YOU TOO, TO LOSE YOUR SISTER LIKE THAT... BUT NOW, MORE THAN EVER, IT'S IMPORTANT THAT YOUR FAMILY UNITES AS ONE!
ARE YOU NAOKI'S FRIEND?
YOU AGREE WITH ME DON'T YOU? PERHAPS YOU CAN TALK SOME SENSE INTO HIM. I CAN'T BELIEVE HOW RUDE HE IS TO ME, WHEN I'M JUST EXPRESSING MY CONCERN FOR HIM AND HIS FAMILY.
I UNDER-STAND, MA'AM...

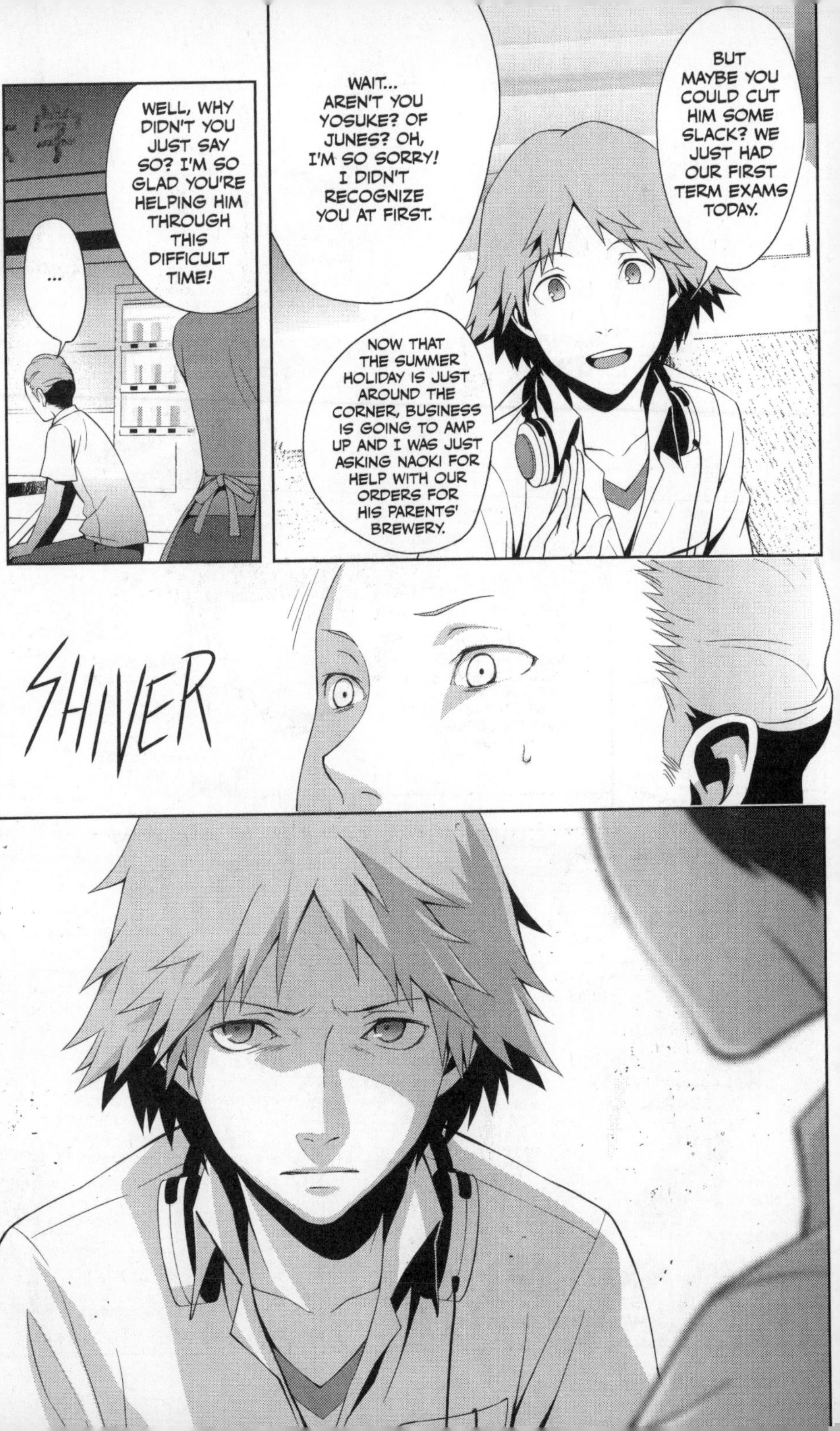
BUT MAYBE YOU COULD CUT HIM SOME SLACK? WE JUST HAD OUR FIRST TERM EXAMS TODAY.
WAIT... AREN'T YOU YOSUKE? OF JUNES? OH, I'M SO SORRY! I DIDN'T RECOGNIZE YOU AT FIRST.
NOW THAT THE SUMMER HOLIDAY IS JUST AROUND THE CORNER, BUSINESS IS GOING TO AMP UP AND I WAS JUST ASKING NAOKI FOR HELP WITH OUR ORDERS FOR HIS PARENTS' BREWERY.
WELL, WHY DIDN'T YOU JUST SAY SO? I'M SO GLAD YOU'RE HELPING HIM THROUGH THIS DIFFICULT TIME!
...
SHIVER

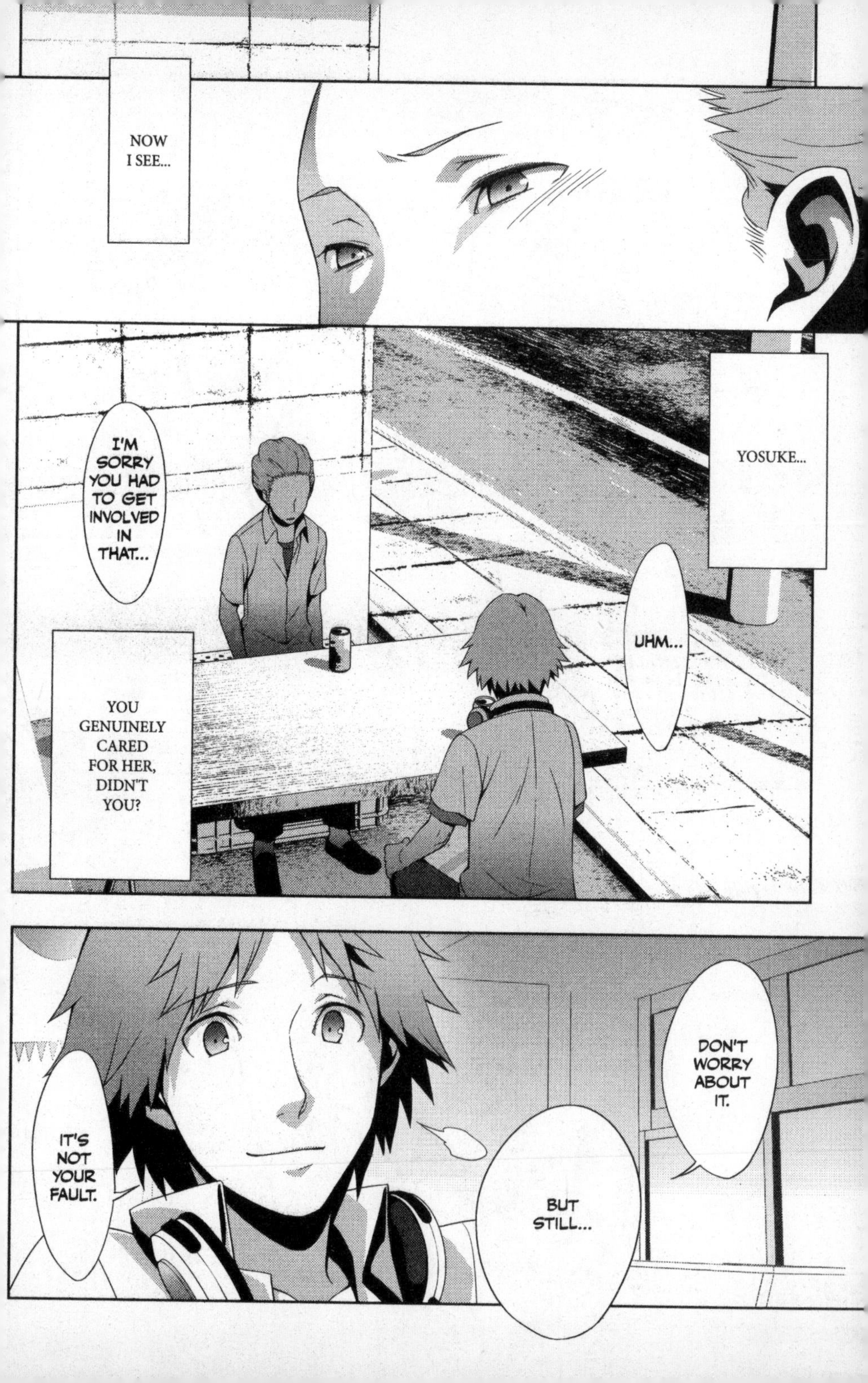
NOW I SEE...
YOSUKE...
UHM...
I'M SORRY YOU HAD TO GET INVOLVED IN THAT...
YOU GENUINELY CARED FOR HER, DIDN'T YOU?
DON'T WORRY ABOUT IT.
BUT STILL...
IT'S NOT YOUR FAULT.

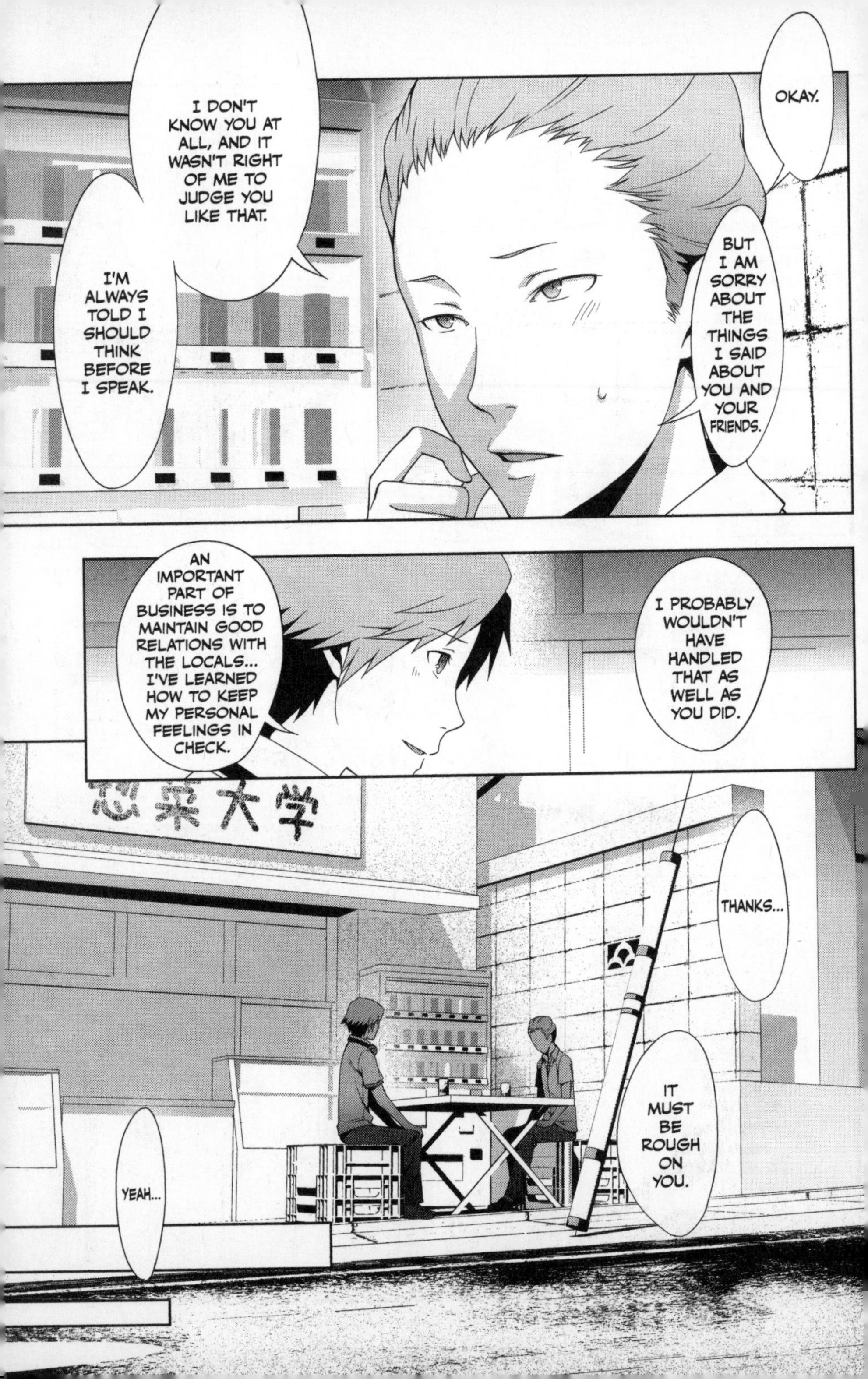
OKAY.
BUT I AM SORRY ABOUT THE THINGS I SAID ABOUT YOU AND YOUR FRIENDS.
I DON'T KNOW YOU AT ALL, AND IT WASN'T RIGHT OF ME TO JUDGE YOU LIKE THAT.
I'M ALWAYS TOLD I SHOULD THINK BEFORE I SPEAK.
I PROBABLY WOULDN'T HAVE HANDLED THAT AS WELL AS YOU DID.
AN IMPORTANT PART OF BUSINESS IS TO MAINTAIN GOOD RELATIONS WITH THE LOCALS... I'VE LEARNED HOW TO KEEP MY PERSONAL FEELINGS IN CHECK.
惣菜大学
THANKS...
IT MUST BE ROUGH ON YOU.
YEAH...

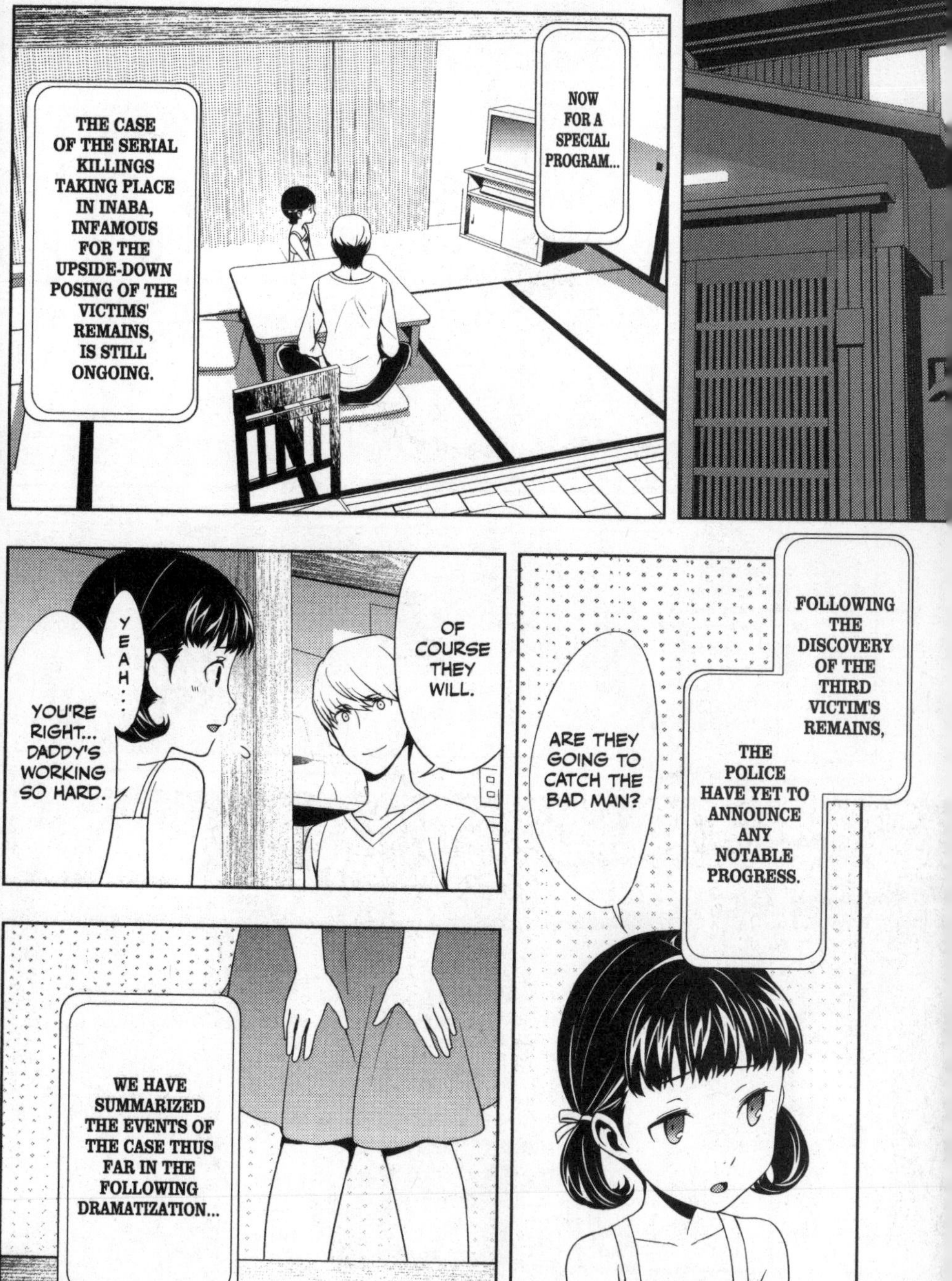
NOW FOR A SPECIAL PROGRAM...
THE CASE OF THE SERIAL KILLINGS TAKING PLACE IN INABA, INFAMOUS FOR THE UPSIDE-DOWN POSING OF THE VICTIMS' REMAINS, IS STILL ONGOING.
FOLLOWING THE DISCOVERY OF THE THIRD VICTIM'S REMAINS,
THE POLICE HAVE YET TO ANNOUNCE ANY NOTABLE PROGRESS.
ARE THEY GOING TO CATCH THE BAD MAN?
OF COURSE THEY WILL.
YEAH...
YOU'RE RIGHT... DADDY'S WORKING SO HARD.
WE HAVE SUMMARIZED THE EVENTS OF THE CASE THUS FAR IN THE FOLLOWING DRAMATIZATION...

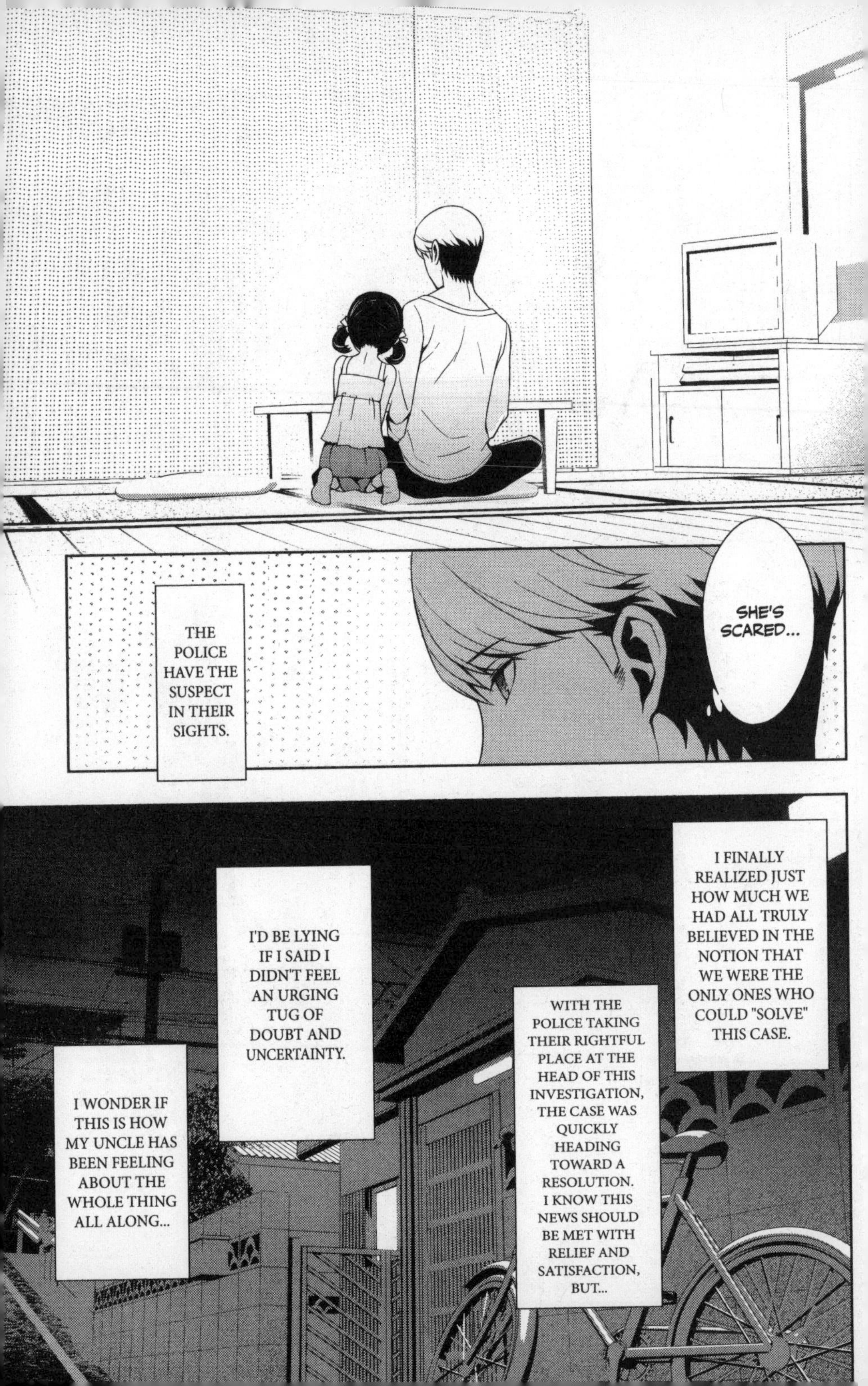
SHE'S SCARED...
THE POLICE HAVE THE SUSPECT IN THEIR SIGHTS.
I FINALLY REALIZED JUST HOW MUCH WE HAD ALL TRULY BELIEVED IN THE NOTION THAT WE WERE THE ONLY ONES WHO COULD "SOLVE" THIS CASE.
WITH THE POLICE TAKING THEIR RIGHTFUL PLACE AT THE HEAD OF THIS INVESTIGATION, THE CASE WAS QUICKLY HEADING TOWARD A RESOLUTION. I KNOW THIS NEWS SHOULD BE MET WITH RELIEF AND SATISFACTION, BUT...
I'D BE LYING IF I SAID I DIDN'T FEEL AN URGING TUG OF DOUBT AND UNCERTAINTY.
I WONDER IF THIS IS HOW MY UNCLE HAS BEEN FEELING ABOUT THE WHOLE THING ALL ALONG...

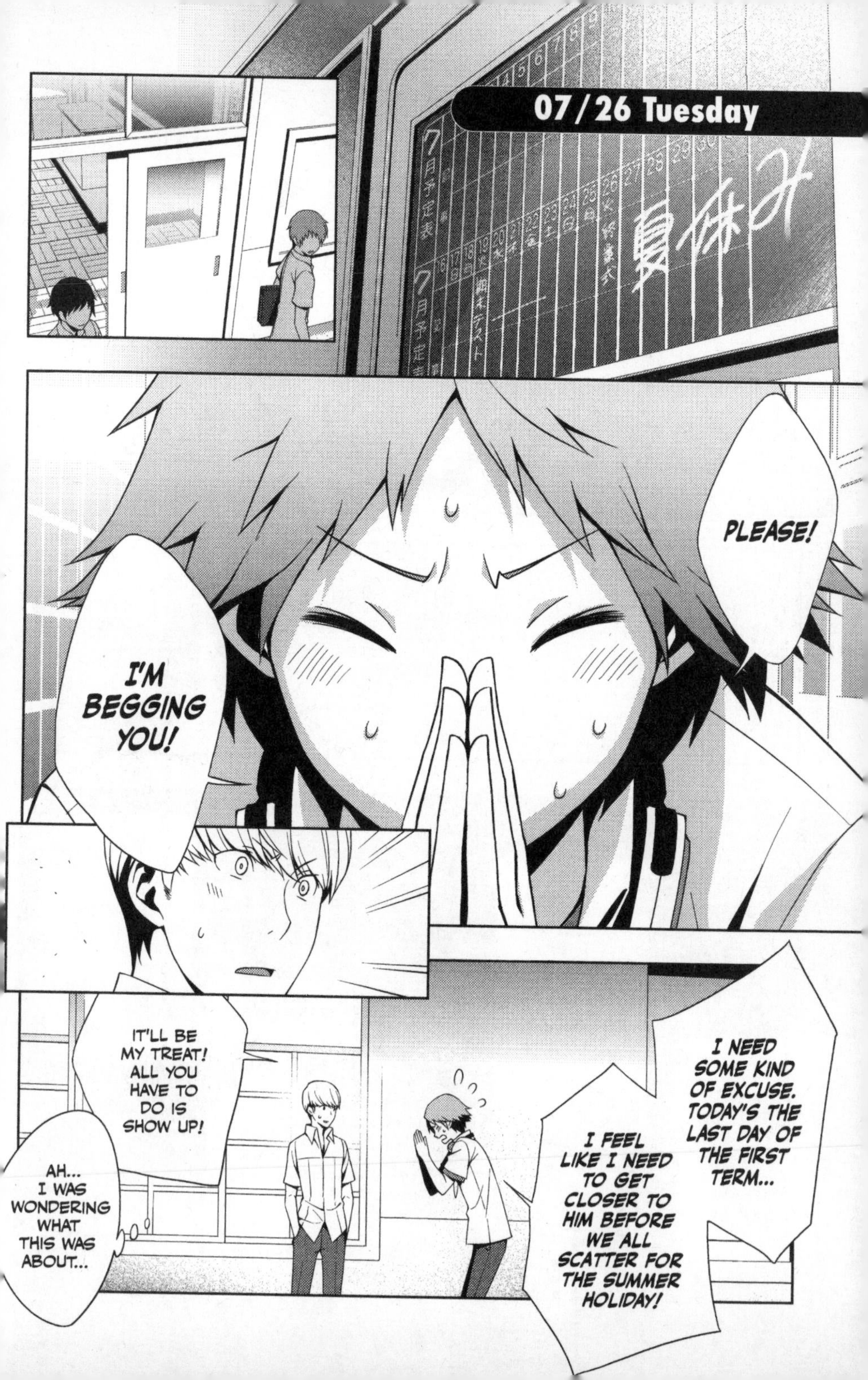
07/26 Tuesday
7月予定表
夏休み
PLEASE!
I'M BEGGING YOU!
I NEED SOME KIND OF EXCUSE. TODAY'S THE LAST DAY OF THE FIRST TERM...
I FEEL LIKE I NEED TO GET CLOSER TO HIM BEFORE WE ALL SCATTER FOR THE SUMMER HOLIDAY!
IT'LL BE MY TREAT! ALL YOU HAVE TO DO IS SHOW UP!
AH... I WAS WONDERING WHAT THIS WAS ABOUT...

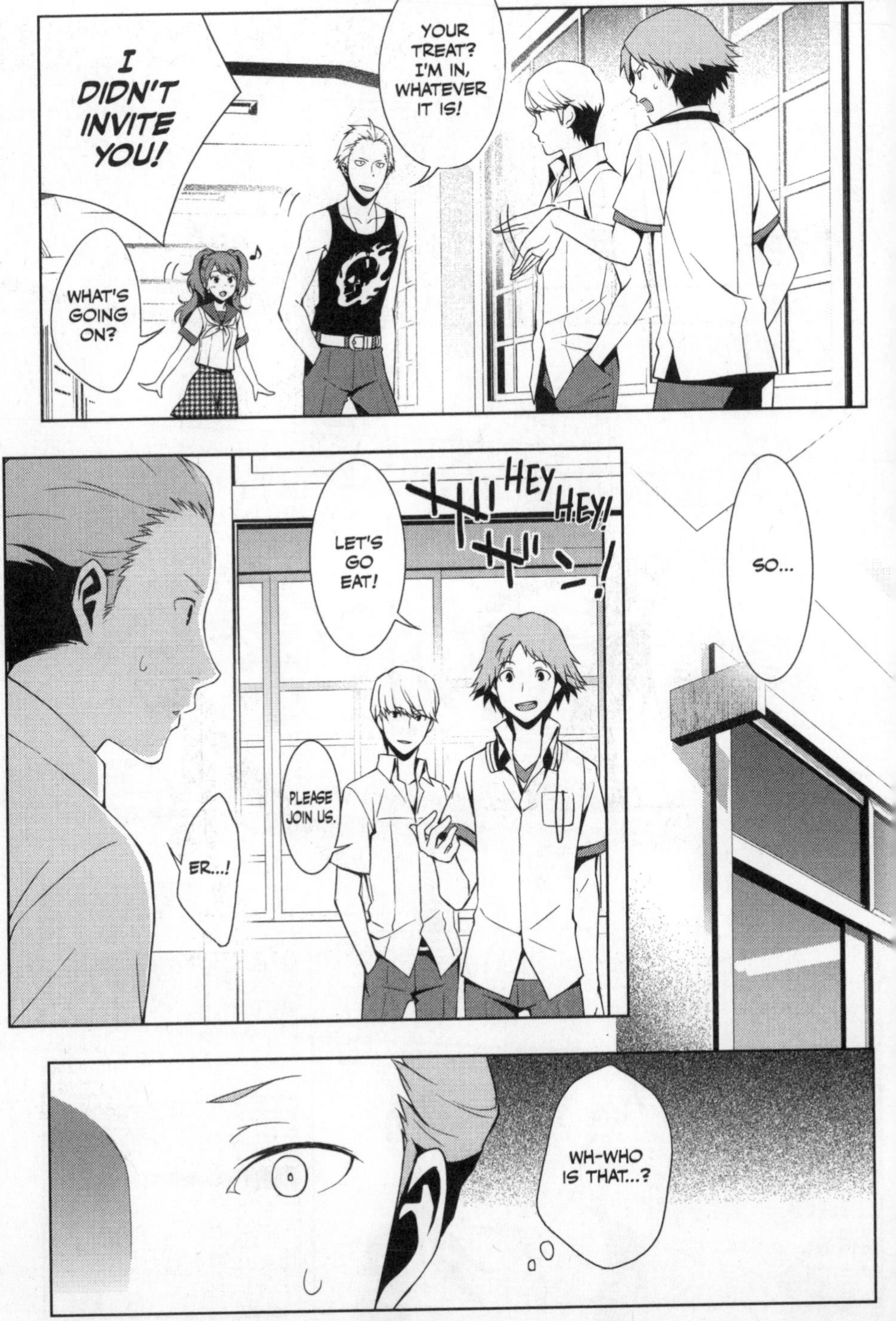
YOUR TREAT? I'M IN, WHATEVER IT IS!
I DIDN'T INVITE YOU!
WHAT'S GOING ON?
SO...
HEY HEY!
LET'S GO EAT!
PLEASE JOIN US.
ER...!
WH-WHO IS THAT...?

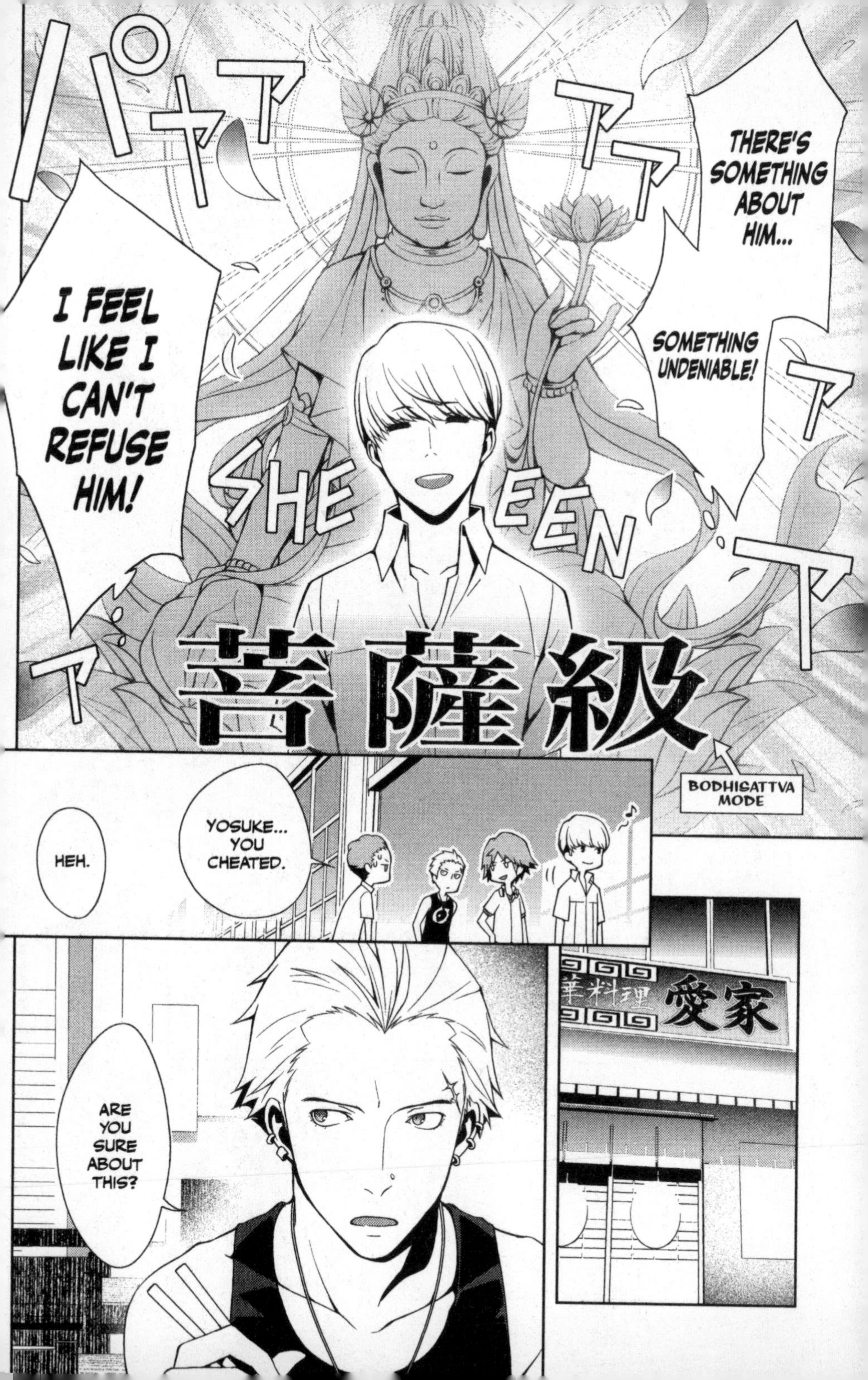
THERE'S SOMETHING ABOUT HIM...
SOMETHING UNDENIABLE!
パァァァァァ
I FEEL LIKE I CAN'T REFUSE HIM!
SHEEEN
菩薩級
BODHISATTVA MODE
YOSUKE... YOU CHEATED.
HEH.
華料理 愛家
ARE YOU SURE ABOUT THIS?

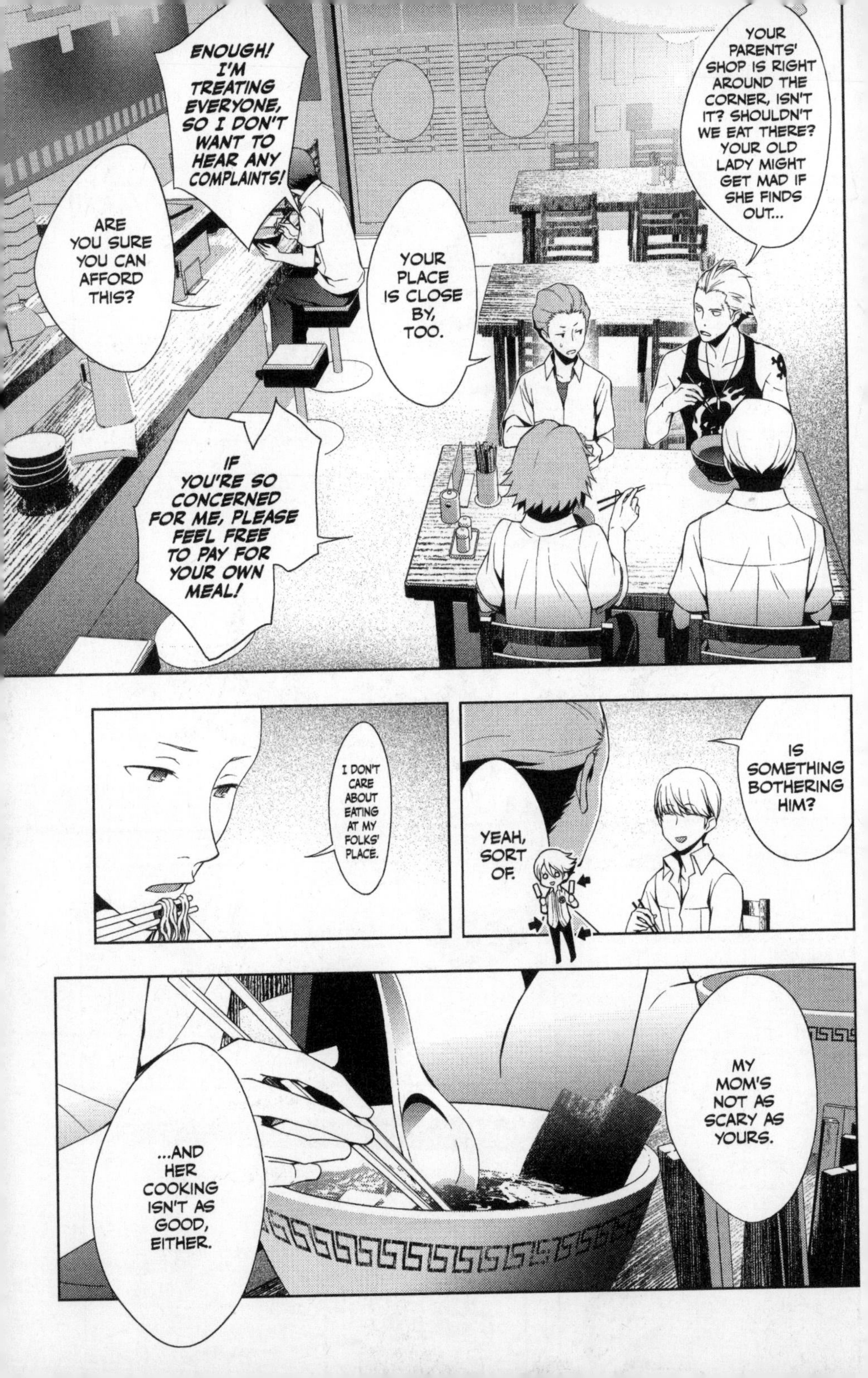
YOUR PARENTS' SHOP IS RIGHT AROUND THE CORNER, ISN'T IT? SHOULDN'T WE EAT THERE? YOUR OLD LADY MIGHT GET MAD IF SHE FINDS OUT...
YOUR PLACE IS CLOSE BY, TOO.
ENOUGH! I'M TREATING EVERYONE, SO I DON'T WANT TO HEAR ANY COMPLAINTS!
ARE YOU SURE YOU CAN AFFORD THIS?
IF YOU'RE SO CONCERNED FOR ME, PLEASE FEEL FREE TO PAY FOR YOUR OWN MEAL!
IS SOMETHING BOTHERING HIM?
YEAH, SORT OF.
I DON'T CARE ABOUT EATING AT MY FOLKS' PLACE.
MY MOM'S NOT AS SCARY AS YOURS.
...AND HER COOKING ISN'T AS GOOD, EITHER.

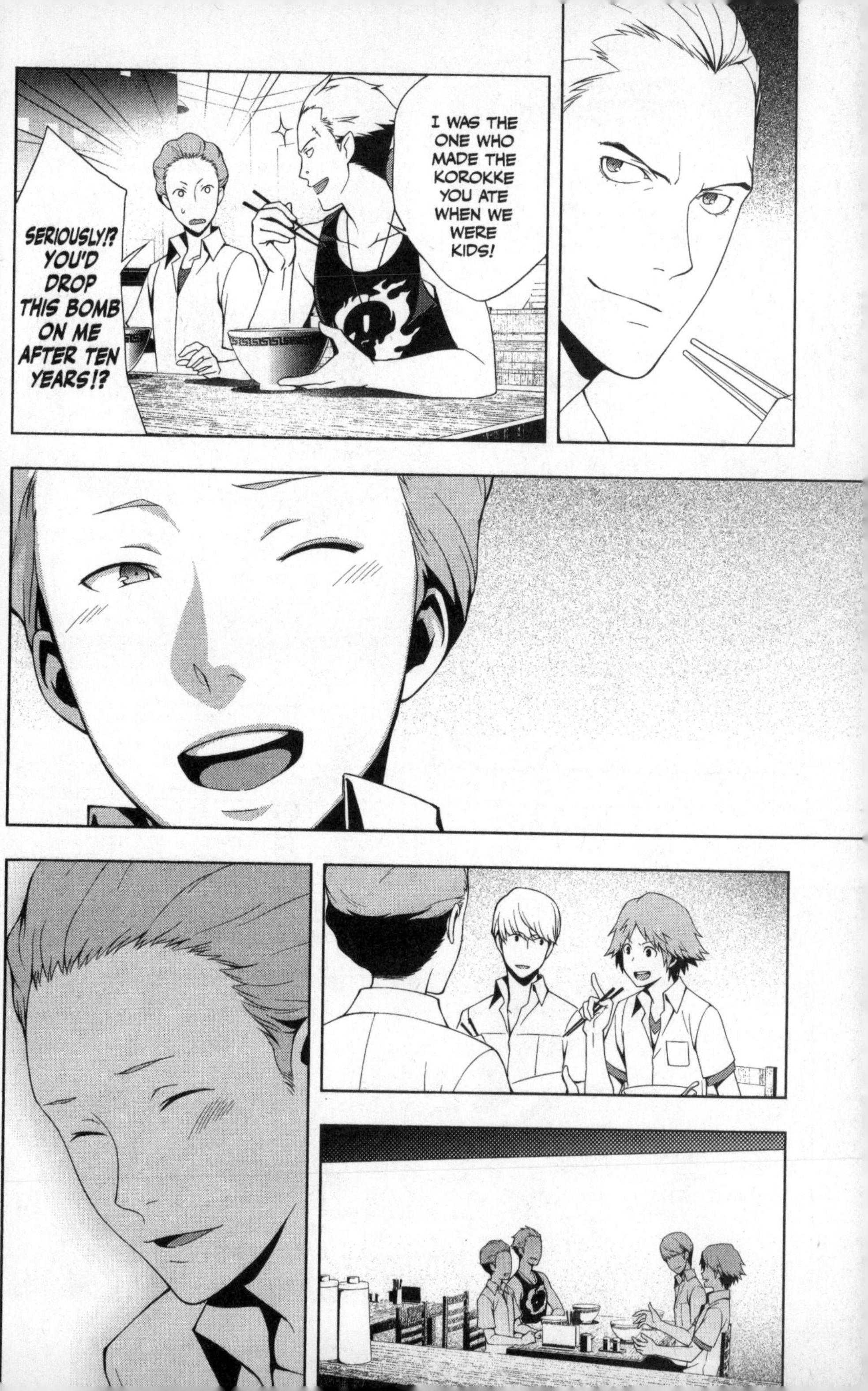
I WAS THE ONE WHO MADE THE KOROKKE YOU ATE WHEN WE WERE KIDS!
SERIOUSLY!? YOU'D DROP THIS BOMB ON ME AFTER TEN YEARS!?

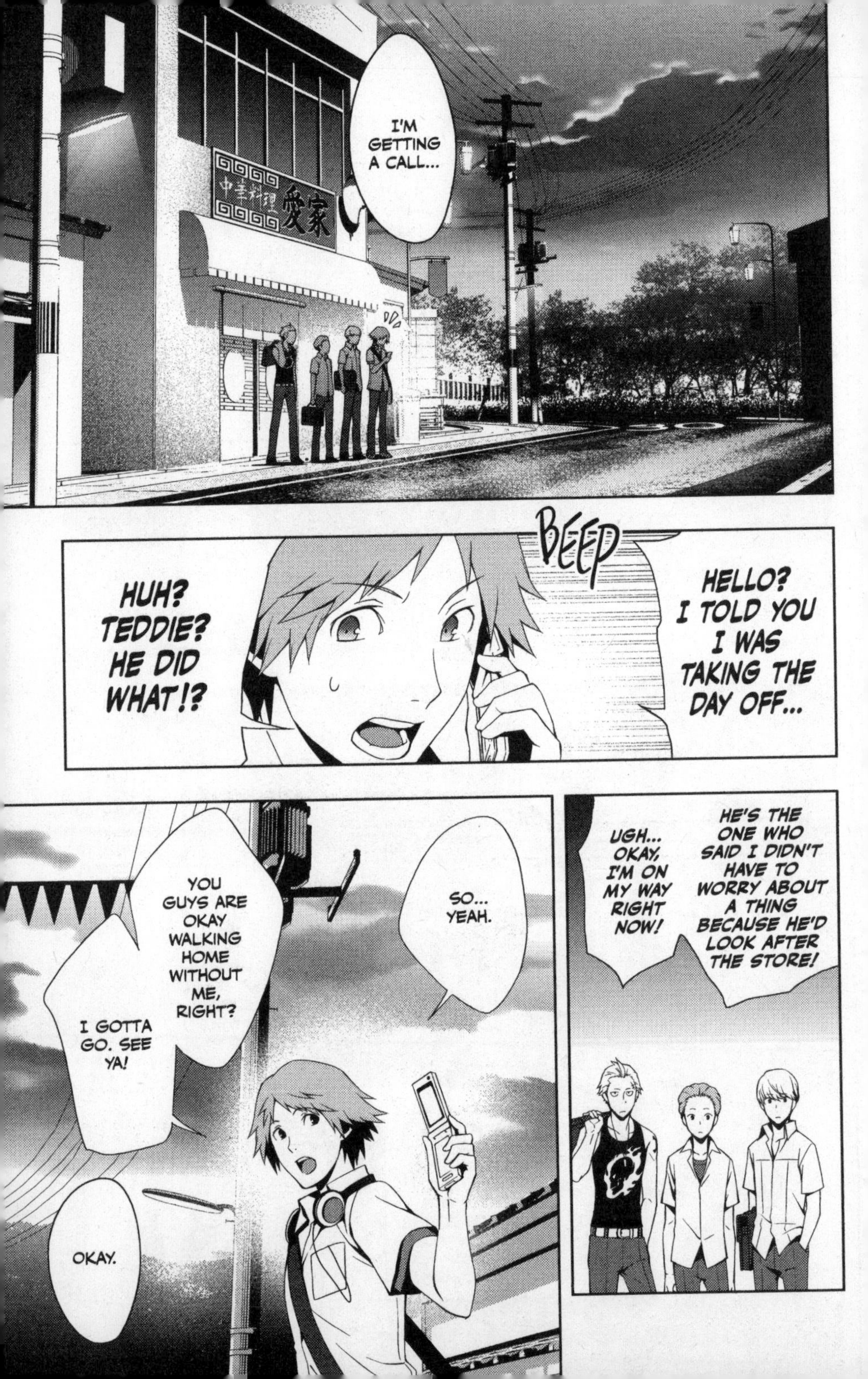
I'M GETTING A CALL...
中華料理 愛家
BEEP
HELLO? I TOLD YOU I WAS TAKING THE DAY OFF...
HUH? TEDDIE? HE DID WHAT!?
HE'S THE ONE WHO SAID I DIDN'T HAVE TO WORRY ABOUT A THING BECAUSE HE'D LOOK AFTER THE STORE!
UGH... OKAY, I'M ON MY WAY RIGHT NOW!
SO... YEAH.
YOU GUYS ARE OKAY WALKING HOME WITHOUT ME, RIGHT?
I GOTTA GO. SEE YA!
OKAY.

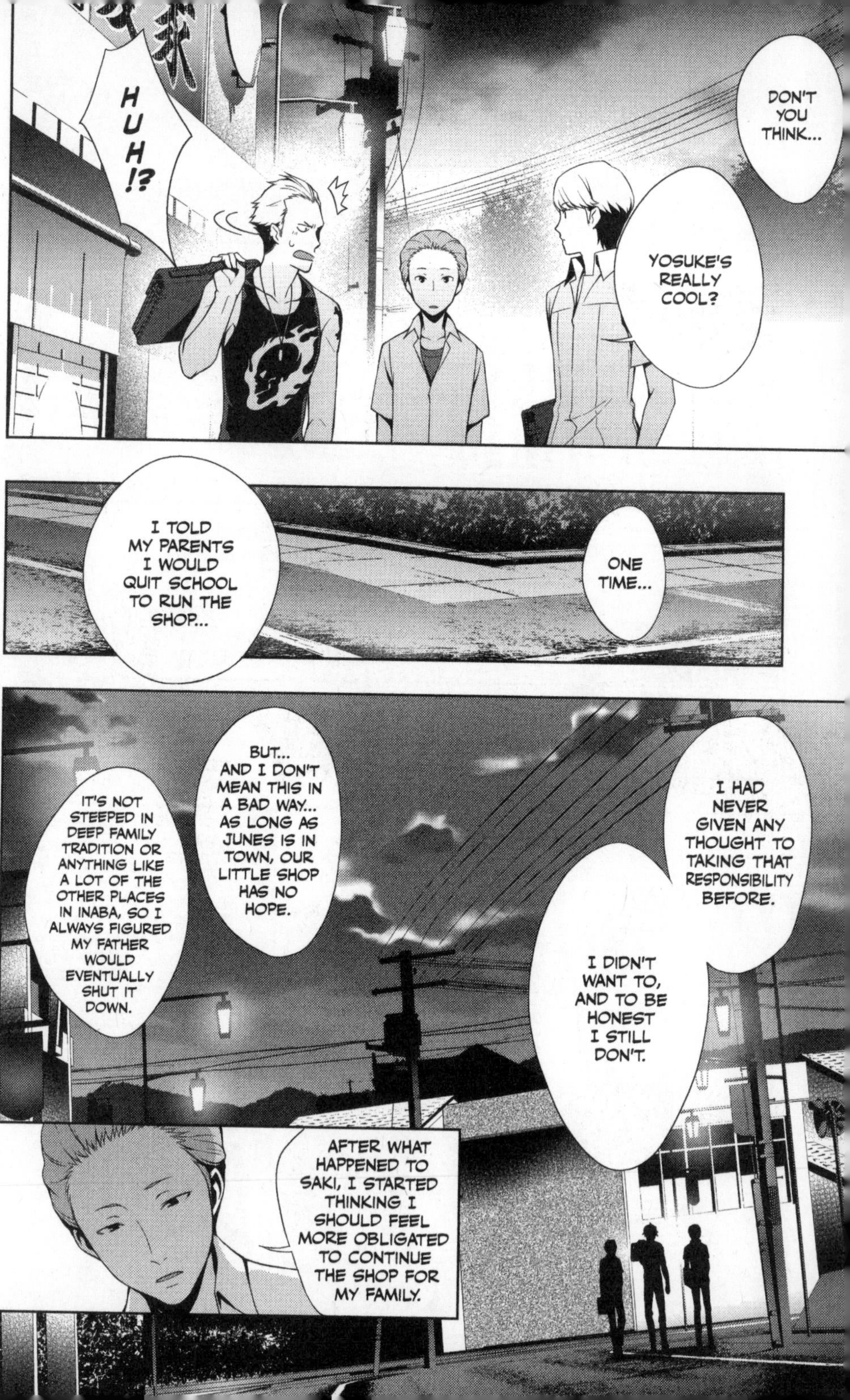
DON'T YOU THINK...
YOSUKE'S REALLY COOL?
HUH!?
ONE TIME...
I TOLD MY PARENTS I WOULD QUIT SCHOOL TO RUN THE SHOP...
I HAD NEVER GIVEN ANY THOUGHT TO TAKING THAT RESPONSIBILITY BEFORE.
I DIDN'T WANT TO, AND TO BE HONEST I STILL DON'T.
BUT... AND I DON'T MEAN THIS IN A BAD WAY... AS LONG AS JUNES IS IN TOWN, OUR LITTLE SHOP HAS NO HOPE.
IT'S NOT STEEPED IN DEEP FAMILY TRADITION OR ANYTHING LIKE A LOT OF THE OTHER PLACES IN INABA, SO I ALWAYS FIGURED MY FATHER WOULD EVENTUALLY SHUT IT DOWN.
AFTER WHAT HAPPENED TO SAKI, I STARTED THINKING I SHOULD FEEL MORE OBLIGATED TO CONTINUE THE SHOP FOR MY FAMILY.

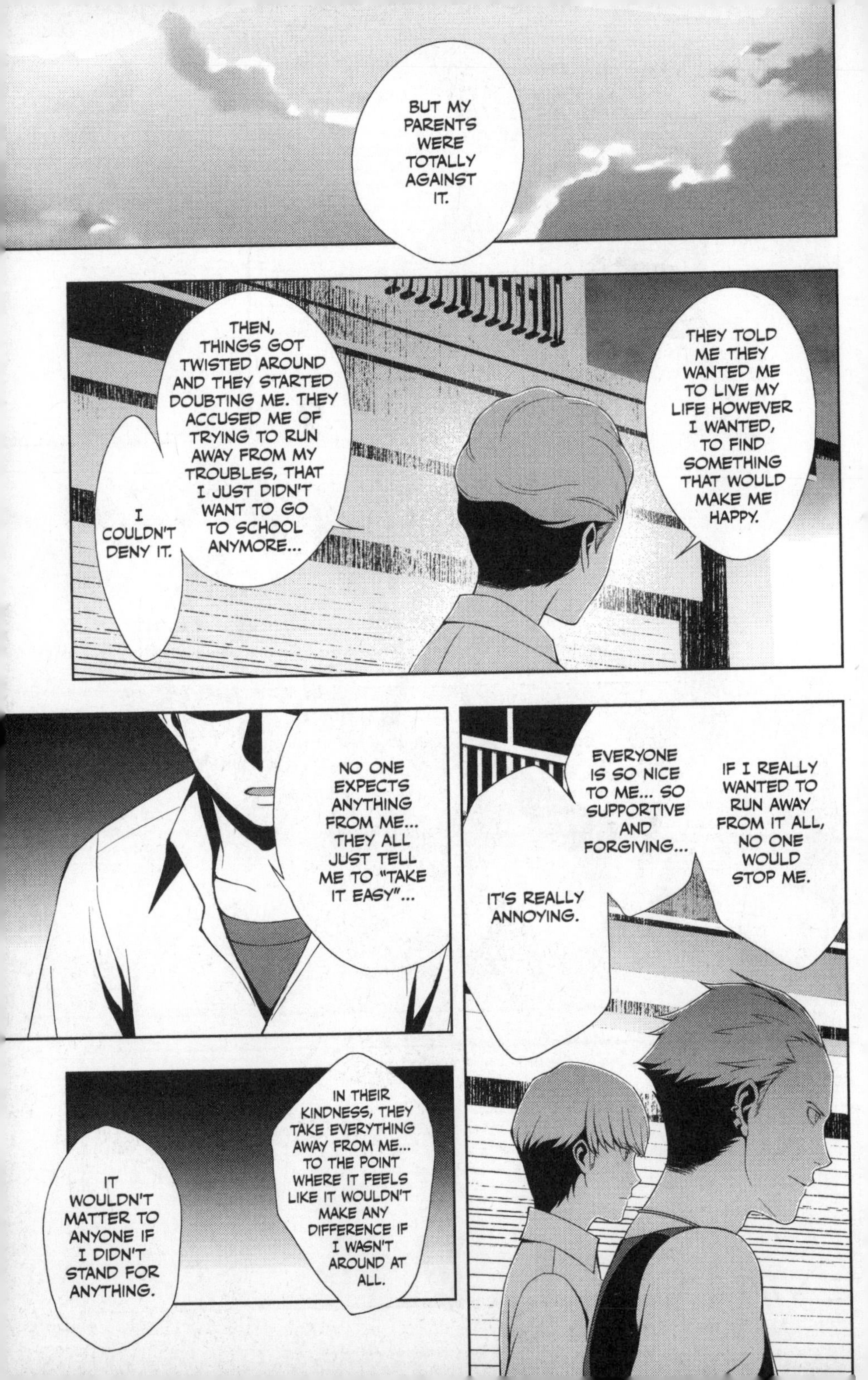
BUT MY PARENTS WERE TOTALLY AGAINST IT.
THEY TOLD ME THEY WANTED ME TO LIVE MY LIFE HOWEVER I WANTED, TO FIND SOMETHING THAT WOULD MAKE ME HAPPY.
THEN, THINGS GOT TWISTED AROUND AND THEY STARTED DOUBTING ME. THEY ACCUSED ME OF TRYING TO RUN AWAY FROM MY TROUBLES, THAT I JUST DIDN'T WANT TO GO TO SCHOOL ANYMORE...
I COULDN'T DENY IT.
IF I REALLY WANTED TO RUN AWAY FROM IT ALL, NO ONE WOULD STOP ME.
EVERYONE IS SO NICE TO ME... SO SUPPORTIVE AND FORGIVING...
IT'S REALLY ANNOYING.
NO ONE EXPECTS ANYTHING FROM ME... THEY ALL JUST TELL ME TO "TAKE IT EASY"...
IN THEIR KINDNESS, THEY TAKE EVERYTHING AWAY FROM ME... TO THE POINT WHERE IT FEELS LIKE IT WOULDN'T MAKE ANY DIFFERENCE IF I WASN'T AROUND AT ALL.
IT WOULDN'T MATTER TO ANYONE IF I DIDN'T STAND FOR ANYTHING.

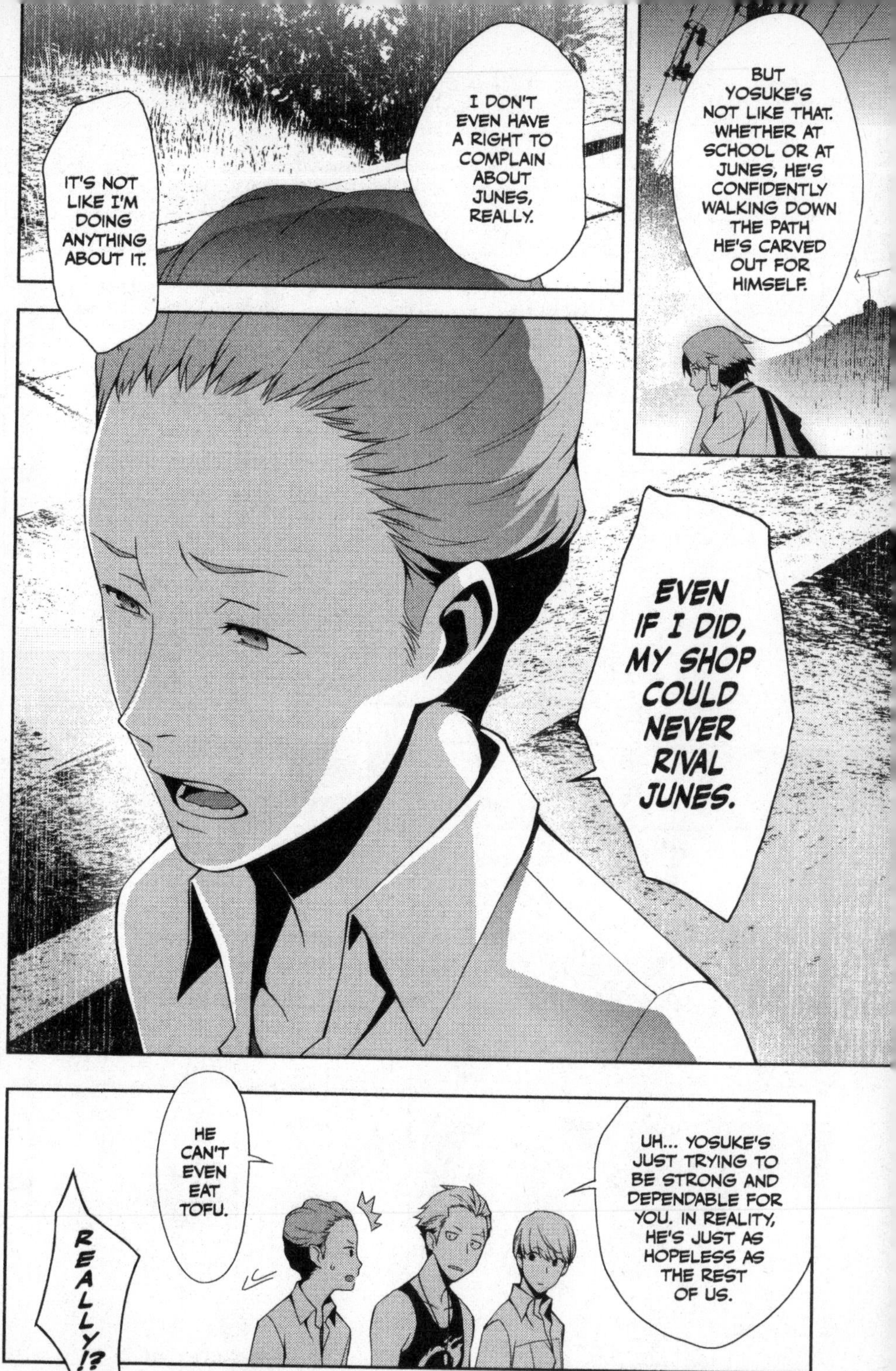
BUT YOSUKE'S NOT LIKE THAT. WHETHER AT SCHOOL OR AT JUNES, HE'S CONFIDENTLY WALKING DOWN THE PATH HE'S CARVED OUT FOR HIMSELF.
I DON'T EVEN HAVE A RIGHT TO COMPLAIN ABOUT JUNES, REALLY.
IT'S NOT LIKE I'M DOING ANYTHING ABOUT IT.
EVEN IF I DID, MY SHOP COULD NEVER RIVAL JUNES.
UH... YOSUKE'S JUST TRYING TO BE STRONG AND DEPENDABLE FOR YOU. IN REALITY, HE'S JUST AS HOPELESS AS THE REST OF US.
HE CAN'T EVEN EAT TOFU.
REALLY!?

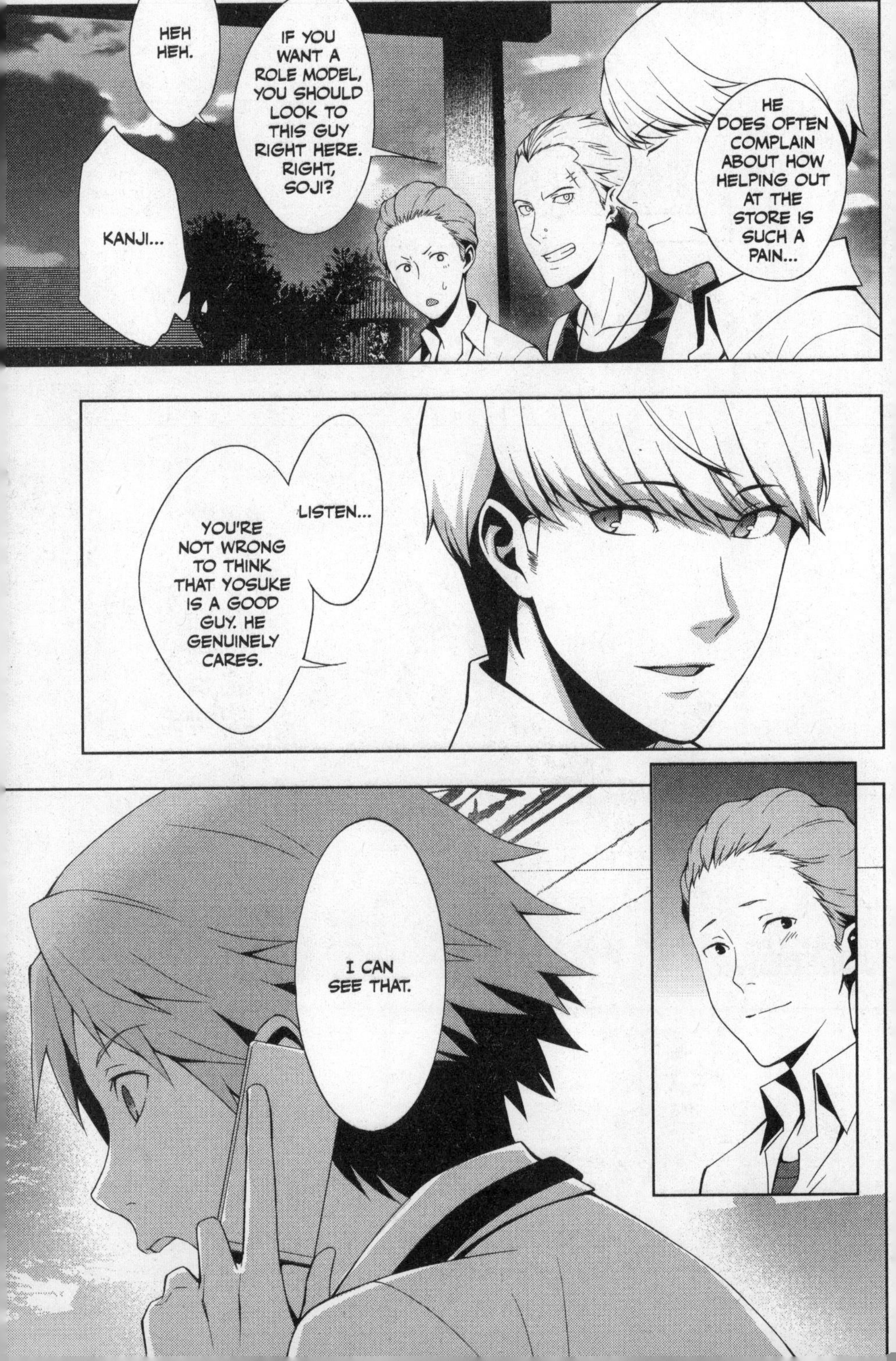
HE DOES OFTEN COMPLAIN ABOUT HOW HELPING OUT AT THE STORE IS SUCH A PAIN...
IF YOU WANT A ROLE MODEL, YOU SHOULD LOOK TO THIS GUY RIGHT HERE. RIGHT, SOJI?
HEH HEH.
KANJI...
LISTEN...
YOU'RE NOT WRONG TO THINK THAT YOSUKE IS A GOOD GUY. HE GENUINELY CARES.
I CAN SEE THAT.

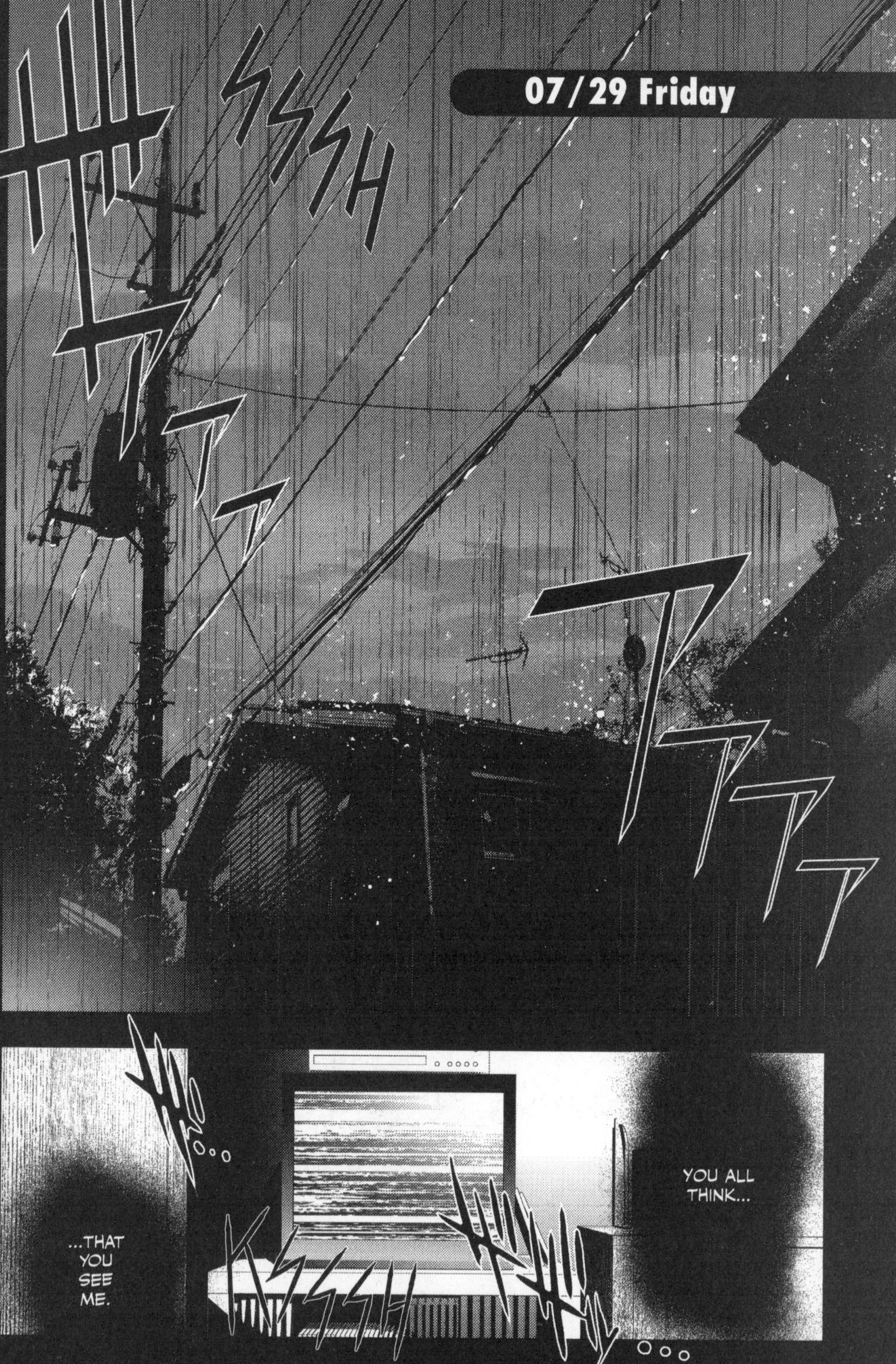
07/29 Friday
SSSH
YOU ALL THINK...
...THAT YOU SEE ME.
KSSSH

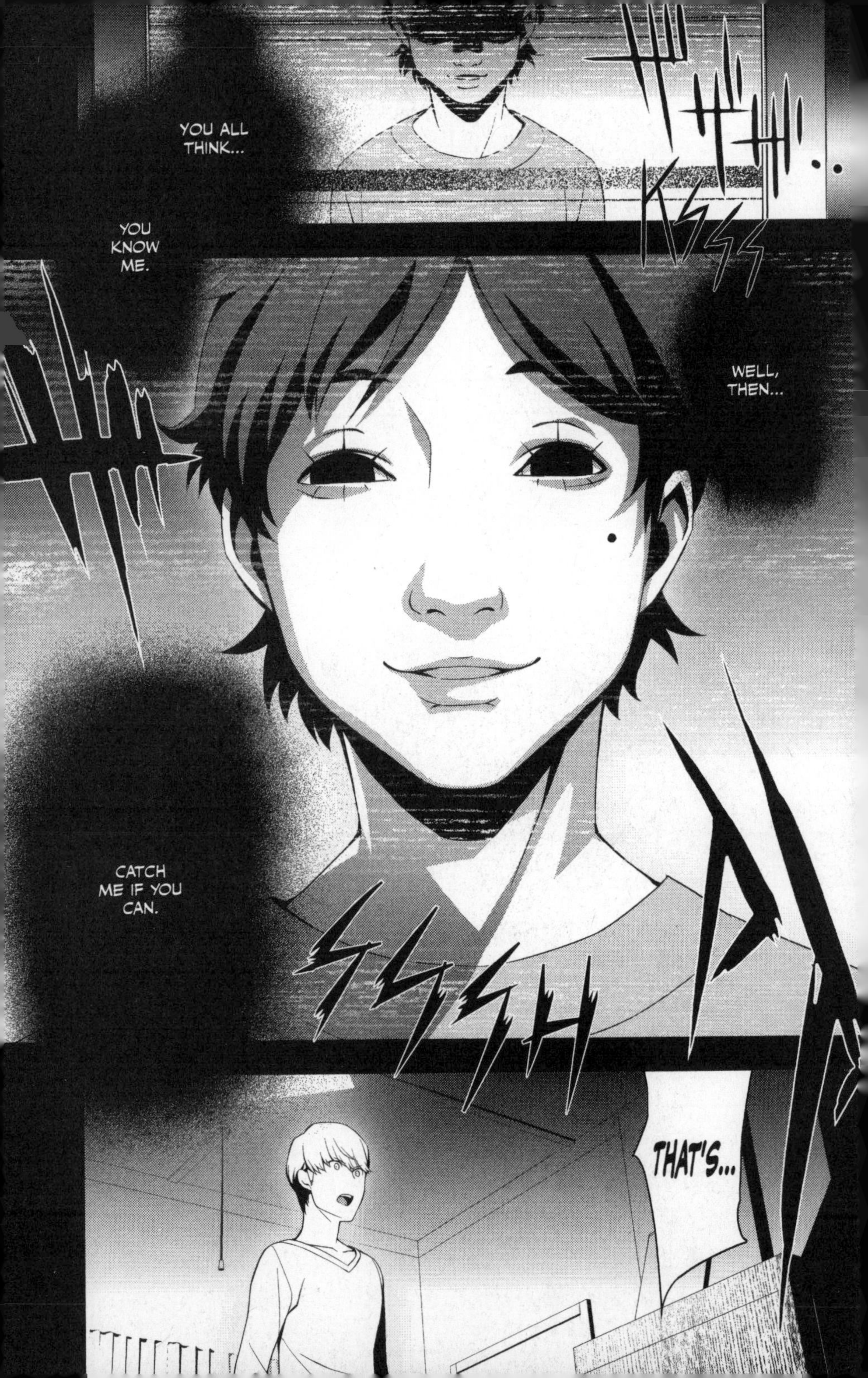
KSSS
YOU ALL THINK...
YOU KNOW ME.
WELL, THEN...
CATCH ME IF YOU CAN.
SSSH
THAT'S...

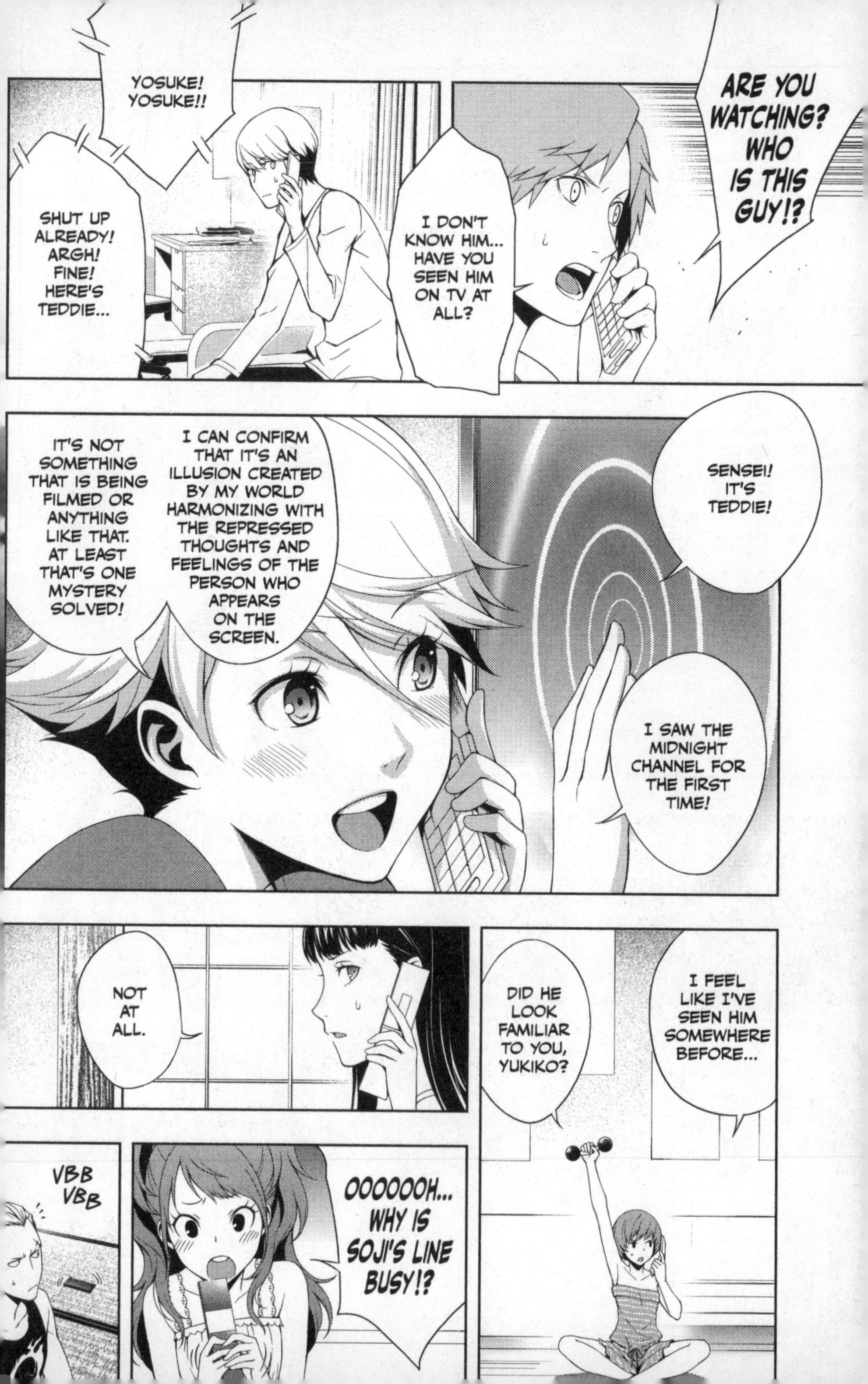
ARE YOU WATCHING? WHO IS THIS GUY!?
I DON'T KNOW HIM... HAVE YOU SEEN HIM ON TV AT ALL?
YOSUKE! YOSUKE!!
SHUT UP ALREADY! ARGH! FINE! HERE'S TEDDIE...
SENSEI! IT'S TEDDIE!
I SAW THE MIDNIGHT CHANNEL FOR THE FIRST TIME!
I CAN CONFIRM THAT IT'S AN ILLUSION CREATED BY MY WORLD HARMONIZING WITH THE REPRESSED THOUGHTS AND FEELINGS OF THE PERSON WHO APPEARS ON THE SCREEN.
IT'S NOT SOMETHING THAT IS BEING FILMED OR ANYTHING LIKE THAT. AT LEAST THAT'S ONE MYSTERY SOLVED!
I FEEL LIKE I'VE SEEN HIM SOMEWHERE BEFORE...
DID HE LOOK FAMILIAR TO YOU, YUKIKO?
NOT AT ALL.
OOOOOOH... WHY IS SOJI'S LINE BUSY!?
VBB VBB

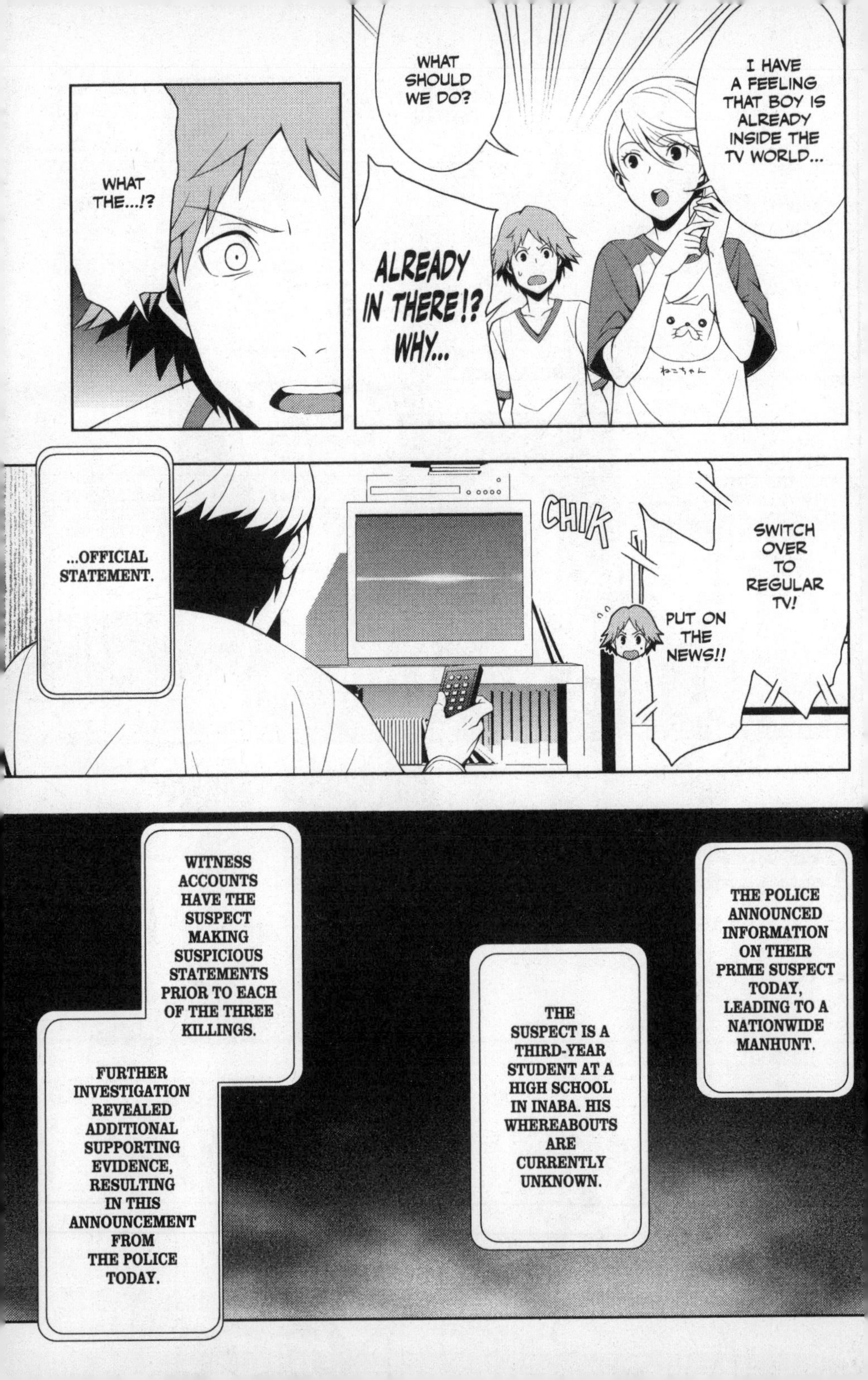
I HAVE A FEELING THAT BOY IS ALREADY INSIDE THE TV WORLD...
WHAT SHOULD WE DO?
ALREADY IN THERE!? WHY...
ねこちゃん
WHAT THE...!?
SWITCH OVER TO REGULAR TV!
PUT ON THE NEWS!!
CHIK
...OFFICIAL STATEMENT.
THE POLICE ANNOUNCED INFORMATION ON THEIR PRIME SUSPECT TODAY, LEADING TO A NATIONWIDE MANHUNT.
THE SUSPECT IS A THIRD-YEAR STUDENT AT A HIGH SCHOOL IN INABA. HIS WHEREABOUTS ARE CURRENTLY UNKNOWN.
WITNESS ACCOUNTS HAVE THE SUSPECT MAKING SUSPICIOUS STATEMENTS PRIOR TO EACH OF THE THREE KILLINGS.
FURTHER INVESTIGATION REVEALED ADDITIONAL SUPPORTING EVIDENCE, RESULTING IN THIS ANNOUNCEMENT FROM THE POLICE TODAY.

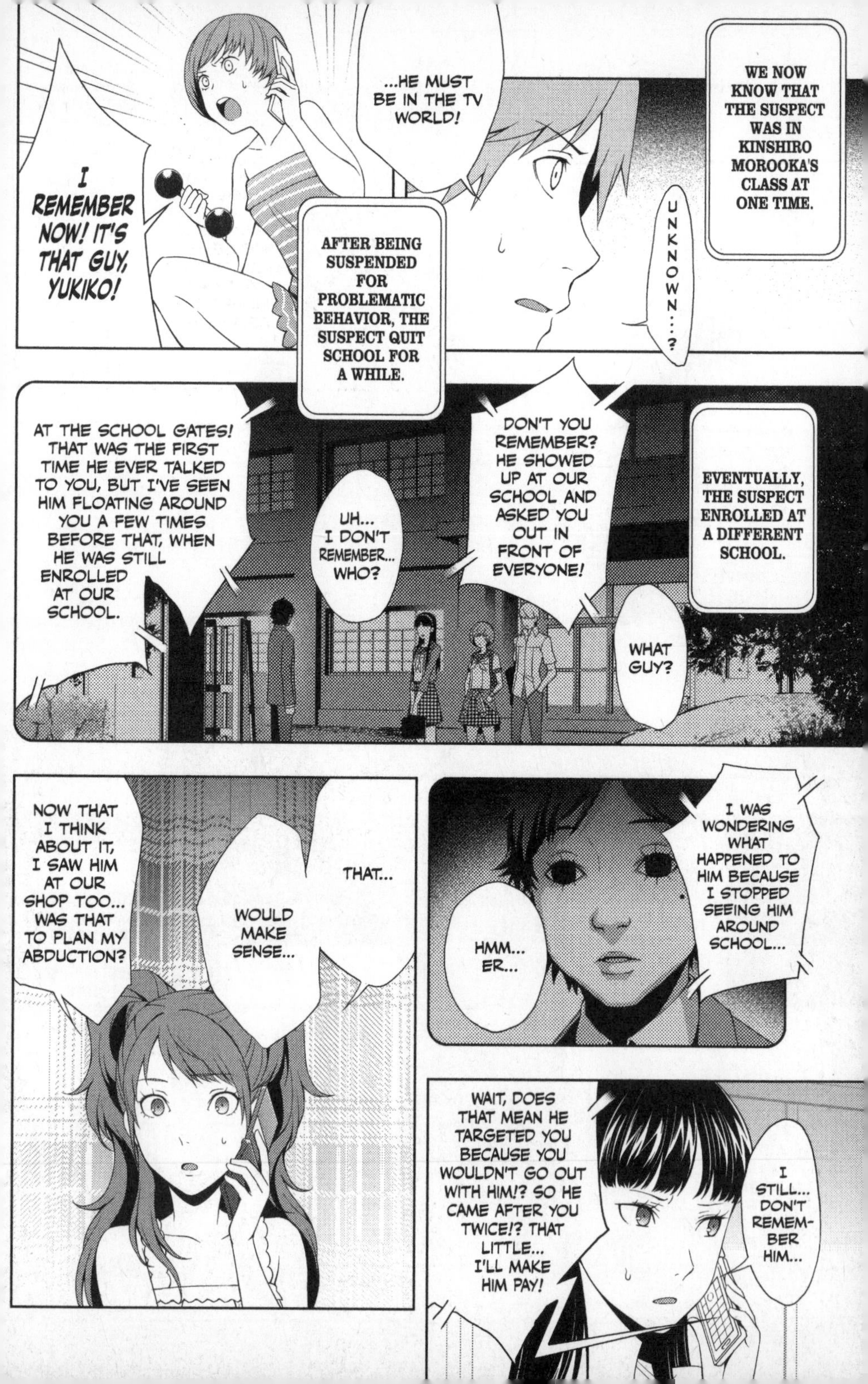
WE NOW KNOW THAT THE SUSPECT WAS IN KINSHIRO MOROOKA'S CLASS AT ONE TIME.
UNKNOWN...?
...HE MUST BE IN THE TV WORLD!
AFTER BEING SUSPENDED FOR PROBLEMATIC BEHAVIOR, THE SUSPECT QUIT SCHOOL FOR A WHILE.
I REMEMBER NOW! IT'S THAT GUY, YUKIKO!
EVENTUALLY, THE SUSPECT ENROLLED AT A DIFFERENT SCHOOL.
WHAT GUY?
DON'T YOU REMEMBER? HE SHOWED UP AT OUR SCHOOL AND ASKED YOU OUT IN FRONT OF EVERYONE!
UH... I DON'T REMEMBER... WHO?
AT THE SCHOOL GATES! THAT WAS THE FIRST TIME HE EVER TALKED TO YOU, BUT I'VE SEEN HIM FLOATING AROUND YOU A FEW TIMES BEFORE THAT, WHEN HE WAS STILL ENROLLED AT OUR SCHOOL.
I WAS WONDERING WHAT HAPPENED TO HIM BECAUSE I STOPPED SEEING HIM AROUND SCHOOL...
HMM... ER...
I STILL... DON'T REMEMBER HIM...
WAIT, DOES THAT MEAN HE TARGETED YOU BECAUSE YOU WOULDN'T GO OUT WITH HIM!? SO HE CAME AFTER YOU TWICE!? THAT LITTLE... I'LL MAKE HIM PAY!
THAT...
WOULD MAKE SENSE...
NOW THAT I THINK ABOUT IT, I SAW HIM AT OUR SHOP TOO... WAS THAT TO PLAN MY ABDUCTION?

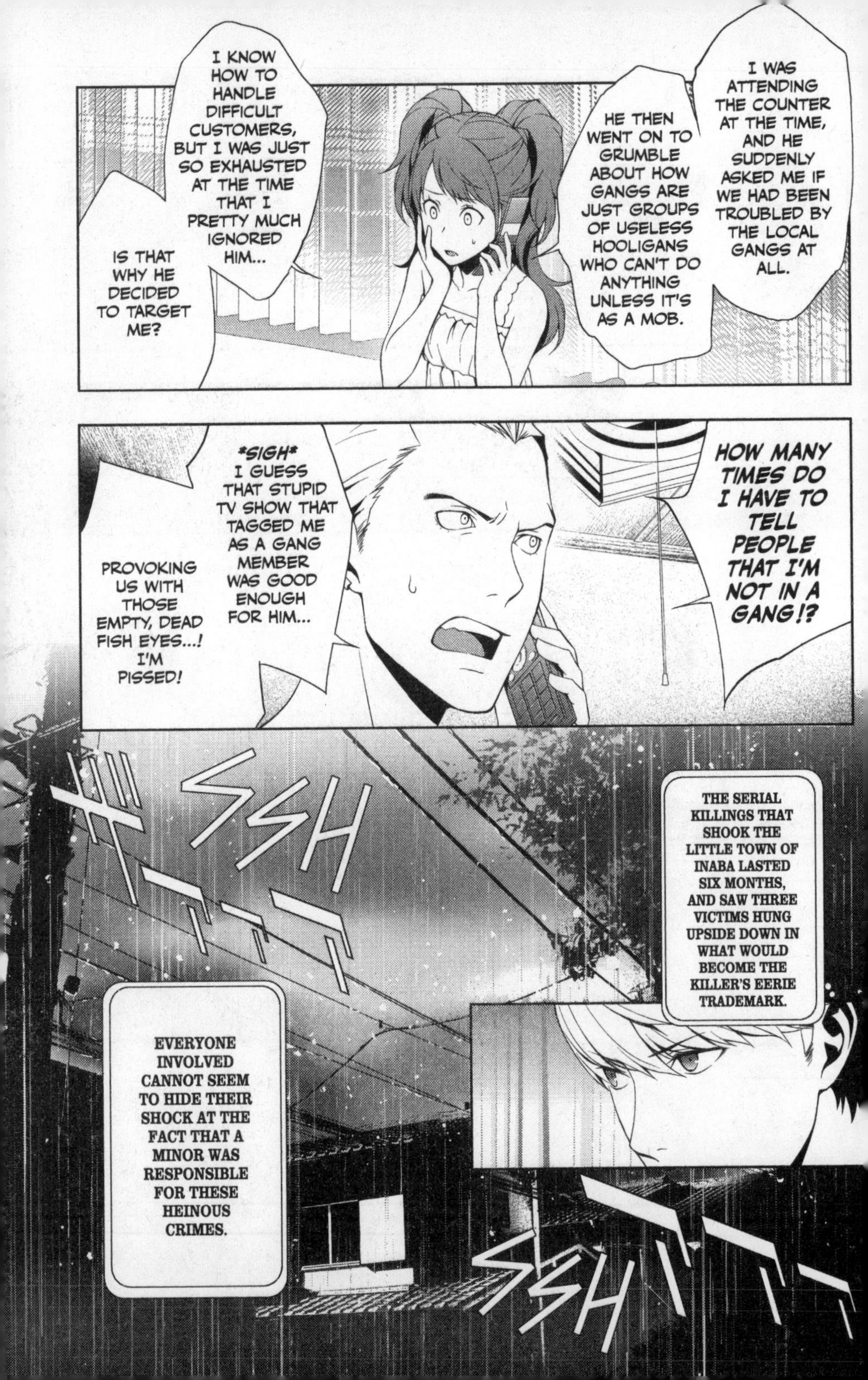
I WAS ATTENDING THE COUNTER AT THE TIME, AND HE SUDDENLY ASKED ME IF WE HAD BEEN TROUBLED BY THE LOCAL GANGS AT ALL.
HE THEN WENT ON TO GRUMBLE ABOUT HOW GANGS ARE JUST GROUPS OF USELESS HOOLIGANS WHO CAN'T DO ANYTHING UNLESS IT'S AS A MOB.
I KNOW HOW TO HANDLE DIFFICULT CUSTOMERS, BUT I WAS JUST SO EXHAUSTED AT THE TIME THAT I PRETTY MUCH IGNORED HIM...
IS THAT WHY HE DECIDED TO TARGET ME?
HOW MANY TIMES DO I HAVE TO TELL PEOPLE THAT I'M NOT IN A GANG!?
SIGH I GUESS THAT STUPID TV SHOW THAT TAGGED ME AS A GANG MEMBER WAS GOOD ENOUGH FOR HIM...
PROVOKING US WITH THOSE EMPTY, DEAD FISH EYES...! I'M PISSED!
SSH
THE SERIAL KILLINGS THAT SHOOK THE LITTLE TOWN OF INABA LASTED SIX MONTHS, AND SAW THREE VICTIMS HUNG UPSIDE DOWN IN WHAT WOULD BECOME THE KILLER'S EERIE TRADEMARK.
EVERYONE INVOLVED CANNOT SEEM TO HIDE THEIR SHOCK AT THE FACT THAT A MINOR WAS RESPONSIBLE FOR THESE HEINOUS CRIMES.
SSH

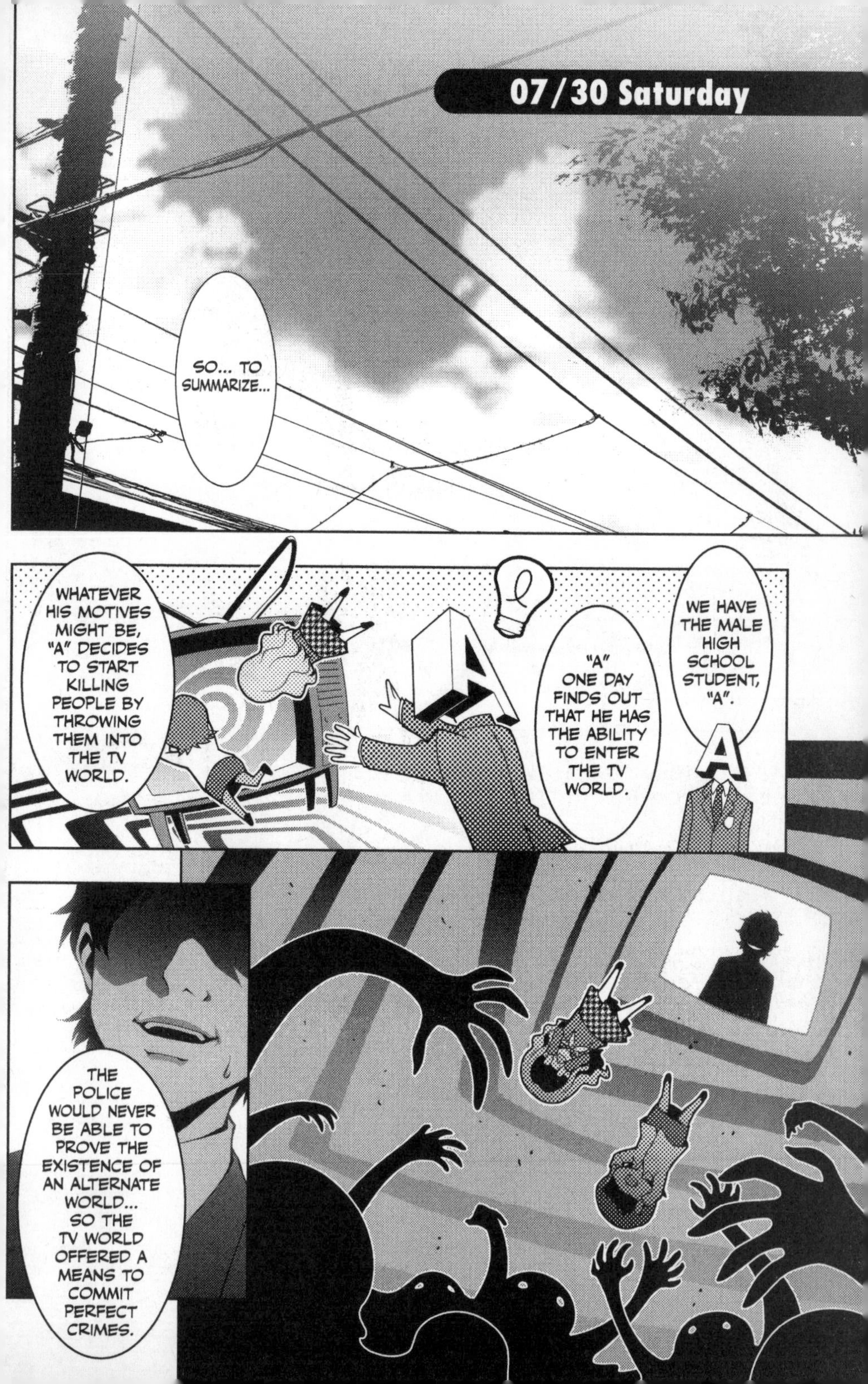
07/30 Saturday
SO... TO SUMMARIZE...
WE HAVE THE MALE HIGH SCHOOL STUDENT, "A".
A
"A" ONE DAY FINDS OUT THAT HE HAS THE ABILITY TO ENTER THE TV WORLD.
A
WHATEVER HIS MOTIVES MIGHT BE, "A" DECIDES TO START KILLING PEOPLE BY THROWING THEM INTO THE TV WORLD.
THE POLICE WOULD NEVER BE ABLE TO PROVE THE EXISTENCE OF AN ALTERNATE WORLD... SO THE TV WORLD OFFERED A MEANS TO COMMIT PERFECT CRIMES.

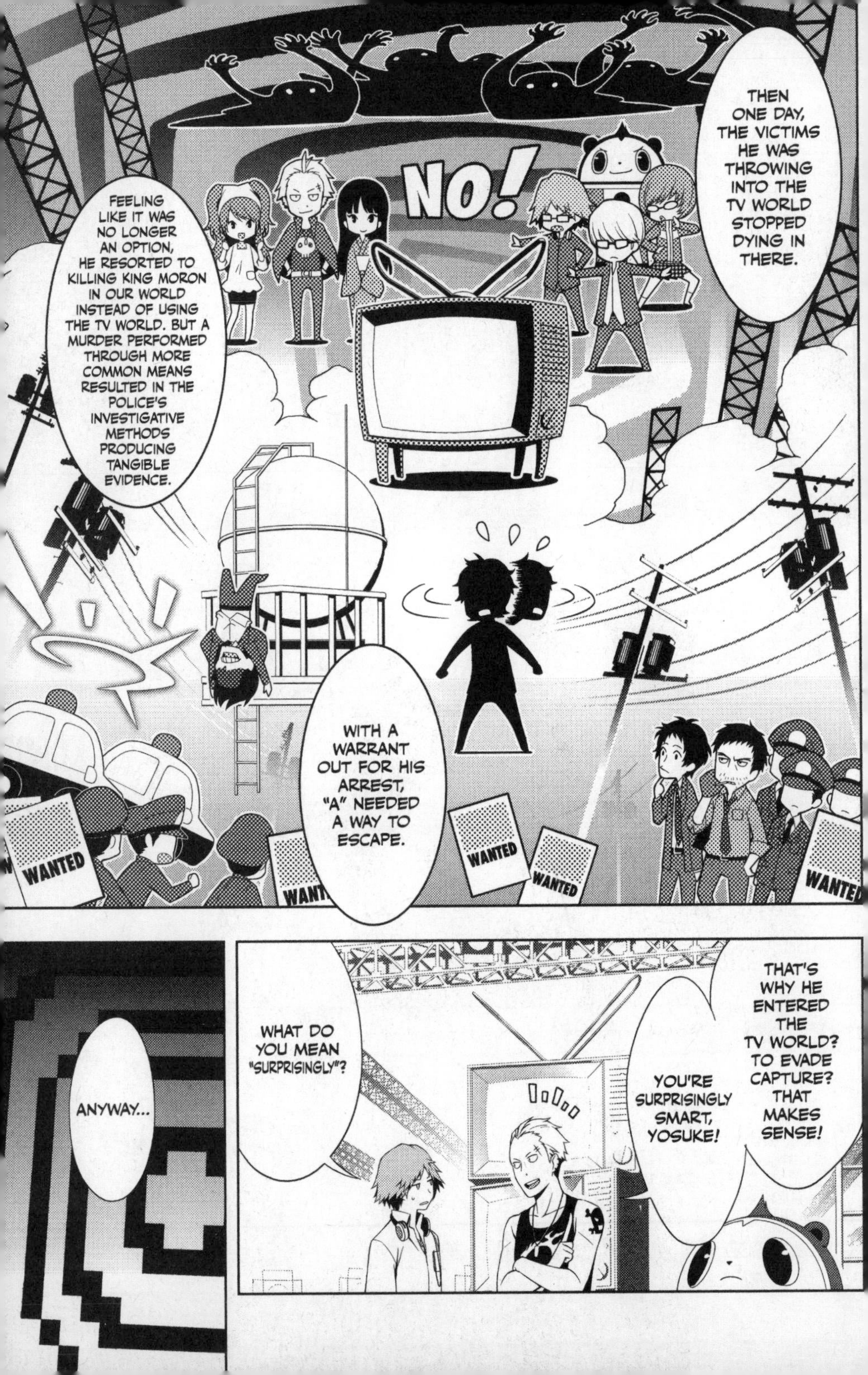
THEN ONE DAY, THE VICTIMS HE WAS THROWING INTO THE TV WORLD STOPPED DYING IN THERE.
NO!
FEELING LIKE IT WAS NO LONGER AN OPTION, HE RESORTED TO KILLING KING MORON IN OUR WORLD INSTEAD OF USING THE TV WORLD. BUT A MURDER PERFORMED THROUGH MORE COMMON MEANS RESULTED IN THE POLICE'S INVESTIGATIVE METHODS PRODUCING TANGIBLE EVIDENCE.
WITH A WARRANT OUT FOR HIS ARREST, "A" NEEDED A WAY TO ESCAPE.
WANTED
WANTED
WANTED
WANTED
THAT'S WHY HE ENTERED THE TV WORLD? TO EVADE CAPTURE? THAT MAKES SENSE!
YOU'RE SURPRISINGLY SMART, YOSUKE!
WHAT DO YOU MEAN "SURPRISINGLY"?
ANYWAY...

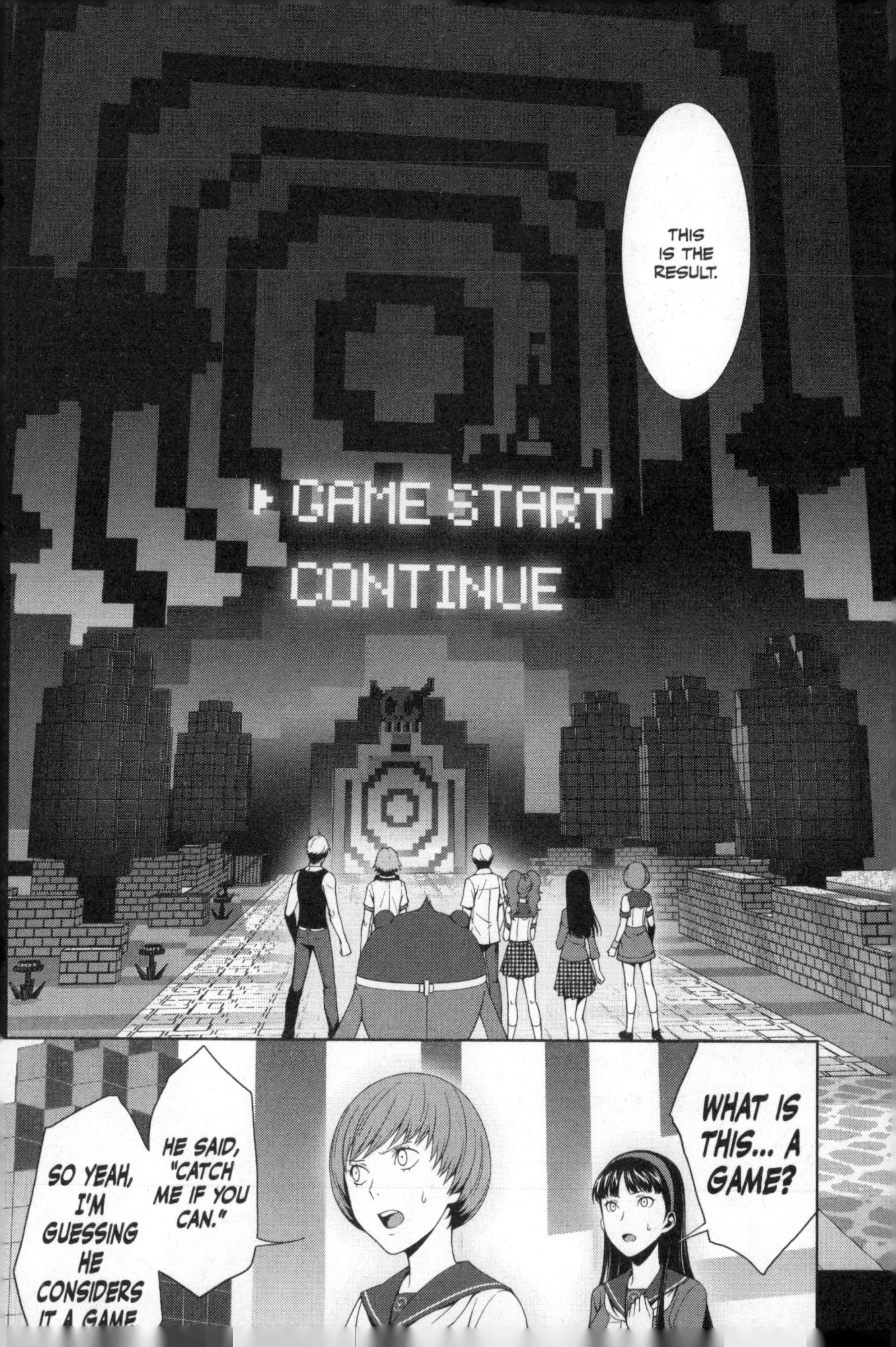
THIS IS THE RESULT.
▶ GAME START
CONTINUE
WHAT IS THIS... A GAME?
HE SAID, "CATCH ME IF YOU CAN."
SO YEAH, I'M GUESSING HE CONSIDERS IT A GAME.

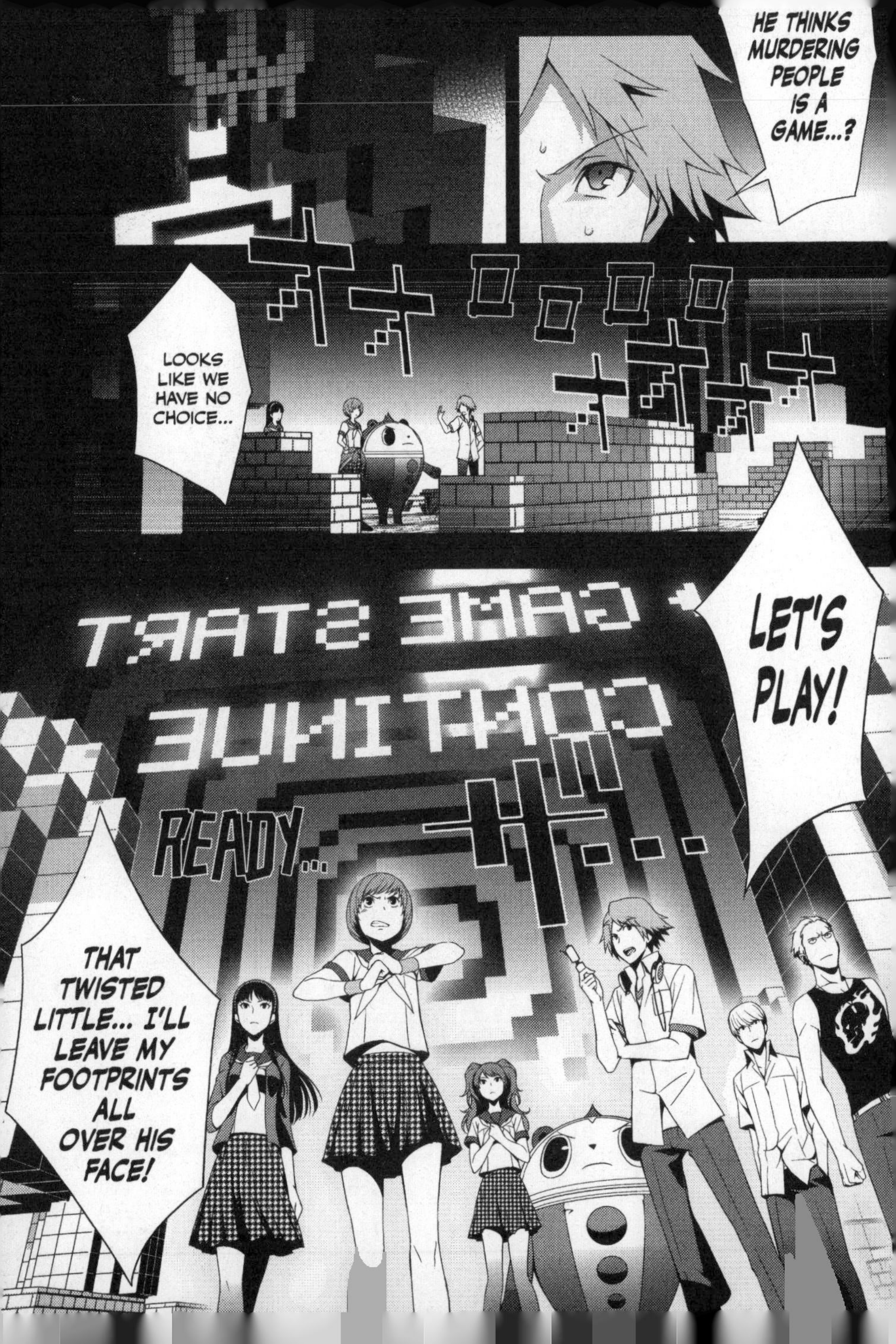
HE THINKS MURDERING PEOPLE IS A GAME...?
LOOKS LIKE WE HAVE NO CHOICE...
LET'S PLAY!
GAME START
CONTINUE
READY...
THAT TWISTED LITTLE... I'LL LEAVE MY FOOTPRINTS ALL OVER HIS FACE!

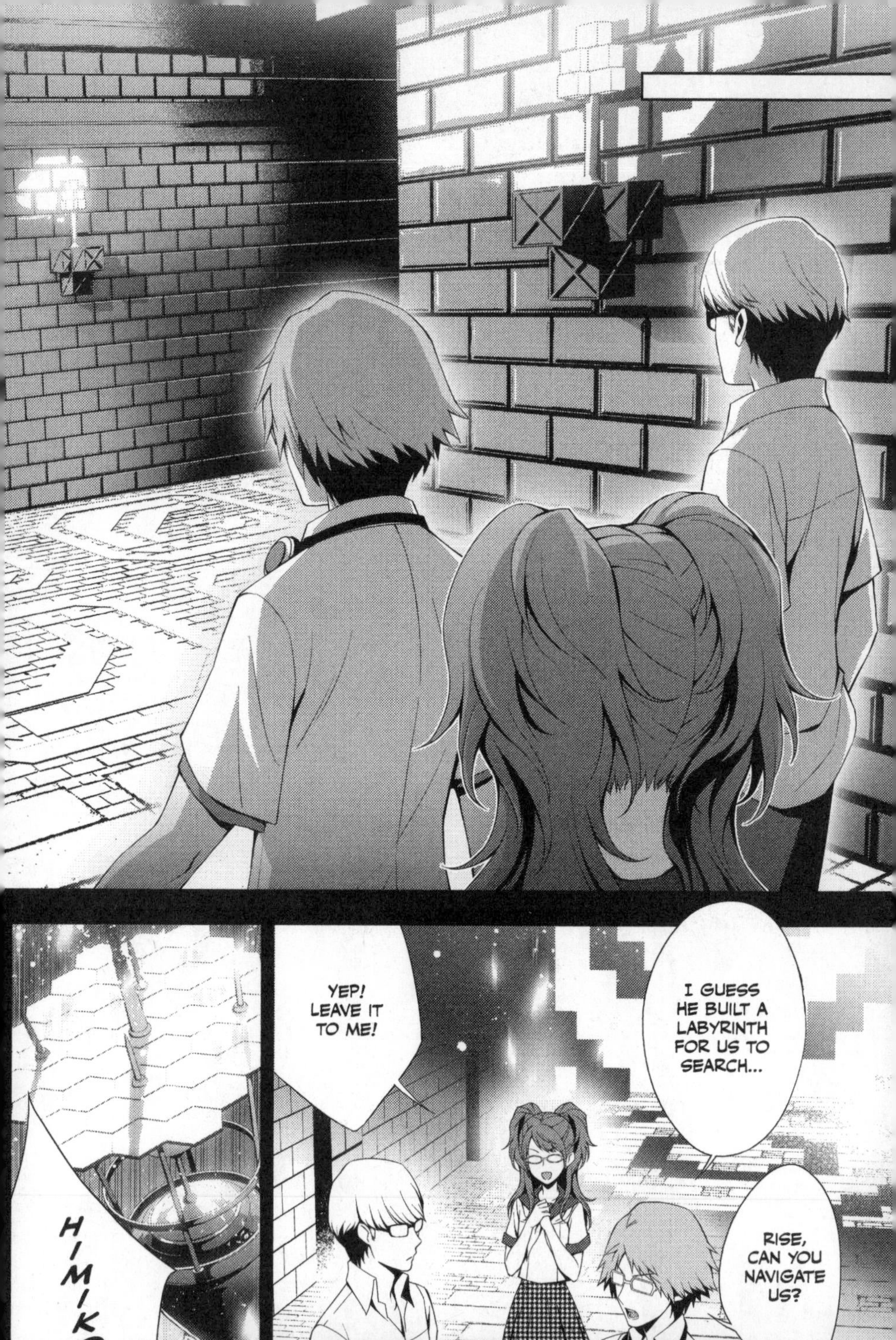
I GUESS HE BUILT A LABYRINTH FOR US TO SEARCH...
RISE, CAN YOU NAVIGATE US?
YEP! LEAVE IT TO ME!
HIMIKO

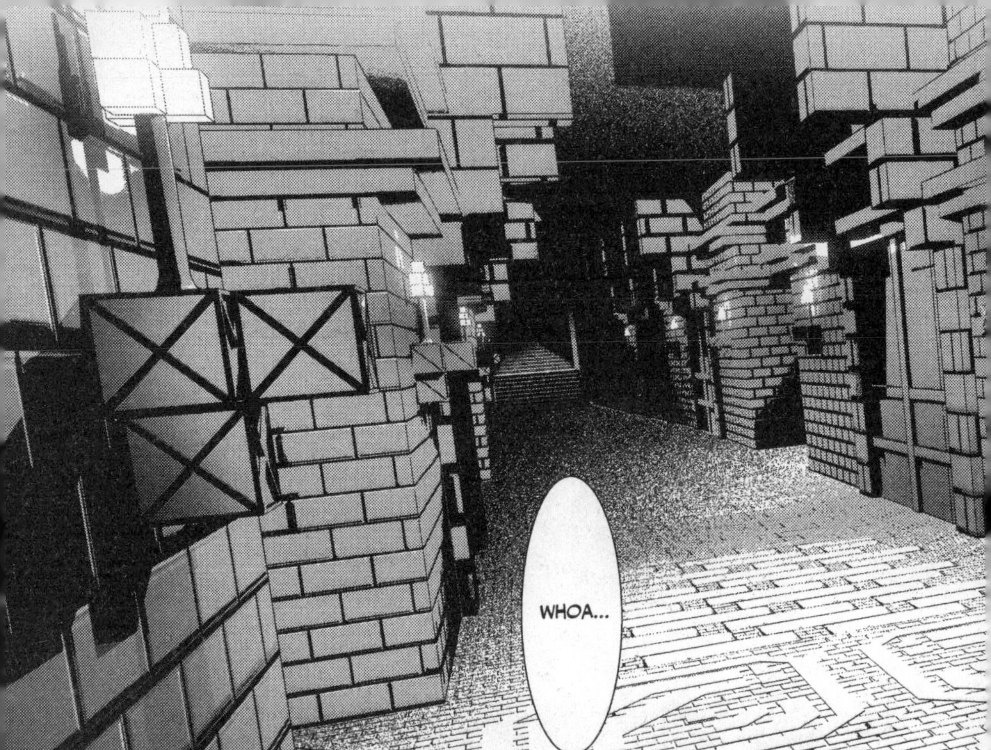
WHOA...

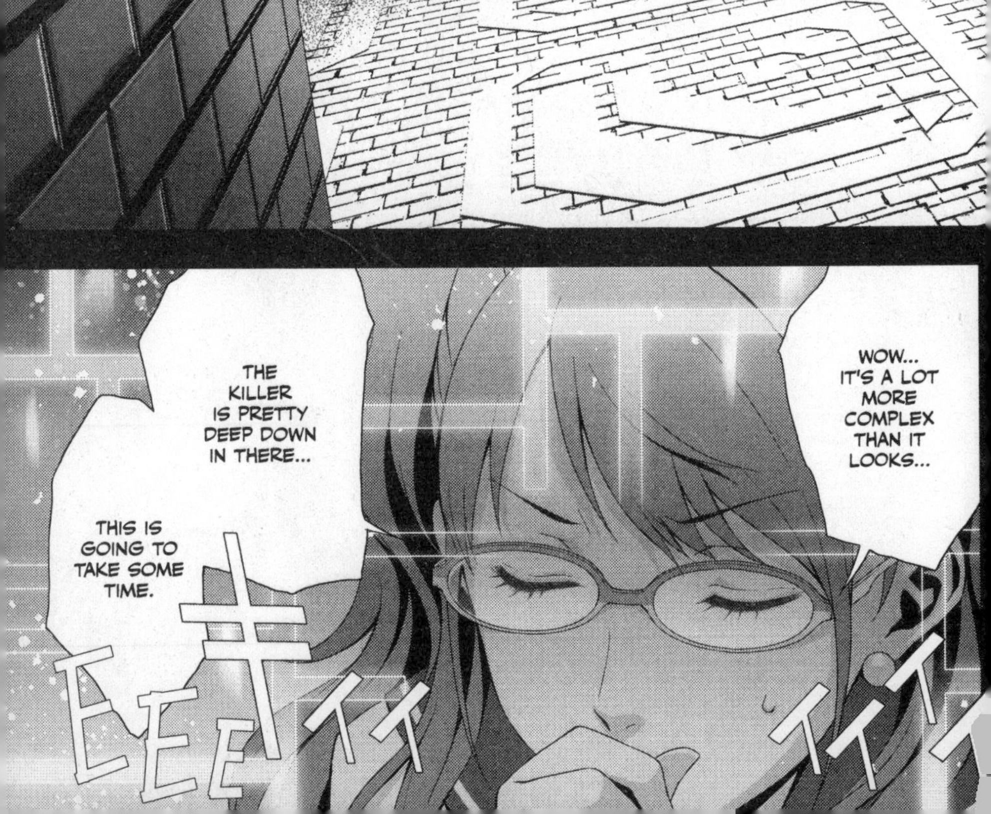
WOW... IT'S A LOT MORE COMPLEX THAN IT LOOKS...
THE KILLER IS PRETTY DEEP DOWN IN THERE...
THIS IS GOING TO TAKE SOME TIME.

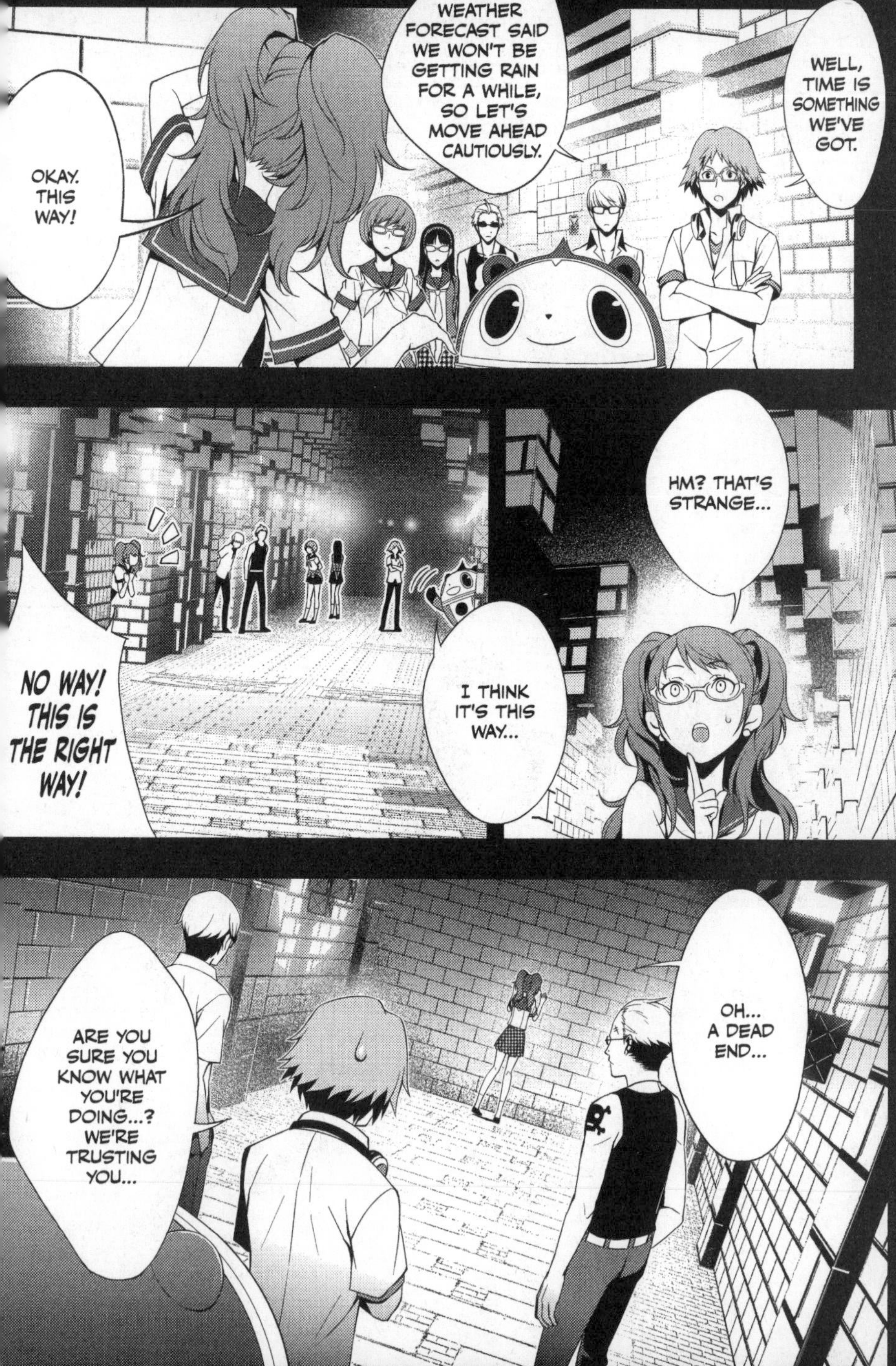
WELL, TIME IS SOMETHING WE'VE GOT.
THE WEATHER FORECAST SAID WE WON'T BE GETTING RAIN FOR A WHILE, SO LET'S MOVE AHEAD CAUTIOUSLY.
OKAY. THIS WAY!
HM? THAT'S STRANGE...
I THINK IT'S THIS WAY...
NO WAY! THIS IS THE RIGHT WAY!
OH... A DEAD END...
ARE YOU SURE YOU KNOW WHAT YOU'RE DOING...? WE'RE TRUSTING YOU...

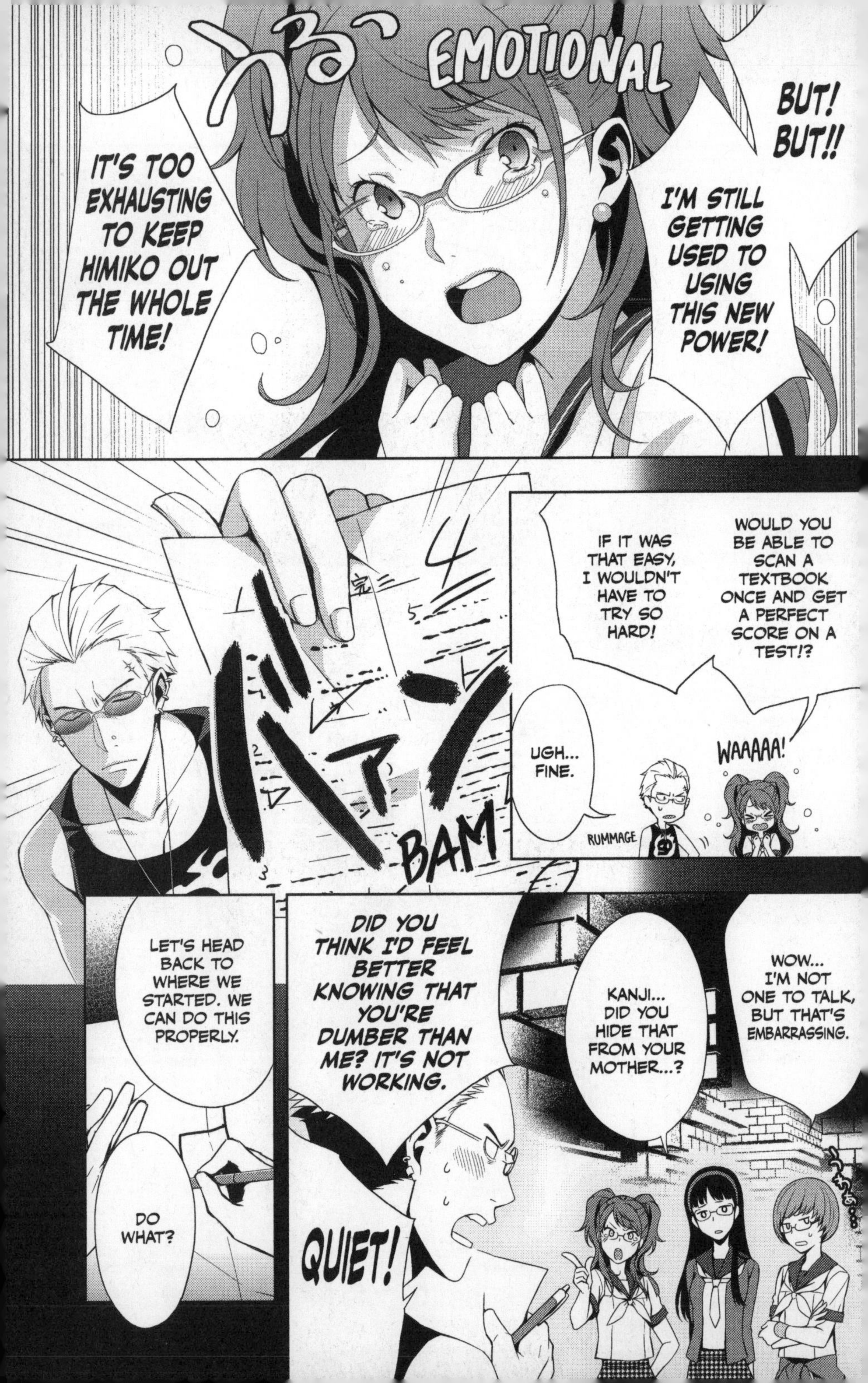
BUT! BUT!!
I'M STILL GETTING USED TO USING THIS NEW POWER!
EMOTIONAL
IT'S TOO EXHAUSTING TO KEEP HIMIKO OUT THE WHOLE TIME!
WOULD YOU BE ABLE TO SCAN A TEXTBOOK ONCE AND GET A PERFECT SCORE ON A TEST!?
IF IT WAS THAT EASY, I WOULDN'T HAVE TO TRY SO HARD!
WAAAAA!
UGH... FINE.
RUMMAGE
BAM
WOW... I'M NOT ONE TO TALK, BUT THAT'S EMBARRASSING.
KANJI... DID YOU HIDE THAT FROM YOUR MOTHER...?
DID YOU THINK I'D FEEL BETTER KNOWING THAT YOU'RE DUMBER THAN ME? IT'S NOT WORKING.
QUIET!
LET'S HEAD BACK TO WHERE WE STARTED. WE CAN DO THIS PROPERLY.
DO WHAT?

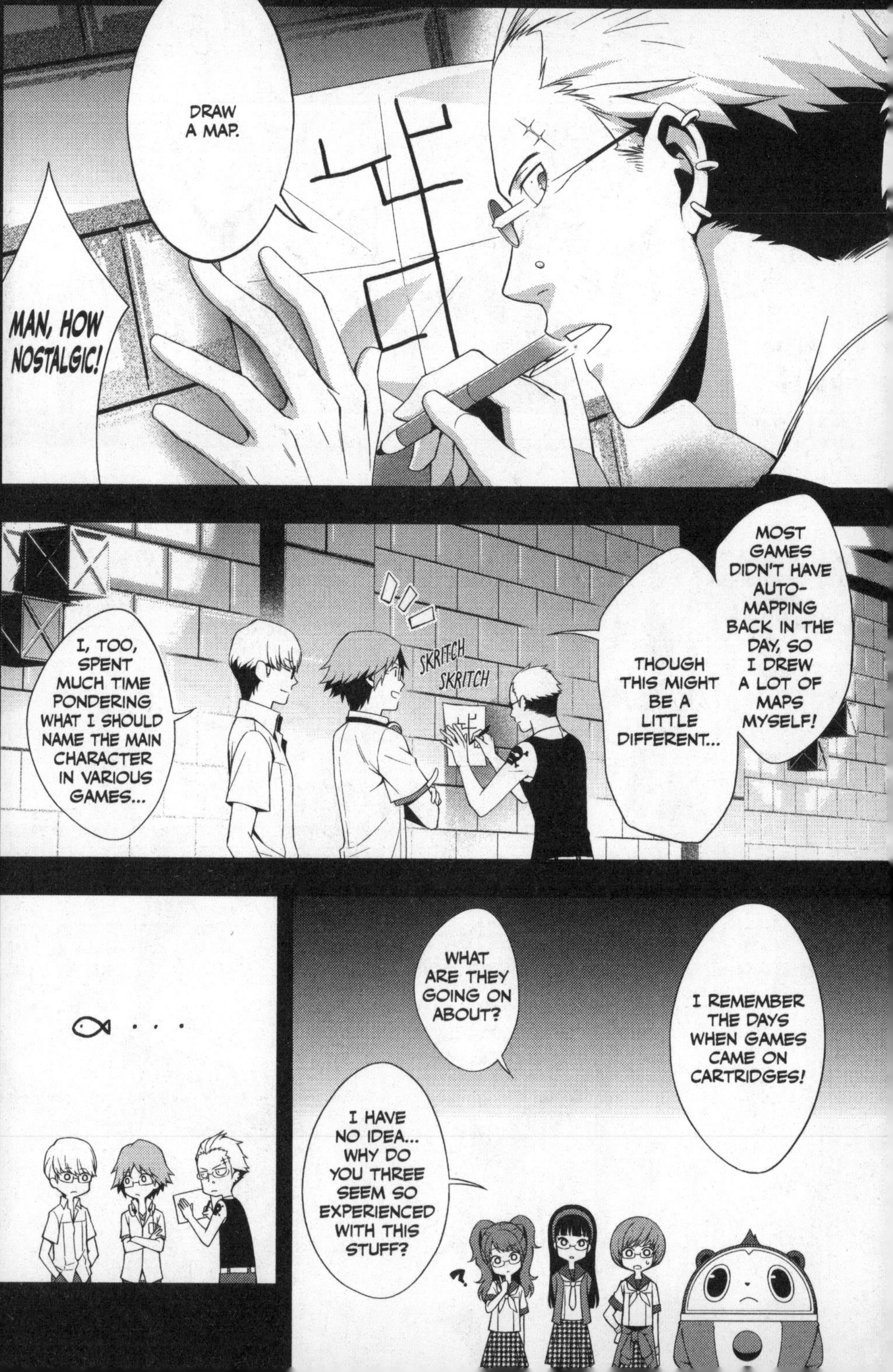
DRAW A MAP.
MAN, HOW NOSTALGIC!
MOST GAMES DIDN'T HAVE AUTO-MAPPING BACK IN THE DAY, SO I DREW A LOT OF MAPS MYSELF!
THOUGH THIS MIGHT BE A LITTLE DIFFERENT...
SKRITCH SKRITCH
I, TOO, SPENT MUCH TIME PONDERING WHAT I SHOULD NAME THE MAIN CHARACTER IN VARIOUS GAMES...
I REMEMBER THE DAYS WHEN GAMES CAME ON CARTRIDGES!
WHAT ARE THEY GOING ON ABOUT?
I HAVE NO IDEA... WHY DO YOU THREE SEEM SO EXPERIENCED WITH THIS STUFF?
...

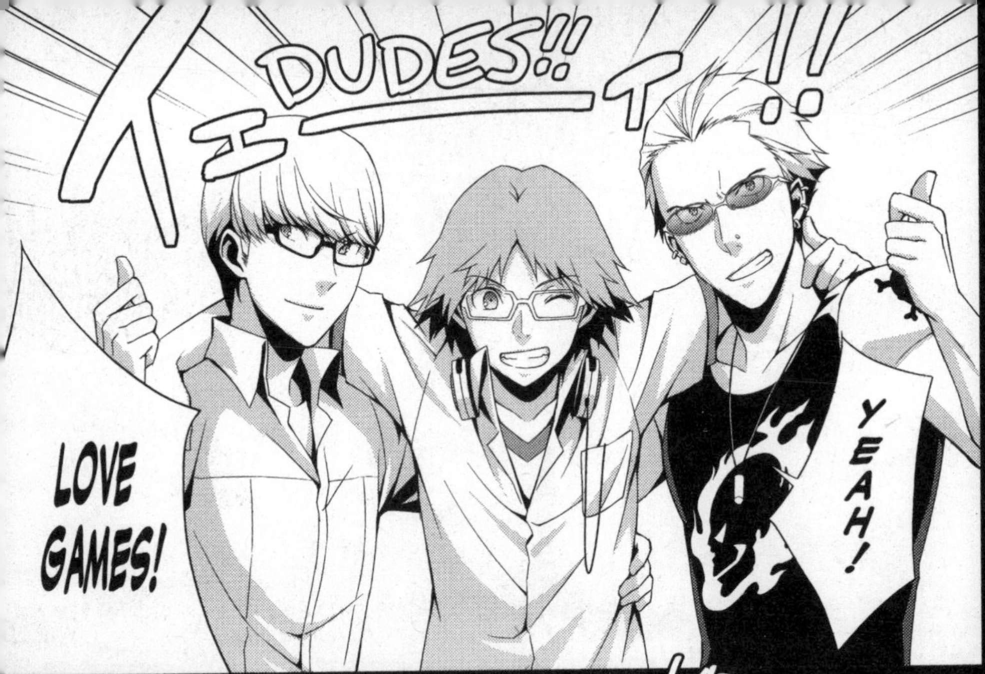
イエーイ!!
DUDES!!
YEAH!
LOVE GAMES!

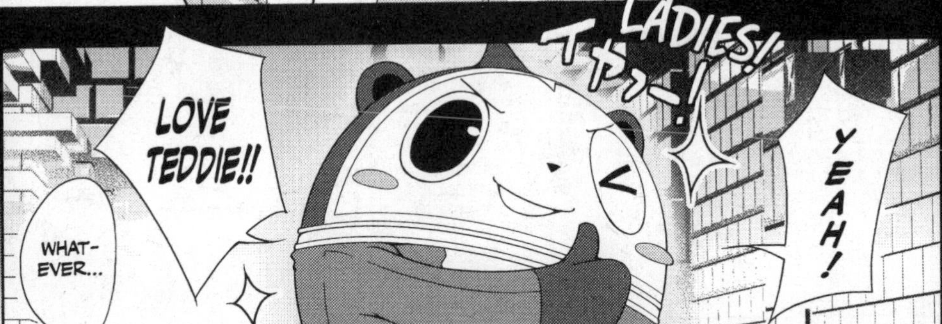
イやっー!
LADIES!
YEAH!
LOVE TEDDIE!!
WHAT-EVER...

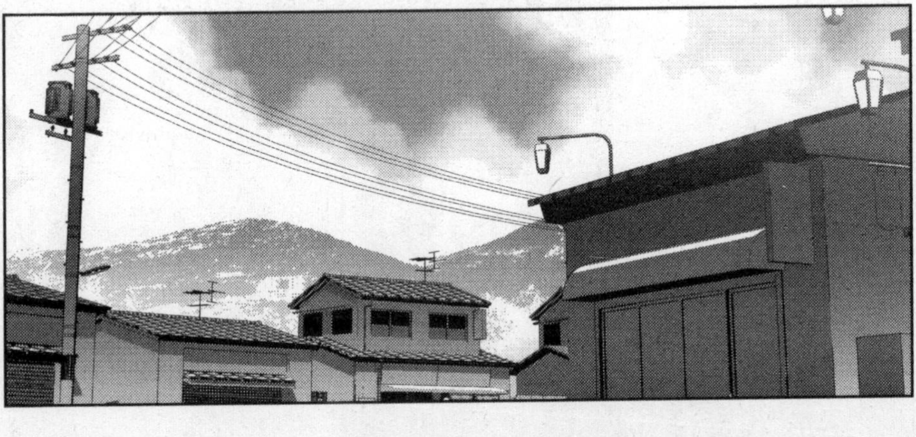

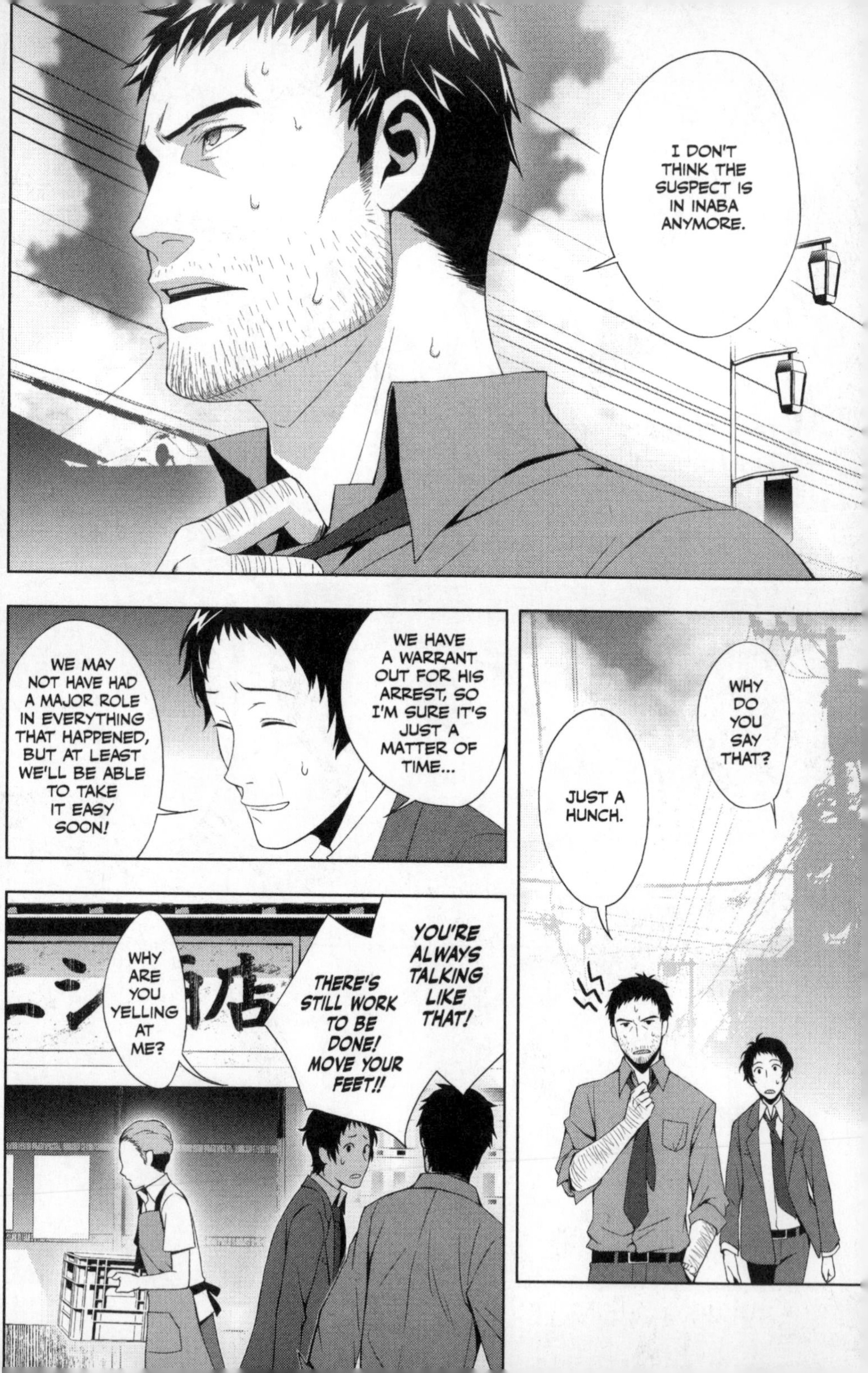
I DON'T THINK THE SUSPECT IS IN INABA ANYMORE.
WHY DO YOU SAY THAT?
JUST A HUNCH.
WE HAVE A WARRANT OUT FOR HIS ARREST, SO I'M SURE IT'S JUST A MATTER OF TIME...
WE MAY NOT HAVE HAD A MAJOR ROLE IN EVERYTHING THAT HAPPENED, BUT AT LEAST WE'LL BE ABLE TO TAKE IT EASY SOON!
YOU'RE ALWAYS TALKING LIKE THAT!
THERE'S STILL WORK TO BE DONE! MOVE YOUR FEET!!
WHY ARE YOU YELLING AT ME?

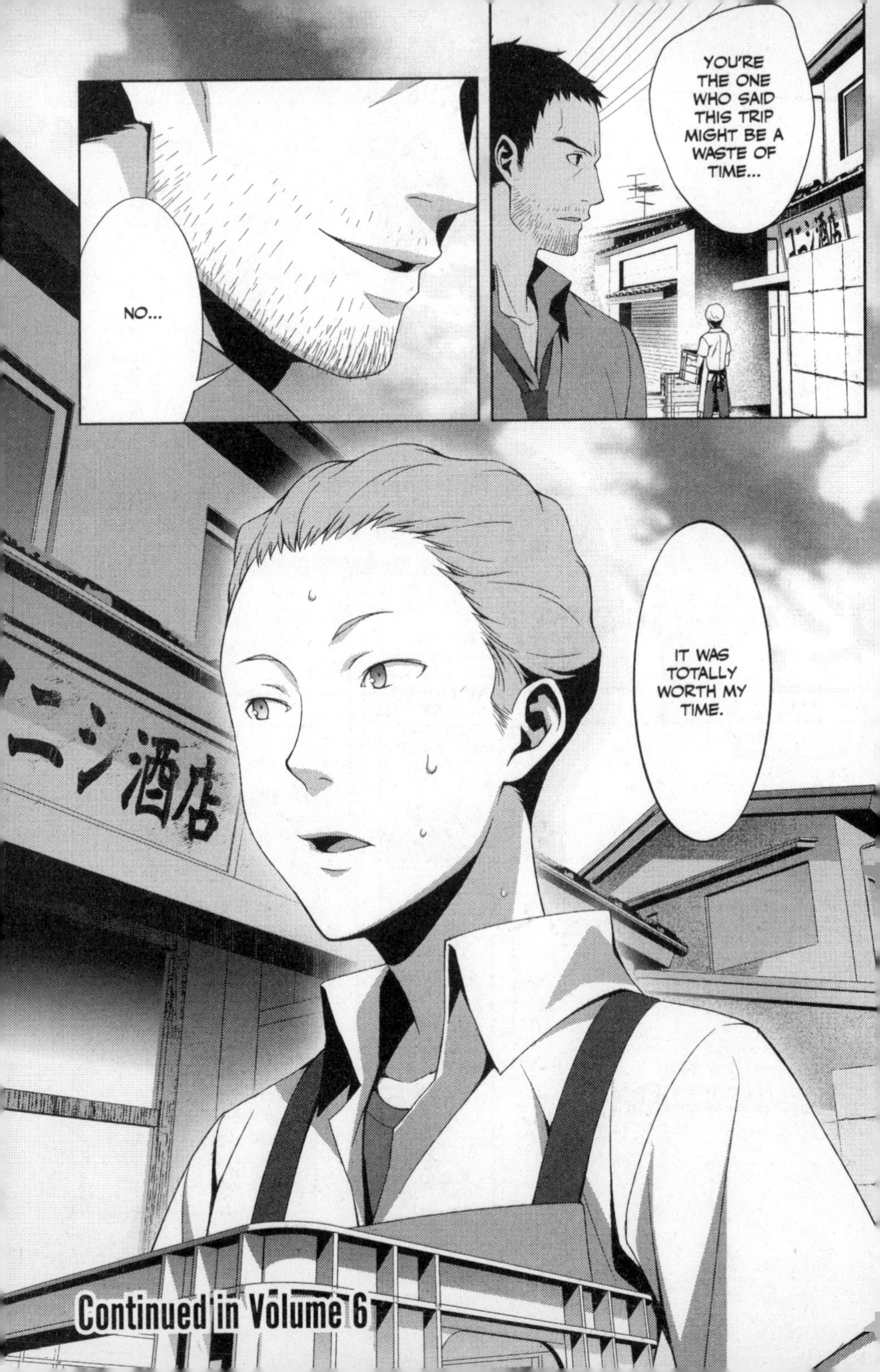
YOU'RE THE ONE WHO SAID THIS TRIP MIGHT BE A WASTE OF TIME...
コニシ酒店
NO...
IT WAS TOTALLY WORTH MY TIME.

Continued in Volume 6

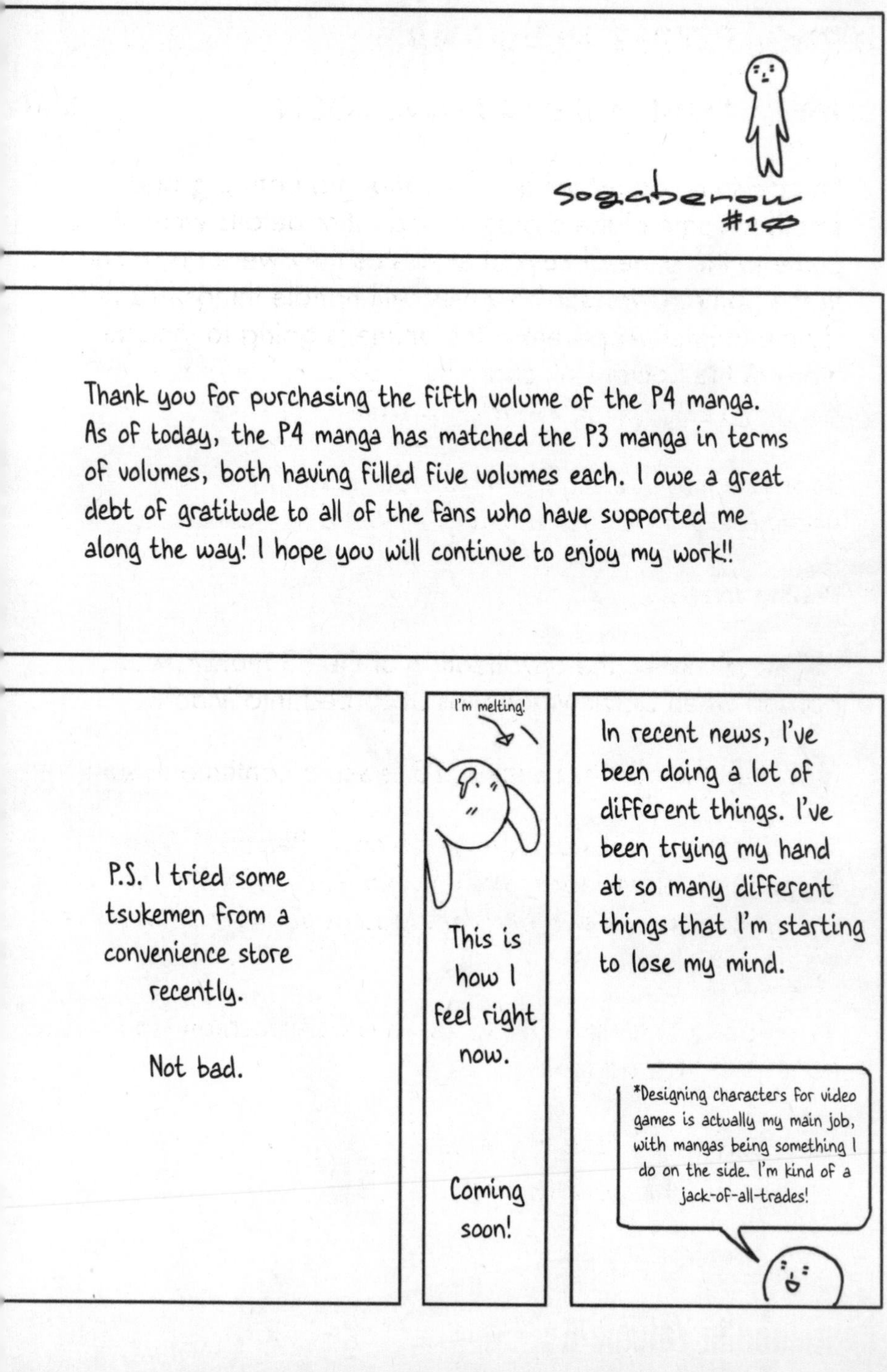
Sogaberow #10
Thank you for purchasing the fifth volume of the P4 manga. As of today, the P4 manga has matched the P3 manga in terms of volumes, both having filled five volumes each. I owe a great debt of gratitude to all of the fans who have supported me along the way! I hope you will continue to enjoy my work!!
In recent news, I've been doing a lot of different things. I've been trying my hand at so many different things that I'm starting to lose my mind.
*Designing characters for video games is actually my main job, with mangas being something I do on the side. I'm kind of a jack-of-all-trades!
I'm melting!
This is how I feel right now.
Coming soon!
P.S. I tried some tsukemen from a convenience store recently.
Not bad.

REGARDING PERSONA

THE P4 ANIME WILL BE STARTING SOON!

I made some adjustments for the manga, both big and small, to some of the dialogue and other details when it came to the general flow of events as they were presented in the game. I wonder how they will handle things like that for the anime? Apparently, the anime is going to include more of the Social Link characters, so as a fan of the game I am definitely looking forward to that!

Shoji Meguro's doing the music for the anime, so that's exciting too. I wonder if they will hold a live concert.

In other news...

As you all know, the serialization of the P3 manga was paused when Black Maoh was absorbed into Maoh.

Now that the dust has settled, P3 is set to continue its run!

The P3 manga will continue in the new "Persona Magazine", slated for release in November. While the P3 manga was on hold, the P4 manga caught up to it with five whole volumes.

I do plan to finish the P3 manga in proper fashion, so I hope you'll take a look!

So with that, I take my leave...
See you in the next volume! (ﾟｰﾟ)

vol.5

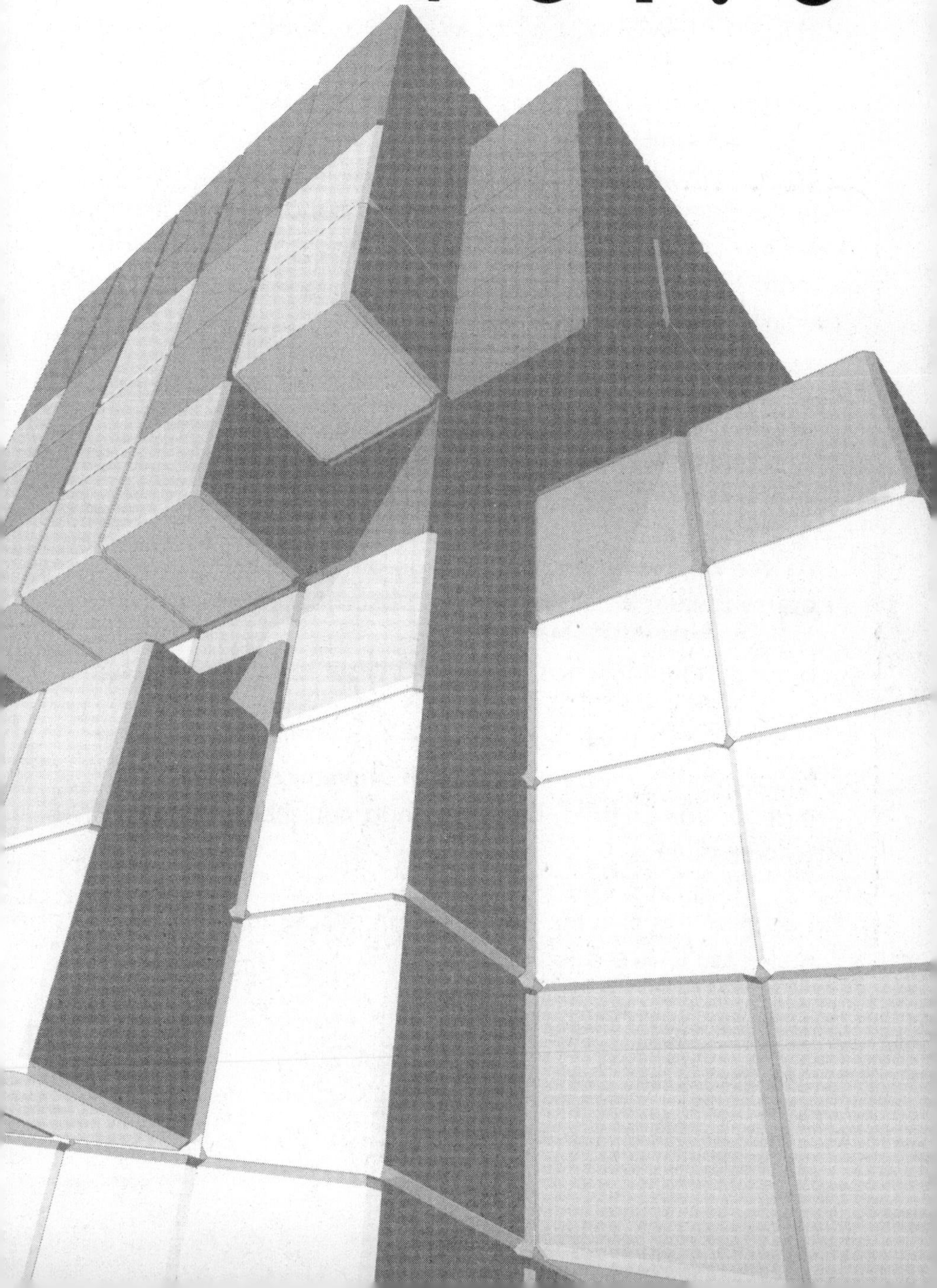

Persona 4

Original Work
ATLUS

Original Art Director
Shigenori SOEJIMA (ATLUS)

Manga / Story
Shuji SOGABE

Production / 3D Modeling & Layout / Art
Ryota HONMA (studioss)

Lead Artist
Haruna AOKI (studioss)

Art Team
Asami SAKUMA (studioss)

Design
Keiko SEKI (SELFISH GENE)
studioss

Editing
Naoki IIJIMA

Special Thanks
Junichi MORI (ATLUS)
Ikuya KOBAYASHI (ATLUS)

PERSONA 4 ORIGINAL STAFF

Persona 4

* Vol.5 : Shuji SOGABE / ATLUS

ENGLISH EDITION
Translation: M. KIRIE HAYASHI
Lettering: MARSHALL DILLON

UDON STAFF
Chief of Operations: ERIK KO
Director of Publishing: MATT MOYLAN
VP of Business Development: CORY CASONI
Director of Marketing: MEGAN MAIDEN
Japanese Liaisons: STEVEN CUMMINGS
                  ANNA KAWASHIMA

ペルソナ4 5
PERSONA 4 Volume 5

©ATLUS ©SEGA All rights reserved.
©Shuji Sogabe 2011

First published in 2011 by KADOKAWA CORPORATION, Tokyo.
English translation rights arranged with KADOKAWA CORPORATION, Tokyo.

English language version published by UDON Entertainment Inc.
118 Tower Hill Road, C1, PO Box 20008
Richmond Hill, Ontario, L4K 0K0 CANADA

www.UDONentertainment.com

Second Printing: January 2023
ISBN: 978-1-927925-82-9

Printed in Canada